P.E.Gibson

LAWRENCE OF ARABIA

A Biographical Enquiry

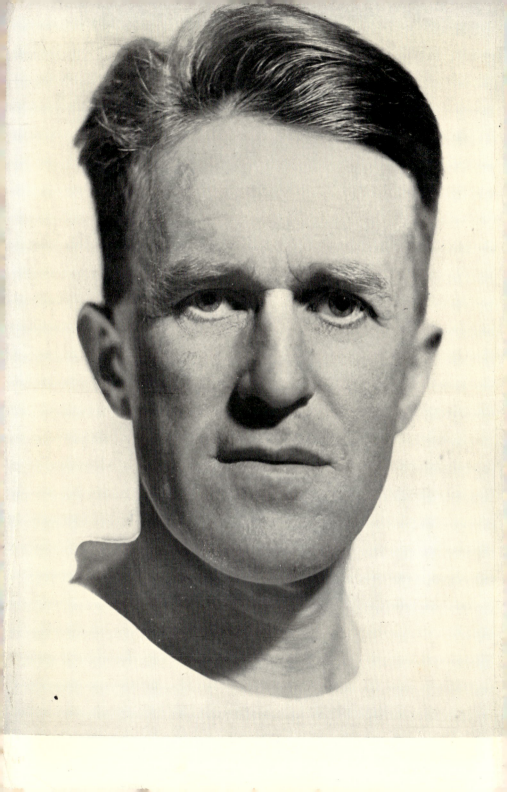

LAWRENCE
OF
ARABIA

A Biographical Enquiry
by
RICHARD ALDINGTON

Untruthful! My nephew Algernon?
Impossible! He is an Oxonian.
OSCAR WILDE

COLLINS
ST JAMES'S PLACE, LONDON
1955

PRINTED IN GREAT BRITAIN
COLLINS CLEAR-TYPE PRESS: LONDON AND GLASGOW

To

J. L. BROWNING

ERRATA

For " Violet " in line 4 please
read " Nancy." The letter referred
to in the 6th line of page 332 was
written not to Lady Violet Astor
but to Lady (Nancy) Astor.

CONTENTS

Contents

ILLUSTRATIONS

MAPS

INTRODUCTORY LETTER TO
ALISTER KERSHAW

My Dear Alister,

You will remember how startled I was when you suggested that I should gratify your admiration for a hero by writing a life of Lawrence of Arabia. I pointed out my unfitness for the task, the enormous amount of work involved, my lack of enthusiasm for military heroes, and above all the fact that Lawrence's life has been written over and over again. What more would there be to say? With that grace of persuasion which few are able to resist you remarked that after the astonishing and unwelcome revolutions of the past fifteen years some new appraisal of Lawrence might be acceptable. And had I not found the Duke of Wellington a far more interesting and attractive character than I had expected? That was true, and I started on my task with doubts of my ability to perform it worthily but certainly with the hope of investigating a hero and his deeds.

In Part III of this book you will find in more detail the account of my investigations into Lawrence's assertion that in 1922 and again in 1925 (when he was a private in the Tanks) he had been offered the post of High Commissioner for Egypt. On investigation I came to the conclusion that this claim was unfounded. I thought it well to obtain the evidence of those most likely to know the truth, and therefore applied to a former Cabinet Minister, Mr. Amery, to the present Lord Lloyd (son of the man actually appointed by the Cabinet as High Commissioner when Lord Allenby resigned) and to Lawrence's friend, Sir Ronald Storrs, who was Governor of Jerusalem after the first war. They were unanimous in dismissing the claim as highly improbable, and though I may not quote I received indirect but equally emphatic disavowal from still higher quarters that Lawrence was ever offered the post. (You will find all the evidence in Chapter Eight of Part III and the references at the end.)

Gradually as I went more closely into the material available I came to the conclusion that this Egypt affair is not a regrettable exception. On the contrary it is but one more example of a systematic falsification and over-valuing of himself and his achievements which Lawrence practised from a very early date. In other words the national hero turned out at least half a fraud. The scope of my projected book was insensibly changed and from a biography it became a biographical enquiry, the facts for which had to be tracked down with the minute care of a literary detective. My enquiries were not helped by the fact that the record is very incomplete and statements are often contradictory. But if this book leads to their publication it will have achieved something, and I am confident that nothing can be produced to shake the exposition of the main facts given here, whatever might have to be modified in detail through the publication of material at present unavailable. In any case nobody is competent to contradict the most important revelations in this book until he has read the MS. letters of T. E. Shaw (formerly Lawrence) to Charlotte Shaw (Mrs. Bernard Shaw) now available in the British Museum.

As I investigated the strange and tortuous psychology of this extraordinary man I felt more and more convinced that sometime in his early life he had been dealt a terrific blow by Fate, some humiliating and painful wound which he was always trying to compensate. In spite of the newspapers, he was something of a mystery man, there was a secret somewhere. You will recollect that a friend of ours hinted strongly to us of a family scandal, and that I refused at first to believe it. Further investigations showed that these hints were well-founded, and the secret which so much oppressed Lawrence's life was the fact of his birth. You will find the evidence in the first chapter of Part I and later chapters on Lawrence's early life.

It is a most invidious and disagreeable task to make public these occurrences in the history of a once fairly well-known family, some members of which still are alive. But without this clue all writings on Lawrence are valueless—or virtually so—for this is undoubtedly the clue to a character which has puzzled two generations. If I have been guilty of bad taste, well, I have been; but I have not betrayed anyone's confidence; the facts I discovered entirely by my own researches. In extenuation I would add that I have presented the evidence as objectively and quietly as possible, avoiding any attempt to exploit a scandal and its personalities, limiting myself to a mere establishing of the fact and its consequences for T. E. 'Lawrence.'

You may feel that I have not devoted much space to the " Arab war," and in comparison with my English predecessors this is true. And yet I have drawn on material which has been neglected by those writing from a purely partisan and nationalist view-point as hero worshippers. Whatever its literary merit (which may be very high) *Seven Pillars of Wisdom* is rather a work of quasi-fiction than of history. In addition to Lawrence's so-called *Secret Despatches* and the *British Official War History*, I have consulted the writings of Jemel Pasha and General Liman von Sanders (neither of whom, however, so much as mentions Lawrence in his account of the Arab war), the various reminiscences in *T. E. Lawrence by his Friends*, the books of Sir Hubert Young and Major N. N. E. Bray who were eye-witnesses, the important and very well-documented work by General Brémond. On the Arab side I have had the Memoirs of King Abdulla of Transjordania (an amiable fantasist) and the more serious though not impartial book of Mr. Antonius, who received much information from King Hussein and King Feisal I. His account of the Akaba expedition from the Arab point of view is especially interesting. I think you will find that even so warm an admirer of the great Lawrence of Arabia as yourself may be forced by the bleak evidence of facts to modify your enthusiasm.

The legend of Lawrence has been built up by nearly all those writers who have taken Lawrence as their subject, whether for a full-scale biography or for a three-page reminiscence. The edifice shows a fairly solid front to the uncritical reader but once it has been examined it is shown to be an inverted pyramid at the base of which stands Lawrence himself on whom the legend rests. My book is therefore a criticism of those writings which have fostered the Lawrence legend. The truth about the man was harder to come by, as no one crack in the edifice revealed the whole truth. I have gleaned the facts by comparison of the sources of the legend first among themselves and then—a more valuable comparison—with writings which were not primarily concerned with Lawrence. So you will see my research has been arduous, and first involved Lawrence's own writings and what has been written about him. Then I tried to cast my net as wide as possible among the works not devoted primarily to a study of Lawrence, and you will see from the list of acknowledgments to be found elsewhere in the book which of these works I have quoted at all extensively. The full extent of my researches will appear from the bibliography and list of sources at the end of the book.

As a book of this sort is bound to invite criticism, I would like to reiterate its purpose and its limitations. I do not pretend to have written the definitive biography of Lawrence, nor is this in any sense a final portrait of the man. Much of the evidence that is necessary for such a task is still not available.

My book is, as the title states, a biographical enquiry and not a biography, and, like John Locke, I have considered it " ambition enough to be employed as an under-labourer clearing the ground a little and removing some of the rubbish that lies in the way of knowledge." The book is primarily an analysis of the career of Lawrence the man of action and of the establishment and growth of what I have termed the Lawrence legend. If I have found that the first was of much less significance than is generally supposed, and the second was largely Lawrence's own doing, this is not to deny that Lawrence was a man of peculiar abilities. If *The Seven Pillars of Wisdom* is to be regarded as a work of the imagination rather than of history, it may well be considered by its admirers all the more remarkable for that fact.

I can't close without especially warm and personal thanks to J. L. Browning and John Holroyd-Reece, to Denison Deasy and to Alan Bird of Wadham for aid, comfort and much valuable research, and, especially, to William Dibben for his patience and skill in finding rare books. But above all, dear Alister, to yourself.

RICHARD ALDINGTON

P.S. The quotations from, and references to, *T. E. Lawrence by his Friends*, are always taken from the original longer edition,

PART ONE

CHAPTER ONE

THE FACTS recorded of T. E. Lawrence's parentage and upbringing are scattered and fragmentary, and the task of tracking them down, and fitting them into some order, is complicated and delicate. More is involved than a conventional curiosity which biographers always have felt or feigned about the antecedents of famous men and women. Rightly or wrongly many of us believe that early influences acting on heredity determine the character of a whole life. In all cases the more we can understand these influences, the better we shall be placed to pass judgment. A narrative which tries to give the facts about this Oxonian Ishmael should begin in the name of Allah, the Merciful, the Compassionate. Not that he would care! Or would he?

There is of course the unresolved debate of Nature v. Nurture, Morgan v. Pavlof, Heredity v. Environment; from which not much is to be deduced except that too little is known for anyone to dogmatise. Still, when a family culminates in a personality so curious as T. E. Lawrence obviously something more is involved than influences which were shared with his brothers. We must invoke heredity, a lucky or unlucky shuffle of the genes. It is surely false, though, to think of any man—or living organism—as the *sum* of his ancestry, he is a *selection* from that ancestry at the hazard of " chromosome divisions," a set of unique inherited qualities which the chances of environment will encourage or suppress, neutralise or warp. If this sounds pedantic, it can't be helped. A stand must be made against attempts to explain Lawrence as a result of " mixed blood," whatever that may be, and such fancies as the assertion that a knack for learning foreign languages may be " inherited " because among the ancestors a man has never

seen were some whose native languages differed from that spoken by
his parents and those about him. This is like Herodotus's nonsense
about the Egyptian baby who spontaneously spoke Phrygian, just as
the " mixed blood " theory is a hangover from Aristotle.

These notions may be safely placed in the area of popular
mythology (a potent factor in Lawrence's career) along with the
theories that he was the son of Bernard Shaw (because he took the
name Shaw in the Air Force), or was a son of Thomas Hardy (presumably because he went to tea at Max Gate), or was descended from
an imaginary " Sir Robert Lawrence," alleged to have crusaded with
Richard of Anjou, or that among his " predecessors " (nice distinction!)
were the British Indian soldiers, Sir Henry and Sir John Lawrence.

Let us look at the evidence available and try to put together a few
facts. In January 1926, when Lawrence was stationed at the R.A.F.
Cadets' College, Cranwell, he received a letter from his old friend and
patron, D. G. Hogarth, asking what he was to say in an article on
Lawrence commissioned by the *Encyclopædia Britannica*. Lawrence
returned a characteristically baffling reply, writing alternately in black
and red ink—what was written in black ink might be repeated but
what was in red ink was not to be published.

Hogarth might say that Lawrence's family did not originate in
Ireland but must not say it came from Leicestershire; he might say
that it had settled near Dublin but not sixty miles to the north-west
and not that this happened in the reign of Queen Elizabeth; he might
say that Lawrence's ancestors included Henry Vansittart (a member of
the Hell Fire Club and one of the early misgovernors of Bengal) but not
that Vansittart was a " rogue " nor that Sir Walter Raleigh was an
ancestor.[1] Why the mystery? In any case the prohibition did not
last very long, since next year Robert Graves was given the Leicestershire and Raleigh information and County Meath was specified. The
same information is given by Liddell Hart in 1934. Graves says that
Lawrence was Irish, Hebridean, Spanish and Norse; Hart says part
English, part Scandinavian. Graves is vague about his mother, and so
is Captain Hart. Though it is anticipating and though I shall have
more than once to call the reader's attention to the fact, both these
biographies were produced in constant communication with Lawrence
who read and passed every line of them. Some of the passages in
Captain Hart's book from which I shall quote were in fact written by

Lawrence himself.[2] The book contains mysterious little hints, such as the assertion that if his father's family felt inclined Lawrence's dream of a certain three hundred pounds a year might come true, and that much of the land round Bovington (Dorset) was owned by relatives of his father from whom he rented a ruined cottage with five acres of land.[3]

Lowell Thomas makes him Scotch, Welsh, English and Spanish, but places his " original home " in Galway.[4] I should perhaps interject that I have Mr. Thomas's personal assurance that Lawrence worked with him on his book.

What are we to make of this mysterious farrago ? No Lawrence family can be traced either in Galway or in County Meath, which of course might be due to lack of records; but the article on Lawrence in the *Dictionary of National Biography*, written by his friend the Oriental scholar and diplomat, Sir Ronald Storrs, tells us that Lawrence's mother was Sarah Maden, the daughter of a Sunderland engineer, brought up in the Highlands and afterwards in Skye. She appears in T. E. Lawrence's birth certificate as Sarah Lawrence, *née* Maden. His mother, " S. Lawrence " gives her date of birth as 1861.[5] No Sarah Maden appears in the national records for 1861, but registration was not then compulsory. The Sarah Maden registered in the County of Lancaster in October 1863 is quite a different person, daughter of a stone-mason. The birth certificate of one of Lawrence's brothers gives the mother's name as " formerly Sarah Junner," and a Sarah Junner was born on the 31st August, 1861, in Sunderland (as Sir Ronald Storrs says), the father being described as a " shipwright journeyman " which a genteel imagination may easily glorify into " engineer."[6] In the same *D.N.B.* article Storrs tells us the important fact that Lawrence's father was " the younger son of an Anglo-Irish landowning family " and that he was " Thomas Robert Chapman, who had assumed the name Lawrence."

One of T. E. Lawrence's beliefs—or at any rate assertions—is to the effect that the best way to hide the truth is to tell half-truths; so there seems a reasonable possibility that some of the information he gave to his friends was true. The reputation of so distinguished a witness as Storrs suggests that the Chapman clue is worth following up. And interestingly enough, the social registers of Burke and Debrett, which know nothing of any family of Irish landed gentry by the name of Lawrence, do know a Chapman family.

The story begins towards the end of the 16th century. At that time there were living two brothers, John and William Chapman, who came from Hinckley in the county of Leicestershire, England, and were distant cousins of Sir Walter Raleigh. Through Raleigh's patronage John Chapman obtained large grants of land in the county of Kerry, Ireland. When Raleigh lost the royal favour John Chapman, it is said, got into money difficulties. At all events, he sold his land to the Earl of Cork for £26,400, which we are told was a large sum of money for that epoch. This John Chapman appears to have died childless, but we are not informed whether he did or did not leave his fortune to his brother William who survived him. In any case, William's son Benjamin was the real founder of the family and its fortune.

This Benjamin was a Roundhead, and during the Great Rebellion joined as Cornet a regiment of horse raised by the Earl of Inchiquin for the Parliament. Benjamin Chapman became a Captain and received from Oliver Cromwell the grant of a large estate in the county of Westmeath. This had been called St. Lucy's, and had been confiscated from the Knights Hospitallers of St. John of Jerusalem, and renamed Killua. Benjamin married Anne, daughter of Robert Parkinson of Andee, and by her had two sons, William who succeeded him, and Thomas who went to America, where possibly his descendants still live. William Chapman 2nd married Ismay, daughter of Thomas Nugent of Clonlost.

We now begin to get definite dates. William Chapman 2nd died in 1734, bequeathing his estate to his eldest son Benjamin Chapman 2nd, who was High Sheriff of Meath in 1733 and of Westmeath in 1751. He married Ann, daughter of Robert Tighe of Mitchelstown (Co. Westmeath) and died in 1779, being succeeded by his eldest son Benjamin Chapman 3rd, under whom the family achieved fresh distinction. He was a Doctor of Laws of Dublin, a barrister, a Member of the Irish Parliament, and in 1782 was created a Baronet for services not specified. In his time the family home at St. Lucy's was renamed Killua Castle. He married Anne, daughter of John Lowther of Staffordstown (Co. Meath) and in 1810 died without children.

The title did not then become extinct, but went to his brother Sir Thomas Chapman, knight, who in 1808 married Margaret, daughter of James Fetherston of Bracklin Castle (Co. Westmeath), by whom he had several children. Their eldest son, Sir Montagu Lowther Chapman,

GENEALOGICAL TREE OF THE CHAPMAN FAMILY

coming from
HINCKLEY, LEICESTERSHIRE

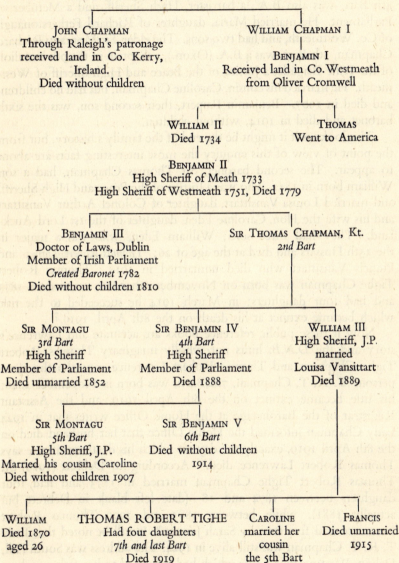

JOHN CHAPMAN
Through Raleigh's patronage
received land in Co. Kerry,
Ireland.
Died without children

WILLIAM CHAPMAN I

BENJAMIN I
Received land in Co. Westmeath
from Oliver Cromwell

WILLIAM II
Died 1734

THOMAS
Went to America

BENJAMIN II
High Sheriff of Meath 1733
High Sheriff of Westmeath 1751, Died 1779

BENJAMIN III
Doctor of Laws, Dublin
Member of Irish Parliament
Created Baronet 1782
Died without children 1810

SIR THOMAS CHAPMAN, Kt.
2nd Bart

SIR MONTAGU
3rd Bart
High Sheriff
Member of Parliament
Died unmarried 1852

SIR BENJAMIN IV
4th Bart
High Sheriff
Member of Parliament
Died 1888

WILLIAM III
High Sheriff, J.P.
married
Louisa Vansittart
Died 1889

SIR MONTAGU
5th Bart
High Sheriff, J.P.
Married his cousin Caroline
Died without children 1907

SIR BENJAMIN V
6th Bart
Died without children
1914

WILLIAM
Died 1870
aged 26

THOMAS ROBERT TIGHE
Had four daughters
7th and last Bart
Died 1919

CAROLINE
married her
cousin
the 5th Bart

FRANCIS
Died unmarried
1915

3rd Bart. died in 1852. Their second son, Sir Benjamin James Chapman 4th Bart. died in 1888. This 3rd Bart. was a B.A. of Trinity College, Dublin, High Sheriff and Member of Parliament. His brother, the 4th Bart. was also B.A., a barrister, High Sheriff, and a Member of Parliament. He married Maria, daughter of Richard Fetherstonaugh of Co. Westmeath, and had two sons. The elder, Sir Montagu Richard Chapman, 5th Bart. was a B.A. (Oxon.), a Captain in the 9th battalion of the Rifle Brigade, a Justice of the Peace and High Sheriff of Westmeath. He married his cousin, Caroline Chapman, but had no children, and died in 1907. Benjamin Rupert, their second son, was the sixth baronet and died in 1914, without children.

This looks as if it might be the end of the family's history, but from the point of view of this enquiry the most interesting facts are about to appear. The second baronet, Sir Thomas Chapman, had a son William born in 1811, who was a Justice of the Peace and High Sheriff, and married Louisa Vansittart, daughter of Colonel Arthur Vansittart and his wife the Hon. Caroline Eden, daughter of the 1st Lord Auckland. They had three sons; William Eden, who was a major in the 15th Hussars and died at the age of 26; *Thomas Robert Tighe*; and Francis Vansittart who died unmarried in 1915. Thomas Robert Tighe Chapman was born on November 6th 1846, married in 1873 and had four daughters; in March 1914 he succeeded to the title which became extinct at his death on the 8th April, 1919.[7]

Now if these public reference books are accurate and Lawrence's story and the *D.N.B.* hints not wholly imaginary Thomas Robert Tighe Chapman and Thomas Robert Lawrence must be the same person. T. R. T. Chapman, 7th Bart., was born in November 1846; his title became extinct on the 9th April 1919, and the Assistant Registrar of the Baronetage at the Home Office writes that in 1924 Lady Chapman informed the Home Office that her husband died on the 8th April 1919, exactly the day on which his death certificate says Thomas Robert Lawrence died.[8] According to Debrett (1919) Sir Thomas Robert Tighe Chapman married in 1873 and had four daughters between 1874 and 18—(date left blank in Debrett but actually 1881), while between 1885 and 1900 Thomas Robert Lawrence had five sons by Sarah Junner.[9] It will be noted that Lady T. R. T. Chapman was still alive in 1924. Her address was South Hill, Delvin, Westmeath, a house which had belonged to her father-in-law.

The names of Sir Walter Raleigh and Vansittart both occur in this family history; the Chapmans did emigrate from Leicestershire to Ireland; and Killua Castle is in Westmeath. On the other hand, the statement that " he was of mixed race " seems curious, as the Chapmans mostly married Anglo-Irish landed gentry like themselves. " His mother was Island Scottish in feeling and education, but her parentage was part English, part Scandinavian," wrote Lawrence to Liddell Hart who included it in his biography.[10]

Lawrence must have given Lowell Thomas the " Galway " and the crusading 12th century " Sir Robert Lawrence." Since his father was really Sir Thomas Robert Chapman, Lawrence with his peculiar sense of humour, would think it funny to invent a crusading " Sir Robert " among his ancestors. And his father's change of name explains why Thomas Edward so contemptuously abandoned " Lawrence " for " Ross " or " Shaw," why he insisted on his friends calling him " T.E.", and even such a trifle as the ' T. E. Lawrence ' (in quotes) on the title-page of *Revolt in the Desert* and on the title-page and binding of Liddell Hart's biography.

This irregular situation of a father who had four daughters by his wife and five sons (of whom T. E. Lawrence was the second) by another woman is obviously the clue to Lawrence's abortive career and tortuous character. Of course the fact must not be abused and dragged in to explain everything—he had his own remarkable gifts, and was as powerfully influenced by his environment in some respects as he violently reacted from it in others—but with this knowledge we can dissipate much of the legendary " mystery man," understand many things which otherwise are enigmatic, and find compassion rather than repulsion for at least some of his questionable actions and traits. " Call me Ishmael! "—the opening words of the *Moby Dick* he took as one of his literary idols—suited him quite as much as Melville. All his life he was helplessly entangled in a secret which was not his, baffled by it, tongue-tied, forced to habits of dissimulation and mystifying.

For a man whose most obvious characteristic was an abnormal vanity—including of course its identical opposite, abnormal self-depreciation—the unwanted possession of the Secret was a Nessus' shirt, a perpetual crucifixion. And it was all the more maddening because intellectually and morally he didn't care, he was emancipated from the obsolescent sense of sin, though he cared immensely for personal, social and mundane reasons. Through it he was led to a false relationship and a clash of personality and will with his mother, from which he eventually retired to the anti-feminine refuge of a barrack room. There were moods when he wanted to reveal the Secret (which after all wasn't such a secret that it wasn't known to some and guessed by more) especially when he had reached such a position of world notoriety that it could not have injured him. He was compelled to maintain the Secret to please the false susceptibilities of others, yet another highly-gifted man sacrificed to 19th-century snobbery, hypocrisy, philistinism and "respectability" in a generation which was supposedly in violent revolt against them, he above all!

Full confirmation of this situation is amply provided by Lawrence himself in some of the large collection of letters exchanged between himself and Charlotte Shaw (Mrs. Bernard Shaw) and lately made available to the public by the Library of the British Museum. The Lawrence letters are catalogued as Additional M/S 45903,4, are contained in five folders and cover the years 1923-1935. They include a large amount of musical and literary criticism of the records and books she sent him, and complaints of the conditions of his life in the R.A.F., but, in Mrs. Shaw, Lawrence seems to have found about the only relationship he really wanted with a woman, that of a substitute mother. Perhaps I should add that Lawrence wanted these letters made available to his biographers even during his life-time, but Mrs. Shaw objected, though she seems to have kept all his letters to her.

The most important letter was written by Lawrence on the 14th April 1927, shortly after the publication of *Revolt in the Desert*, when he had been exiled to Karachi where he was evidently lonely, cut off from all his intellectual friends, and, according to him, a self-constituted prisoner in the camp seven miles outside the town. This intellectual loneliness must have been hard to bear even for a man so self-centred and so self-sufficient, and perhaps prompted the confidence. But he had already confided other personal secrets to Mrs. Shaw, and an even stronger motive must have been the wish that in his lifetime at least one sympathetic person should have his version of the tragedy which he felt had ruined his life—somebody sufficiently important to see that in due time the information was handed on. This must have been in his mind, because only about two weeks earlier he had written Mrs.

Shaw that sooner or later somebody would want to write his biography and that unpublished letters would be the main source. Mrs. Shaw has preserved what he wanted known and could find no other means to pass on.

The letter contains frank and penetrating (but in no way resentful or exaggerated) judgments on both his parents, to which we shall have to refer when we come to consider the effect of their characters on him. The more important was the mother, who had had a strict Calvinist upbringing in the Isle of Skye and had been a children's nurse. Lawrence says that an overwhelming sense of sin and guilt possessed her because Lawrence's father had left his wife to live with her; and that she strove to atone for her sin by making him and her sons intensely religious.[11] One of them became a missionary.

The second child of this union was Thomas Edward, who according to his mother was born in " the small hours " of the 16th August, 1888. He was registered as born on the 15th by his father, whose name is given as " Thomas Lawrence," by occupation " gentleman," with the address of Gorphwysfa, Tremadoc, Carnarvon, Wales.[12] The only significance attached to this birth in Wales is the fact that, when Lawrence became an Oxford undergraduate, the chance of his birth-place being Wales enabled him to be entered at Jesus College which was usually frequented by Welshmen. Lawrence was only just over a year old when he left Wales, and for a number of years the family lived a wandering life. Between 1889 and 1891 they lived in Kirkcudbright (Scotland) for nearly two years; after three weeks in the Isle of Man and three months in Jersey, they lived in Dinard, France, until the spring of 1894, when they returned to England, first to Langley on the edge of the New Forest (Hampshire), and afterwards, in September, 1896, they settled permanently in Oxford. According to one school of thought, the moving of young children from one place to another is supposed to give them " a sense of insecurity." If so, this may possibly have been one of the several factors he mentions which determined in later life his taking refuge in the " security " of the R.A.F. ranks.

A good deal has been made of Lawrence's precocity, and examples have been collected both from those who knew him in his early years and from his own writings. It must be confessed that many of these are trifling, and the solemnity of his hagiographers (one might call them the Lawrence Bureau) so unsuspecting that the instances they cite often strike an outsider as either ludicrous or highly improbable or both. Before going any further I must warn the reader of some Lawrence peculiarities which will have to be often stressed. He was vague about numbers, except when it suited him to be precise; from quite early times he liked to tell romantic or Irish stories—Milesian tales, they might be called—about himself and his astonishing achievements; and he had so practised and abused the habit of " leg-pulling " or " kidding " that he confesses that he had himself lost sight of the boundaries dividing fact from fiction. If he did not know when he was or wasn't telling the truth, how can others ?

Probably the tangle can never be sorted out, and that is exactly what Lawrence wanted—at one and the same time this confusion gratified his vanity, his sense of superiority, and diverted attention from the " Secret."

We learn from his mother's reminiscences that Lawrence was big for his age, a strong and active child who could pull himself over the nursery gate before he could walk, and that before he was three he learned the alphabet simply from listening to the lessons given his elder brother.[13] His elder brother assures us that at the age of five Lawrence could read the newspaper upside down, and that this accomplishment in later life enabled him to practise the economy of reading the newspaper of the man opposite in a train. He climbed a steep ladder into a loft at the age of two, and later led the others in a twelve foot jump from the top of a shed. He invented stories for them, in which their animal toys played the part of soldiers defending a tower.[14] Before he was six he had picked up a child's fluency in French at Dinard; at seven he was taken on a steamer to see the ships of the Royal Navy at the Spithead Review, disdained the sight, and was found reading Macaulay in the cabin; before he was ten he had learned to take rubbings of the sepulchral brasses he went to see in English churches.[15] Add to this that before he was eight he could swim and ride a pony and was an energetic tree-climber.

These little facts are vouched for by others, and certainly indicate a certain precocity of mind and body. To these may be added Lawrence's own references to his early childhood, all implying a fabulous precocity. In later life he told one correspondent that he was able to read at the age of four, mainly police news, he said; and that he began learning Latin at five.[16] He improved on this in conversation with Liddell Hart, and claimed that he "knew French as a boy, and could read and write before he was four.[17] When he joined the R.A.F. and was transferred to Farnborough after his recruit's course he became impatient at being compelled to spend nine months on photography. Characteristically, he complained direct to R.A.F. Headquarters in a personal letter to Air Vice-Marshal Swann (whom he had met once), explaining that he was "already as good as the men passing out," and adding that he had been taught when he was four by his father whom he described as a pioneer photographer.[18] Moreover, in June, 1931, he wrote a naval officer that his father had yachts and that he used to go sailing with him—again from his fourth year.[19] He told Liddell Hart that he had learned to handle boats from his father, a keen yachtsman.

Photography and yachting are certainly unusual acquirements for a child of three. But "at the age of four" and "in my fourth year" should not be taken literally, and mean nothing really more than "when I was a child." Lawrence was always vague about numbers and dates (there are virtually no dates in his history thesis or in the narrative of his war book) either because he was too lazy to bother, or affected disdain for such petty accuracies. It was seldom that he reported any fact or episode involving himself without embellishing them and indeed in some cases entirely inventing them. If he wished to put himself forward as an infant prodigy his Irish imagination took no more account of years than in other stories it took of probability or common sense.

When Lawrence was eight and his eldest brother ten—with others coming along—there arose the problem of education. Clearly something more serious was required than lessons from an English governess or French monks and gymnastic classes at St. Malo. The decision was made to move to Oxford where there was a High School, from which in due course the boys might hope to pass on to the University. They settled at 2 Polstead Road, which remained the family home until 1921.

The influence of Oxford on T. E. Lawrence was very strong indeed. It was never really shaken off, though modified in the war, and definitely repudiated in the "common man" phase of the Tanks and the R.A.F., when he even attempted to change his Oxford accent into "garage English." Oxford, he declared, was "heaven"—from eighteen to twenty-one. Not much of its ancient glamour touched him during his school days, and that glamour itself had been considerably vulgarised even in 1896. Max Beerbohm, who came to Oxford that year as an undergraduate, considered it " . . . a bit of Manchester through which Apollo had once passed," and " in a riot of vulgarity " he found " only remnants of beauty."[20]

Some of the " memories " of Lawrence's schooldays embalmed in print are very trifling—thus we are told that the four boys all wore the same dark blue and white striped jerseys, and rode to and from school on bicycles always in line and in order of seniority.[21] Possibly this shows that posing and publicity began early. More to the point is the question of how much he owed to his school. It was not what in England is called a Public School (i.e., a private and expensive school for the upper class) and hence carried none of the old-school-tie prestige.

The suggestion has been made that, with his very lofty standards of what was due to him, Lawrence resented having to attend this " townee " school; but, so far as I can discover, no positive evidence for this has ever been brought forward. But Lawrence's account of this school is in sharp contrast with that of his brother who praises the headmaster as " marvellous," the staff as " excellent and willing," the governing body of dons as " splendid," and adds: " The statement has been made that Ned did not enjoy his schooldays, but this is quite a mistake."[22] Lawrence himself did not share this view. He said that apart from reading, writing and French (which he knew before he went to school) what he learned came from the books he read for himself—" school was usually an irrelevant and time-wasting nuisance which I hated and contemned."[23] In the autobiographical letter to Hogarth already quoted, Lawrence says that at school he was educated " very little, very reluctantly, very badly."[24] This is perhaps only another example of having too high a standard and of making a good story, for he could hardly have learned Latin and Greek or even mathematics and history by private reading. He is said to have won prizes every year.[25] Nevertheless he failed to get a history scholarship at St. John's College, though later he managed to win a history exhibition.[26]

What are we to make of this violent repudiation of his school-days, this haughty disclaimer of any obligation to instructors who evidently are only too anxious to claim him as theirs? It is almost as contemptuous as Gibbon's stately disdain for " the monks of Magdalen." Yet

Lawrence did not disdain his University years; and his success as an undergraduate must have depended on his former training. It is said that after 1900 the scholarships he won at school paid all his fees for education. But what are we to make of his statement that he " worked at mathematics until nearly 18," when he changed to history,[27] if compared with the positive declaration of his friend and school-mate T. W. Chaundy (afterwards a lecturer in mathematics) that Lawrence encouraged Mr. Chaundy to do his algebra for him?[28] Yet when at the end of his school career he took the Oxford Senior Local exam., he is said to have passed in nineteen different papers, was 13th among the 120 Firsts out of 10,000 competitors, first in English Language, third in Scripture.[29] Lawrence in later life evidently wanted it to be thought that he had done this purely on his own without any real assistance from the school.

It is tempting to write this off as just another example of his " Ishmael " attitude—the contemptuous brushing off of conventional authority and institutions, the wish to owe everything to himself alone—and no doubt that must be taken into account. But behind this is the undeniable fact that much of what he learned out of school was more important to his life than what he learned in school. Never mind his " before I was four " nonsense. To have learned to use a camera was more useful than mathematics and Latin for illustrations to his thesis and the very ample photographic records of his part in the desert war. So, too, early experience with yachts and canoes may have helped his later work of testing speed-boats. He unconsciously helped to make himself, and wanted to believe—or others to believe—that he had done it all. But were these achievements so remarkable?

He never had any interest in any branch of biology, unless a brief phase of collecting fossils be so considered, and turned away in boredom from a collection of wild birds to study the latrines of a medieval castle. The intense preoccupation with religion in his home put into his hands the *Oxford Helps to the Study of the Bible*, and his school gave him as prizes two books on ancient Egypt. With his own pocket-money he bought Layard's two volumes on Nineveh, which may have stimulated his interest in the Middle East, for along with the account of his excavations Layard tells his readers something of the history and geography of the area with lively accounts of contemporary Turkish and Arabian life.[30] It is characteristic that with his almost complete indifference to natural science he picked up some of its technical terms and long afterwards was able to use them correctly.[31]

While he was still only in the fifth form, and presumably about fifteen, Lawrence was already well-known for his interest in archæology. With another school-fellow he spent his pocket-money in buying up old coins, bottles and pipes found by Oxford workmen digging foundations, and cycled to local churches taking heel-ball rubbings of the brasses which he hung round his room. The two boys haunted the local museums (especially the Ashmolean) and libraries, and worked up theories about church and college architecture. From copying brasses they went on to study any fragments of biography they could find about the people commemorated. They dabbled in heraldry and armour, visiting the Tower of London and the Wallace Collection; and from these went on to medieval enamels and tooled leather, illuminated manuscripts, the then recently discovered relics of ancient Crete, William Morris's Kelmscott Press, which passed on to ambitious projects for a new printing of Froissart with illustrations by contemporary artists. Gradually Lawrence's particular interests concentrated on Gothic architecture and especially medieval castles and fortifications.[32]

Now if all these interests and explorations really occurred when Lawrence was only fifteen they form another set of examples of the precocity which is claimed for him—though of course the same thing would be equally true of his companion, C. F. C. Beeson, who shared them with him.

All this is credible if the period is not set back too far and if we refrain from mythologising Lawrence into an infant Hercules strangling cultural serpents in his cradle. The interests themselves are the usual schoolboy " collecting " and " exploring " manias conditioned by residence in a university town filled with antiquities and antiquarians. From an early age, say 14-15, Lawrence frequented the Ashmolean, and imitated it within his means—brass-rubbings for sculpture, coins and bottles for ushabtis and ancient pottery. Whether instinctively or from imitation he agreed with Oxford, as we have seen, in his indifference to natural science. If his youthful cycling had as objective a church with old tombs instead of an afternoon's fishing or looking for birds' nests, that again was wholly in keeping with the spirit of the place. The turning of his antiquarian interests towards the Middle

East is easily explained by the religious atmosphere which surrounded him both at home and without, whether " worshipping " at St. Aldate's or parading with the Church Lads' Brigade. Middle Eastern archæology was approved, not as proto-history or science or art, but because it was held to show that the Bible is true. Fortunately he found a more intelligent view when he came to know personally the Ashmolean keepers, Hogarth and Leeds.

At this point we come on one of those stories which Lawrence told about himself to his friends and hagiographers. These anecdotes, which are never to his disadvantage, whether explained as the Milesian tales of a wild Irishman unable to see the absurdity of his assertions, or as " leg-pulling," do not recommend Lawrence as a good witness, but did serve the purpose of self-advertisement. Here is the story:

> " Lawrence's knowledge must be pretty extensive. In six years he read every book in the library of the Oxford Union—the best part of 50,000 volumes probably. His father used to get him the books while he was at school and afterwards he always borrowed six volumes a day in his father's name and his own. For three years he read day and night on a hearthrug, which was a mattress so that he could fall asleep as he read. Often he spent eighteen hours a day reading, and at last got so good at it that he could tear the heart out of the most formidable book in half an hour."[33]

Unfortunately for this story, 6 books a day for 6 years doesn't make much more than 13,000; to read 50,000 in that time he would have had to perform the impossible feat of reading 25 a day for 2,000 days—and what about going to school and lectures? A less fantastic version of this tale turns up in V. Richards' *Portrait* and in Liddell Hart's book, with the 50,000 omitted, but with the borrowing 6 books a day in his father's name and his own retained, and the poetic thought that Lawrence " sensed " a subject as a bee finds nectar.[34] Evidently Hart had done some figuring, and examined Lawrence on the subject; whereupon Lawrence explained that Graves had quite misunderstood him about the Oxford Union books, what Lawrence meant was that he had read all the books he wanted to read—he had not, for example, read any of the theological books, of which there are many.[35] And Liddell Hart gently rebukes Graves for " faulty proof-reading "—a side-stepping of the issue. But, as a matter of fact, Lawrence " read

31

and passed every word of" Graves' book, " though he asked me to put a sentence in my introduction making it seem that he had not."[36] And, again according to Graves, Lawrence gave him the whole paragraph, including the 50,000 books, the father's borrowing when Lawrence was at school, the 6 a day, the reading day and night for six years " often 18 hours in a day reading " and " the tearing the heart out of a book in half an hour.[37]

The sentence to which Graves refers runs as follows: " Unfortunately, owing to pressure of time my completed typescript could not be submitted to Shaw before publication, and I apologise to him for any passages where my discretion has been at fault."[38] We hear much of Lawrence as a " wonderful friend." In this case he furnished Graves with stories (the 50,000 books tale is very far from being the only one) which any reader might reasonably query, " read and passed every word " and then " asked " the biographer to make an ambiguous statement which exonerated Lawrence and left the responsibility to his friend. It was, to say the least, unscrupulous of Lawrence to compel his friend to a seeming responsibility for the many false or exaggerated stories of his own superiority which Lawrence foisted through him on a credulous public.

CHAPTER TWO

IN SPITE of numerous reminiscences, the account we have of Lawrence in his boyhood is not satisfactory. It is really more a portrait of his interests than of him, and the evidence is weakened by the fact that none of it is contemporary while the accounts were mainly written in an atmosphere of posthumous hero-worship heightened by the sense of loss at his recent death. Naturally, these early friends tend to recollect evidence of his precociously developed intellectual powers. The fact that the collection of published letters is incomplete may partly account for the peculiar impersonality of the earlier ones, which contain so much about his antiquarian interests and so little about himself. No childish letters have so far been produced (if any exist) and the earliest is dated two days before his 17th birthday—he is at Colchester on a cycling tour with his father, they have visited the Roman gate and the churches, on which Lawrence gives his learned opinions, with sketches.[1] The letter shows a strange lack of warmth and human interest, as if written mainly to preserve a first-hand memorandum of his church and castle hunting.

There were other sides to his highbrow schoolboy's life, among them his fondness for feats of endurance and daring, which went along with a habit of getting himself knocked about and of contracting more or less preventable illnesses. Although he disdained cricket and football and seemingly anything which might be called " sport " except cycling, swimming, canoeing and, later, revolver-shooting, he liked wrestling with other boys. This may or may not have some psychological significance, but the relevant fact is that in one such scuffle he broke his leg just above the ankle. According to

Graves, this happened when Lawrence was 16, i.e., some time between August, 1904 and 1905. At one period of his youth Lawrence took up vegetarianism and is said to have maintained it for three years. If this was simultaneous with the accident, the calcium shortage of vegetarianism might account for both the break and the slow healing.

However that may be, he lost a term at school, and spent the time reading and " doing poker-work." The ankle was still troubling him as late as 1911, when he was on a walking tour near the Euphrates.[2] He was certainly still a vegetarian in 1907, when he wrote from France that he was living on milk, bread, and such fruits as peaches, apricots and cherries.[3]

The shock of this broken leg is supposed to account for the fact that he did not grow very much afterwards, some saying that he stopped at 5 feet 3 inches (Lowell Thomas), some at 5 feet 5½ inches or 5 feet 6 inches (Robert Graves). The average height of males in Great Britain is 5 feet 6 inches, so there was nothing abnormal about that. But if his growth really did stop at 16, then there was something unusual, since the average human male goes on growing until about 20. The fact that the growing ceased soon after the accident does not necessarily imply a relation of cause and effect. There may have been other reasons.

A priori, it seems strange that a man of exactly the average height of his countrymen should have struck so many people as being small; but this certainly is the case. The explanation may be that his head was definitely large in proportion to his slight body, that he had light hair and blue eyes, and looked several years younger than he was. The precocity of his childhood was followed by an arrested psychological development, leaving him with certain perpetually adolescent traits. He carried through life the self-consciousness which is characteristic of so many Englishmen, above all at the adolescent stage when in that environment nature and nurture are at cross-purposes. Some say he could not look another man in the eyes, and that his own eyes were in constant furtive movement. He had a low apologetic voice, a silly giggle, a schoolboy grin, a habit of playing stupid practical jokes, and above all a perpetual " kidding " so that " I could hardly tell my own self where the leg-pulling began or ended."[4]

To all this he added the assertion that he was " sexless," but that, after all, is not a condition of adolescence. On the contrary.

34

The question is—how much of this was genuine, how much pose? And do not start away from the word " pose " as unfair, a pre-judg-ment, an attributing of motive. It is Lawrence's own word for himself. Among the many, many things this self-absorbed man said about himself at various times, he wrote from Arabia towards the end of the war (July 1918) that the war-time things he had been doing " in fancy dress " were all " part of the pose "; adding, " how to reconcile it with the Oxford pose I know not."[5] If words mean anything those words mean that he admitted two of the most important periods of his life—Oxford and the War—were play-acting, a pose. From this we may infer that he had little real and lasting conviction in either phase, whether intellectualist or military, he had no real centre to his being. Can a man be part adolescent and part adult? For, behind that mask, real or assumed, was a watchful and clever adventurer waiting always for the moment when he could assert his superior will, an almost fanatical will which had no other purpose than its self-assertion, and therefore took for granted that the moment of success was also the moment of feeling " absolutely bored."[6]

If, however, we accept these adolescent traits as genuine, self-conscious but not wilfully deceptive, then we must accept the paradox of a human being remaining partly adolescent while becoming partly adult—the will to power and the mechanistic skill whether in leader-ship, intrigue or mere machinery becoming enormously developed at the expense of the vital impulse and all the emotions, discoveries and enjoyments that go with it. Lawrence described himself as " a cold Englishman "—a doubling up of human chilliness. Look at his *Letters*, usually cold as a fish, with hardly an expression of warmth even to his mother in his early youth. They have plenty of calculated flattery and an assumption of moral superiority and sensitive right feeling, into which by implication he admits his correspondents and friends, as in *Seven Pillars* he admits his fellow-fighters, maintaining the Arabs on a slightly lower plane and excluding negroes altogether, being " hurt " that they " should possess exact counterparts of all our bodies."[7] In all of it there is as little vital warmth as there is wit in his special English adolescent " humour." But—not to be led astray by evidence of the consequences of this self-baffling psychology—might it not be the result of some emotional rather than physical shock, some inner conflict which could not be resolved, a longing to remain boyish and therefore unaware of a suffering, a humiliation, a resentment coming at the moment of maturing perception? In a sentence—might not the main clue, though perhaps not the only one, to Lawrence's peculiar psychology lie in his relation to his parents, in his discovery of what they thought their sin and its irreparable wrong to him, as well as to the dissonances set up in him by the influence of two powerful and opposite human personalities?

There is a contrast, worth noting, between the accounts of his parents given by Lawrence to the three biographers who published in his lifetime, and the account he wrote to Charlotte Shaw* which to his disappointment she would not allow Graves to see.[8] Following Lawrence's lead, (he dismissed the book which he had himself collaborated in as "fantastic,"[9] and even before it was published, tried to protect himself by saying he expected it to be a "fulsome thing"[10]) Lowell Thomas's *With Lawrence in Arabia* has been treated with contempt. Liddell Hart does not mention it; Graves dismisses it as "inaccurate and sentimental,"[11] but since Lawrence collaborated with Thomas on the usual terms of disclaiming the help given by a note in the book, who is to blame? In any case little is said in Thomas's book about Lawrence's father, and less about his mother. Thomas Lawrence is here said to have been a "great sportsman," at one time owner of estates in Ireland, who lost "most of his worldly possessions during the Gladstone period" when he "brought his family across the Irish Sea to Wales."[12] Lowell Thomas's book says that Lawrence's mother did not wish him to go to Syria, but eventually consented and "allowed him two hundred pounds for the trip." (According to Lawrence, the family income at the time was £300 or £400 a year). Her visit to China as a missionary with her eldest son in the 1920's is mentioned, and is true.[13]

Graves has "County Meath," the "Leicestershire stock," "Sir Walter Raleigh," "great sportsman," and "mixed blood," for the father. He met the mother and admired her strong character and personality. Her features he found like those of Lawrence. He mentions the China mission, and records an utterance of Lawrence's mother which should be of interest to psychologists: "We could never be bothered with girls in our house." Graves thinks that

* She was much offended by a letter from Graves about Lawrence, the only offence in which was that Graves rightly refused to be treated patronisingly by Shaw.

Lawrence's house saw so few women because of this atmosphere.[14]

The much longer and more detailed account of Liddell Hart's book (written by Lawrence himself) is more outspoken, and gives valuable information to any reader who has the clue while hiding it from others. Lawrence there speaks of his " adopted surnames," which " did not belong," and they are: Lawrence, Ross, Shaw. He shows his resentment at the ambiguous situation of himself and his brothers in a bitter sentence where he says that his father's family " seemed unconscious of his sons, even when after his death recognition of their achievements might have done honour to the name." What name? He had just repudiated " Lawrence," so that he must mean " Chapman." The five brothers, Lawrence proceeds, were taught to be self-sufficient, but after the war when two were killed the others could not rid themselves of their loneliness—but was it only after the war? Lawrence wrote that when he was asked how he stood the company of his fellow-airmen in the barrack room he might answer that he was at home again in his boyhood days. He adds that to claim the lower class as his birthright hardly coincided with the truth.[15] Of course, he never thought of himself as a plebeian, except for purposes of self-dramatising.

Lawrence's rhetorical style strains for effect and the avoidance of the stereotyped phrase, and in the end so often achieves a near rather than clear statement; and here he was being intentionally " mystifying." But it seems a fair inference that he resented very much indeed being ignored by his father's family after ' Lawrence ' of Arabia had become world-known. True, he claimed that he didn't mind, but he meant from the point of view of conventional " morality." Humanly, socially, personally, he cared intensely and understandably.

What Lawrence wrote about his parents in this book of Liddell Hart's is even more interesting, and in spite of mannerism and " mystification " much more nearly authentic than what he gave the two previous biographers. His father, he says, was reduced to " a craftsman's income " by his " self-appointed exile," but then " the landowning pride of caste " would not permit him to work for money. With five children the " family's very necessaries of life were straitened," and they could only live because the father " denied himself every amenity " and the mother " served the household like a drudge." His mother, he says, was Calvinist, ascetic, " a woman of character and keen intelligence," she possessed " iron decision " but was " charming, when she wished." She kept to herself and did not allow her children to know their neighbours. There was a " difference in social attitude " between the parents, for the father was " courtly, but abrupt and large," a man who " shot, fished, rode, sailed " with the " certainty of birthright experience," and " never touched a book." It seems that he carried his disdain for work so far that he never wrote a cheque himself—or was this a precautionary measure?[16]

There is another factor influencing the character of Lawrence's father which is of importance to our enquiry. He had been reared in the surroundings of the Anglo-Irish aristocracy and developed the outlook of that class. Then this naturally self-confident and sociable sportsman had been compelled because of the situation created by his second ménage to cut himself off from his very roots.

The dominant personality of the two parents was obviously Lawrence's mother, with whom Lawrence had in common not only such an obvious physical feature as their strikingly blue eyes, but also significant traits of character. The most significant of these is her strong will-power, which had not only enabled her to draw Thomas Chapman away from his family and from the surroundings he loved, but enabled her to raise herself to such a status as to be an equal mate for a gentleman. The letter Lawrence wrote to Charlotte Shaw from Karachi which has been referred to earlier completes the picture of his parents traced in Hart's biography. Lawrence's views of his mother's influence on his home and up-bringing are of vital importance in assessing his own temperament and character. He says that his mother's Calvinist conscience compelling her to make him atone for their sin she converted this typical Anglo-Irish squire to the habits of a person of her own back-ground. A woman who could do that must have possessed remarkable qualities, and above all a strength of will superior perhaps even to the ruthless will of her famous son. He said that her devotion to the father of her children was not lessened by the fact that he was a perpetual reminder of her sin in taking him from the other woman —indeed her success had its pleasures as well as its pangs, while her attitude towards her children could not but be affected by her religion and a state of mind which was utterly convinced of its own rightness. The couple were terrified at the prospect of their secret being discovered, especially by the children. Of course it inevitably came to their ears. It seems possible that in the case of T. E. Lawrence we might link the shock of discovery and the burden of keeping the secret to himself with his running away to join the Artillery and certainly with his being given a small bungalow to himself, so that he saw as little of his family as possible. Although they maintained a smooth façade to the outer world the difference in background between the father and the mother and the social difficulties inherent in their life together must have led at times to strain, a strain of which Lawrence felt himself the nervous victim.[17]

In this situation, so incapable of any solution, lies the chief cause of Lawrence's bitter futile tragedy. It was at once so trifling in the scheme of things and so overwhelmingly important in the narrow society of the day. The misfortune was double. In the first place was the single but incalculable shock of discovering the " state of sin " acting on a gifted, intensely vain and susceptible youth—a shock which, in spite of his assertion that it did not affect him, obviously left reverberations of resentment throughout his life. In the second place, there was this conflict of which he speaks, inevitably created by the opposing influences of two such different types of parent. Under such stresses—given the additional burden of conventional Oxford—natural human weaknesses and faults became exaggerated and incorrigible. The invisible but unpassable circle of loneliness drawn about his childhood became a fixed habit—" I'd rather be a prig than be sociable."[18] He hid his feelings of guilt under the mannerisms of the Oxford poseur. The high-spirited self-esteem of youth became a derisive pride (" the colossal bladder of my vanity ") which scorned while it craved notoriety. Natural impulses were lost in the cultivation of a consuming will-to-power which was to compensate for all inferiority and yet always dropped to apathy or disgust at the moment of achievement—the will was not exercised to an end, it was itself the end. Hence the craving to be liked, which led to so deliberate and calculated a building of " friendships separated by bulk-heads."[19] Hence, too, a defensive callousness which offended even so devoted a patron as Hogarth. Hence, obviously, the need for mystification and more or less absurdly improbable anecdotes about himself accepted and broadcast by " the Lawrence Bureau."

But doubtless the reader has already seen the danger that his undeniable shock and suffering may be forced to explain everything in the man and his life, as is the case too often with the formulas of psycho-analysis. Human minds and bodies, aspirations and sympathies, cravings and revulsions, are not as simple as that. But to attempt to tell the story of Lawrence while ignoring this situation is like putting on Hamlet without the king and queen and above all, without the haunting ghost.

Lawrence admired and imitated his genial, aristocratic father; rebelled with all the strength of his powerful will against the strong will of the mother he thought so remorselessly religious. His father was said to have been among the best snipe and pheasant shots in Ireland and a yachtsman.[20] Was it mere coincidence that Lawrence in his younger days made himself a first-class revolver shot (pheasant shooting being hopelessly beyond his means) and in later life an expert in speed boats? It is perhaps far-fetched—and yet perhaps not —to see even in Lawrence's over-strenuous cycling an attempt to live up to paternal stories of " hard riding " in the hunting field. For the cosmopolitan there is wry humour in noting how members of even the most unimportant politico-economic group conceive themselves superior to all the others on the usual fallacious racial prejudices. Here the Anglo-Irish stand high, and in his wanderings Lawrence found no man equal to his own English, which he attributed to his father's " blood " in him. Lawrence wrote Graves that he never looked at a man's face, nor recognised one; he thought this was " hereditary," because once in the street his father had trodden on Lawrence's foot in passing and had apologised without recognising his son.[21]

Nowhere is the link between father and son more noticeable than in their attitude towards work and money. By his unorthodox rashness the father was reduced as we have seen, to a " craftsman's income "—meaning an " artisan's wage "?—but his " landowning pride of caste " would not allow him to do any work for his children and their mother. This imitation feudalism in the 19th century was obviously an anachronism, dating from the Dark Ages. In that epoch of perpetual civil war the knight's overlord gave him land and serfs to work it for him, and forbade him to work on pain of derogation in order that no peaceful means of gain should mitigate his military efficiency and ferocity. In the 19th century the only people who had any justification for maintaining this knightly " pride of caste " against work were the regular officers of the Royal Navy and Army; and we shall have often to note Lawrence's intense bitterness against " regular officers." Why? It must have been that he felt himself in every respect their equal, and indeed one of them, except for the one derogation which had debarred him entry to their aristocratic enclosure. But by 1880 the ancient exemption hardly applied to those land-owning scions who merely amused themselves with shooting and fishing and so forth. As gentlemen and nothing else they rather laid themselves open to the taunt of Lawrence's friend G. B. Shaw in *Man and Superman:*

> " BRIGAND: I am a brigand. I live by robbing the rich.
> TANNER: I am a gentleman. I live by robbing the poor. Shake
>   hands."

Inadequate as was the " craftsman's income," as he did not earn it, the money must somehow have been wrung from reluctant Irish tenants.

In his later years probably no one would have agreed with Shaw more thoroughly than Lawrence, but by that time the genteel pose which he had taken over from his father had become second nature. He would have liked an income but was determined not to work for it (" there is nothing so repulsive as working merely for a living—only things are so bad just now that many people are doing that in despair. I refuse to do it . . .")[22] and resented the fact that his father's family wouldn't give him £300 a year.[23] In his early days he had nothing but scorn for " professionalism " in the arts and in politics,[24] and he asserted that he had taken no money for his book and had used his pay only " for official purposes." The whole obsolete attitude was one of the self-created obstacles with which he tripped himself up; but he certainly derived the prejudice from his landowner father. Perhaps Lawrence's vagueness about facts and numbers had the same origin.

If Lawrence's father was at one time a hard drinker (as he asserts), his son certainly did not imitate him in that respect. And it is easy to see why. While the father might boast unscathed of his skill in snipe and pheasant shooting, yachting and riding, he would not have dared to recall old carousals before the fanatically teetotal mother. Indeed Lawrence throughout life maintained prejudices which show a curious

ignorance of the physiology of taste. As late as 1934 he feels inclined
" to smile at these wine-palates " and goes on to make the absurd
assertion: " They deprive themselves of the faculty of judging between
waters, by coarsening their throats with fermented drinks—and that
is a loss of their tastes."[25] How did he know? And did he really think
we taste with our throats? As one who preferred Acqua Vergine to
Acqua Marcia, Hilaire Belloc (whom he was attacking) might have
felt inclined " to smile at " a connoisseurship of water based on Arab
wells contaminated by camel urine and the chlorinated water-tanks
of Army camps. Here of course the mother's influence is palpable,
though he did evade it once to the extent of saying that gin (of all
things!) " has the most beautiful limpidity of anything on earth."[26]
Though Lawrence yielded to the extreme religious compulsion of the
household in his youth, he told Liddell Hart that he had discarded
conventional religion and " did not notice its loss."[27] If it is much
harder to point to specific instances of this maternal influence than in
the father's case, it was none the less there, perhaps the more formidable and permanent as it was something to be resisted or evaded at all
costs. " I can't live at home: I don't know why: the place makes me
utterly intolerable."[28]

Lawrence believed that he had known about the situation
at home before he was ten. It seems a tender age at which to
understand, face and suffer such a complication. This " before I was
ten " is very likely a rhetorical expression deriving from Lawrence's
vagueness over numbers. But, whatever the age at which he did
become aware of this trouble, one cannot help connecting with it a
curious episode which has been mentioned but left unexplained by
Lawrence and his biographers. Readers of the *Letters* must have
puzzled over a sentence in a letter to Lord Wavell written just after
Christmas, 1923, when Lawrence was a private in the Tank Corps.
After commenting graphically but unfavourably on the drinking
habits of the troops, he adds: " The old army, in my recollection, did
at least carry its drink. Don't you agree? "[29] This " old army "
reference struck me as a curious remark, and I had nearly dismissed it
as one of Lawrence's usual mystifications, when I suddenly recollected
a sentence in Liddell Hart's biography which was more precise but not
very generous with details: " In his teens he took a sudden turn for
military experience at the urge of some private difficulty, and served

for a while in the ranks."[30]   This sentence, as it turns out, was based on two statements made by Lawrence himself. In the first he says that about 1906 he enlisted in the Artillery and " did eight months " before he was bought out. In the second he says he ran away from home and served in the Artillery for six months—the discipline didn't worry him but he was terrified by the fighting of his fellow-soldiers at the week-ends.[31]

Of course this might be dismissed as one more of Lawrence's leg-pulling " Milesian tales," in which case it has no significance. If it is true, then it must have been (as he says) somewhere between August, 1905, when a published letter shows him on a cycling trip in England, and August, 1906, when he was in Brittany. He was then 17 and under age and presumably a little under height, but when recruits were badly needed such small difficulties were then overlooked. So far as I can find there is no other reference to this experience in the *Letters* or the reminiscences of his friends. If, in spite of the lack of any corroborative evidence but that one allusion to the " Old Army " in his letter to Wavell, Lawrence's story is accepted as true, then it is surely rather striking evidence of his early interest in soldiering and a first attempt to deal with some seemingly insoluble " private difficulty " by trying to hide in the ranks. As to the motives for his running away— we might draw obvious inferences from the remark to Graves that home life made him " intolerable," while his mother's attitude had made him shrink from a home where he felt he could call no secret his own.

A break in his studies may perhaps have taken place at just this time, since Lawrence said he changed from mathematics to history when he was " nearly 18."[32]   At the same period (i.e., just after his presumed release from the Artillery), his parents seemed to have realised that they had to deal not only with an exceptionally gifted, but also exceptionally self-willed and independent youth, who, if he was to be kept from further rash adventuring of this truant sort had to be given exceptional treatment and freedom. It was when he began to read history that his parents had built for his exclusive use a two-room bungalow in the garden of Polstead Road, where at the time of writing it still exists.[33]

The usual explanation for Lawrence's changing from an attic in the house to this bungalow is that the growing boys over-filled the house— but, if so, why was it not given to the eldest son ? Lawrence allowed

Graves to write that " to avoid surveillance later he refused to sleep in the house," but also passed the statement that he built the bungalow with his own hands, which is obviously untrue. The only thing he did was to hang the walls with sheeting of the type used in workhouses to make them sound-proof, but the place was much more comfortable than the average room in an Oxford college, having running water, electric light, a house telephone and a stove. Here, it is said, he did all his University work, wrote his thesis, and (in 1914), wrote his share of *The Wilderness of Zin*.[34]

His mother says that there is " not a word of truth " in the stories that after reporting in at midnight he would be " out at night till all hours, and come and get in by a window." Vyvyan Richards, his closest Oxford friend at that time, has a very different story. Lawrence, he says, woke up at night like a cat—there is plenty of confirmation of this detail in later life—and on winter nights would go and dive into an icy river and run back dripping and grinning all over his face. On being introduced by Lawrence to his mother, Richards had the pleasant experience of hearing himself derisively introduced as the performer of Lawrence's own midnight and clandestine irregularities.[35]

Such trivialities may seem hardly worth recording, but their significance lies not in the episodes themselves but in the psychology they reveal, the reactions of Lawrence's highly susceptible temperament to the fate imposed on him at birth. Already, at 18, he had developed his *farouche* independence and personal loneliness, self-discipline and self-punishment—sometimes real, sometimes imagined —a reckless derision and almost clownish mockery at life's futilities and pretences.

It is easy to understand Lawrence's view that such a couple as his parents would have been well-advised not to produce children.[36]

CHAPTER THREE

THE INFLUENCE of Oxford—by which of course they mean the
University and its institutions—on Lawrence was decisive, as
most of his friends agree. The attraction of University life
induced him while still at the High School to enjoy—a little fearful of
the risks perhaps—breaking the school regulation forbidding the
pupils to visit undergraduates' rooms in college.[1] Lowell Thomas
thought that Oxford had " left its indelible mark " on Lawrence, and a
fellow-graduate feelingly describes him as " the perfect Oxonian."[2]
Yet his entrance to the University was not quite so smooth and
effortless as might be supposed from the stories of his alleged success in
passing examinations. Lawrence, as already mentioned, told Liddell
Hart that he had " worked at mathematics until nearly 18," and then
changed to history.[3] Perhaps we may infer that he did not work very
hard or had not much aptitude for mathematics, since he had
" encouraged " his schoolfellow, T. W. Chaundy, to do his algebra
for him.[4] And if he had spent six months away from school by running
away from home to join the Artillery, the loss of time may have
affected his work adversely. At all events, the change to history was
not a success, and he failed in the examination for a History Scholarship
at St. John's College.[5]

The date of this John's examination is not recorded, though possibly
it was in June, 1906. In August of that year he made his first independent trip to France, and on his return either began or continued to
receive lessons from a history crammer, L. C. Jane, who later became a
lecturer in the international politics school at Aberystwyth.[6] The
crammer reports that Lawrence would not read the obvious books,
but only the more obscure ones, and that while his interests were very

45

wide, they were chiefly medieval. He took no interest in later periods, though he did once read a work on the French Revolution. Jane did not think Lawrence was "a scholar by temperament" and thought his work always unusual without any sign of conscious effort to make it so. Lawrence liked to ask him unexpected questions and then watch his crammer's expression without comment. He usually visited Jane between midnight and 4 a.m.[7] So much for the good obedient son who was always in at midnight. Another friend adds that Lawrence often went on excursions after midnight and then returned home climbing in quietly through the window and steeping himself in a hot bath till daybreak.[8] It is perhaps worth recording that Lawrence always kept in his miscellaneous collection of books a copy of a work edited by Jane. This was the King's Classics edition of a translation of Jocelin de Brakelond's *Chronicle*, 1907, in which the editor wrote the inscription: "He who strives to please all men, deserves to please none."[9] As late as 1922 Lawrence occupied himself in trying to obtain for his former crammer a post, possibly the lectureship just mentioned.[10]

In February, 1907, after this intensive course of history cramming, Lawrence tried again, and this time won an exhibition at Jesus College, perhaps given preference by the examiners over other candidates because he had been born in Wales.[11] It is a possible inference, that Lawrence, after his neglect of the obvious books, would not have won the exhibition on his historical scholarship alone, though an enthusiastic friend asserted soon afterwards that "he knows all the history there is."[12] At all events, from 1906 until 1910, Lawrence's life conformed to the usual university pattern—he kept his terms at Oxford and spent the summer holidays abroad, in France or in Syria.

Very little is recorded of Lawrence's studies as an undergraduate. He spent only one term in College, after which he lived in the Polstead Road bungalow, cultivating his reputation for eccentricity and reading per diem whatever number of books unconnected with his official studies the reader's credulity will allow. A fellow undergraduate visiting Lawrence's rooms in College during his first term records with awe that Lawrence was out and "the only signs of him at all were a few strange books—of early French poetry chiefly."[13] It gives one a melancholy idea of what an English undergraduate of 1907 thought "strange books" when you reflect that (for instance) the

Chanson de Roland is now read in class by French schoolgirls. About the same time that he was devouring voraciously 50,000 books of the Oxford Union Library he " spent nearly three years reading Provençal Poetry and medieval Franch chansons de geste."[14] His only reference to Provençal literature, so far as I recollect, is when he tells his younger brother, William, " if you can read history and Bertrand together you would not dream of following Ezra Pound."[15] " Bertrand " of course is Bertrand de Born (whose castle Lawrence afterwards visited) and the other reference presumably to Ezra Pound's poem *Altaforte*. At his death Lawrence's library contained no works of Provençal literature either in the original or translated. On the other hand it contained no less than seventeen authors of the *langue d'oïl* up to Villon, of which eight are original texts, eight translations, and one text and translation. But of course he read many library books, and A. W. Lawrence mentions his possessing translations of *Huon of Bordeaux* and *The Four Sons of Aymon*, now no longer in the library. These, and no doubt others, must have been discarded or lost. The dates of purchase or publication show that Lawrence still kept his interest in medieval French after the war.

Lawrence's tutor at Jesus has left no opinion on his attainments in scholarship, unless his answer to Lawrence's apology for missing an appointment that it had given his tutor time for an hour's useful work is considered as such.[16] The remark is something of a chestnut in academic snootiness, so need not be taken too seriously. Professor Ernest Barker, who gave Lawrence special tuition in medieval history towards the end of his undergraduate course, could not remember any of Lawrence's essays but came to the conclusion that Lawrence was not an " historical scholar " in the normal sense of the phrase. The professor thought Lawrence was not interested in history for its own sake, but that he took the Oxford History School " because it was the next hurdle in his path at the time." The same, he thought, was true of Lawrence as archæologist, for whom that field of academic research, like history, was " not an end or a career, but a phase and an experience."[17] With this may be compared Lawrence's claim to " the practice of my ten years' study of history " in the Synopsis to his war book.[18] On the other hand the tradition at Oxford is that he was considered one of the most brilliant students of his year,[19] and if he behaved with studied eccentricity he was merely imitating the example of some of his intellectual pastors and masters. Lawrence's own remarks on his studies are very characteristic:

> "I left my special subject (the Crusades) till the last two weeks of the last term. It was mostly done while the examination was actually in progress in three all-night sittings: special subjects, if you know all but the facts, are a matter of simple cram."[20]

Knowing all about subjects except for the facts seems dangerous knowledge. But if little is recorded about Lawrence's official studies, there is luckily a good deal of scattered information about his unofficial activities; and though there is the usual difficulty, if not impossibility, of sorting out the facts from the "knowledge," the attempt must not be shirked. These may be roughly sorted out as adventurous, antiquarian and æsthetic.

Like other outstanding individualists Lawrence disliked the organised games which form so essential a part of the English "public school" system. In one of his *Letters*[21] Lawrence expresses disapproval of "the public school type," though one would say he possessed and even exaggerated some of its characteristic traits. But he certainly was not what in the schoolboy slang of his day was called a "muff." He excelled at such individualist efforts as revolver shooting, cycling, photography, and canoeing. He was reckless about getting himself hurt, or beaten up, and careless of his own health to an extreme degree with an only too public school disregard for precaution.

His accident in wrestling has been already discussed, and his cycling feats will be mentioned later. Cycling, transmuted to motor-cycling, lasted his life-time. Canoeing did not outlast the immediate pre-war days when he took a canoe to the Euphrates and upset himself and two Arabs at the hazard of their lives. Before that epoch, about 1908, he and a friend, H. F. Mathers, upset their canoe on the Cherwell during a winter flood, and as Lawrence had his legs wrapped in a rug he would have been drowned if his friend had not pulled him to the bank. The same friend was present at the over-advertised canoe trip down the under-ground Oxford sewer, the Trill Mill stream. From published accounts I had reached the baffling conclusion that there must have been two or even three first occasions on which this exploration took place. It seems that earlier accounts simply failed to mention that there were three canoes. According to Mr. Mathers's recollection,

The two-roomed bungalow in the garden of
No. 2 Polstead Road, Oxford.

ROBERT GRAVES in *Lawrence and the Arabs*

" To avoid surveillance he refused to sleep in the house at all, but
used a summer-house in the garden (he built it himself) as his
bedroom.

S. LAWRENCE (mother of T. E.) in *T. E. Lawrence by His Friends*

" When he began history a separate study was needed, so we had
a very pretty well-built bungalow of two rooms made for him at
the end of the garden."

the party included, besides Lawrence and himself, a future bishop (A. T. P. Williams), a future canon (E. F. Hall) and V. Richards. The sixth person was probably T. W. Chaundy, who has also left an account. The main purpose of the trip seems to have been to *épater les bourgeois* of Oxford by firing blank pistol-shots under the gutter gratings in the streets. It cannot have been very perilous since it was afterwards frequently repeated by Oxford girls, but then *il n'y a que le premier pas qui coûte*.[22]

As to climbing—Graves made the statement that Lawrence was " said to have invented the now classic climb from Balliol College to Keble College,"[23] but when questioned by Liddell Hart, Lawrence made the much more guarded statement that he " climbed towers and roofs to get photographs."[24] That is certainly supported by his photographs and contemporary letters. Speaking of Lawrence's lack of interest in natural science, C. F. C. Beeson says that Lawrence found nothing worth studying in Jurassic cliffs or plantations of trees—they were to him only material for climbing.[25]

As we shall see when we come to glance at his undergraduate trips overseas, Lawrence liked to mingle his antiquarian and æsthetic hobbies with strenuous exercise, and if he could find an opportunity for some unnecessary feat of endurance, so much the better. (Even as a schoolboy he had enjoyed smashing some—presumably flimsy— church pews which interfered with his access to a monumental brass). As he grew older and the spirit of the place acted on him he developed more and more into the typical Oxford æsthete without losing the antiquarian interests which indeed played a dominant part in Oxford medievalism and æstheticism. He enjoyed the sensation of lawlessness when discovered trespassing with a friend in search of a tumulus or, in the style of Harrison Ainsworth, collecting mouldering human bones in a church crypt. Another friend was made to visit ancient stones near Oxford or the prehistoric earthworks of Dorchester or a Roman road.[26]

Almost inevitably, at that period, Lawrence became a Pre-Raphaelite æsthete, and the influence of William Morris lasted in one form or another all his life. The modern myth which makes William Morris an etiolated and languishing dreamer of dreams is inexact. His contemporaries thought he looked like a sea-captain, and his friends noted with encouragement that when he went down into his cellar he always returned with two bottles in each hand. At one time he turned himself into a socialist stump talker; at another interest in the sagas took him to Iceland. He was an Oxford medievalist with a difference, a man who worked with his own hands to build and furnish the house he dreamed of for his beautiful wife, an artist-craftsman in literature, the main inspirer of what used to be called *art nouveau*, the reviver of fine printing. In his old age he turned from narrative poems to prose romances of imaginary past times written in a style of mannered archaistic simplicity. His *News From Nowhere* is a roseate dream of the past thrown into an improbable future, for what he was really attacking was not so much capitalism as ugliness, and what he wanted to destroy was not class distinctions but industrialism. He ended up as a master printer producing books, mostly reprints of medieval works, at socialist prices running from ten to thirty pounds, at his Kelmscott Press.

Like Oxford and Morris, Lawrence looked back wistfully to the past. "He lived in a world of old things, castles, churches, memorial brasses, pottery and books—books—books."[27] Among the books were those of Morris, of which he still retained sixteen at the time of his death. Morris's name often turns up in his letters, and in answering a questionnaire he gave Morris as his favourite author.[28] During the war he wrote to Vyvyan Richards: "I'm always trying to blow up railway trains and bridges instead of looking for the *Well at the World's End*"—the title of a Morris romance about the search for the fountain of youth. But, Richards tells us, the Morris book which Lawrence most enjoyed was *The Roots of the Mountains*.

The idea of that book no doubt came from the scanty traditions of the Teutonic tribes about the period of the Hunnish invasions. The "folk" of Burgstead are shown leading a Nordic-Arcadian life as pastoralists, woodsmen, hunters and craftsmen. They dwell communally in "halls" and sleep in "shut-beds," hold "things" and "folk-moots," parade with tribal banners like a Swiss *braderie*, and blow mightily on anachronistic "slug-horns." Their young women are called "mays" and fight gallantly in battle. The hero is called "Face-of-God" and the rival heroines "The Bride" and "Sun-Beam." A love-story is woven into the military tale of the redemption of lost tribes of the "kindred" from the Huns who are massacred to the last man with platonic bloodthirstiness.[29]

At intervals throughout his life Lawrence dreamed and talked of setting up and himself working a hand-press in a "hall" modelled after Burgstead and similar Morris fantasies. To this end he bought some of the 14th-century timbers from an old Oxford Hall when it was pulled down, but never used them. He bought the land in Essex where his friend Richards—the sharer of this dream—had actually built himself a hut for a printer's press. That was after the war, but in undergraduate days they had planned a hall with the carved king-posts, rafters and purlins from the old Oxford Hall like those of old Lisieux,[30] and with "shut-beds," labelled 'Meum' and 'Tuum.'

In the undergraduate days he and his friend combined the cult of Morris with a strenuous expedition through mud and snow to visit what they had heard was "the perfect Morris house" at Chipping Camden in the Cotswolds. There Lawrence exulted over "the large living-room with the old open chapel roof," the "low galleries screened with Morris chintz," the "long refectory tables and shelves full of the Kelmscott printings," the "Morris tapestries," the "special oak lectern" displaying the Kelmscott Chaucer, and the "very handpress Morris himself had used."[31] Later, after his first visit to Syria, the Morris hall idea was abandoned, and he and another friend were to live in a windmill by the sea, printing "rather precious books," by Pater and Arnold, each copy to be bound differently for each improbable customer "in vellum stained with Tyrian dye."[30] And when long afterwards he produced the special edition of his war book each copy was indeed differently bound, not in vellum stained with Tyrian dye and not by Lawrence, but in expensive designs by the best-known London book-binders.

Yet when it came to the point Lawrence always backed out at the last minute from any such joint undertaking. In 1912, for instance, he wrote Vyvyan Richards from Carchemish about his "superb scheme for building a wooden house in Epping Forest," begging him to "do everything, and let me come home at Xmas to rapture over all. I have more hopes than ever before. Sail in, and carry out all to your content and I will be more than acquiescent. How is the type-cutting? If you are hewing logs in a forest, your hands are probably ruined for six months. No matter in the world."[33] Fifteen months later all his enthusiasm has ebbed away in an awkward confession that "I cannot print with you when you want me. I have felt it coming for a long time, and have funked it. You know I was in England for a fortnight this summer, and actually found myself one afternoon in Liverpool Street coming up to you . . . and then went back again."[34]

The persistence of this æsthetic dream of emulating the poet-craftsman-printer and dwelling in a William Morris world is as curious as the failure to carry it out, except in odd details or amateurishly, is pathetic. That he obstinately held to his preference for Morris against the current opinion in the 1920's is the more remarkable since he usually followed docilely the fashions of literary London. Lawrence was not a poet, he was a high-brow with an immense respect for poets, as romantic as Swinburne. E. M. Forster relates how Lawrence was scandalised by the suggestion that another world war would destroy all civilisation and all poetry, and remarked primly " that poetry is indestructible."[35] Graves records that Lawrence thought of poetry as a mastery of the technique of using words rather than of the poet's special approach to life and thought.[36] (It is surely a happy alliance of the two?) Neither was he a craftsman nor a printer. He tried his hand at wood-carving, at copying in brass the lantern in Holman Hunt's *Light of the World*, (or in Paton's *The Man with the Muck Rake*), at sculpting a naked Arab boy in stone, at sketching castles. They were all more or less failures. Most competent printers agree with David Garnett (a director of the Nonesuch Press) in thinking Lawrence's production of his own book " a monstrous example."[37] Yet, in 1927, he wrote Graves: " I've wished all my life to have the power of creating something imaginative: sculpture, painting, literature: and always I've found my gift of expression inadequate to the conception I felt." So much did he want achievement even in the lower activity of printing that he persuaded himself he had actually done what he only dreamed. In an unpublished letter to Henry Williamson, Lawrence apologised for typing: which he says he hated as he claimed that his long experience with print had taught him to respect it.[38] He should have said that his experience was not with print but of talking about printing, for all he ever did as a printer was to have one book set up by the " Monotype " process.

How far this Morris æstheticism was a conscious attempt to escape from the religious servitude imposed on him can only be a matter of conjecture. Though he rebelled against it and at one time claimed to hold the " chilly creed " of " nihilism "[39], orthodox religion of the Anglican type was heavily imposed on his youth, and seems to have endured up till the time when he left Oxford at the age of 22, in 1910. We are told that he was a regular worshipper at St. Aldate's, where he profited by the teaching of the Gospel by one of the Canons there while he himself took the Sunday school classes twice each Sunday.[40] This began while Lawrence was still at school and involved a walk to Folly Bridge twice every Sunday, a distance of five miles in all. The Sunday school teaching may have gone on until 1910, certainly lasted well into his undergraduate days since he corresponded with his Sunday school boys when he went on his cycle tours. Every year he took the boys on a rowing treat up the river, and in the winter invited them to his home for an evening when he taught them a game in which they had to pick up sixpences with their mouths from a bath of warm water two inches deep, kneeling beside the bath with their hands behind them.[41]

His elder brother says that for two or three years Lawrence was an officer in the St. Aldate's Company of the Church Lads' Brigade, and since he could not be an " officer " until he was 19, this must have been from the end of 1907 on. The Church Lads' Brigade was founded by a retired Colonel, and its sponsors include Field-Marshals and Arch-bishops—indeed the Church Lads were known as " the bishop's boys." The idea apparently was to present religion to ardent youth with all the glamour of military life, or perhaps vice versa. At any rate, the exact performance of religious duties was inculcated along with the use of uniforms, bands, drills, parades and route marches. The training was probably more military in Lawrence's day that it is now, since a tendency for the military to overtop the religious interests was checked in the pacifist year 1936. The ultimate effect of this service on Lawrence seems to have been rather on the negative side. In later life he wrote unsympathetically of soldiers who thought they could reconcile the religious life with their profession, and eagerly pressed the Labour M.P., Ernest Thurtle, to abolish obligatory Church parades.[42] He went further, and protested against the use of the word " supernatural " in connection with himself: " I do not believe that. There is no more rational being than myself alive."[43] But, as elsewhere, his most ve-hement protest was against the strong-willed and very religious mother who he considered had imposed all these things on his youth. He resented his mother's repeated attempts to make him religious. Christianity was ruined for him by her persistence.[44] So much of

Lawrence's life was rebellion against and escape from that dominant personality and its ambience! If we accept his own story of his running away to join the Artillery " about 1906," then that must have been his first effective if desperate reaction, a rough sanctuary from which he returned only on terms which gave him a bungalow to himself and the freedom of Oxford. Even from that situation he insisted on an annual escape overseas, which progressively extended from Brittany and Normandy to the Mediterranean and then to Syria.

CHAPTER FOUR

According to one of his contemporaries, Lawrence's parents had complete trust in their sons and each year gave them a sum of money for their holidays and let them go where they liked.[1] If the family really lived on £400 a year (just about £55 a year each) the sum cannot have amounted to much. And in fact, Lawrence spread stories of his fabulous economy in travelling expenses which are partly confirmed but more often contradicted by his own letters at the time. In point of fact T. R. T. Chapman inherited £25,000 from his brother who died in 1915, and T. R. Lawrence left £17,700.

He was still a schoolboy when, in August 1906, he crossed to Brittany, and when joined a few days later by his friend, C. F. C. Beeson, went on a cycling tour. Each carried on his bicycle a small basket covered with American-cloth, a waterproof and a pair of boots. They also had a volume of Viollet-le-Duc's *Dictionnaire Raisonné*.[2] Viollet-le-Duc was the antiquarian architect who repaired and restored (some people said over-restored) so many French cathedrals and *châteaux-forts* during the Second Empire. Among his other works was one on Military Architecture which was translated into English by B. MacDermott in 1879.

Lawrence mentions this book in his thesis, *Crusader Castles*, but it is impossible to say if he read it as early as 1906—it was reprinted in 1907. The point is that at eighteen Lawrence was already making a study of medieval castles, a fact confirmed by C. F. C. Beeson who says they spent many hours at such places at Lehon, Montafilant and Tonquedec drawing ground-plans and making diagrams of peculiarities of style. He adds that Lawrence was chiefly interested in the minds of the people who had planned these defensive works and in seeing to what extent their intentions had been put to the test by history.³ Their main intention was to keep out their enemies, in which they were not always successful, and after the development of artillery the castles became useless. It is said that in one year the then newly-developed French artillery of Charles VII retook from the English sixty castles each of which had cost them a four to six months' siege. The interest therefore was purely antiquarian, and had only a remote connection with the principles of modern warfare. On the other hand, that he concentrated on this military subject, from choice and long before he thought of making it a subject for a thesis, is one more example of Lawrence's interest in the army and matters military.

The letters written home—nearly always to his mother—during this trip on the whole, show an earnest young highbrow with a very literary approach to life. Moonlight on the Channel reminds him of Tennyson's "long glories of the autumn moon" and at Dinard he thinks of Milton. He has been reading Ruskin's *Stones of Venice*, which he finds masterly; as a result he is not surprised to find Renaissance styles dropping out of favour.⁴ He writes a patronising and dogmatic letter to his younger brother on the subject of excavating earth mounds, and finds difficulties evidently in getting what he wanted in France, and in trying to adapt Breton ways of living to his vegetarian and teetotal fads. He could not get "a decent drink," which made him very thirsty, the apples were "uneatable," the only other fruits were pears and plums, though he had a "glorious feast" of wild blackberries. There was no milk in Brittany—"not obtainable anywhere." The dangers of too puritanical an attachment to the strict doctrines of teetotal vegetarianism in a strange land showed themselves by his getting diarrhœa through eating too many plums and developing Malta fever by being for once successful in his hunt for milk, by getting goat's milk.⁵ The Malta fever may have been later than this first trip, but he certainly had it before 1909. Even on this excursion he showed signs of his life-long habit of being unnecessarily strenuous and getting himself knocked about—in climbing a castle he said he "impaled" himself and tore his face on thorns, and that he cycled to Fougères on the hottest day of the year, 107° in the shade, according to his romantic arithmetic.⁶

In April, 1907—after he had won his exhibition but before actually joining his College—Lawrence made a cycling tour round the Welsh castles. Nothing of much interest is contained in his letters. He told his brother of sitting down to make a sketch, and " you know it takes a lot to make me do that." He gave his mother a broad hint that he wanted a camera, and said he found himself better if he limited himself to two meals a day and a glass of milk at one o'clock.

He got his camera—or was allowed to use his father's—in August of that year when they visited France together. Lawrence speaks of a whole day from six in the morning till seven in the evening spent in photographing Richard I's Château Gaillard, during which he took ten photographs. He had found it a hard day and some of the photographs most difficult to take.[7] Study of the castle decided Lawrence that Richard I was far greater than usually supposed and the big fortress was to him undoubtedly a work of genius.[8] Separating from his father, Lawrence made his way to Angers by way of Le Mans. He rode back to St. Malo by way of Le Lion d'Angers and Rennes in a day, and boasted to his French friends at Dinard that he had ridden 250 kilometres in a day. By the route he took it is 123 kilometres from Angers to Rennes, and 69 from there to St. Malo (where there is a ferry to Dinard), so we can allow him only 192 instead of the 250 which (he said) caused his friends to exclaim: " *Oh là-là, qu'il est merveilleux.*"[9] He had said the year before that to be alone " makes such an addition to one's enjoyment of nature and her prodigal loveliness."[10] He evidently still thought so since he visited the Château de Fougères by moonlight, and felt that " the dream of years " had been fulfilled by a night spent at Mont St. Michel. The romantic in him is shown by what he wrote of that visit:

" It is a perfect evening; the tide is high and comes some 20 feet up the street. In addition the stars are out most beautifully, and the moon is, they say, just about to rise. The phosphorescence in the water interests me specially."[11]

When did Lawrence decide to offer a thesis on the castles of the crusaders in Europe and Syria? Various dates have been suggested, from the summer of 1907 (before he even started his course), down to just before his final exams, so that he could make up for his failure to read the usual books.[12] The earliest piece of evidence I have found comes from a letter dated 23rd August, 1908, in which he praises the castle of Niort and adds: " Nothing could possibly have been more opportune or more interesting for my thesis."[13] For, as in the year before, he spent several weeks of July and August, 1907, in a really extended tour of castles, sometimes along roads deep in dust, sometimes toiling over hills, sometimes battling against head-winds and pelting rain and hail or wilting under the summer heats of the Midi until he likened his miseries to a combination of those of Sisyphus, Tantalus, and Theseus.[14] With a like energy he noted, sketched, ground-planned and photographed the castles which were to prove his thesis—for he had wisely formed his theory first and then set out to look for the evidence.

From the letters now available his journey can be followed place by place from Le Havre to Aigues-Mortes and back by the western roads. Whether the itinerary was given him by some older man, such as Hogarth or his tutor, or whether he worked it out for himself from the castles he wanted to see, it was a very good one. Unfortunately with his limited funds and mania for speed he tried to accomplish in six or seven weeks more than could have been seen properly in as many months, with the natural result that he had to admit he had no time for sight-seeing, apart, that is, from his castles. Of course at this date it is not possible to say which of the alternative routes he chose and whether he diverged, but in view of his habit of exaggerating his exploits we may note that, roughly speaking, he reported kilometres as miles. Thus, in a letter to his friend Beeson from the Hôtel du Nord, Cordes, near Albi (Tarn), he says he has had 38 punctures and come 1,400 miles[15] although the route on the map is only about 1,500 kilometres. A week later at the Grand Hôtel du Midi at Chalus (Haute Vienne) he reports that he has ridden nearly 2,000 miles to date[16] and from the maps the total distance does not seem much more than 2,100 kilometres.* It is claimed that he could do 180 miles a day.[17] As a matter of fact what Lawrence said was that *if* he had no luggage he *could* do 180 miles a day.[18] This would be 288 kilometres, quite a bit above the average of what the champion cyclists of Europe are asked to do in the Tour de France race. The 100 miles a day he claimed for his 1908 tour seem from the map to have been about 100 kilometres, but all the same it was a tremendous cycling achievement for an amateur.

This speeding along the roads was probably even more of an

*These kilometre figures are given only as approximate, but the calculation has been made to favour Lawrence.

attraction than seeing France and visiting castles, much as he genuinely enjoyed that. But speed was a lifelong passion with him, almost the only experience which seemed to alleviate his neurasthenia. It was a nervous stimulus which he seemed to experience as physical pleasure; "I could write for hours on the lustfulness of moving swiftly," he told Robert Graves.[19] After 1914 he rode a motor bicycle but at the time we are considering it was a pedal bicycle, a model with dropped racing handles and a top gear of unusually high ratio.[20]

Those who have come to realise Lawrence's irresistible propensity to dramatise his exploits and advertise himself will not be surprised to know that he circulated a very quotable little story about this bicycle which has been vouched for by his friends. Thus, Vyvyan Richards says Lawrence had "a light little racing bicycle, which was built by Lord Nuffield when plain Mr. Morris at Oxford. The two of them put their heads together to perfect the design."[21] Towards the end of his life Lawrence told Canon Hall that "the diminutive bicycle, specially built for him by Lord Nuffield's own hands for his first wanderings across France, had been stolen outside All Souls."[22] And Professor A. W. Lawrence speaks of his brother's "bicycle, a three-speed machine with one unusually high gear, built to his order in a shop at Oxford by Mr. Morris, who subsequently became famous in the motor industry."[23] Unfortunately for this story, Lord Nuffield assured David Garnett that he "gave up making bicycles before 1900."[24]

There can be no doubt that all three statements just quoted were repeated in complete sincerity and good faith, because the writers believed what Lawrence told them. Obviously they only knew of these stories because they heard them from Lawrence himself, as V. Richards himself admits, adding significantly "yet none of these stories was ever told against himself."[25] Of course, it can and will be said that hitherto these exaggerations and untruths I am pinning on Lawrence are trifles, and so they are, though truth itself is not a trifle. But it so happens that they can be convincingly shown to be untrue, while in other cases one may be perfectly certain the tales are false without having complete evidence to prove it. But what are we to think of a man so self-centred, so—there is no other word for it—conceited, so avid of *réclame* at any price, that he would stoop to such trifling deceits? And if he would deceive in trifles, for the sake of a worthless astonishment and admiration, what guarantee is there that he did not do likewise in more important matters where he cannot be so convincingly checked? And further, what is the value of a reputation which is based on a multitude of just such disprovable or suspect stories? There is a difference between deliberately inventing stories, trivial or otherwise, in order to show off, and the mistakes, lapses of memory, inaccuracies to which all men are liable, not to mention the variations in tastes, beliefs and thought at different ages.

The most important and influential part of this trip (which had other important moments for him) was his stay at Aigues-Mortes, the 13th century fortified base for the 7th crusade, begun by Louis IX and completed by his successor. It was too late (1240-1280) to be of use to his thesis, unless indeed he later compared its comparatively flimsy walls with the immense ruins of Chastel Pèlerin (1218) near Haifa. But Aigues-Mortes was Lawrence's first contact with the Mediterranean. He felt, he wrote his mother, as if at last he had reached the way to " the South and all the glorious East." He saw " Greece, Carthage, Egypt, Tyre, Syria, Italy, Spain, Sicily, Crete . . ." before him. " I must get down here—further out—again! Really this getting to the sea has almost overturned my mental balance, I would accept a passage for Greece to-morrow."[26] Possibly much of this emotion is " literary " like his schoolboyish echoing of Xenophon's " Thalassa! Thalassa! " when he thought he caught a glimpse of the sea from Les Baux. But at any rate he did go to the Middle East the very next year in the face of considerable difficulties and hardships.

Evidently relying on Lawrence's stories, Liddell Hart says Lawrence contracted malaria " probably " when " sleeping out in the marshy delta of the Rhône," when he was sixteen. Lawrence in fact was nearly 19 at the time. Moreover, he wrote a very long letter to his mother on that Sunday, the 2nd August, 1908, and mentions not only the mosquitoes but the curtains round the beds to keep them out. The enormous clouds of mosquitoes in the Camargue and its neighbourhood—impossible to realise for those who have not experienced them—would speedily have driven him to the shelter of a hotel and a net if he had tried to sleep out. (The " sleeping out " was just one of his tales; the letters show he was staying in hotels). But Lawrence was badly bitten—" I'm one huge bite "—and was infected with malaria in consequence. But this was not the malaria which recurred throughout his life. The Camargue malaria is comparatively mild and is said to last only nine years. There is every reason to think he was re-infected with a more serious type next year (1909) in Syria.[27]

Nobody will deny the energy and plain fare of Lawrence's French tours, but the stories have been over-played. He made five recorded tours of France and did not object to Graves saying that he had made eight.[28] He adds " on practically nothing." Vyvyan Richards is more precise: " He used to wander about France on his little light cycle, living on half a franc a day—' Plenty of berries at that time of the year,' he explained."[29] Another friend gets him down to " 2½d. a day," or 25 pre-1914 centimes. He certainly lived cheaply on milk and bread, cherries, apricots, peaches, pears, but only until the evening when " more solid stuff is consumed."[30] Another letter expresses a hearty British contempt for the menus of the Tarn region, but leaves one to infer that he had abandoned vegetarianism and was eating meat, since he accuses the Hôtel du Nord, Cordes, of giving him " a plough-ox or two," and " stewed infant or monkey."[31]   At Cordes he paid " 3 francs a night," and at Montpazier paid 1fr. 50c. for a " huge room with editions of Chateaubriand, the Corneilles, etc., a glorious Renaissance window . . . all comforts desirable."[32] Nobody is going to suggest that this was luxury, but it is different from the Lawrence Bureau picture of the sternly self-disciplined preparer for mighty deeds sleeping out and living on " a few pence a day."

He let himself in for real hardship and apparently some danger in the next year (1909) when, contrary to the advice of Hogarth and Doughty, he decided to tour the castles of Syria and Palestine on foot, in summer, and alone, without a companion or dragoman or baggage animals. Trying to sort out the facts from the self-created legends is, as usual, a complicated and ungrateful task, but it has to be attempted. We may dismiss at once such tales as that he " shortly after landing, adopted native costume and set out barefoot for the interior . . ." and " wandered off alone, along the fringe of the Great Arabian Desert."[33] Nor, except for the season and method of travelling, was there anything unusual or exploratory in his journey. With his letters home and a contemporary Baedeker it is easy to follow his trail and the places he visited. Afoot and with a special interest (i.e., castles) he did not follow altogether the usual tourist routes, but constantly crossed or

touched them. When he says that in parts of his journey he seemed
" to have been the first European visitor,"[34] he probably meant that in
the villages of the Jebel Akrad (which he is describing) no European
had asked the peasants for the pilgrim's dole of food and shelter.

It is said the idea of travelling thus cheaply was given him at
Oxford by " a half-Irish Arab,"[35] or as another describes him, " a
Syrian Protestant clergyman . . . the Rev. N. Odeh,"[36] from whom
he " picked up a smattering of conversational Arabic."

Certainly for such a journey he must have had some knowledge of
Syrian Arabic and probably his claim that he knew only " 80 words "
is as much a romantic understatement as his claim that he eventually
" knew 12,000 words " sounds fantastically exaggerated.[37] He was
certainly not penniless, since on one occasion he was able to pay seven
pounds for a carriage drive.[38] Vyvyan Richards says that Lawrence's
father gave him a lump sum, " out of which he bought a revolver and a
special camera costing £40." Richards remembered " his delight in
the perfect instrument," adding that Lawrence bought the cheapest
passage to the East, and—banked the rest.[39] According to David
Garnett, Lawrence went on the P. & O. liner *Mongolia*, from England,
on which the second-class single ticket at that date was £11.
These figures suggest that he may have been given £100; Lowell
Thomas says £200. A complication is introduced by Lawrence's
later statement to Graves that on his way to Syria he stopped in Paris
and bought a copper watch for ten francs, the copper watch being an
essential stage property in one of his Syrian stories. Obviously he
could have picked up the *Mongolia* at Marseille, but why spend a fare
of thirty-two shillings extra merely to buy a copper watch which he
could have bought in England? A plausible motive for his going to
Paris—if he did go—would be to look at the Museum of sculpture and
casts at the Trocadéro where there was also a collection of architectural
drawings by Viollet-le-Duc and the curator was M. C. Enlart, both of
them authorities on medieval castles. But he could not have travelled
by Paris and Marseille and at the same time have passed Gibraltar (as
Garnett says) on the same journey. Garnett, writing with unpublished
letters before him, is no doubt correct; in which case the copper
watch bought in Paris on the way to Syria is simply another one of
Lawrence's *ex-post-facto* embroideries or myths.[40]

For his protection Lawrence carried a letter (*irade*) from the Turkish

Government ordering all local officials to give him aid, obtained for him by the head of his college, Sir John Rhys, through the good offices of Lord Curzon. This was not a Foreign Office but a personal service to Rhys, as Curzon was not at that date in the Government. But without this protective letter Lawrence would certainly have been arrested by the Turkish police long before he had carried out his plans. Possibly this precaution was suggested by D. G. Hogarth, who also advised his consulting Doughty and a relative of Hogarth's, H. Pirie-Gordon, who had visited some of the Crusader castles in 1908, who lent Lawrence an annotated map of Syria he had used himself, and gave him photographs of castles taken on his journey.[41] He cannot then be accused of failing to collect expert information before starting or of throwing himself recklessly into an unplanned adventure.

Most of Lawrence's long walk that summer can be easily traced on the map from the information in his letters, except that the fact that one letter is missing leaves an uncertainty as to how he went from Haifa to Tripoli on his way north. Of course, he did not do as much as he allowed people to say. He visited 36 castles[42] and if in print he was credited with " visiting, and photographing in detail, some fifty," why, so much the better for the legend.[43] He had to traverse very mountainous country, and found Syria most difficult going, Esdraelon and the plain around Baalbek being the only flat places in the whole country.[44]

So much, en passant, for psychological " interpretations " of Lawrence based on his alleged " love of the Syrian desert " which is assumed to be as flat as the plains of Argentina. Perhaps he exaggerated when he wrote that in one day's march he " went up and down the height of Mt. Blanc," but that is certainly much closer to the truth than the boundless, empty plain idea. In Palestine he did not limit himself to castles, but walked all the way down the west shore of Lake Tiberias and some way down the Jordan Valley before turning seaward towards the great castle of Belvoir, after which he saw Nazareth on his way to Haifa.[45]

He was not wholly dependent on natives, and indeed seems to have met plenty of Europeans. He spent four days with the English doctor to the Jewish Mission at Safed, and speaks of meeting Irish women and Scotch women and some Americans from Sidon ; and he asked for hospitality at the American Mission School of Jebail, the ancient

Byblus, not far from Beirut. He has left even more detailed accounts of how he fared with the natives of Syria than with those of France. After describing the two sorts of very thin bread, used as " a dipper " for boiled wheat or " leben " (sour milk) he goes on to relate how the natives fed him. In the morning he was given hot sweetened milk with thin brittle bread, and a bowl of prickly pears which he found most refreshing. Bread and water only at mid-day, but, occasionally, figs, grapes and water-melons. There were also tomatoes and cucumbers. (How he avoided finding all these in the Midi of France where they super-abound in August is one of the many mysteries). In the evening he got bread or sour or sweetened milk. Very frugal fare, though when he stayed with priests they gave him stews and various types of meat-messes. He slept either in the house or on the roof or verandah on quilts stuffed with feathers, wool and fleas in equal proportions. Sometimes the people accepted money, sometimes not.[46] It is hardly surprising after this to learn that when Professor Barker saw him at a lecture in Oxford in October, 1909, he was thinned with hardship.

The expedition brought its accidents and adventures. Lawrence, at the end of his journey, wrote to the head of his college, saying that he had counted on two attacks of malaria but had had four. One or more of these may have been a return of the Camargue malaria, but it seems likely that he was mosquito-bitten again and infected with a worse type of malaria.[47] In September-October, 1918, during the advance across country partly traversed by Lawrence, the British army's malaria cases doubled in number and were " for the most part of a malignant type."[48] Possibly his stay with Dr. Anderson at Safed may have included treatment, though he seems to have been careless about his malaria—not realising, perhaps, that every malarious person is a potential source of infection to others. Someday perhaps Lawrence's medical history will be reconstructed by a competent physician. Meanwhile, the layman can only point to a possibility that his repeated attacks of malaria and other infections, not to mention broken bones, may cumulatively have had some effect on him in later life, i.e., a decline of physical energy reinforcing a native indolence and psychological depression or nervous exhaustion.

The " adventures " on this trip have been exaggerated, highly publicised, and constantly repeated. One of these was reported by Lawrence in a letter soon after it occurred:

" By the way, I took the escort abused above because I was shot at near Masyad: an ass with an old gun: I suppose he was trying it. At any rate he put in a shot at about 200 yards, which I was able to return rather successfully: for his horse promptly bolted about half a mile: I think it must have been grazed somewhere: at any rate he stopped about 800 yards away to contemplate the scenery, and wonder how on earth a person with nothing but a pistol could shoot so far: and when I put up my sights as high as they would go and plumped a bullet somewhere over his nut he made off like a steeple-chaser: such a distance was far beyond his old muzzle-loader. I'm rather glad that my perseverance in carrying the Mauser★ has been rewarded, it is rather a load but practically unknown out here."[49]

There is nothing in that plain narrative (written to his mother) which sounds either improbable or extraordinary. Seeing that Lawrence was " in European dress and brown boots,"[50] the " ass with the old gun " may have hoped to combine religious merit with profit in Bedouin style by despatching an infidel. It will be noted that all Lawrence claims here for his return shots is that one of them may have grazed the horse. But this was far too humdrum an event for circulation among his friends and admirers, and he certainly showed a picturesque imagination in some of the sensational versions which he told his friends and which were put into print in a book published for the benefit of a " Charitable Trust." Let us look first at the version he handed out to a guileless Syrian schoolmistress, with whom he had been making light of his alleged sufferings and dangers, and even joking at them. He had had " many narrow escapes from death at the hands of cruel Kurds and Turks; " or so he modestly confessed. For instance, one day in " wild mountains " he met a " huge cruel-looking Turk " who instantly shot at him but luckily missed. Whereupon Lawrence, " to frighten the man," aimed his revolver at the Turk's little finger so accurately that it was slightly wounded. " The giant stood spell-bound," as well he might, whereupon the young hero

---

★ This pistol must have been smuggled, for in 1909 the importation of firearms into Turkish territory was forbidden.

bound up the Turk's finger and " patted his adversary on the back to show his goodwill." Chivalry went still further, for Lawrence " shared the little money he had with him, and the two went down the mountains together as friends." On which the schoolmistress reflects that it was the story of David and Goliath over again, except that " the weapon that won the day for Lawrence was that of friendliness, in which he so firmly believed."★[51]

A bluffer and more hearty version is given by Sir Leonard Woolley. The scene is staged on the sea shore near Latakia just after a bathe, when suddenly a bullet cracked past Lawrence. Looking up he saw a man about fifty yards distant taking aim at him for a second shot, whereupon Lawrence picked up his revolver, " shot the fellow through the right hand, tied up his wound, kicked him " (out of sheer " friendliness," no doubt) and " sent him about his business." Whereupon the great archæologist reflects that Lawrence " had indeed a cool indomitable courage."[52] As was shown in the episode, (related, apparently, only to Vyvyan Richards), of Lawrence on a high wall " fending off with a revolver in one hand a hostile mob ready to stone him from below and manipulating his camera with the other."[53] Just try taking snapshots with one hand.

This history of the cruel Turk won over by " friendliness " must not be confused with the history of the " covetous Turkman " which appears with varying details in both his official biographies. There was probably a basis of fact to it. H. Pirie-Gordon says that when Lawrence returned the borrowed map he " apologised for the bloodstain on it."[54] In his letter of the 24th September, 1909 from Aleppo to Sir John Rhys, Lawrence says that the week before he had been " robbed and rather smashed up " and that before he would be fit to walk again " the season of rains would have begun." In a postscript he asks that his father should not be told of the robbery, and adds that the " *irades* " (i.e., official letters) were so effective that " the man was caught in 48 hours."[55]

Vyvyan Richards' recollection of the story as told him by Lawrence on his return is that Lawrence found himself followed by a native on " a deserted stretch," whereupon he " knew " he would be attacked and that " a bout of fever " gave him little hope, but he nevertheless

★ i.e. " I'd rather be a prig than sociable."

kept on, and " when the fight came he refused to shoot the robber as he might have done." They fought three rounds and Lawrence was much struck by " the sound Shakespearean way " in which they both by common consent rested between the rounds![56]

Graves and Liddell Hart include the mysterious copper watch bought in Paris, at the sight of which the villagers are said to have murmured ' Gold.'[57] In Graves the Mauser becomes a Colt; in Hart, a Webley. In Graves, the Turkman cannot shoot Lawrence with his own pistol because " the safety-catch was raised; " in Hart, Lawrence " pulled out the trigger guard, so collapsing the pistol." In both the robber is frightened off by a shepherd, whose arrival stopped him as he was battering Lawrence's head with the pistol or stones. In Hart, the lost property is recovered by the Turkish police " after a lengthy argument." In Graves, more details are given. He tells us frankly that there is no truth in the story " of a desperate fight and the burning of the village," and puts forward the tale that Lawrence with his " *irade* " collected 110 men, whose ferry-fare across the Euphrates from Birejik he had to pay, that Lawrence, heavy with fever, slept while police and villagers wrangled, and that the robber was eventually employed under Lawrence at the Carchemish excavations.[58] The version told Pirie-Gordon says that in this contest Lawrence lost most of his clothes and all his money, had to work his passage to Marseille, where he landed with enough money to reach Oxford.[59]

According to the University rules, the thesis on castles which was the outcome of all this travel and drama had to be submitted to the examiners in the Easter Vacation of 1910. If Lawrence carried out the intention expressed in his letter to Rhys he was back in Oxford by the 15th October—and so far as is recorded escaped any fine for being a week late. He thus had between five and six months in which to write his thesis, but in a letter to a younger brother written in mid-1911 Lawrence says: " I left my special subject (the Crusades) till the last two weeks of the last term. It was mostly done while the examination was actually in progress in three all-night sittings: special subjects, if you know all but the facts are a matter of simple cram."[60] This is perhaps a little ambiguous and has led some readers to think he claimed to have written the thesis in three nights during the examination. But actually he does not say so, and possibly he wrote the thesis first and then mugged up the facts afterwards for the other papers. The result in any case was successful since he secured his degree with first-class honours in Modern History, as was still possible at that date. Whatever its merits as an undergraduate thesis, the claims made for it since his death would seem to be exaggerated.

It will not be expected that a non-specialist would venture to offer an opinion on a subject so technical and abstruse, and I can only record the opinions of those more competent. The Oxford " authority " of the time was Sir Charles Oman, who spent some twenty years writing a history of the Peninsular War. He also wrote (among other works) a *History of the Art of War in the Middle Ages,* which Lawrence described as " altogether futile; " Lawrence affected to despise him as totally ineffective. He tried to pretend that Oman was a relic of the past and not worth wasting time on, since he was a charlatan, an imbecile and a smatterer.[61]

It was Oman's opinion that the builders of the Crusaders' castles were influenced by the art of fortification which the Byzantine Empire had developed from Roman tradition. Lawrence took the opposite view—the Crusaders already had the knowledge and carried it with them from the west. Oddly enough, in thus challenging the accepted view, Lawrence was carrying out Oman's own advice to pupils trying to provoke the interest of a jaded examiner: " Always, if you can, begin with some statement that rouses his attention, an error in common vogue that must be denounced, or a conclusion that must be justified, however contrary it may be to received opinion. But these theses or criticisms must at all costs have some originality . . . "[62] Accordingly, Lawrence challenged Oman's views, though not by name, at the very opening of his thesis.

According to one authority this thesis was of such distinction that it was difficult to find anyone competent to judge it;[63] while Graves on the other hand tells us that " the examiners were so impressed that they celebrated the event by a special dinner at which Lawrence's tutor, Poole, was the host."[64] From Professor A. W. Lawrence we learn that " one of the judges of the thesis urged the University Press to publish it, saying however that not one of the photographs could be spared; " but unfortunately the Press decided the work would be too costly.[65] But Liddell Hart says Lawrence refused to publish the thesis because " it was only a preliminary study and not good enough to print."[66] In a letter of January, 1911, Lawrence tells a friend that his camera was stolen before he was able to take any interesting photographs, but promises to send his thesis " if it re-appears in time for next term."[67] Text and photographs were eventually published in a limited edition in 1936, but competent scholars refused to sponsor it.

More recently (1950) a new book on this aspect of military architecture has been published by Robin Fedden under the same title of *Crusader Castles*. In his bibliography Fedden says of Lawrence's book that it is " stimulating, but often inaccurate," and after mentioning Lawrence's views in his text decides that " the truth probably lies somewhere between these two extremes. The Crusaders both learnt much and brought much with them."[68] Professor Louis Bréhier holds firmly to the old view that the progress of fortifications dates from the crusades. "The Byzantine and Arab types of military architecture," he writes, " were the result of age-long experience of the art of war, and were imported from Syria into France and the whole of the Occident." And he enumerates technical features, including machicoulis which, he says, came from Palestine.*[69] But of course what really mattered was that Lawrence got the Honours degree.

* Since writing the above I have seen the article in the 1929 Baedeker on Islamic architecture, written by Professor K. A. C. Cresswell, one of the greatest living authorities. Speaking of the Bab en-Nasir gate at Cairo, built A.D. 1089, he says it is "defended by a pair of machicoulis, a device in fortification not found in Europe until the end of the 12th century. . . . Practically every architectural feature of these fortifications can be traced to N. Syria, and their inspiration. as fortifications, is Byzantine."

CHAPTER FIVE

THE TAKING of his degree and the consequent ending of his life as a pupil seem to have left Lawrence with nothing much to do for the remainder of 1910. There is no evidence available that he had any practical plans for a profession or for getting down to work—which certainly seems indicated in an able-bodied young man between 21 and 22 in a numerous family represented as living in such obligatory parsimony. But, of course, we have to remember the imperfection of the printed testimony, letters having been omitted or censored; with the curious result that for this very year 1910 the editor of the *Letters* notes that he has "not been able" to publish Lawrence's letter on Chartres cathedral although "it is the most beautiful and emotional of his early letters."[1] The omission of his "most beautiful and emotional letter" is certainly a rather baffling piece of selection, and the reader must always remember that we are working on a noticeably incomplete record. In any event, it would be a mistake to suppose that the absence of any evidence of wanting to work meant that Lawrence was without ambition. One of the early recollections of him by someone who was not a member of the regular Lawrence Bureau speaks of his "intense ambition."[2] This is supported by a photograph of Lawrence and his brothers in 1910 reproduced in *Crusader Castles*,[3] showing an intent concentrated look on his face often to be seen in over-ambitious youths. And the stronger the ambition, the less likely was he to have any definite plans for gratifying it.

In this uncertainty it was very natural that the young man should have thought of carrying on his studies and taking another degree. It is said that his bicycle tours of northern France in June and August and

70

a two-day trip to Rouen in November were made with the idea of writing a thesis on the medieval pottery which he had begun collecting as a schoolboy. According to David Garnett, Lawrence knew more about the collection of pots at the Ashmolean than any of the Staff. They seem to have been rather a feeble lot at Oxford in those days— no history examiner capable of marking a thesis on medieval military architecture, nobody at the Ashmolean acquainted with its pottery. The same thing must have been true of the British Museum department of Greek bronzes, if we may credit the story Lawrence told of the head of Hypnos which he claimed " he had found in a rubbish heap in Italy, so precious that it travelled in his bunk while he himself slept on deck . . . twin almost to that in the British Museum; indeed he was asked to exchange them as his seemed the more perfect. But it was found after to be a reproduction . . . " Lawrence mentions possessing this head in August, 1910, at which date there is no evidence he had ever been to Italy unless he landed at Messina in 1909, which seems unlikely as the P. & O. did not stop there. Pre-1914, bronze copies of the Hypnos were regularly on sale in Museum Street, London, in Paris, and in Naples. The B.M. staff of 1910 must indeed have been incompetent if they could not distinguish at a glance between a modern copy and a genuine Greek bronze in their own keeping.[4] What E. T. Leeds (assistant-keeper of the Ashmolean from 1908) says about those days is that he remembers Lawrence coming into the Museum on " some self-appointed task " such as " re-labelling a large collection of brass-rubbings " or " discussing and assessing the date and sequence of medieval pottery."[5] There is nothing about picking up ancient Greek bronzes from Italian rubbish heaps.

This period of transition from a life of dependence to employment as assistant-archæologist at Carchemish seems to form an appropriate lull for looking over his early letters. Later in life Lawrence admitted that all his letters were consciously adapted to the person he was addressing and wanted to influence. Everything he did was conscious, deliberately planned and willed, except when fate or accident tripped him up, or at least so he would have us believe. But in this conscious adaptation in letter-writing he was after all only exaggerating what everyone does more or less unconsciously; and in any case the process is not very obvious in his early letters. The trouble here is that, as with every collection of letters, the record depends on the hazard of preservation; and no young man puts much of himself into his letters home or even to his friends. A calculating temperament will produce calculating letters. Complete silence on some topic or ambition is only partial evidence that it was not in the writer's mind. The biographer can only go upon what is expressed by the letter-writer.

The main impression to be derived from these early letters (in which may be included those written between 1910 and 1914) is that they reveal a young man of scholarly habits (since the professors will not allow us to call him a scholar) with literary and art-craft ambitions and taste mainly of a late Pre-Raphaelite sort, tending to early Georgian. This conventional Oxford character was doubled, not by a conventional sportsman, but by an energetic cyclist and pedestrian who liked going to rather out of the way places where the fare was rough and scanty, who was reckless about his health and would endure hard usage and even being knocked about without complaint. There is nothing incompatible in the two characters, as witness the many wandering scholars or even scholar soldiers, such as e.g., Richard Burton. In addition, these early letters have the interest of showing Lawrence as a writer before the development of his too consciously rhetorical style. The young æsthete is very much in evidence when he writes to his mother of his " joy " in reading at night and " I know that nothing, not even the dawn, can disturb me in my curtains .. . . And it is lovely too, after you have been wandering for hours in the forest with Percivale or Sagramors le desirous, to open the door, and from over the Cherwell to look at the sun glowering through the valley-mists." And after some fancies about books taking on some of the personality of their reader he winds up:

" Imagination should be put into the most precious caskets, and that is why one can only live in the future or the past, in Utopia or the *Wood beyond the World*."[6]

The references are to Malory, Thomas More and Morris but the tone of the passage is nearer that of Oscar Wilde's *Intentions*. In the next letter, written from Carentan as the former was from Andelys, he translates his emotions at the interior of a Gothic cathedral into terms of Ruskin:

" Take someone with you, or go alone to Rheims, and sit down at the base of the sixth pilaster from the West on the South side of the nave aisle, and look up between the fourth and fifth pillars at the third window of the clerestory on the north side of the nave."[7]

Excellent! The Master himself could not have been more precise and authoritative but the writer seems to stumble into a different key as he proceeds:

" Take all the direction in at a gulp, and find yourself looking at an altogether adorable mist of orange and red, such a ruby and such a gold as I have seen nowhere else in glass . . . One can imagine saints and angels and medallions and canopies, but without the smallest reason or foundation."[8]

The reader half-expects the next sentence will be a call to Lawrence's friend to come and cool his hands in the twilight of Gothic things.

Lawrence said of himself at a later date that he only wrote well when excited, and after the war it seemed that he was too often excited only by what was violent or horrible or disgusting. The quotations just made, which could easily be multiplied, show that before the war the exact opposite was true. Not that he failed to attempt purple patches in *Seven Pillars* and even in *The Mint*, but they are usually stilted and over-mannered compared with his frank enjoyment of horrors in his maturity or the equally frank plagiarisms of his youth.

In the earliest of these letters Lawrence took pleasure in quoting Greek but soon dropped the habit, perhaps because he thought it pedantic, and even in his stilted ecstasies over Athens writes only one word in Greek characters. Italy and Italian art are not mentioned, and I think, no painter's or sculptor's name except Rossetti. He speaks with pleasure of finding a low-price series of French books, quite well-produced too, which would enable him to read Molière, Racine, Corneille and Voltaire.[9] In another letter he says he has bought (and is carrying on his bicycle) two volumes of Montaigne, *Tristan and Iseult*, *Jehan de Saintré*, the xiiith cent. fabliaux, de Nerval and a French anthology.[10] Two of these were still in his library at his death, with his initials and the date, 1910.

In 1929 Lawrence told Liddell Hart that he had " studied war since about 16 years of age, because filled with idea of freeing a people and had chosen Arabs as only suitable ones left."[11] Lady Gregory mentions in her memoirs having heard something of the sort from the Shaws, with the addition that Lawrence had at first been uncertain whether he should liberate the Irish or the Arabs.[12] There is a letter which shows that he had thought about the strategic part played by the castles during the crusades, though he nowhere mentions the vital fact that the castles were built in an effort to compensate for lack of man power, nor makes the inference that they must have been built by slave labour. There is other evidence of his military interests. But, although he speaks freely in these letters of his academic, æsthetic, art-and-craft and literary interests, there is absolutely no mention or implication of this politico-military ambition to " liberate the Arabs." So far as the contemporary evidence goes, his interest in the Middle East came from the needs of his thesis and then from the chance given him by Hogarth to work at Carchemish. It is perhaps worth noting that as late as August, 1910, he wrote a friend asking about the price of second-hand copies of Hogarth's *Wandering Scholar in the Levant*, and Doughty's *Arabia Deserta*.[13] In March, 1911, he had not yet found a copy of the Doughty for he writes: " The book will be necessary, for I must know it by more than library use, if ever I am to do something of the sort."[14] From which we may surely infer that his ambitions at the time were still literary, especially since in January of that year he wrote:

> " You will see I think, that printing is not a business but a craft. We cannot sit down to it for so many hours a day any more than one could paint a picture on that system. And besides, such a scheme would be almost sure to interrupt *The Seven Pillars of Wisdom* or my monumental book on the Crusades."[15]

Here, incidentally, we get a glimpse of Lawrence's life-long objection to steady hard work, and his belief that arts or crafts can be successfully practised without it. This *Seven Pillars* was not the book we have but was a book written in his youth about his experiences in seven cities of the Middle East.[16] It was no doubt fanciful at least in part, since one of the seven cities was Medina, which he could not have visited.[17]

Towards the end of 1910 these months of uncertainty were changed for a definite occupation which took him back to the Middle East, and the thesis on medieval pottery if it ever was really planned, was laid aside for ever. Lawrence was elected to a Magdalen demyship worth £100 a year for four years. This was arranged for him by D. G.

Hogarth, himself a fellow of Magdalen, who had raised funds for the exploration of the Hittite mound of Carchemish (the modern Jerablus) on the Euphrates, to the east and slightly to the north of Aleppo. As assistants Hogarth engaged for the coming season R. Campbell Thompson and Lawrence, so the demyship was obviously meant to supplement the small salary which was paid only during the working season.

For some reason Lawrence told Graves that his first meeting with Hogarth was just before starting on his 1909 Syrian walk; while he told Liddell Hart that he had attracted Hogarth's attention much earlier by work at the Ashmolean pots. Lawrence had been going to the Ashmolean from at least as far back as 1903, so Hogarth must have heard of him before 1909 even if they did not actually meet until then.[18] Hogarth was one of those " hide-thy-life " Oxford scholars who seems to have been successful in evading any attempts which may have been made to publicise him—there is not much to be learned from the tribute in the careful pages of the *Dictionary of National Biography*. He is said to have been an accomplished linguist, but too modestly says himself that he did not know Arabic very well. He was a Magdalen don, and married, with a child; and became keeper of the Ashmolean. He had worked with Arthur Evans in Crete, and wrote the article on *Mycenæan Civilisation* for the *Encyclopædia Britannica* in 1902. In more recent editions this heading is changed to *Aegean Civilisation* and brought up to date by A. J. B. Wace. His *Penetration of Arabia* is a history of the discoveries and knowledge brought back by European scholar-adventurers from Niebuhr in 1761 down to Doughty and the Blunts. Though a " popular " book (one of the *Story of Exploration* series) it is well-documented, conscientious, impartial and a work from which anyone who is not a specialist may learn. It was published in 1905. In 1922 Hogarth published a short history of Arabia, which unfortunately stops with the revolt of Sharif Hussein in 1916, on which Hogarth might have given valuable information.

In the *Wandering Scholar* (the book just mentioned which Lawrence was trying to buy) there is a hint of Hogarth's donnish eccentricity in the fact that the preface to the second edition apologises for the lack of dates in the travel narrative, while his essay on Egypt and Egyptologists bristles with prejudice. It was that perhaps which helped

to turn his attention towards the Hittites, who were a discovery if not
an invention of Oxford. So far back as 1879, A. H. Sayce, the wealthy
parson-don of Queen's College, and then Professor of Assyriology,
had been discussing some unknown inscriptions and sculptures when
he had a "sudden inspiration" and pointed out that they were "in
precisely the same style of art as those of the monuments of Ivriz and
Carchemish . . . which I called Hittite."[19]* Hogarth had been collecting "Hittite seals" for the museum, and had asked Lawrence to buy
any he could in 1909. Hogarth's name is chiefly connected with his
work as archæologist at Ephesus and Carchemish, and as a war-time
creator of the Arab Bureau.

Such was the train of events which sent Lawrence back to the
Middle East for much of the period between December, 1910, and
November, 1918, and such the scholar-patron to whom Lawrence
said he owed every decent job he had in his life except for his time in
the R.A.F.[20] It is a matter of guess-work to ask why Hogarth selected
Lawrence, who, as he himself admitted, was not, like Woolley, a
trained archæologist[21] or, we may add, like Campbell Thompson; but
he had shown much amateur interest as well as intellectual tastes and
there is a strong presumption that Hogarth hoped to train him up as a
successor. In addition to this, though Lawrence often offended and
repelled people by his mannerisms and posing and "leg-pullings"
he could when he chose turn on a personal charm which many people
found irresistible. One admirer speaks gushingly of "the intoxication
of his dear companionship."[22] It is obvious that it must have been
so, even if every allowance is made for the adulation lavished on him
after he became a national hero. Hogarth must have known or guessed
something of his secret, and felt that the young man would be happiest
away from Oxford and England; and certainly Lawrence always said
the Carchemish years were the happiest of his life.

For some reason Lawrence left England ahead of his colleagues, in
December, 1910, on a ship which enabled him to spend a day each in
Naples, Athens and Smyrna, and a week in Constantinople. Reaching
the spiritual home of all good Oxonians he was considerably fluttered
and found that he had walked into the Parthenon "without really
remembering who or where I was. A heaviness in the air made my

---

* I find that as early as 1876 Sayce read a paper on some inscription which he said were
"Hittite." See *The Hittites* by O. R. Gurney, 1952.

eyes swim, and wrapped up my senses; I only knew that I, a stranger, was walking on the floor of the place I had most desired to see, the greatest temple of Athene, the palace of art . . ."[23] a perfectly conventional reaction. Constantinople gave him a more tempered delight, though he thought it much finer than Damascus, and was thrilled with the mosques with their blue and gold and cream and green tiles. The yellow glazed pottery of " *exactly the shapes in England in the xivth century*," delighted him.[24]

From this plethora of culture and æstheticism he passed to the homely simplicity of the American Mission at Jebail where he intended to stay for six weeks or more to learn Arabic and Assyrian! But by the end of February he was off again, this time with Hogarth, on another culture-tour by train from Haifa to Damascus and Aleppo; and so on to Jerablus and the Carchemish mound. Although some half-hearted attempts had been made there many years before, the season of 1911 was still experimental, as Hogarth wanted to find out whether from his point of view the mound would be worth fuller exploration. Carchemish was really only a secondary site. The most important Hittite centre was Boghazkeui, but as British archæology could not raise the £3,000 required, the Germans got it, and Winckler (who was working there in this same year of 1911) eventually discovered about 10,000 fragments of tablets inscribed in Hittite. There were jealousies between the English and German archæologists, and between the archæologists and the German engineers who were then bridging the Euphrates at Jerablus for their Berlin to Baghdad railway. If we may believe Lawrence's letter and Woolley's reminiscences the English archæologists spent much energy quarrelling with and trying to bully the local Turkish authorities; the German engineers fought with their Arab employees; and the natives fought with each other. Gertrude Bell, who came to visit the Carchemish expedition in Hogarth's absence after she had been staying with the Germans at Ashur (the modern Kalaat Shirgat), gave great offence by telling Campbell Thompson that in comparison with the Germans their archæological methods were " prehistoric."[25] On the other hand Sayce says that but for the accidental visit of the Englishman, Garstang, to Boghazkeui, " we should never have known even the little we do about its archæological history."[26] So much for the courtesies and camaraderies of historical science. I can only add that such reference books as I have looked at say a great deal about Winckler and his discoveries and very little about Hogarth. Sayce himself, who visited Carchemish at this time, and in his reminiscences mentions innumerable celebrities, makes no reference whatever to Lawrence.

Life at Carchemish was not very strenuous, at any rate in 1911, if we may rely on Lawrence's letters home. It seems to have been the half-occupied idleness which he always preferred to the exactions of real work, especially when the half-idleness was irresponsible and yet had possibilities of sudden excitements and opportunities for playing jokes on the ignorant and superstitious workmen. Nominally, Lawrence was put in charge of the pottery, but wrote that he was " playing " with it, and, finding little to do, felt he was superfluous for most of the day while the evenings were spent in doing the odd jobs that could have been done during the day.[27] Later he told Graves photography and sculpture were also jobs in which he specialised, which must have been the case, for his letters mention both.[28] He told Liddell Hart that he knew all about the pottery and had made a complete stratification from the surface to 30 feet down.[29] But, as he also told Liddell Hart, he enjoyed doing nothing, and did not think he needed action to drown his sense of the futility of everything.[30] Woolley has recorded that he would sometimes find Lawrence and all the workmen sitting down and talking, and when he protested Lawrence " would grin and asked what anything mattered."[31] Some called it nihilism and some called it loafing, but doubtless by any name it was popular with the down-trodden wage-slaves.

Woolley, who did not take over the direction of Carchemish until the next year, says that Lawrence was very good with the Arab workmen. He invented competitions, setting one group of workmen against another, and two hundred running and screaming men would achieve half a day's output in an hour.[32] A very scientific method of excavation! It was Lawrence also who allowed them revolver cartridges to fire when a discovery was made. The handy man in Lawrence found odd jobs to occupy him from the beginning. He says he showed them how to make black and red paint, how to keep all light from a dark slide, that he made a camera obscura, re-wormed a screw without a die, refitted a plane-table, replaced the wick-turners on a lamp, set up a derrick made out of poplar poles and rope, to get on her legs a fallen Ishtar.[33] Although in September, 1912, Lawrence wrote: " I can't yet talk Arabic,"[34] Woolley referring to precisely the same period says Lawrence " spoke Arabic well " and was " always trying to improve his knowledge of the dialects," and could " talk freely " with the workmen. Lawrence's ability to read, write and speak Arabic has been much debated, but it is obvious that from 1911 on he must have been able to speak and understand colloquial and some dialect Arabic. Without them he could not have done many of the things he did do, e.g., he certainly could not have controlled gangs of labourers.

All this to the contrary, it would be a mistake to under-estimate either Lawrence's enthusiasm for his new post or his rapidly growing knowledge as an archæologist. It is true that early in 1912 Hogarth sent him to Petrie in Egypt for what might be called an instructional course in what were then modern methods of excavating, recording and preserving fragile finds. But that was normal for a new recruit, and then perhaps Gertrude Bell had been right and Hogarth had realised that their methods were a little " prehistoric." A non-specialist can have no opinion on such points, but anyone reading Lawrence's letters from Carchemish must feel his enthusiasm and his interest in technicalities. Evidently, like successful advocates and politicians, Lawrence possessed the ability to mug up and master a subject rapidly and convincingly, only to drop it and let it fade as soon as the interest or need had gone. This may be one if not the chief reason for the conflicting evidence (including his own) about his knowledge of Arabic, i.e., he let it drop away when no longer interested.

While there were doubtless other reasons for wanting to be out of England and in Asia Minor (such as vague plans for founding a Doughty-like book on the lives of the desert hunters and tinkers, the Sleyb)[35] enthusiasm for the work might help to account for his decision to remain in the district during the summer of 1911. He had mentioned to Hogarth that he thought of staying through the winter because it would help him to acquire an Arabic dialect which would prove a useful disguise.[36] But the true reasons were more personal and intimate. In June the British Museum, disappointed with results or without funds, had decided to close down the Carchemish expedition, after sending the excavators to report on Tell Ahmar where there had been a ford from time immemorial—as Baedeker says, " travellers will admire the dexterity of the boatmen."[37] Lawrence decided to make his way back to Aleppo on foot, by a circuitous route.

Before looking at Lawrence's diary of this tour, it is necessary to introduce the two friends Lawrence chose from among the Carchemish workers. By far the more important of these, and indeed probably the great love of Lawrence's life, was the donkey-boy or water-boy, Dahoum, also known as Sheik Ahmed. He was called Dahoum, the dark one, because he was very fair. His name often appears in Lawrence's pre-war letters; he and Lawrence lived and travelled together, and it is said that Dahoum, who died during the war, was the mysterious " S.A." to whose memory the dedicatory poem of *Seven Pillars* is addressed. David Garnett says that Dahoum was " a charming boy of remarkable and individual character who had, on his own account, taught himself to read a few words."[38] Graves briefly mentions him as " a younger man called Dahoum " and I cannot find any reference to him in Liddell Hart's book. Not one of these writers had ever met Dahoum. Woolley, who did know Dahoum, says he was a boy of about fifteen, not particularly intelligent but remarkably handsome, and with a body of perfect proportions. Lawrence's Arabic teacher at Jebail, who met Dahoum when he was about eighteen, says he was greatly attached to Lawrence whom the Arabs regarded as their friend and brother.[39] Lawrence became interested in Dahoum during this first season, for in a letter to Hogarth he describes Dahoum's terror at having to drink a Seidlitz powder which he considered " sorcery." A few days later Lawrence wrote to the American mission asking for a few simple books for a boy of fifteen—" our donkey-boy " with whom " I have had quite a success."[40] This must be Dahoum, who is also mentioned in a letter of December 1911; as having had malaria and being about to remain at Carchemish alone with Lawrence in July 1912; and as having been with him on the Sinai expedition in early 1914. He was one of the two Arabs Lawrence brought to Oxford and lodged in his bungalow in 1913. In that year, after the season of work, Sir Leonard Woolley writes that Lawrence had Dahoum pose as model for a crouching nude figure which Lawrence carved from the local limestone. Sir Leonard comments that the mere making of an image was looked at askance, but the portrayal of a naked figure proved to the Arabs that Lawrence was a pederast, a view that was widely held by them. Sir Leonard

Lowell Thomas

Lowell Thomas (back to camera) meets Emir Feisal (hand raised in salute). Between them stands T. E. Lawrence

[*Taken from a strip of film now in the possession of the War Office*]

Woolley hastens to add that the charge had no foundation.[41] According to his friend, Vyvyan Richards, " Lawrence showed a like affection for other youths too, both in Arabia and after his return to England."[42]

The other friend was the foreman Hamoudi, " tall, gaunt, with a thin sandy beard cut short, long-armed and immensely powerful,"[43] who had in his youth provoked other men to fight for the sheer pleasure of killing them. He admitted to six or seven murders, and had been an outlaw for years, " a very suitable person to initiate Lawrence into the Arab world of action."[44] This was the other Arab brought to England by Lawrence, his companion on two or three of his earlier excursions, after which Lawrence was either accompanied by Dahoum or went alone. According to Hamoudi's post-war recollections Lawrence's first trip from Jerablus was to Nisib and beyond, disguised as Hamoudi's servant, but it is difficult to fit this in chronologically and it may have been later.[45]

At all events Lawrence's diary shows that he was alone when, after separating from Campbell Thompson at Tell Ahmar, he set out on foot " on a Wednesday about July 12." The diary goes up to the 13th August, but the walk lasted only until 29th July when Lawrence collapsed with dysentery (or possibly mild typhoid) at Jerablus. So long as Lawrence was living with one of the older Englishmen at the excavations his health and diet were more or less looked after for him. But as soon as he was on his own he seems to have neglected even the elementary precautions demanded of a European in such a country in summer, and to have travelled without any medical supplies. When he fell ill, as he did even in the war, from a miserable diet and self-neglect, he seems to have done nothing about himself and to have pushed on until he collapsed. This was very brave and pertinacious, but was it intelligent? A sick man is inefficient. Of course, the namby-pamby " health " fussing of British and Americans to-day is so contemptible that any sane person left is more likely to sympathise with Lawrence's neglect than with their craven molly-coddling. But the fact that he was ill nearly all the time makes this diary a depressing little document. Indeed the wonder is that he was able to keep a diary at all.

On the second day of his walking tour he was already " a little feverish "—he doesn't say from what, but probably from the toothache which kept him awake on the night of the 15th July after a day mostly

spent in measuring and photographing the castle at Urfa. The chief
of police there insisted he should have a guard, and remonstrated with
him for travelling alone. Two days later he had an abscess and swollen
cheek, and when he reached Harran his tooth was worse, his face sore
and swollen, and his feet very tired. By the 22nd his tooth was better
but his feet were sore and festering. On the 23rd he was better and
received a message from Dahoum to the effect that " the Kala'at was
sad," whatever that might mean. Kala'at, the castle, had perhaps
been a rendezvous. Then Lawrence had a festering hand, his once
broken ankle collapsed, and on the 27th: " Left foot to-day altogether
right "—a bit ambiguous, but one sees what he means. His right foot
was in a bad way; his right hand had begun to fester where it had
been bitten. The only comfort was that his left hand had now healed.
He reached Jerablus on the 28th where he was warmly welcomed with
enquiries as to whether there would be more work and when would
the railway come, and stayed with Hamoudi. On the 29th he had
a sharp attack of dysentery, fainted twice, and when he got back
to the village had to admit that even he could not continue to tramp.
In fact he was so weak and fainted so often that he had to make great
demands on Hamoudi. Lawrence's only diversion as he waited for a
carriage to take him to Aleppo was the daily visit from Dahoum which
he carefully recorded. On the 3rd August Lawrence realised he must
return to England, but Hamoudi suddenly dropped his hospitality,
refused to lend a horse, and wanted Lawrence to move to
Dahoum's house. Lawrence's messenger had come back from Birejik
with the cheerful news that he could not get a carriage or any help
from the town-doctor or from the Turkish governor. Eventually with
Dahoum's help Lawrence got away, crossed the river, and found a
carriage to take him to Aleppo, which he reached on the evening of
the 5th August.[46] While waiting on the Syrian bank of the Euphrates
for some form of conveyance he consoled himself by reading about the
Holy Grail.

In an interview, granted after Lawrence's death to one of his
friends, Hamoudi gave a roseate account of these events, mixing
up Lawrence's itinerary, transposing to near Jerablus in 1911 the
theft of Lawrence's camera in 1909, making the thieves his own
tribesmen, and casting himself for the part of Lawrence's saviour in
distress, despite the dangers from the Turkish Government if a

European died on his hands. It is strange that this warrior, whose one regret was that Lawrence had not died in battle, is nowhere recorded as playing any part in the Arab revolt; but perhaps he changed his name.[47]

Thus, Lawrence's second attempt at foot travel in Syria ended even more unhappily than the first. Much drama might be evolved from being knocked on the head by a " huge, cruel " Turkman, but there is no particular romance to be extracted from a combination of dysentery with a heavy bout of malaria, which was the condition in which he reached Oxford from Beirut in late August. While protesting that he was not ill, he had to confess that he still could not walk a hundred yards, and could get upstairs only " crab-wise." He was trying to stave off the malaria by taking quinine until he could get the arsenic treatment which he felt would effect a definite cure. (Although no longer in use, arsenic at that time was sometimes prescribed in the treatment of malaria). Lawrence's one consolation was that Hogarth was hopeful of subsidies for another season, " as a result," Lawrence boasted, " of the wonderful pottery discoveries of the last two months " of which he of course had been in charge.[48]

CHAPTER SIX

THE SUCCESS of Hogarth's attempts to raise money for the continuation of the Carchemish expedition soon brought results to Lawrence. He was evidently in good spirits, and seemingly recovered from the troubles of his summer expedition, when he wrote that he was going first to the excavations, then to Egypt to work under Flinders Petrie, and later arrange for the arrival of Leonard Woolley, the new head of the expedition.[1] The expedition in fact was continued until the outbreak of war in 1914.

Lawrence's behaviour towards others was always calculated, especially on a first encounter. With those who approached him as social or intellectual inferiors he was usually affable and friendly, turning on his famous charm; deferential to the point of asking their advice, and yet unable to resist trying to dazzle them with tales of his real or supposed grandeurs. His advance seems to have been different with those who, lacking the indisputable authority of an Allenby or a Winston Churchill, for one reason or another might consider themselves his superiors. Here his method was to lurk behind his giggle and Oxford voice, and then suddenly " to provoke the instinctive response of those he encountered to a sudden challenge to some established dogma, dignity or practice."[2] The idea was to take them off guard, probe for a weak spot, and try to take advantage of any weakness.

For some reason, possibly because Petrie was unimpressed when Lawrence joined him for instruction in January, 1912, he decided the professor must be reported as ridiculous. Thus, there is what is hopefully called " a good story " to the effect that to find

Petrie he must go where the flies were thickest.[3] Lawrence also allowed the tale to be printed that he presented himself to Petrie in football shorts and a cricket blazer, and was told with heavy irony that they did not play cricket at his camp. Liddell Hart explains that the irony was greater than was intended, as Petrie's failure to distinguish between the garbs of the winter and summer games was surpassed by Lawrence's hatred of all games.[4] Well, if boys don't play cricket in shorts, neither do they play football in blazers, nor indeed are blazers usually displayed by those who can play neither game. Besides, if he was as quick as is reported, Petrie might have guessed that this flashing of the Magdalen blazer was a hint that he was no Oxonian, but merely Professor of Egyptology in the *petit bourgeois* university of London.

Lawrence disliked having to be up before dawn and returning to camp at night after having to work all day down in a 50 foot shaft. And Hogarth, with his violent prejudice against Egypt and Egyptology, would not be displeased by jeers at the professor's work and methods. Petrie seemingly gave Lawrence the task of cutting out and waxing a small skeleton—no doubt, to teach him the technique. Lawrence reported derisively that he had persuaded Petrie the skeleton and its " rags of clothing " in a " rotten wooden box " were just what the Ashmolean wanted: " Besides, it is really almost complete: when we lifted it up one of the feet dropped off and a lot of toe-bones from the other, but you would hardly notice that in a dark corner." He thought Petrie's work very carelessly done compared with the work at Carchemish.[5] How careful they were at Carchemish is illustrated by the report of a woman visitor that hot coffee was there served in ancient Hittite cups without handles, and when she hesitated to pick hers up for fear of dropping it, Lawrence laughingly remarked that even if she did the British Museum would thankfully accept the pieces.[6] According to Graves, Lawrence found Egypt dull, but so much impressed Petrie that the professor asked him to come another year to the camp.[7] It may be so, but what Lawrence wrote at the time was that Petrie offered to raise funds for Lawrence to dig for hypothetical and problematical ancestors of the ancient Egyptians at Bahrein in the Persian Gulf, considerably more than a thousand miles away.[8]

In the early spring of 1912 Lawrence was joined at Carchemish by Leonard Woolley who has since made so great a reputation as a field archæologist. If we may believe their own reports, these two young men seem rather to have abused their status under the then existing Capitulations* by behaving to the natives and German engineers with considerable truculence. Allowance must be made for the high spirits of youth and the exasperation of dealing with bureaucrats, as well as the exaggerations incidental to Lawrence stories. David Garnett tells us that he has " reason to believe that many of the stories about Lawrence's practical jokes at the expense of the Germans are apocryphal."[9] If those were the only apocryphal stories . . . ! And not all the Carchemish stories are about the Germans, anyway.

Lawrence began this new season with a failure which Woolley settled with a revolver; or so they said. The local Turkish governor had been ordered to allow no unauthorised work on the site, and had installed a military guard who refused to allow Lawrence to start building a house. When Woolley arrived, he was told that the permit for the excavations was in the name of Hogarth, and such permits were not transferable. After much wrangling and threats of arming his men, Woolley got his order by pulling out his revolver and threatening to shoot the official! Another wrangle arose from their lack of a clear title to the land, and the claims of one Hassan for stones dug from the site given to the Germans. When Lawrence attended the Turkish Court to argue the case, his papers were seized, and soldiers sent to stop further movement of stones. Once again the two Oxonians used their revolvers. While Woolley covered the judge, their cook, Haj Wahid, intimidated the spectators with two revolvers, and Lawrence rushed into the next room and recovered his papers from the local governor under threat of shooting him. When the Turkish officials in Aleppo complained to the British Consul, it is alleged that he said it was a pity the judge and governor had not been really shot instead of only threatened! When the Court served the archæologists with a writ ordering payment of thirty pounds, they simply tore it up.[10] Such was the insolence of Turkish officials to courteous British intellectuals under the pre-1914 Capitulations.

This series of rows with the Turks was accompanied by a premature war with the Germans who, it seems, were always in the wrong and

---

* Pre-1914 Consuls in Turkey had the privilege of Ambassadors, and exercised jurisdiction in all matters of civil legal dispute between their nationals. Disputes between foreigners and Turkish subjects were decided in Turkish courts with the aid of the dragoman of the foreigners' consul.

are always made to look ridiculous in the stories. Yet in the early days relations had been good. Under date 8th August, 1911, Lawrence relates that during dinner at Barron's hotel, Aleppo, he called a Jew sitting opposite him a pig. This caused a terrific uproar from the Levantines dining there which was only appeased by some tough German railway engineers threatening to throw the Jew in the river if he or his friends said another word.[11] This mutual and racial sympathy faded in a squabble over the disposal of the Carchemish rubble which the Germans wanted for their railway. Other stories include one of the Germans flogging Ahmed (Dahoum ?) for quarrelling with their foreman. The tale as told is that Lawrence forced the German engineer to apologise publicly to the Arab hand. The Lawrence-approved books of Graves and Liddell Hart attribute this remarkable triumph to Lawrence's " small deadly voice " or " ominously quiet voice."[12]   Woolley says Lawrence threatened to flog the German unless he apologised, and when the chief engineer told Lawrence he " dared not," Lawrence " pointed out that there was good reason for assuming that he both dared and could."[13] In July, 1912, there was a bloodless fight between Arabs and Kurds.[14] A more serious affray occurred early in 1914, between Germans and Kurds, in which a man was killed and eight or eighteen or twenty wounded. The archæologists intervened, and arranged the payment of blood money for the murdered Kurd. Lawrence passed the statement of Graves and Liddell Hart that he and Woolley were offered Turkish decorations for their share in this episode, but refused.[15] Woolley on the other hand, who was there, reports nothing about decorations and merely says that the investigating Turkish Vali thanked them for having kept the Kurds in order, but the two Englishmen gave all the credit to their native followers.[16]

Turning from this " lighter side " (as Woolley calls it) of life at Carchemish we naturally reach the heavier topic of archæology, which was at any rate the ostensible reason for their being on the mound. How good was Lawrence as an archæologist, what did he achieve? In those days, it seems, Lawrence did not like being labelled " an ordinary archæologist,"[17] though what greater distinction his ambition then desired he does not say. Still, in December, 1913, he expected to be at Carchemish for four or five years and then to " go after another and another nice thing."[18] The great attraction of

Carchemish to him was that it was "a place where one eats lotos nearly every day "—i.e., where there was little to do and pleasant conditions for doing it.[19] Thus, it is a fair inference that he enjoyed field archæology when it did not involve the steady hard work exacted by Flinders Petrie and when easy-going methods allowed him to "enjoy doing nothing."[20] Woolley says that Lawrence's work in the field was "curiously erratic." Sometimes he would take detailed notes which unfortunately could not always be followed by other people, and then again he would make fun of some work and dismiss it in a few words. And Woolley mentions a row of sculptured slabs which were dismissed in this easy fashion. Lawrence's miraculous memory— which Graves tells us was "almost morbid"—is vouched for by Woolley who says that he was able to fit a small fragment of a Hittite inscription, which had just been discovered, to a similar piece out of the many hundreds found months before and put away in their store-room. He could also remember a particular piece of broken pot dug up the season before and where it was found and what was found with it, although the fragment had been dug out and the notes on it made by Woolley. A "phenomenal" memory indeed.[21]

His Oxford tutors, as already mentioned, did not think him "a scholar by temperament" and believed that he took up history because it was a hurdle that had to be taken at the time. Professor Barker thought he took up archæological work in the same spirit, and Leeds, coining a phrase, thought that at Carchemish Lawrence saw "a happy opportunity to explore new avenues."[22] Lawrence wrote no articles for archæological journals, which activity indeed would have inter-fered with his "lotos-eating."[23] Lawrence's contributions to *The Wilderness of Zin*, from the nature of the book, are more topographical than archæological; and in any case the book was hastily thrown together by Woolley and Lawrence (chiefly Woolley) allegedly to camouflage Captain Newcombe's unauthorised military surveying in Turkish territory which looked like, even if it was not, espionage. When Liddell Hart praised *The Wilderness of Zin* as "lucid and well-expressed" and so forth, Lawrence cut him short with the remark that Woolley wrote most of it and edited the rest.[24] And yet in his Preface to the report, written after Woolley had joined the army, Lawrence says: "In Mr. Woolley's absence I have revised parts of his work where I was competent to do so, and have left it untouched else-where."[25]

After the war well-meaning people of eminence offered Lawrence various important sites for excavation not realising that he had lost interest in archæology, did not want such work, and was not competent to direct modern excavations, since at Carchemish he had left all the responsible work to Woolley. He was always having to find excuses for refusing these and other offers after the war, since what he really wanted to do was to live in England doing a minimum of work—he would have liked someone to give him £300 a year.[26] He said that he had been invited to 'an Eastern principality' but had refused.[27] This typically mysterious claim is left indefinite. It may have meant India or may have meant an alleged scheme " to clear the Assyrian palace under Jonah's tomb " in Feisal's Irak; and here the excuse for doing nothing was that his presence in Irak would have been politically embarrassing.[28] He told Captain Hart that he was not allowed to visit France, Turkey and other countries[29] but (even if that was true) he did not have to traverse them to get to Irak. When his friend Storrs, as governor of Cyprus, offered Lawrence the post of Director of Archæology in Cyprus, obviously none of these excuses held good; and Lawrence refused " because of what he chose to imagine the social obligations of an official there."[30] Lawrence's story that Feisal would arrange for a popular saint to have a revelation that Jonah was buried somewhere else, so that Lawrence could excavate the site, was probably another of his tales.[31]

Thus Lawrence lost interest in archæology as turn by turn he lost interest in other subjects, or lacked energy and perseverance to follow them up. Even in the Carchemish days his peculiar schoolboy jocosity and what's-the-good-of-anything attitude may be noted in his informal letters to Hogarth. To give one instance only, Hogarth—who, under correction, does seem to have been more a museum collector than a scientific archæologist—wrote Lawrence telling him to buy a Hittite cylinder. To which Lawrence replied that he had already done so, adding flippantly that he was not sure if it was " Hittity," in fact he thought it wasn't.[32] It may be questioned whether such nonchalant and irresponsible service was what the British Museum and Magdalen thought they were paying for.

This type of jocosity tended to express itself in elaborate hoaxes and silly practical jokes which rather suit a malicious schoolboy than dignify " the Greatest Englishman of his generation." When Hogarth was coming out to Carchemish on one of his periodical visits Lawrence carefully prepared his reception. He got together some odds and ends of lace and a quantity of cheap pink satin ribbon. Hogarth's mud-walled room was hung with lace curtains tied up with pink bows, one of which was fastened to the mirror. A make-shift dressing-table was spread with a tray of hair-pins and a pin-cushion, while the bath-room which consisted of nothing more than a tiny room with a tin bath on a concrete floor, was enriched with little bottles of cheap scent. Hogarth, we are told, was furious at this joke, but Lawrence, " who never laughed out loud," was highly amused for weeks.[33] What, it may be asked, was the point of this exquisite jest, which amused the great man for so long? Well, Hogarth was married, and Lawrence did not much like his male friends to associate intimately with women. (" Bother all women, they seem to upset the people I like."[34]) So the turning of Hogarth's quarters into what Lawrence evidently thought a brilliant parody of a matrimonial bedroom was no doubt planned to satirise Hogarth for his deviation from undiluted masculinity.

Readers may feel that this " pulling the leg " of Hogarth was more silly than malicious, and hardly worth the trouble. But what are we to think of the " joke " played upon Woolley which caused Lawrence so much " ingenuous pleasure," such " infectious amusement? " Woolley was sick with malaria, and went to bed early in the hope of " sleeping it off." Through the whole of a wet, stormy and feverish night he was kept awake vainly trying to discover the cause of a maddening noise which made sleep impossible—Lawrence had fixed to the top of his tent a wind-vane cut from a biscuit-tin which screeched throughout the night.[35] Next day Lawrence showed such " infectious amusement " at the success of his brilliant little plot that even Woolley himself had to enter into the joke.[36] He must have been easily placated.

It was wholly in accordance with sporting Oxford tradition to accept smilingly such Attic jests as the two recorded above, but just as all the imaginative stories Lawrence told about himself invariably tended to his honour and glory, so the practical joke always had to be on his side. If by chance such a thing happened as a practical joke at his expense, then it was an unpardonable outrage. One day when he was walking at some distance from Carchemish on the Syrian side of the Euphrates, he went up to some young Kurdish women who were drawing water and asked for a drink. Whether on this occasion he was wearing the gay Arab belt with extra large tassels to emphasise his status as an unmarried man, is not recorded; but he usually then wore such a belt. Perhaps that offended them; perhaps he had stumbled ignorantly on some exclusively female territory, calling for vengeance such as Malinowski records of his savage women with such lurid details; perhaps they had heard the gossip about him and Dahoum; or perhaps they too merely wanted to play a humorous practical joke. At any rate, pretending that they wanted to see if he was white all over, they fell upon him and stripped him nearly naked with bluff familiarity before they allowed him to escape. When he got back to camp he did not, as such a sportsman surely should, hasten to share this admirable little practical joke with his friends; on the contrary, he kept it to himself, and though he did eventually tell Woolley, it was not until much later and still with humourless indignation. It is added that he never went that way again.[37]

Wonderful as was Lawrence's "charm," it does not seem to have been so apparent before the war as after the publicity of the Lowell Thomas film-lectures. Woolley did not think he impressed a casual acquaintance, and he himself had the impression that Lawrence was essentially immature; his head was disproportionately large for his small body, and he had an apologetic smile. When the Arabs had done anything to displease him they knew that they could always recover his favour by giving him flowers.[38] Sir Ernest Dowson, head of the Surveyor-General's office in Cairo, was similarly impressed. When Lawrence entered the Cairo office in his customary attire (no Magdalen blazer here) grinning half-apologetically and gave a little bow of introduction, Dowson's first thought as a loyal servant of the Crown was: "Whoever can this extraordinary little pip-squeak be?" After the conversation, which Dowson forgot, one question remained grimly in his mind—was his visitor a "real or pretended clown?"[39] There is some doubt about the date of this interview but it was certainly very soon after the Carchemish days.

Lawrence wore his hair very long in those days, and only considered it too long when it hindered his eating.[40] He took pleasure in wearing startling clothes, and Woolley thought that this fondness for being "dressy" never really left him. On the other hand we have testimony and even photographic evidence of his occasional carelessness in dressing. The photograph opposite page 48 of *T. E. Lawrence by his Friends* shows him supposedly in the Oxford Officers' Training Corps, an unkempt young soldier in a badly-fitting tunic with slovenly puttees. Contrast this with the photograph opposite page 428 of Graves' book, an extremely dressy R.A.F. ranker on a motor-bike, with immaculate puttees, breeches "taken in" at the knees, and tunic altered and close fitted by the squadron tailor—a complete Hollywood soldier. In Carchemish days he evidently enjoyed wearing conspicuous clothing, and even in Feisal's army he distinguished himself from the "tulip bed" effect of his brightly clothed followers by dressing in "immaculate white," the costume of dignity in the East. His younger brother, W. G. Lawrence, who saw him at Carchemish in September, 1913, describes him as wearing " white flannels, socks and red slippers, with a white Magdalen blazer."[41] Even in the rough, horse-shoe-shaped hut in which they lived on the mound, Lawrence dressed for dinner, but in anything but the conventional stiff shirt, black tie and dinner jacket. After carefully brushing his long hair, he put on a white shirt and shorts and a white and gold embroidered Arab waistcoat. On top of this a gorgeous cloak of gold and silver thread, said to be worth sixty pounds but bought for a song from an Aleppo thief. Thus splendidly attired he would sit after dinner and read Homer or Blake or Doughty's poems. At that time he had a very critical taste in Arab dishes, and, strangely enough for one who despised food so loftily, there is much gastronomic talk in his letters. A Roman mosaic had been moved to make a floor for the hut, and Lawrence bought expensive oriental rugs to spread on it, as well as two arm-chairs of black wood and white leather, which he had had specially made for him in Aleppo, chairs which matched his William Morris tapestry and Kutachia pots.[42]

From December, 1911, until June, 1914, Lawrence was in England only during Christmas 1912, and for about two weeks in July 1913, when he brought Dahoum and Hamoudi to Oxford. The remainder of that period was spent at Carchemish, with a certain number of excursions, by far the most important of which was the survey of the Sinai area with Woolley under Captain Newcombe. Lawrence passed Graves' assertion that pre-1914 he "wandered all over Syria and the Near East,"[43] and Liddell Hart states that he knew "like a book Syria, North Mesopotamia, Asia Minor, Egypt and Greece."[44] Wild exaggerations! Much nearer the facts is the quotation from his own words in which he says that he travelled always with someone from the Carchemish people (the *Letters* show it was Dahoum) "taking a few camels on hire-carrying, sailing down the Syrian coast, bathing, harvesting and sight-seeing in the towns."[45]

He told Hart that he had spent two weeks (at some unspecified date) working as a checker to a coaling ship at Port Said ; this is confirmed by a passage in *Seven Pillars*.[46] But he was never more than on the fringe of the real desert, and hardly ever out of the Baedeker area. During the same period pre-1914, Leachman, for instance, rode from Baghdad to Aleppo by mule, had discovered the Wadi Khar, had ridden in Arab clothes with the Roalla and Anaizeh, had watched their fights with the Shammar, and had met Ibn Rashid, though he failed to reach Hail. Later he rode 1,300 miles through Kurdistan and Anatolia, from Baghdad to Aleppo, went through Palestine, and rode on camelback the 540 desert miles from Dumair (near Damascus) to Baghdad in nine days. He had made another journey of 1,300 miles through the Central Arabian desert, had managed to reach the Wahabi "capital" of Riadh (which even Doughty did not see) and made friends with the great desert chieftain Ibn Saud. The main journeys were recorded in the Royal Geographical Society Journal, and received the acknowledgment of a medal.[47]

Gertrude Bell, a friend of the Lawrence Bureau, has been widely advertised; but who except the same Journal has recorded Captain Shakespear's great journey across Arabia from Kuwait to Suez?

A canoe with an outboard motor was brought out to Syria by Lawrence, in which he made trips on the Euphrates, on one occasion as far as Rakka, the Nicephorion of Seleucus 1st, which in June, 1913, Lawrence was hoping to excavate for the Turkish government. In June, 1912, he announced he was going to Tell Halaf, a Hittite town then being excavated by the German, Oppenheim, who himself visited Carchemish in mid-July. Tell Halaf is close to the town of Ras-el-Ain on the river Khabur about fifty miles south of Veransherh. Oppenheim offered Lawrence his relay of post horses, which covered in thirty-six hours what would normally have taken six days, but for once Lawrence's love of speed abandoned him, and he refused them.[48] Instead, he went to Jebail with Dahoum to be near his missionary friends, where he spent about three weeks walking in Arab dress, for which when there he had to find excuses.[49] Elsewhere he mentions a visit to a Kurd chief about thirty miles across the Euphrates.[50] Though the record of the letters is incomplete, Lawrence is shown by them to have spent so much time at Carchemish that not much is left for excursions, though possibly there may have been some which have gone unrecorded.

Readers of *Seven Pillars* have puzzled over a phrase in the description of the Deraa flogging, in which Lawrence speaks of himself as " moaning in wonder that it was not a dream, and myself back five years ago, a timid recruit at Khalfati, where something, less staining, of the sort had happened."[51] Five years from 1917 take us back to 1912. This may be linked up with a curious story Lawrence told Liddell Hart (in 1933) that he and " one of his workmen " (possibly Dahoum) had been " lured " to an unspecified place near Birejik to see a " statue of a woman seated on the backs of two lions." As this district was " too north for Arabs " they were arrested as deserters and " kicked downstairs into a lousy dungeon," whereby Lawrence was " bruised all up one side " and his companion got a sprain. Next morning Lawrence bribed their way out.[52] Khalfati is not very far from Birejik, but David Garnett links the reference to the Turkoman attack in 1909. A curious coincidence is that in his 1911 diary Lawrence mentions going to see " a stone of a woman holding her breasts. Proved to be a miserable Roman sepulchral relief,"[53] and photographed a lion broken in two at Harran. Birejik was the town where Woolley and Lawrence had carried on their revolver flourishing and had scored their triumphs over the Turkish Governor. It seems strange that Lawrence and Dahoum should not have been recognised so near Jerablus (Carchemish) as Khalfati.*

What is more remarkable is that a person so susceptible and self-important as Lawrence should apparently have made no attempt to obtain redress or revenge for this insult and assault, and it is all the more remarkable since (according to Sir Hubert Young) Lawrence had

---

*Evidently this story was circulating during the war, for the French secret report on Lawrence (August 1917) says there was a rumour that Lawrence had been conscripted by the Turks at Urfa and did not escape for three weeks (Brémond p. 160). This, if true, would explain the puzzling word " recruit."

made himself at Jerablus an "unofficial Qonsolos, or representative of the great British Government."[54] An instance of this is recorded by Young, who stayed at Carchemish with Lawrence and his younger brother for a week in September, 1913. One day they came upon some Kurds who had been dynamiting fish. Lawrence went up to the biggest of the Kurds and ordered him to pick up the fish, to tie them in bundles, and to come to the police station. The Kurd was singularly unimpressed and replied: " What is this? Who art thou? I know thee not. I know not thy father nor yet thy mother. I gather up no fish. I tie them in no bundle. Moreover, I come not with thee to the police station." What you might call a comprehensive raspberry! But Lawrence, aided by his brother, seized the man's arms and tried to drag him off, while the callous representative of the Indian Army looked on. A shower of stones, " one of which caught Lawrence in the side and nearly broke a rib," and the drawing of a knife by one of the Kurds suggested to Young that they had better let the man go. Which they did; but Lawrence immediately went to the local Turkish police inspector, threatened to get him dismissed if the men were not arrested, and suggested that they should be flogged. Young winds up: " Whether they were really flogged, or even taken into custody, I have no notion. But the incident gives some idea of the way in which this solitary young Englishman, who had no official position whatever, had begun even in peace-time to strike out a line for himself."[55]

Well . . . Nor was this story one of those Lawrence poured into the ears of his easily impressed friend, Richards, who was told by Lawrence—he did not himself witness it as Major Young did—a rather different version of a similar episode. Lawrence, having crossed a stretch of desert, had paid off his camel-man, only to hear him crying in distress as three Turkish gendarmes tried to steal his money under pretence of various dues. Lawrence, instantly returned, protested, and when that failed " with a signal to the camel-man he suddenly attacked the gendarmes." Needless to say, Lawrence " was good for two at least " and the camel-man for the other, and the Turks were disarmed of their carbines and marched unresisting to the governor's room. When the governor realised who his visitor was (in spite of his wearing Arab costume) he " collapsed " (why?) and protested that his policemen should be " degraded, deprived of their arms." Lawrence interrupted him: " I have done that, and here are the arms, and outside in the road are the gendarmes themselves. Don't let it happen again."[56] It was very unfortunate he hadn't that plucky camel-man around when tackling the Kurds, for one can't help thinking that Young by his professional attitude of strict neutrality rather let the Qonsolos down.

Major Young's mention of the presence in Carchemish of Lawrence's younger brother William, calls attention to a letter he wrote to a friend in October of 1913, which relates *une ténébreuse affaire* which is hard to make clear owing to its curious mixture of testimony. At the same time, it gives a glimpse of what a genuine British Qonsolos of those days was prepared to do or was credited with allowing—the same gentleman, by the way, who is alleged to have regretted that Woolley and Lawrence had not shot the Turkish governor and magistrate. William Lawrence tells his correspondent that one of his brother's greatest friends was the Kurd, Buswari, who, only four months earlier had massacred 8,000 people at Urfa, Adan and Nisib, at the last of which T. E. Lawrence had been present in disguise. During the Balkan War of 1912-13 (when the Bulgarians seemed on the point of capturing Constantinople) this Buswari and another Kurd " planned the sack of Aleppo, actually arranging which should have the loot of which houses, and apportioning two bankers' houses, great collectors of objets d'art, to Ned," i.e., T. E. Lawrence. The young man is clearly relating not what he witnessed himself but what his brother had told him, for the style of the anecdote is unmistakable.[57] Woolley tells us that the Kurds at that time had planned to sack Aleppo, killing the Germans at Jerablus on their way. Whereupon Woolley anxiously sent for Buswari, who lavishly promised him a guard of 2,000 men. In Aleppo Woolley met Buswari's son and another Kurd making a list of the richest houses to rob. Now, as David Garnett points out, the massacres referred to had happened before Lawrence ever landed in Syria, so he could not have been in Nezib in disguise; and Woolley in his tale does not mention Lawrence's name even.[58] From which it may be inferred that Lawrence, having heard of the massacres and learning the Buswari story from Woolley, put them together in a brotherly tale to his own greater glory, by attributing them all to himself.

This, however, is not the end of the Tale. The British Consul in Aleppo is said to have been warned by Lawrence and Woolley of this

"He would turn away when he saw the
lens pointing in his own direction....
Frequently Chase snapped pictures
of the Colonel without his knowledge, or just at the instant that he
turned and found himself facing the
lens and discovered our perfidy."

LOWELL THOMAS (1924) in
With Lawrence in Arabia

"We never had the slightest difficulty
persuading T. E. to pose for Harry
Chase's camera."

LOWELL THOMAS (1937) in
T. E. Lawrence by His Friends

One of the illustrations that appeared in
Lowell Thomas's *With Lawrence in
Arabia* over the caption "Lawrence
occasionally visited enemy territory
disguised as a gipsy woman of Syria."

approaching sack—but Woolley does not mention any of this story. According to the Consul's wife, the chance of the Consulate being defended by the Turks was slight, so at Lawrence's suggestion the Consul agreed to allow Lawrence to smuggle in rifles from a British gun-boat at Beirut. With two naval officers Lawrence managed the gun-running without being discovered. She goes on to say that she had rifles under all her divans, but nevertheless thought that Woolley and Lawrence might have been "pulling their Consul's leg." She adds that it was a sound scheme, and that the rumour that the British Consulate was so armed would have frightened off the Kurds. But if Buswari and his men were such friends of Lawrence that they had allotted him two houses to plunder where was the necessity for arming? Where the naval officers got the rifles, and who paid for them is not stated; and the fact that gun-running is illegal doubtless did not worry a Qonsolos of those spacious days.[59]

In later life Lawrence spoke of these Carchemish years as the happiest he ever knew. Carchemish was "the perfect life."[60] Even if allowance is made for the human tendency to idealise the epoch of lost youth and the obvious contrast between post-war chaos and pre-war tranquillity, we can see that here at least he was telling the truth—the Carchemish life did suit his peculiar temperament and alleviated the unhappy conditions of his existence. At Carchemish he was wholly free (except for letter-writing) of the home life he found so unendurable and of his mother's expectations of him which he could not meet, however much he wished. He was devoted to Hogarth and got on well enough with Woolley, who did all the real intellectual work of the expedition while allowing Lawrence to do much as he wished, yet without excluding him from such work as pottering with the ceramics and photography which really interested him. What Lawrence himself called his "Oxford pose,"[61] of æstheticism and dressing up was not interfered with. In the off season he could wear his Arab bachelor's girdle with the extra-large tassels of celibacy, amuse himself with Dahoum, and treat the villagers "in lordly fashion,"[62] as the sole representative of the distant English authority which employed them on easy labour and distributed lavish baksheesh. Lawrence must have enjoyed his holiday excursions with Dahoum, though they cannot have been anything like so extensive or frequent as he implies and his panegyrists assert.

Lawrence as we have seen, later allowed Liddell Hart to say that he had travelled " always with someone from our Carchemish digging gang " (obviously Dahoum) taking " a few camels on hire-carrying, sailing down the Syrian coast, bathing, harvesting, and sight-seeing in the towns."[63] His letters, on the other hand, show him settled at Carchemish or visiting his English-speaking friends at Jebail and Aleppo, so that there is difficulty in finding time for these other activities unless indeed they occurred at no great distance from Jerablus. He did not really have " five years "[64] of wandering about the Middle East, but, (apart from his walking tour in 1909), merely the off-seasons of two and a half years, made the basis of his claim that he " came to know Syria like a book, much of North Mesopotamia, Egypt and Greece."[65] The available evidence shows that before August, 1914, Lawrence had spent one day each in Athens, Naples and Smyrna, about a month with Petrie in Egypt, a week in Constantinople, and did not wander farther east of the Euphrates than Harran. The " sailing down the Syrian coast " story was told to Vyvyan Richards where it became " a journey by boat up the Palestine coast " with the picturesque addition of Lawrence's collapse in delirium from malaria, only to regain consciousness "in an Eastern hall stretched luxuriously in a deck-chair listening to a Beethoven sonata echoing divinely through the large spaces."[66] Time must also be found for Lawrence in these off-seasons to supplement his income by " casual earnings of a queerly varied kind,"[67] including the two weeks at Port Said as a coal checker, his " getting in touch with the members of the various Arab Freedom societies," and a visit to Kitchener in Cairo to warn that unwary soldier of the danger to the British Empire of allowing any other European power to control Alexandretta.[68] It should perhaps be added that Lawrence's " basic intention " on these wanderings " was always to write a strategic study of the Crusades," and that his anti-Turkish sympathies were not limited to the Arabs. The Kurds had " encouraged him to ride in their ranks " while Armenian revolutionaries "had come to him for help and advice and he had dipped far into their councils."[69]

Altogether, he must have been a much sought after and most self-important young man as well as a happy one during this epoch of his life. At the Jebail American Mission School, which he made his second home, Lawrence was known as " the Encyclopædia " from his wide knowledge.[70]

At Carchemish (Jerablus) he came out of his "absorbed and discomforting aloofness" and devoted himself to his guests, on whom he made different impressions. A woman visitor speaks of his "intensely blue eyes" and "gold hair," and thought he looked "a young man of rare power and considerable physical beauty."[71] On the other hand, an Armenian of his own age thought him "a frail, pallid, silent youth" with a "shut-up Oxford face," and found him "impressive, disturbing, disagreeable" in the "exquisite temple of culture" created by himself and Woolley.[72] When Major Sir Hubert Young, spent the week of 1913 with Lawrence at Carchemish they passed the days "in clambering over the mound, bathing in the Euphrates, carving figures out of the soft limestone, and above all talking." They tried vainly to make out the meaning of Hittite inscriptions, and practised revolver shooting with a matchbox for a target at thirty paces, at which accomplishment Lawrence easily beat the professional soldier. Many years later Young expressed his surprise that in their all-day talks they never mentioned "strategy and the art of war," though they were uppermost in Young's mind, and Lawrence, as he subsequently told Liddell Hart, had been closely studying all the best-known writers on warfare since he was sixteen. This friendship with a regular officer is the more interesting since Lawrence afterwards came to dislike the type so much, though Young thought that he earned Lawrence's highbrow friendship by his casual use of the word "boustrophedon," a Greek word which literally means "Turning like oxen in ploughing," but is used of ancient methods of writing which go alternately from left to right and right to left.[73]

Whether Lawrence was really "in touch with the members of the various Arab Freedom societies,"[74] or had "dipped deep" in anybody's secret political councils remains a question. It is obviously useless to look for any contemporary evidence since nobody would put into writing dangerous information which might be betrayed. The story of Buswari and the alleged plan to loot Aleppo seems to have been taken over by Lawrence from Woolley with numerous embellishments, and seems to be the chief basis for his supposed alliance with the Kurds, unless indeed, Captain Hart refers to the Qonsolos episode. What help the Armenian committees thought to obtain from a junior archæologist of pronounced æsthetic tastes and meagre income is not stated, and the other hints are too slight to take hold of. In *Seven Pillars*, Lawrence describes the secret societies—the Ahad and the Fetah—but there makes no claim to being in touch with them, and on a later page merely says that he had " seen something of the political forces working in the minds of the Middle East."[75] Indeed, the chief if not the only pre-war pronouncement of Lawrence's about the topic of " Arab freedom " (which we are given to understand had been the main object of his life since schooldays) is a chance remark in a letter written in April, 1913, at the end of the first Balkan war; " As for Turkey, down with the Turks! But I am afraid there is, not life, but stickiness in them yet. Their disappearance would mean a chance for the Arabs, who were at any rate once not incapable of good government. One must debit them with algebra though." The tone of these remarks does not appear to indicate either high hopes or lofty admiration for " Arab freedom."[76]

In contrast to these uncertainties, there is considerable information about the expedition made by Woolley and Lawrence, with Captain (afterwards Colonel) Newcombe of the Royal Engineers in January and February of 1914, along the then Turkish-Egyptian frontier. Under threat of war England, in 1906, had compelled the Turks to give up to Egypt a large quadrilateral of desert land north of the Suez Canal, between the Mediterranean and the Gulf of Akaba. A military survey and maps of this area had been nearly completed in 1913 by the British War Office and the Survey of Egypt, the field work being done by military officers.[77] When it came to the point of carrying the survey to the other side of the Turkish frontier, a difficulty arose. It could hardly be that the Turks would allow map-making by British officers in Turkish territory,[78] and they might with some justification consider such activities as espionage. Honesty being the best policy, the decision was made to call on the Palestine Exploration Fund to send an archæologist to make a survey of this Bible land (to be written up later in their " slightly devotional " annual publication) under cover of which Captain Newcombe could continue his military work. Woolley was first selected for the task, but as he could not be spared for three months, Lawrence was added to divide the work with him.[79]

None of the intellectuals writing on Lawrence has expressed the faintest regret or indignation at this official abuse of science and religion in order to screen politico-military activities in the underhand manner that has since become so deplorably frequent, though the Director General of the Survey of Egypt attempts to apologise for it on the grounds that it was equally valuable for " peaceful " as for " defensive " purposes;[80] and Captain Newcombe received orders from Kitchener himself to cease surveying when the Turkish officials discovered the real nature of the survey and ordered the governor of Akaba to forbid it. Nor is any explanation given of why these two junior archæologists were asked to go on the survey instead of one of the genuine specialists in Biblical archæology. How far the alleged archæological survey was in fact only a piece of camouflage,[81] is indicated by the admissions in Lawrence's preface that he and Woolley were not " Semitic specialists," that they were so ignorant of the subject that they arrived in Sinai without having even heard of the names of the scholar-travellers who had preceded them, and consequently duplicated their work.[82] Yet this connection with the Egypt Survey and the maps Lawrence prepared for their joint report were essentially useful to him in the autumn of 1914, serving as an introduction to the War Office which enabled him to start his war service as a commissioned officer on the Staff instead of as an officer cadet or in the fighting ranks. When after the outbreak of war Lawrence described the survey as " a very fortunate stroke,"[83] he was thinking of it perhaps from a military point of view, but it was also a very fortunate stroke in his own career.

From Woolley's narrative and Lawrence's map, the first part of their journey can be closely followed. They took Dahoum with them from Carchemish, and reached Gaza on the 6th January, 1914. They remained at Gaza only one day to buy the equipment needed, and on the 7th met Newcombe at Beersheba, but without reporting to the Survey headquarters in Cairo. The little expedition spent three days at Beersheba, then on January 11th moved south to Khalasa where they stayed four days; from the 16th to the 23rd they were at the ruined Byzantine town of Esbeita, from which they moved south-west to El Auja which is just on the Turkish side of the frontier. They then doubled back, re-crossing the Darb el Shur, (the old caravan route from Palestine to Egypt) and moving just inside the Turkish frontier to Bir Birein, where Woolley and Lawrence temporarily lost their camels. After further wandering on either side of the frontier, Woolley and Lawrence separated on the 8th February near the Egyptian Government post of Kossaima.[84] Newcombe says they spent only four or five days in his camp, during which all his daylight hours were given to surveying, and after dark until midnight in listening to the discussions of the two archæologists.[85] He was particularly interested in their investigation of Ain Kadeis, thought by some to be the Kadesh-Barnea of the Old Testament, on which there is a note by Lawrence in their report.[86] This report tentatively places Kadesh in the region of Kossaima, which includes Ain Kadeis, after ruthlessly jeering at the American, Trumbull, for his description of the place,[87] which might possibly have been better supplied with water in 1882 than in 1914.

When Lawrence takes up the narrative after his separation from Woolley at Kossaima all dates cease, so that we do not know how long he and Dahoum were in walking the hundred miles or so on the Egyptian side of the frontier to the coast and Akaba—I say " walking " because Newcombe says that at this period Lawrence preferred walking to riding either horse or camel.[88] Obviously it was some time in February when Lawrence joined Newcombe at Akaba, where the Turkish governor informed Newcombe that he had definite orders from Constantinople to forbid the surveying in his district. Lawrence, Newcombe adds, was " surprised and even hurt " that the officer obeyed the order; but evidently complaint had been made to Cairo, since Kitchener by telephone called off the military survey.[89]

At the same time Lawrence was forbidden to take photographs and " to archæologise," and was not allowed a boat to visit the island called by the Crusaders, Graye, and now Kureijeh, or Jeziret Firaun (Pharaoh's Island), which lies off the Egyptian coast opposite Akaba according to Lawrence, near Wadi Taba, but according to the 1912 Baedeker " opposite the mouth of the Wadi Kureijeh," an hour and a quarter farther south. This prohibition he took as a challenge, and contrived to cross the 400 yards to the island with Dahoum on empty ten-gallon water tanks borrowed from Newcombe.

Lawrence wrote a careful account of the island ruins, only to find that he had been anticipated by " the French Fathers."[90] The next day he and Dahoum were expelled from the district by a Turkish police-man, from whom they managed to escape in Wadi Araba. The two boys took that route in preference to the usual trip (Baedeker, Route

22) up the old Roman road through Wadi Ithm or Yetem to Maan. The escort must have stuck to them for sixty or seventy miles if, as Lawrence says, they only got rid of him (or them) "in the ravines about Mount Hor," or Jebel Harun, the burial place of Aaron according to Semitic mythology. Lawrence's official account of this journey is vague, and not easy to follow on his own map. He had arranged to meet Woolley in Aleppo on the 1st March, but had to borrow the railway fares for himself and Dahoum from two English tourists at Petra.[91]

An embellished version of these events is contained in Lawrence's letter " to a friend," written from Damascus on the last day of February, 1914. The camels which, according to Newcombe and Woolley were lost near Ain Kadeis on the 27th January, are here lost on the way to Akaba, where Lawrence arrived " alone and on foot, since my idiot camels went astray," but " By Jove, I was glad to see a tent." To reach " Pharaoh's Island " Lawrence " puffed a zinc tank full of air " (how is that done?) and accompanied by Dahoum, splashed his way with planks as paddles, across half a mile (400 yards in his official version), of sea infested with " hungry sharks." The escorting policeman of Newcombe's version becomes " a lieutenant and half a company of soldiers," whom they " dodged " and " slipped " until " the desired happened, and the last one left us, and I spent a splendid morning all in peace on top of Aaron's tomb in Mount Hor." Lawrence then speaks of shooting a partridge and of spending a " bitterly cold " night " with a huge wind " curled up with Dahoum " in a knot under sheepskin cloaks."[92] Jebel Harun is well over 4,000 feet high, so that a strong wind in a February night must have been very uncomfortable and fully justified their feeling " cold and cross as bears."

Lawrence and Woolley had only just returned to Carchemish at the beginning of March, to start what proved to be Lawrence's last season as a working archæologist, when they became involved in the riot of the Kurdish and Arab railway workers against their German employers, already briefly referred to earlier in this chapter. Woolley has given an account of this in his *Dead Towns* book, and there is an even longer description by Lawrence in a letter written to the poet, J. E. Flecker, with whom Lawrence had made friends at Beirut in

August, 1911, shortly after Flecker's marriage. In June, 1914, Flecker was very ill and depressed, dying in fact of consumption in a Swiss sanatorium, and Lawrence's letter was written (from England) in response to an appeal for news. Apart from Lawrence's usual inability to give figures correctly there is no serious discrepancy between the two accounts, though he writes in a schoolboyish vein of partizanship for his side against the other side, with even such schoolboy phrases as " an awful rotter," " shoot the bounder," " the German idiots," " to biff that," " we of course were inwardly chortling." The dispute arose from a mistake about a man's pay, and in the subsequent shooting a man was killed and many wounded. The dead man had belonged to Buswari's Kurds, and Woolley eventually arranged with Buswari for the payment of blood money for the murder, and compensation to the wounded. A comic touch in these ugly happenings is alleged from the fact (?) that the Aleppo authorities misunderstood a telegram about " the firing " and sent out the Fire Brigade instead of the soldiers. But both Woolley and Lawrence were in some danger from rifle fire as they and their headmen (Haj Wahid and Hamoudi) tried to prevent the riot from spreading—one of the wounded was a boy to whom Lawrence was speaking when he was hit.[93]

At the end of that season both archæologists left for England. In 1919 Woolley returned to Jerablus as political officer, and in December of that year continued his work as archæologist at Carchemish, after more than a five-year interval.[94] Lawrence never saw the place again.

I have not been able to determine how much Lawrence contributed to the British Museum published Report on Carchemish. The text of Vol I (1914) was written by Dr. Hogarth with a short preface by Sir Frederick Kenyon. The text of Vol II (1921), " The Town Defences " was written by Sir Leonard Woolley. The title-page of the whole work mentions that the excavations were " conducted by " Woolley and Lawrence. Sir Frederick says that Woolley and Lawrence " co-operated with " Hogarth in producing the book. Hogarth (Vol I. p. 24) quotes a story told to Lawrence by unnamed person or persons about the origin of the modern tribes round Jerablus. Woolley says he had Lawrence as assistant from 1912-14 and that a " Jerablusi, Dahum, was trained by Lawrence to act as photographer, and as such did excellent work." After 1920 the photographer was P. L. O. Guy. Although the published texts seem to be entirely the work of Hogarth and Woolley, it is a fair inference that they may have used Lawrence's notes to an extent which cannot now be determined. Moreover, some if not most of the photographs may have been the work of Lawrence or his pupil, Dahoum.

CHAPTER SEVEN

Now THAT we have brought Lawrence to the brink of the 1914-18 war, of which he became eventually the great popular British hero, it seems advisable to halt for a moment to consider what we have learned about him. That he was physically stronger than his low height and slight body suggested; that he took little or no care of his health but had great endurance in resisting the numerous illnesses which resulted; that he was an Oxford æsthete and something of a scholar, assistant to Leonard Woolley, and skilful with his hands; that he liked wearing bright clothes and Arab costume, could drop his feeling of racial superiority and get on terms with Arabs and some Kurds, liked making excursions in Syria with his Arab boy, Dahoum—all these have their significance. More fundamental is that he was the illegitimate son of an Anglo-Irish baronet, bitterly resented his social inferiority, and longed to compensate for it by some great achievement. If he was what is called " a born soldier," the frustration through his birth and poverty of a career as a regular officer would account for many things in his make-up. Behind his self-consciousness, the diffident Oxford manner and schoolboy behaviour was a watchful adventurer of intense ambition, a mind of versatility and skill, an unscrupulous will-to-power, a wilfulness impatient of control, a self-assertiveness which was allied with contempt. We must add to this that in his carefully calculated relationships which seemingly never became intimacies he kept each in a watertight compartment and presented himself in a certain predetermined rôle;[1] and that he possessed what is called " Irish charm " or as he once put it " some quality that he could turn ' on or off like a tap ' which appealed to people."[2]

But the most startling and disconcerting trait in Lawrence's character is the propensity which seemed uncontrollable in him to put out highly embellished stories of himself and his doings which after circulating among his credulous friends—and doubtless receiving additions thereby—eventually found their way into print as part of the story of the great Lawrence of Arabia. The preceding pages show a few instances of this habit, which endured until the end of his life and coloured his recollections of childhood. It is seldom that these stories are wholly invented. There is generally a foundation of fact which when reported immediately in a letter to someone he was not particularly eager to impress is often credible though not especially remarkable—but sooner or later this would be worked up by Lawrence into stories to his own glorification, stories which were untrue in precisely those parts which made them sound extraordinary and made him sound remarkable. The reader must be careful to distinguish between the invented newspaper stories which began to appear in print as soon as Lowell Thomas made him famous, and those he invented and circulated himself. His friend Vyvyan Richards who has published some of the latter (though with a growing suspicion of their authenticity), says: " Few men have gathered after them so great a train of stories as he, serious and comic, and the greater proportion could only have come from his own lips; yet none of these stories was ever told against himself—his supremacy must never seem to suffer."[3] Exactly so, and they made his popular reputation.

Lawrence went further than this. Having put into circulation such embellished stories through the credulity of one or more friends and profited by the renown as an extraordinary person they brought him, he would repudiate them sometimes (many he stuck to) or complain that he was persecuted by publicity. His curious duplicity in this respect went so far that he persuaded Lowell Thomas and Graves to publish statements freeing him from responsibility for the statements and stories he had given them. As I shall show later, Lowell Thomas was repudiated by Lawrence (who pretended scarcely to have known him) and was sneered at by Lawrence's friends. On a separate page in Mr. Thomas's book appears the notice:

" The Publishers desire to state that Colonel Lawrence is not the source from which the facts in this volume were obtained, nor is he in any way responsible for its contents."[4]

Believing this—as who would not?—I wrote Lowell Thomas through an American friend saying (among other things) that I assumed Lawrence had " contributed nothing in the way of editorial suggestions to film or lecture." To this Lowell Thomas replied:

" Your guess is one hundred per cent wrong. He helped me in a lot of ways on the lecture that I gave a couple of thousand times. He also worked with me on my book. At that time he was exceedingly anxious that no one should know this."[5]

When I come to discuss the Lowell Thomas lecture and book I shall put forward some internal evidence to show that Mr. Thomas must have been helped by quotations from documents Lawrence alone could supply, as well as by stories which must have been contributed by Lawrence and his friends or derived indirectly from them. It is not my business to explain why Mr. Thomas consented to have his publishers insert the untrue statement I have quoted. But this is not all. Robert Graves's book, *Lawrence and the Arabs*, as already pointed out contains this statement from him: " Unfortunately, owing to pressure of time, my completed typescript could not be submitted to Shaw," (i.e., T. E. Lawrence), " before publication, and I apologise to him for any passages where my discretion has been at fault."[6] But in the two volumes published after Lawrence's death which contain notes by Graves and Captain Hart on their collaboration with Lawrence, and the help he gave in the writing of their respective biographies, Graves admits that this statement gives a wrong impression. I quote his words:

" Lawrence read and passed every word of the book, though he asked me to put a sentence in my introduction making it seem that he had not."[7]

Certain passages of this book were written by Lawrence himself,[8] as also was the case with Hart's book. Captain Hart, as Graves later pointed out,[9] was more thorough in checking Lawrence's statements than either of his predecessors, and, as his notes show, under his questioning Lawrence denied, withdrew or side-stepped some of the ridiculous stories he had himself invented or over-embellished. All three of these writers wrote in good faith, accepting what Lawrence told them. Lowell Thomas spoke and wrote as a war propagandist, charged by his government to find something to counteract German anti-British propaganda in the U.S.A.—his business was to find British war heroes. When even he blenched and asked Lawrence point-blank whether stories Thomas had been told about him were true, Lawrence laughed " with glee," and replied: " History isn't made up of truth anyway, so why worry? "[10] A tender literary conscience might have started at those words, the cynicism of which needs no comment. As I shall be able to show in more detail later on, Lawrence, having got what he wanted—and more than he bargained for—out of Thomas, proceeded by implication to disown him, to pretend he had scarcely known him, and to complain—as, for instance, he did to Graves—that " butter of the Lowell Thomas sort does not keep very well: and its quotation at tenth hand is painful."[11] But most of the butter came originally from Lawrence or the Lawrence Bureau. Probably Graves and Hart never knew that Lawrence had collaborated with Lowell Thomas, just as Graves complained that Lawrence never told him that he was collaborating in Hart's work. After that book came out Lawrence tried to soothe Graves by saying he would rather have Graves than Liddell Hart, though he had also said elsewhere " how much he appreciated Hart's biography and wished that none others had been published."[12] By the time the Hart book was ready the device of pretending that Lawrence had nothing to do with such works on himself had worn thin; and in any case he must have realised that Liddell Hart would not lend himself to such false dis-claimers as Thomas and Graves had weakly permitted. Therefore, in that book Lawrence's " notes and comments " are acknowledged, but the author takes responsibility for his opinions. But in spite of his care, Hart's book contains many stories which should have aroused his suspicions.

The difficulties of a biographer trying to discover the facts are baffling, discouraging and at times insuperable. If Lawrence's state-ments were all false the task would be comparatively easy; but they are not. Some are true or seem true; some, in fact many of them, are at least partly true; others are or seem to be quite unfounded. But with the imperfections of the record, (many documents and letters are still unavailable), there is need for much caution—evidence might turn up to justify a story or a statement which a priori looks improbable. In any case, a distinction must be made between the newspaper talk about Lawrence, and the stories which can be definitely traced to him or to one of his personal friends. I am concerned only with the latter; the newspaper stuff is only important because of the annoyance it undoubtedly was to him in later life—a Frankenstein monster he himself had been the chief agent in creating.

The business of a biographer is to tell a life-story and thereby also to portray a character by gathering, arranging and interpreting the discoverable facts about his subject. Where the facts are uncertain or contaminated or embellished, as in this case, the biographer finds himself in the position of counsel who puts his client in the box only to discover a faulty witness; or, if that seems too lofty a comparison for so humble a labour, he may be likened to a bricklayer who finds some of the bricks given him true and straight, others faulty and misshapen, and yet others crumbling to dust when handled. Whatever Lawrence's part in the 1914 war it can probably never be estimated exactly because so much of the evidence rests on his own testimony. Lawrence has recorded that Lord Allenby could not determine how much in him was " genuine performer " and how much " charlatan,"[13] and Lord Wavell comments that Allenby never solved the problem; but " always suspected a strong streak of the charlatan in Lawrence."[14] Lloyd George more vaguely hints a similar opinion.[15]

From this arose the necessity for careful checking of all the claims and picturesque anecdotes which were circulated directly by Lawrence or indirectly by him through his more or less credulous friends. But in so doing the biographer must keep in mind that no man is rigidly consistent and accurate, especially a man like Lawrence whose unstable temperament is illustrated by the constant variations in his scrawled handwriting; that everyone changes with the passage of time, so much so that a man of forty looks back with some astonishment and dismay at his half-forgotten self of twenty, unless indeed roseate idealisation of the past sets in early; that the universal miseries of life induce fibbings and subterfuges in us all, and that in our letters we all tend to vary our expression according to the person addressed. He must keep in mind the old fable of the shepherd who cried " Wolf " too often, and remember that Lawrence may sometimes be speaking the truth. Above all, he must recollect that many of the embellished tales are not without some basis of fact, and avoid denying all Lawrence's accomplishments because they were outrageously exaggerated. He was, for instance, a very good revolver shot, though he did tell an absurd tale of intentionally shooting a man in the little finger, and the different and highly-coloured versions of the episode he circulated do not mean that no such encounter occurred. His bicycle was not designed by Lord Nuffield and himself, as he claimed, but he did have a light racing bicycle, and did cover long distances, though demonstrably in some instances (and probably in most) not as long as he asserted.

Now that Lawrence's habit of circulating these tales about himself has been demonstrated—at any rate in the pre-war period and, as we shall see, it certainly did not disappear in 1914—and his method of getting them into print has been explained, it is inevitable to ask why he did this. The psycho-analyst will have his confident explanations, among them that Lawrence was a peculiar example of the "God-man complex." Professional psychologists of other schools will have other explanations, and strictly orthodox psychiatrists possibly others. A careful study of Lawrence's psychology, taken with what has been recorded of his medical history, by some really competent specialist, would be of great interest and doubtless enable us to understand and to condone much which now seems merely impudent. Meanwhile from the standpoint of common sense and common knowledge we may point out that a certain amount of boasting, more or less, is usually inseparable from that stage of adolescence which Lawrence so queerly seemed in some respects never to outlive. In some recorded cases this boasting becomes pathological, as in the so-called "J-3 murder case" in France where a gifted lad was shot by a jealous friend because he boasted (quite untruly) of imaginary wealth and achievements. The significant thing is that the youth's companions believed all he said without any hesitation or critical enquiry, which was also the case with Lawrence. We can go further, and say that such boasting is a universal human failing or trait, from young Red Indian braves to elderly retired mariners and field officers. What is different in Lawrence's case is that the stories were told deliberately, and found their way into print while he persuaded two biographers to publish statements misleading their readers into thinking he had no responsibility for them. If it be asked why these stories were believed by his biographers and by the numerous friends who have left their personal memories, the answer is perfectly simple. Not one of these stories was published until after Lowell Thomas's propaganda had worked up public hysteria to an almost unprecedented extent, and had made Lawrence the popular war hero, creating an atmosphere in which such stories were readily acceptable, on the strength of achievements which Lowell Thomas himself had not witnessed—his lecture and his book are based on what he was told by Lawrence and Lawrence's friends. I shall have to recall later on how difficult all this makes any fair and honest account of Lawrence's actions in the war, especially if you remember that *Seven Pillars* is itself a propaganda book, full of rhetorical writing and fine sentiments but vague about dates, facts, effectives, and self-confessedly suppressing some facts and altering others.

Some of the Lawrence stories so far discussed (e.g., the Hypnos head story and the 50,000 books), are absurd and trivial, but they happen to be among those where Lawrence can be shown definitely to be romancing. It is necessary to establish his record in this respect because in other and more important cases there cannot be or is not at present such definite proof that he was romancing or inventing. After what has been and will be demonstrated, some—perhaps many— readers may feel that the onus of proof lies elsewhere, that it is now up to the Lawrence Bureau to prove the truth of what he and they have advanced as facts. As an example of the self-glorifying story which cannot be definitely disproved but which sounds highly improbable, let us look into the much-publicised interview between Lawrence and Kitchener which is alleged to have occurred before the war. As it links up with a claim (supported also by no evidence beyond Lawrence's own assertions) that early in 1915 he was the real author of the strategic plan for a landing at or near Alexandretta, the enquiry is not without interest.

The first mention of this interview occurs in Lowell Thomas's book. According to this, Lawrence " with his intimate knowledge of history" thought that the proposal to run a branch line to Alexandretta from the main Berlin-Baghdad railway was " a bold Prussian threat against British power in Asia " and therefore instantly hurried to Cairo, " demanded an audience with Lord Kitchener " and asked him why " Germany had been permitted to get control of Alexandretta."[16]

Unfortunately for posterity no film or photograph exists to show the expressions moving across Lord Kitchener's swivel-eyed features as he was thus bluntly challenged by an unknown non-military Oxonian of twenty-five. According to Thomas's version of Lawrence's tale there was no explosion but the mild reply: " I have warned London repeatedly, but the Foreign Office pays no attention. Within two years, there will be a World War. Unfortunately, young man, you and I can't stop it, so run along and sell your papers."[17] Why " sell your papers?" What papers? Can this refer to the well-known practice of Oxonians who help to pay their way through college by hawking copies of the *Saturday Evening Post* on Carfax? However that may be, the story itself was told to Mr. Thomas by " Major Young, of the Near Eastern Secret Corps," whatever that was. Probably Major Sir Hubert Young of the Indian Army is meant, but his book, *The Independent Arab*, is discreetly silent on this tale. It is, however, repeated by Graves (and hence with Lawrence's knowledge) in agreement with the assertion that Lawrence was " a student of world politics," of which there is not the slightest evidence in his pre-1914 letters and writings, and with the change of Kitchener's last words to: " So run along, young man, and dig before it rains."[18] Thus, through Graves, Lawrence gave his acquiescence to a story which Lowell Thomas had already picked up from someone in a slightly different form, thereby glorifying himself as one on familiar terms before the war with the ruler of Egypt, as a student of world politics and one intimately acquainted with history.

But did this interview ever take place? It is true Lawrence was in Egypt with Petrie in 1912, when Kitchener was Consul-General, but when Liddell Hart asked Lawrence at what date he met Kitchener, Lawrence replied that he " first met Kitchener in 1913 and again in 1914."[19] It is only negative, but there is no evidence that Lawrence was in Cairo at any time during 1913-14 until December, 1914, and Sir Ernest Dowson has certainly mis-dated Lawrence's first reporting for duty at the Surveyor General's office. Of course, it is possible that Lawrence did make a brief trip to Cairo between January, 1913 and June, 1914 (when Kitchener left for good), and that the journey went wholly unrecorded at the time. He may have had an interview, even, though it seems quite incredible that he could have refrained from boasting of having met so eminent a person to some of his friends;

yet not one of the pre-war letters or reminiscences mentions it. Lowell Thomas only heard the story in 1918, by which date Kitchener was dead. Not the least incredible part of the tale is that a man in Kitchener's responsible position would have been so utterly indiscreet as to prophesy a World War to a casual civilian caller aged 25.

And how unaware Lawrence was of the approaching catastrophe is proved by his 1913 letter, already quoted, in which he hopes for several more years at Carchemish and then another and another " nice place." If a man so important as Kitchener had really warned him that a war was coming, how could Lawrence have indulged in such false hopes?

In the 17th-18th century vogue of " the ruling passion " psychology Lawrence's would certainly have been set down as amour-propre, vanity. But, as La Rochefoucauld, one of its chief exponents, pointed out, vanity is a universal passion; and it is not necessarily to be condemned, since it may be and often is a strong motive to effort and action. What is curious in Lawrence's case is that he was so lacking in pride that he was quite content to let himself be celebrated in anecdotes which he knew to be untrue or exaggerated since he himself had originated them and connived at their circulation. Yet this preposterous vanity co-existed with a desire to be thought modest and retiring in the English Public School boy tradition; and indeed in some moods it became partly genuine when he discovered what a nuisance newspapers and public made of the notoriety he himself had so eagerly courted. But the familiar propaganda which represents him as the shrinking victim of a notoriety thrust upon him against his will is just one more myth—of his own creation.

PART TWO

CHAPTER ONE

THE OPENING of the first world war in August, 1914, found Lawrence in Oxford. Since, in December, 1913, he had written his friend, Richards, that Carchemish would last another four or five years[1] and his letter to Flecker from Oxford just before the war speaks of returning to the East in two or three weeks,[2] is it unreasonable to infer (as I have done in the last chapter) that he had not really been given any warning by Kitchener, and that the war was as much a surprise to him as it was to most people? Unless, of course, it is argued that these remarks were deliberately inserted in his letters to conceal from others his private inner knowledge of the course of events. It might also be argued that his return to England just before the murder of the Archduke Ferdinand points in the same direction— had not Kitchener also gone home on leave about the same time, being providentially caught and brought back to the War Office by a special message from the Prime Minister just as he stepped on the Channel boat to regain his post in Egypt? But how improbable an explanation in Lawrence's case!

There was, however, another if minor reason for Lawrence's presence in Oxford that summer. As already mentioned, his preface to *The Wilderness of Zin* confesses that when he and Woolley went to make the archæological survey of Sinai he had never even heard the names of the learned travellers who had preceded them.[3] Obviously these works had to be run through before the report could be issued; there had been neither books nor time for the research during the Carchemish season; but Oxford and London possessed the requisite libraries. According to Lawrence, in a note written about 1933, Turkey though not, in August, 1914, in the war was not too pleased about the Sinai survey and therefore Kitchener, who had throughout been behind the survey, insisted that the report on the archæological results of the Expedition be produced by the Palestine Exploration Fund as soon as possible as " whitewash."[4] Kitchener certainly had been interested in the survey. It has already been recorded that he sent a telephone message to Captain Newcombe at Akaba to stop the survey when the local Turkish governor objected, and it was Kitchener who, as a subaltern in 1878, had begun the survey. Indeed, according to Lord Wavell (who ought to know) the Staff used Kitchener's maps on the Palestine front until 1916.[5] But if the camouflage of the two archæologists and their obscurely published report was really Kitchener's device, it was hardly worthy of his reputation. Did he think such trifling espionage a casus belli? Moreover the " white- wash " was pretty slow in appearing, if the intention of publication was really the hopeful thought that " Turkey " would in consequence believe that the survey had not been military but purely archæological. The script was not even sent to press until December 3rd,[6] by Lawrence, who mentions that the maps for the report were being prepared at the War Office; although in another, unfortunately undated, letter, he says that if it were published it would probably be confiscated; " and I shall have to do the confiscating."[7] Lawrence does not say by what authority a temporary second lieutenant in the Map Depart- ment was given power to confiscate books. That he was merely show- ing off to his correspondent is clear from the fact that a few weeks later he wrote to Hogarth telling him to get the book out as fast as he could.[8]

This alleged order from " K " to complete and publish the report is of some interest since it is one of the two reasons put forward to explain why Lawrence did not immediately join up as a fighting soldier. The other reason will be examined a little later. Nobody will accuse Lawrence of physical cowardice, of any conscientious objection, to wars in general or that war in particular. Writing on his thirtieth birthday, 15th August, 1918, he said " four years ago " (i.e., August 1914), " I had meant to be a general and knighted, when thirty."[9] In a letter written in September, 1914, he feared the Turks were not contemplating war. (As a matter of fact, " the Turks " had signed a secret treaty of alliance with the German Government on the 2nd August, which made their eventual entry into the war against England

CHAP. I]   *A Biographical Enquiry*

certain). Omniscience and the air of being at the very centre of things with private knowledge of the secrets of high policy were among Lawrence's mannerisms at all times. So it is not surprising to find him writing importantly from his garden bungalow in Oxford any scraps of gossip he had picked up from Hogarth and other dons to a friend (in America!) as his own inside knowledge of what " England " and " we " had decided to do about Turkey. " We " he says, intend " to let Turkey have fiscal and economic rights over foreign property," while retaining from the Capitulations (which the Turkish Government had abolished), " the personal inviolability and sanctity of the foreign houses." Should the Turkish Government refuse these suggestions " England will not go to war," but " Greece and Roumania will look in, after having promised Bulgaria a slice for her benevolent aid; " presumably under pressure from the British Government, for " then of course," if " Turkey attacks us," well, " we would be justified in self-defence."[10] Since when had the Cabinet taken to confiding the secrets of its policy and future actions to obscure Oxonians? Ten days before hostilities began between Turkey and the Entente, Lawrence wrote: " Turkey seems at last to have made up its mind to lie down and be at peace with all the world. I'm sorry, because I wanted to root them out of Syria."[11]

The political judgment and prescience of those remarks are only equalled by the military acumen which failed to realise that the armies of France and England in September, 1914, had only just avoided a fearful military disaster, and had suffered casualties which made an immediate offensive impossible. And yet, as we have seen, Lawrence in his youth had shown impulses towards the military life and an interest in soldiering, the more remarkable since they are not often to be noted in his type of intellectual æsthete. His running away to enlist in the ranks of the Royal Artillery may or may not be one of his stories, but his association with the Oxford Church Lads' Brigade and O.T.C. is authenticated. Again, the stories of his physical endurance and fakir-like abstinence from food are obvious exaggerations of the familiar type, but he certainly cycled and walked strenuously and ate frugally on his French and Syrian tours. Then, his self-training as an expert revolver shot is interesting, and still more so the fact that a day or two after the opening of the 1914 war, a friend saw him practising rifle-shooting on a range his younger brother had made in a disused clay pit in north Oxford.¹² All this may reasonably be held to show a wish if not an aptitude for soldiering, the frustration of which partly explains his resentment against regular officers—they had been privileged to be what he by his birth was debarred from.

His intellectual preparation for warfare was even more thorough and unusual than his attempts at practical training. No contemporary records have been preserved, since these studies are not once mentioned in any pre-war records nor in any reminiscences of that epoch, and the first public mention of them occurs in Lowell Thomas's book, for Lawrence's own remarks on the subject do not appear in *Revolt in the Desert*. Lowell Thomas was told that Lawrence had made " an exhaustive study of military writers," from " the wars of Sennacherib, Thotmes and Rameses," down to " Napoleon, Wellington, Stonewall Jackson, von Moltke and Foch." And Lawrence himself told Mr. Thomas that " in the irregular war which he conducted against the Turks," he had found Cæsar and Xenophon more useful than Foch.¹³ Passing to Graves, we learn that Lawrence's tutors did not require him to read up any campaigns later than Napoleon's but he had read " most of the more modern military writers, such as the great Clause-witz " (who, by the by, first saw service on the Rhine in 1792, and was Thielmann's chief of staff at Waterloo), von Moltke and " the recent Frenchmen, including Foch." Here again Foch is denounced, in this case on the grounds that he had " lifted many of his chief principles from an Austrian report on the 1866 campaign."¹⁴

Next, we have Lawrence's own statement in *Seven Pillars* in which he condescendingly explains that " of course he had read the usual books, Clausewitz, Jomini, Mahan, and Foch," and " like any other Oxford man had played at Napoleon's campaigns, worked at Hannibal's tactics, and the wars of Belisarius."¹⁵ When questioned by Liddell Hart on this topic Lawrence opened out freely. He had, he explained, begun reading books on war at—it seems inevitable—an exceptionally early age, fifteen. He had read Creasy, Henderson, Mahan, Napier, Coxe, technical treatises on castle building, Procopius, Demetrius Poliorcetes, and " nearly every manual of chivalry "— whatever that may mean. His " period was always the Middle Ages " but from Clausewitz (whom he read in 1905-6) he worked back to Napoleon, Guibert and Saxe. He had visited every 12th century castle in France, England and Wales, went " elaborately into siege-manœuvres via Viollet-le-Duc," had seen Valmy and "tried to re-fight the whole of Marlborough's wars."[16] In Hart's book these military authors are increased by Vegetius, Goltz, Willisen and Bourcet. Liddell Hart informs us that the only copy of Bourcet known in England is at the War Office, but does not tell us how the undergraduate Lawrence came to read it, and he appends a note of admiration to Lawrence's revelation that he had actually " browsed " through the thirty-two volumes of Napoleon's *Despatches.* Moreover, he assured Hart that he had " visited Rocroi, Crécy, Agincourt, Malplaquet, Sedan " and had followed " step by step " the Crusaders in Syria.[17]

Well, there you have the story, or rather the stories. It seems a formidable preparation for minor guerrilla warfare with Bedouins along the Hejaz railway. At his death there was only one of these books in Lawrence's library, a three-volume English translation of Clausewitz published in 1911, six years after he read the book in 1905-6. The two volumes of Procopius he had were part of a then complete set of Loeb classics given to him by Lord Riddell after the war: but not kept up to date. The record may be lacking, but there is no mention in the published letters or by friends or relatives of any visit by Lawrence to the battlefields named. If the ambiguous phrase about trying to re-fight all Marlborough's battles means that he went over the actual sites, then he must have made entirely unrecorded journeys to Belgium and Germany—and where chronologically are these to be fitted in?

A possible clue to all this ostentatious militarist erudition may be derived from Lawrence's curious remark about Foch's having derived his principles from an Austrian report on the 1866 campaign. Why the 1866 campaign particularly? In Hart's book Lawrence is quoted as saying that he learned of these books through his tutor, R. Lane-Poole,[18] but in a private note to Liddell Hart he mentions that he had been " fortunate in having access to the advice of Oman and Lane-Poole."[19] Now, there was at Oxford a University Kriegspiel Club, of which Oman was long an enthusiastic member, which " played war-games in the German style on the old set of Prussian official maps for the campaign of Sadowa . . . " i.e. the 1866 campaign! The " most resolute and bloodthirsty tactician on the map " Oman tells us, was as might be expected, the professor of theology. He goes on to say the " Kriegspiel " remained one of his recreations for many years and that afterwards he was " a frequent umpire in the bloodless battles of the younger generation."[20] Here we have a possible source for Lawrence's portentous parade of military authorities; and if introduced to the Kriegspiel Club Lawrence could easily have overheard the learned discussions of these high-brow warriors in their arm-chairs—making them his own as he usually did make his what he picked up from others. Similarly he may have " tried to re-fight the whole of Marlborough's wars " in the Kriegspiel manner without actually visiting the battlefields. Or is it all an invention by Lawrence?

Unfortunately, in spite of this unique fund of military learning, Lawrence, in 1914, could not apply for the only appropriate post of Field-Marshal with any hopes of success. But before we examine the evidence as to what he did do, the reader must again be warned that censorship has been at work. The editor of Lawrence's *Letters* tells us that " the record of the war years in Lawrence's private letters is a fragmentary one, and I have not been allowed to use all that I wished to publish."[21] Whether the publication of this suppressed material would or would not materially alter the record as it now stands is obviously a matter of pure conjecture, and for any certainty we must await the pleasure of those who are withholding the evidence, whatever it may be, probably nothing of any interest. At all events, the letter of political prophecy already quoted (18th September, 1914), shows that Lawrence had not yet entered the Army; " I am writing a learned work on Moses and his wanderings; for the Egyptian people say they want me but not yet, and the War Office won't accept me till the Egyptian W.O. has finished with me."[22] This is none too clear, but it seems to mean that while he was engaged in some way to the " Egyptian War Office " the parent body in London would not have him; it also implies that he had already sought a Staff office appointment.

When, after the war, the writing up of Lawrence's exploits began, a different story was put forth. According to the version given to Lowell Thomas, Lawrence tried to enlist as a private, but the Medical board " looked at the frail, five-foot-three, tow-headed youth, winked at one another, and told him to run home to his mother and wait until the next war."[23] Graves, who was unaware of the collaboration of Lawrence with Lowell Thomas, " corrects " the statement that Lawrence was rejected for physical reasons. What he reports is that

Lawrence tried to join " an Officers' Training Corps at Oxford " and " tried again in London " but failed because of " a temporary glut of recruits."[24] Another version, not necessarily in contradiction to the above, is sponsored by Sir Ronald Storrs in the *Dictionary of National Biography:* " On the outbreak of war in 1914 Lawrence, being below standard height (then raised to 5 feet 6 inches)* obtained but a sedentary commission on the Geographical Section, General Staff of the W.O."[25] This was evidently the story Lawrence told his war-time friends. Colonel Newcombe says: " On the outbreak of war, I had to leave the completion of my maps and reports to go to France; Woolley soon became an Artillery Officer, being rather taller than T. E. Lawrence. . . . Lawrence being too short for the required standard at that time, offered his services to finish and edit my reports and maps."[26] Vyvyan Richards says that Lawrence and Woolley both tried to enlist at the outset, but were told to complete their report first; " when Woolley joined up " Lawrence found he was not eligible since the minimum height limit had been raised to check temporarily an excessive rush of recruits."[27]

It is perfectly true that even in August there was such a rush that some units could do no more than take particulars of many volunteers, and that in the late autumn or winter the standard height was temporarily raised to check the flow of recruits for whom there was neither equipment nor training personnel—I think to 5 feet 8 inches, but I may be wrong. Liddell Hart has the same rejection for height story[28] but in the notes made for his book from Lawrence's talk and other sources we read: " Did not try to enlist. Worked on Sinai book, then W.O. Sinai map."[29] And that Lawrence did not try to enlist for active service is corroborated by the note on Hart's script published in the *Letters.* There Lawrence says that he and Woolley (after completing *The Wilderness of Zin*) wrote to Newcombe " and asked his advice about a war job." Such jobs were very difficult to get, but Newcombe " told Cox, of the Intelligence, about us, and got our names on the waiting list." Waiting list for what? Obviously " a job " in Army Intelligence, for " Woolley lost heart, waiting, and wangled a Commission in the Artillery."[30]

According to Lawrence, Hogarth then introduced him through an intermediary to Colonel Hedley, the head of the Geographical Section at the War Office, all of whose subordinate officers were then being

* It was weeks after the outbreak of war that the height standard was temporarily raised.

t'aken for France. According to Hedley, there were no intermediaries, and Lawrence turned up unsponsored and said the Army would not take him because he was too small. Hedley then promised to get him a commission.[31] According to Liddell Hart, Hedley already had " heard some good stories about Lawrence " from Newcombe, which one can well believe. They are not lacking here. Lawrence evidently told Liddell Hart that some time elapsed between his entering the War Office and receiving a commission in order to pass off the story that he was sent wearing civilian clothes to take some maps to General Rawlinson, who " nearly had a fit when he saw me," and said " I want to talk to an officer." Whereupon Hedley said he must have a commission, which he obtained without a medical examination; which surely implies that the commission was not for fighting ?[32]

But in a letter from Oxford, dated 19th October, 1914, Lawrence tells his correspondent that he and Woolley were doing nothing— although they were full of intentions.[33] The Army List for November-December, 1914, lists Lawrence's appointment under date, 23rd October, 1914, as " Temp. 2nd Lieut.-Interpreter." It may of course have been ante-dated, but why "interpreter" in the Map Department. That he intended to stick to office work in which he could find some object that would offer him a proper opportunity for his special gifts and intelligence seems clearly indicated by the remark in an un-dated letter after he joined the War Office Staff. This was to the effect that the Staff could hardly get rid of him as he knew their secrets. Although he had no definite appointment, he had hopes.[34] He was not unique in preferring to exercise his ingenuity against the enemy rather than becoming cannon fodder, but it is typical that he would not admit it. Lawrence's conception of his duties was strictly personal, for when told to provide a map of Sinai he put together and delivered the 68 manuscript sheets—" some of it was accurate and the rest I invented," which obviously would save troops many casualties.[35] The reader will perhaps not be surprised to learn that within three weeks Colonel Hedley admitted to somebody that young Lawrence was running his entire department.[36] And it is a fact that all the other officers of the department had gone to the front.[37]

The cloud of respectable witnesses to these recruiting stories would seem to settle the matter beyond dispute, until we realise that all repeat stories originating in Lawrence and not what they personally observed. On the other hand that solitary and neglected " did not try to enlist " in Liddell Hart's notes was evidently contradicted by Lawrence after the writing of Hedley's letter.[38] From the point of view of the Lawrence legend it was evidently right and decorous that the hero should have tried to do his bit as a private or subaltern in a line regiment. The height story was a perfect alibi, though the exact date on which the standard was raised is nowhere given—I am assured that it was in fact not raised until after Lawrence went to the War Office, but the item is unimportant. Lawrence's patriotism was always self-assertive rather than self-sacrificing, and it is not denied that he was " intensely ambitious " at this time. If he really hoped to become a general, it was an immense step upward to start the war on the Staff and to avoid the waste of time involved in rising by merit above the mob of temporary second lieutenants. That Sinai survey was indeed, as he said, " a very fortunate stroke "—for him. And there is the irrefutable fact that with Newcombe in France and Woolley in the Artillery, Lawrence was the only man in England who knew anything about that last season's survey. If the Entente had not declared war on the Turkish Government—as Lawrence feared it might not—then he had a second line for promotion; and if it did, well, he was at the centre of things, and not likely to be overlooked when an expanded Intelligence was thought necessary in the Middle East.

There seems to have been something irregular—at least from the bureaucratic point of view—about this commission as Second-Lieutenant Interpreter. Lawrence informed Liddell Hart that in 1919 " someone " told him he had never been properly commissioned.[39] In 1922 he wrote to Bernard Shaw that he had " had the utmost difficulty in getting a gratuity of £110 from the War Office when they demobilised me."[40] Lawrence's numbers are to be taken with caution, but if this sum is correct (which it may be) then this was a ridiculously small sum for a man with Lawrence's length of service (nearly five years), with two years as a temporary field officer. It was the gratuity of a second lieutenant with about eighteen months' service. It would be interesting to have this explained. Perhaps, from a bureaucratic point of view, the period when he sat at a desk in Cairo was military service; and the period when he was Political and Liaison Officer to Feisal, blowing up trains and scurrying about with Bedouin Arabs in conditions of discomfort and occasional acute danger, not military service? Or was it the penalty of getting into the Army by way of the Staff instead of the recruiting office? Or did they get his dossier mixed up with that of the other Thomas Edward Lawrence who was gazetted a second lieutenant in the Royal Sussex Regiment in 1918? In any event the fact—if it is a fact—does not imply much official esteem for his war services.

Since Lawrence was not in the Army when he wrote his letter of the 19th October, and the Army List gives the 23rd as the date of his commission, it is practically certain that this was his date of entry, about a week before war was declared by England and France on the Turkish Government. This was another "most fortunate stroke" in Lawrence's war career. If Turkey had remained neutral, he must inevitably have been sooner or later forced out to France, most probably to meet the fate of his two younger brothers. Captain Hart tells us that the regular Intelligence service at Cairo was so poor that for competent information about the Turkish Army they had to rely on the superior knowledge of a journalist, Philip Graves. He adds that Colonel Hedley recommended Lawrence as an officer ideally suited for Intelligence work in Egypt.[41] However that may be, this new situation meant that anyone with any knowledge of the Middle East and (especially) of the right people in England was sure to be sent out. Marmaduke Pickthall, possibly the greatest Oriental scholar of them all, had to be left out because he was more pro-Turkish than pro-British, and, like Philby, eventually became a Moslem. But a less rabid Turcophile, Aubrey Herbert, M.P., was selected to go to Cairo, with another M.P., George Lloyd, afterwards Lord Lloyd, and Clayton and Storrs—the real brains of all this complex Middle Eastern intrigue. Newcombe was brought back from France, Woolley and Lawrence were warned, and the whole party set out in December, Newcombe and Lawrence going ahead of the others on the 9th December. Later, they were joined by Hogarth and Gertrude Bell, and eventually were absorbed into the Arab Bureau. This transfer brought Lawrence promotion to the rank of Staff Captain with seniority of the 15th December, 1914. Thus in seven weeks Lawrence had reached a rank which might have taken years to attain if he had actually joined the British Army as a friendless private or second lieutenant on the Western Front.

Although there is absolutely no contemporary evidence available that he had any such thought, it is the fact that after the war Lawrence claimed that " since about sixteen years of age " he had been " filled with the idea of freeing people and had chosen Arabs as the only suitable ones left."[42] But if this was so, it is surprising that for two years of the war Lawrence limited himself to Intelligence work at a desk in Cairo, with no more active service efforts than leaves and official Cook's tours to Athens, the Senussi Desert and Kut el Amara.[43] Even when he visited the Hejaz with Storrs for the first time in October, 1916, it was with no intention of fighting, since he told Feisal that his " duties in Cairo excluded field work " but that " perhaps " his chiefs would let " me pay a second visit later on."[44] (In fact, as we shall see when the time comes, he was considerably surprised when Clayton told him bluntly he had got to go back.) This does not look like any burning enthusiasm for taking up the practical military work of " freeing a people."

As a matter of fact Lawrence merely went from the map department in London to the map department in Cairo.[45] The reaction of the bureaucrats there (" who is this extraordinary little pip-squeak? "[46]) has already been noted.

G.H.Q. at that time was in the old Savoy Hotel at Cairo, about two miles from the offices of the Egyptian Survey at Giza; and Lawrence used a motor bicycle for riding to and fro as well as for later visits to the Government Press at Bulaq. Dowson remembered him as an insignificant second lieutenant, his light hair ruffled, his cap askew and with no belt.[47] He proceeded at once to assert himself by severely criticising the system of transliterating Arabic place names which had been set up (as Lawrence probably knew) by the Director of the Reproduction Office, W. H. Crosthwaite, who had studied the subject for months and had discussed it with the experts.[48] What Lawrence's qualifications for criticism were then is not clear, but his knowledge of written Arabic could not have been great.[49] And when he himself later was challenged on the discrepancies of transliteration in *Seven Pillars*, he retorted angrily that he spelt his names as the mood took him to show how little he thought of the systems.[50] It is not surprising that Crosthwaite was taken aback at his impertinence, while Logan, the head of the Map Compilation Office in Cairo, was gravely insulted at having to take orders from a newly appointed amateur fresh from England. This sudden attack on Crosthwaite's methods was characteristic of Lawrence's strategy in trying to establish a superiority over people he met.[51]

Further on in the same essay Sir Ernest Dowson has a passage of rather striking severity. He says that it was not merely the pompous and the incompetents who were alienated by Lawrence's ways. There were men of first-class ability and sound common-sense who objected to his frivolous and impudent attitude. They thought his wearing of Arab dress histrionic and melodramatic, and considered him an actor whose cheap exploits were the result of the power of the gold so lavishly put at his disposal.[52] We are not told whether these men were civilians or soldiers (doubtless both), for there is evidence that many professional soldiers disliked him as much as he pretended to despise them. This dislike later produced from Lawrence and his adherents a corresponding over-valuing of his achievements, and among these adherents were a few professional soldiers. One such enthusiast remarks moderately: " In my considered opinion, Lawrence was the greatest genius whom England has produced in the last two centuries."[53]

Turning back from these opinions to the more difficult search for fact, we get from Sir Ernest Dowson some idea of what Lawrence's duties were during his approximately two years in Cairo. These duties, according to Dowson, were various, but chiefly those of a liaison officer in the over-complicated organisations set up during the war. Lawrence was the link between the Survey of Egypt on one side, and on the other Military Intelligence and (after February, 1916) the Arab Bureau. The dealings of the Royal Navy and Mediterranean Expeditionary Force with the Survey also passed mainly through Lawrence, because such a course was convenient. With time a widespread organisation was created to collect material for maps and other records, and this usually came through Lawrence to be co-ordinated and made use of under his direction. There were also demands for facsimiles and special reproductions, among them the much-advertised set of stamps for Sharif Hussein of the Hejaz. Similarly, Lawrence was the link between G.H.Q. and the Egyptian Government Printing Press. Throughout his period of service in Cairo, Lawrence visited the Survey at least two or three times a week and often several times a day. Dowson adds that no one ever complained about Lawrence, and

" Lawrence usually dressed in robes of spotless white "

praises his resourcefulness and his ability to turn his mind to any work, his enthusiasm and his capacity to get his own way when his own way seemed vital to him. Furthermore, Lawrence possessed a rare and valuable quality—his presence had a stimulating effect on the men in the offices and workshops, so that when they were working very long hours there was a noticeable heightening of morale after his visits.[54]

This testimony is not only creditable, it is even credible. Obviously Lawrence must have carried out his Cairo duties competently or he would not have been allowed to keep his post—greatly as incompetence, particularly in the higher ranks, appears to have been condoned in that war area; but hundreds of other officers performed duties of equal or greater importance without being celebrated as supermen. Not much information about his work in Cairo can be found in Lawrence's contemporary letters, partly no doubt because of war-time censorship (though he completely ignored this in writing to Hogarth) and partly because, as I must again remind the reader, existing letters have been suppressed. Evidently, at first it was all clerical work, for in January, 1915, he mentioned that he was tied to an office-desk all day putting together scraps of information and preparing geographies from details carried in the memory.[55] In early February, he claims he has been in his office from 9 a.m. until 10 p.m. writing all day.[56] He is said to have collaborated with Philip Graves in producing an official handbook on the Turkish Army.[57] In July he supplements the office information by saying that he also lives in trains, interviews Turkish prisoners, and supplies information, but chiefly works at map-drawing and geography.[58] Evidently in April, 1915, he still had no intention of taking any active part in the fighting, since he wrote to Hogarth that he had no training as a field officer, and thought it would be " bad form " to go fighting up to Constantinople.[59] By " field officer " Lawrence probably meant a regimental officer in the field, though why he thought fighting up to Constantinople should be " bad form " is a baffling query.

Something must be said in elaboration of Lawrence's remark about interrogating prisoners. Early in February, 1915, Turkish forces made an unsuccessful attack on the Suez Canal. Most of these belonged to the Turkish 25th Division, which had been recruited from the Damascus area, and obviously some at least of the men must have come from villages which Lawrence and Dahoum had visted. If the questioner could speak some words in the local dialect and could show a knowledge of local people (as in some cases Lawrence could), the chances of obtaining information from ignorant, homesick men were probably increased. And in the case of these prisoners of the 25th Turkish Division, Lawrence was peculiarly fitted for the task of questioning them.[60] But was he able to converse with the Turkish-speaking soldiers in their own language? An anecdote told by Dowson implies that Lawrence had some knowledge of Turkish,[61] and the like is implied by his working on the Turkish order of battle with Philip Graves, who of course knew the language very well. It was claimed that they knew all there was to know about the Turkish Army.[62] Perhaps so, but one hesitates over some of Lawrence's more sensationally lurid statements about the Turkish Army; for instance that nearly half among some of the groups of prisoners who were examined proved to have venereal disease which they had acquired from their officers.[63] Towards the end of the war, the state of the Turkish rank and file in Syria and Palestine was pitiful indeed, but if they were so degraded at the beginning of the war, their four years' successful resistance does not seem very creditable to the troops attacking them.

By this time it is probably unnecessary to inform the reader that the story of Lawrence's activities in Cairo was not originally put out with much sobriety and care for fact, but in a series of stories and unproved claims which betray the familiar sources of the Lawrence of Arabia legends. There is, for instance, the story of the two generals who, in Lowell Thomas' version, spent hours in the map department " poring over inaccurate charts " and would after forming their plans invite suggestions from " the insignificant subaltern " who " not infrequently " replied: " While there are many excellent points in your plan, it is not feasible except at the expense of great loss of time in building roads for transport of supplies and artillery, and at needless expense of lives in maintaining lines of communication through the territory of hostile native tribes."[64] There is no doubt that Lowell Thomas had a pleasing knack of brisking up Lawrence's anecdotes, but while he must be praised for the form he cannot, as usual, be blamed by the Lawrence Bureau for the matter. Shorn of its more picturesque absurdities (the generals humbly going to the map department instead of having the " charts " brought to them is specially pleasing), the same tale with modifications reappears in the Lawrence-approved Graves' book. Here the wretched generals are treated pretty roughly, and deservedly humbled. Lawrence interrupts them as they discuss a reported movement of Turkish troops with a sharp crack of the whip: "Nonsense; they can't make the distance in twice the time you give them. The roads are bad and there's no local transport. Besides, their commanding officer is a very lazy fellow."[65] Is it surprising that Liddell Hart reflects exultantly that if Conan Doyle had been born a generation later "he would have found in Lawrence an apt model from which to create Sherlock Holmes?"[66] You know my methods, Allenby; apply them.

The likeness to Sherlock Holmes becomes even more striking when we come to consider the prisoner of war stories. Liddell Hart assures us that Lawrence's success in obtaining information was "uncanny." Lawrence modestly explained it away as elementary: "I always knew their districts; and asked about my friends in them. Then they told me everything."[67] But were all the prisoners captured by the British from the 25th Turkish Division and all the 25th Division friends of Lawrence's friends? Obviously not, and we have the testimony of Graves to prove it. "An ugly-looking ruffian" (writes Graves) arrested as a spy, said he was a Syrian—though why that should be an alibi escapes me. Lawrence, "overcoming his usual aversion to looking a man in the face," said: "'He's lying; look at his little pig eyes! The man's an Egyptian of the pedlar class.'" Whereupon Lawrence "spoke sharply in the pedlar's dialect'" (suppose you screeve or go cheap jack?) and the man "admitted who he was." Again an unnamed colleague of Lawrence's showed him a "fine-looking Arab" as "one of the real Bedouin." But Lawrence said: "No! He's not got the Bedouin walk or style. He's a Syrian Arab farmer living under the protection of the Beni Sakhr tribe." "And so it proved,"[68] says Graves. Positively, Holmes, this is black magic.

David Garnett says Lawrence spent his time in Cairo and was the centre of great preparations for the most incompetent military operations.[69]

We now come to the History of How Lawrence Planned the Alexandretta Landing, and the History of How Lawrence Arranged the Surrender of Erzerum. Though later in time, the surrender of Erzerum may be taken first. When Liddell Hart asked Lawrence how he came to receive instructions to accompany Aubrey Herbert to Kut, Lawrence replied:

"I had put the Grand Duke Nicholas in touch with certain disaffected Arab officers in Erzerum. Did it through the War Office and our military attaché in Russia. So the War Office thought I could do the same thing over Mespot. . . ."[70]*

This is made more definite by Graves: "As a matter of fact, the capture of Erzerum had been 'arranged'—Colonel Buchan's novel *Greenmantle* has more than a flavour of truth. . . ."[72] And Liddell Hart brings the two together: "In the spring of 1916 he had a long-range hand in a more important matter, the 'capture' of Erzerum by the Russian Caucasus Army after a curiously half-hearted defence. . . ." And Buchan's *Greenmantle* is cited with the sage warning that "fiction has often a basis in fact."[72] And in the "Lives" of T. E. Lawrence, fact would seem to have an uncommonly large escort of fiction.

I take the following facts from the narrative of Mr. M. Philips Price, the *Manchester Guardian* war correspondent in Russia during that war. The Russian Caucasian Army had been reinforced to make 175,000 men, while the Turks had withdrawn two divisions and three batteries of artillery to defend Baghdad; they had failed to return the heavy guns used in the defeat of the British on Gallipoli, and had allowed many officers to go on leave. The Russian offensive approached Erzerum so rapidly that the field commander, General Eudenitch, asked the Grand Duke Nicholas to be allowed to work out a plan for the capture of Erzerum with General Przjevalsky, who for many years had been military attaché in Erzerum, and knew the forts and surroundings well. The Russians advanced through snow-drifts and over ice without regular food supplies, and the 4th Russian Caucasian Division on the 12-13th February had to cross a pass 10,000 feet high and lost 2,000 front-line soldiers by frost-bite. A wireless message from Abdulla Kerim Pasha, commander of the 3rd Turkish Army, to Enver Pasha was intercepted: "the condition of the 3rd Army is serious; reinforcements must be sent at once or Erzerum cannot be held." The Russian commander did not wait for the 4th Division, and, seeing Turkish reinforcements on the way, attacked at once, and, after very bitter fighting, captured Erzerum.[74] Nothing

---

* In *Seven Pillars* this claim is reduced to "reasons not unconnected with the fall of Erzerum."[71]

whatever is said of the surrender being " arranged," but Price does mention that the Arab and Syrian troops were unfitted for such a strenuous winter campaign.

The reader will remember that Lawrence claimed that his " arrangement " for the surrender was sent through the British military attaché, but does not mention his name. This is very strange, because in 1916 the British military attaché on the Caucasus front was A. P. Wavell, afterwards Lord Wavell, later a personal friend of Lawrence's. Wavell's *Encyclopædia* article on the Campaign in the Caucasus, strange to say, does not even mention Lawrence and knows nothing whatever about an " arranged surrender." What he does say is this: " The Russian capture of Erzerum was one of the finest feats of arms of the whole war. . . . Its capture on February 16th, was mainly the result of a turning movement from the north, the 2nd Turkestan Corps, under Przjevalski, the ablest of its Russian corps commanders on the Caucasus front, who had an intimate knowledge of Erzerum, where he had spent fifteen years as military attaché."[75]

If the fall of Erzerum was due to Lawrence's intervention, why did his friend, Lord Wavell, not mention the fact in his authoritative account of the battle? Above all, since Wavell was the British military attaché through whom Lawrence claimed that he " put the Grand Duke Nicholas in touch with certain disaffected Arab officers in Erzerum "? Is it conceivable that such a soldier as Wavell would describe an " arranged " surrender " as one of the finest feats of arms of the whole war "? On the other side, we have only the unsupported statements of persons with no first-hand knowledge of the event, and their vague reference to a novel by John Buchan. If any real evidence of the truth of Lawrence's tale exists, it has not yet been produced.

The Alexandretta or Gulf of Iskanderun landing is a rather more complicated story, but worth trying to unravel, since it is one of the many cases in which Lawrence claimed—directly and through his friends—to have initiated a policy or strategic plan which was not his, while the confident, not to say brow-beating, assertion of his priority was accepted by the world as true and went to build up the Lawrence of Arabia legend. Let me begin by reminding the reader of Lawrence's (already quoted) letter in which, he exults at knowing War Office secrets so that they " can't sack me," and also the lofty manner in which he confidently handed out as his own the (erroneous) political prognostics which he must have picked up from dons, since at the time he wrote he was not even in the Army and could have had no confidential knowledge of what " England " or " we " were going to do. In other words, Lawrence picked up secrets, nor did he have any scruples about giving out as his own what he picked up from others. In addition, there is the fact of his Francophobia, a hatred and an envy so irrational, so irresponsible and so unscrupulous that it is fair to say his attitude towards Syria was determined more by hatred of France than by devotion to the " Arabs "—a convenient propaganda word which grouped many disharmonious and even mutually hostile tribes and peoples. This Francophobia seems strange in one who claimed to have spent three years reading French and Provençal medieval literature, whose early letters show so much interest in contemporary French writing, and who translated a French book after the war. The difficulty is partly but not completely resolved by Woolley, who says that, after a long stay in the Lebanon (possibly the three weeks with Dahoum, " walking about in Arab dress " in Jebail), Lawrence " felt a profound jealousy of the part" which the French " played or wished to play in Syria," and adds that long before the Sykes-Picot agreement Lawrence " was an enemy of France in the Levant, and that sentiment was the key to many of his later acts."[76] Lawrence was not the only British officer with such feelings. Fashoda, with Lord Salisbury's ultimatum threatening France with war, was then only sixteen years in the past, and the feelings prompting that action still remained—the French were to be kept out of the Eastern Mediterranean. More specifically, the violently anti-France letters from Lawrence I am about to quote were written to D. G. Hogarth, and received without protest from him, and Hogarth became the Director of the Arab Bureau with all its avowed and concealed influences on British policy.

The Gulf of Iskanderun or Alexandretta Bay is at the top of Syria, where the coast-line turns sharply to the west along the shores of Cilicia. The first reference to it in Lawrence's letters is a request to Hogarth for " a print of any photos of Beilan you have,"[77] made on the 15th January, 1915. Beilan was a small town of between 7,000-8,000 inhabitants, 10 miles from Alexandretta, and near " the Syrian gate " the mountain pass to inland Syria. It is a reasonable inference that Lawrence had been told to collect information for a map sheet of the district, but had then not grasped the significance of the order. On the 18th March, Lawrence wrote Hogarth an uncensored private letter excited in expression and highly indiscreet in contents, since over a month before the landing at Gallipoli (25th April), it contains the words: " the Australians and New Zealanders, and some Indians are going to the Dardanelles, with the French, and Ian Hamilton's army."[78] No wonder the Turks were ready on Gallipoli when such indiscretions occurred! Evidently Lawrence was now in possession of highly important secrets, and clearly a most untrustworthy person to have them, for the letter is filled with confidential military information. In this letter he puts to Hogarth, as a new idea of his own, the plan for a landing near Alexandretta, and violently urges Hogarth to try to impose this plan upon the War Office and the Foreign Office. The Turks, he says, "have only 50,000 disaffected troops in Syria," but " we " have conceded Syria to France, which however must not be allowed to hold Alexandretta, since " in the hands of France it will prove a sure base for naval attacks on Egypt," and " if Russia has Alexandretta, it's all up with us in the Near East," and, since the French will " probably be under Russia's finger " in the future, Lawrence deems it " absolutely necessary that we hold Alexandretta." After mentioning eminent persons who favour this scheme, Lawrence proposes that someone should " suggest to Winston that there is a petrol spring on the beach . . . huge iron deposits . . . coal." With 10,000 men, he adds, the British in Alexandretta would be impregnable. Six words, concerning high officials, are cut from this letter.[79]

These promptings—with additions which will be considered later —were continued in other private letters to Hogarth, the last dated 26th April, which seems to indicate that Lawrence did not then know the landing had just been made at Gallipoli. But, in letters to another correspondent, he shows that he had not abandoned hope of the Alexandretta enterprise. The question is, was Lawrence the author of this strategic plan? He certainly made the claim, and in writing: " I am unrepentant about the Alexandretta scheme which was, from beginning to end, my invention, put forward necessarily through my chiefs (I was a 2nd Lieutenant of 3 months seniority!). Actually K. accepted it, and ordered it, for the Australian and N.Z. forces: and then was met by a French ultimatum."[80] As Lawrence was commissioned on 26th October, 1914, three months bring us to January, 1915, when " the chiefs " through whom Lawrence " necessarily put forward " his strategic plan were Dowson, Lt.-Col. Clayton and eventually Lieutenant-General Sir J. Maxwell. And we find, in fact, the following words in a telegram from Maxwell to Kitchener:

> " If any diversion is contemplated, I think the easiest, safest, and most fruitful results would be one at Alexandretta. There . . . we strike a vital blow at the railways and also hit German interests very hard . . . Alexandretta would not want a very large force. All other places—Rafah, Jaffa, Acre, Beirut—are too far from the Turkish lines of communication."[81]

This looks like a striking piece of evidence in Lawrence's favour, but unfortunately for his claim that the plan was his invention " from beginning to end," the telegram was sent off from Cairo on the 4th December, 1914, i.e., five days before Lawrence even left London for Cairo. In any case, the idea was not a new one even in December, 1914. Maxwell and Kitchener had " more than once discussed the project before the War."[82] The plan of a landing at Alexandretta was frequently discussed. It came up again in October, 1915, when the evacuation of Gallipoli began to look inevitable, and Kitchener came out to the Mediterranean on a tour of inspection. Maxwell's idea of a " not very large force " was more than the 10,000 named by Lawrence; it was 100,000. The Royal Navy objected that another 400 miles of sea communications would be opened for them to protect, and that anyway there were not enough lighters and small craft if Gallipoli was to continue. And finally the French intervened.[83] It is possible that Lawrence's unproven stories that he had met Kitchener in 1913 and 1914 may have been brought forward after Kitchener's death to bolster the claim (put out by Lawrence) that Lawrence had " warned Kitchener " about Alexandretta before the war. It is significant that Liddell Hart does not advance this claim for Lawrence. He says that Kitchener " mooted the idea of a landing near Alexandretta," but needed a large force, and that, from August on and again three weeks after the opening of war with Turkey (i.e., mid-November, 1914), the whole question of defending Egypt by an attack on the Dardanelles was raised, not by Lawrence, but by a much more likely person—Winston Churchill.[84]

This enquiry may be rounded out by the interesting fact that Sharif Hussein after the war claimed that the Alexandretta landing was *his* plan and " he had never understood why his advice was neglected."[85]

These letters to Hogarth in 1915 have been extravagantly praised as showing Lawrence's great political realism and that " he had already planned the campaign which he was to carry to a victorious conclusion three years later."[86] The latter remark begs the question as to who really defeated the Turks in 1918. At the date he wrote these letters, he was, of course, as an intelligence officer, in possession of secret information about Syria, Palestine, Arabia and Mesopotamia, and did not scruple to reveal it in his private letters to Hogarth. It seems likely that he interviewed some of the British spies or knew them, since in April (1915) he sent to England a medieval dagger pommel which had recently been bought in Jerusalem,[87] and which could only have been bought by some such agency.

At that time the Hejaz had not rebelled, though Lawrence a little prematurely announced, in March, 1915, that the " Sharif had almost declared himself"—fourteen months before the event. (The complicated intrigue between Sharif Hussein and the British had in fact been under way for some time at that date.) But a week later, Lawrence is more interested in Idrissi, the ruler of Asir, who " if anything like as good as we hope," Lawrence thought could " rush right up to Damascus, and biff the French out of all hope of Syria."[88] Now, under Clayton's suasion, Idrissi had performed a useful service in November, 1914, by declaring against the Turks and thus cutting their communications with Yemen—an action which helped to save the incompetent British force in Aden. But it was wildly over-optimistic to think that Idrissi's forces, even supposing they could move through the Hejaz in the Sharif's name,[89] were capable of such an achievement as capturing Syria; and, in fact Idrissi did nothing more active in the war than to " contain one weak Turkish division."[90] What this letter shows only too clearly is the disastrous rivalry between the British in India and the British in Egypt, as well as the personal Francophobia of Lawrence himself. It is hard to see the political realism of preparing for " a renaissance of the Turk when he has lost Constantinople " (which " he " hasn't yet lost), or, with the defeats at Gaza, Gallipoli and Kut still ahead, to reflect (20th April, 1915), " Poor old Turkey is only hanging together. People always talk of the splendid show she has made lately, but it really is too pitiful for words. Everything about her is very, very sick. . . ."[91] Well, with considerable aid from the Russians and some from the French, the British Government expended 750,000,000 pounds, passed well over a million troops in all through that war area, and took four years to defeat this "very, very sick" Turkey. The "political realism" of Lawrence's remark is not very apparent. Of course, the idea of incorporating the aid of the discontented Arabs in the war against Turkey was to some extent carried out (there was never any rising or mutiny of Arab troops), but then the idea had been formulated and negotiations begun before Lawrence ever reached Cairo. Certainly, his criticisms of the slowness and incompetence and lack of initiative in the British Middle Eastern forces were only too bitterly true. It is perhaps worth noting that when a French Mission was sent from Paris to the Hejaz in August, 1916, Philippe Berthelot's last words to the chief officer were: "The greatest service you could do us would be to get some action out of the British in the East."[92]

CHAPTER TWO

THE SCARCITY of Lawrence's personal letters during the war period leaves us with little knowledge of his private life during the years at Cairo which in retrospect he described as "glorious." By April of 1915, the group of men who had gone to Cairo with Lawrence had broken up. Lloyd and Herbert had gone with the Gallipoli expeditionary force, and Woolley was at Port Said. Newcombe remained in Cairo for some time before returning to France; but unluckily has cut short his memories of Lawrence at the moment of leaving London in December, 1914. The fullest and pleasantest glimpse we have of Lawrence at this time is in the memoirs of Sir Ronald Storrs, unfortunately not contemporary notes, or at best notes re-written after Lowell Thomas and the outbreak of hagiography.

It seems safe to say that Lawrence's complaint to Hogarth that he was working fourteen hours a day represented only a very temporary rush. He found plenty of time to read—always Greek or Latin books —in Storrs's flat, and he also borrowed books. Lawrence is said to have liked listening to Storrs as he improvised on the piano, and never tired of walking the bazaars or visiting mosques. He went round the Arab Museum with Storrs looking for "motifs" which might be used for the issue of Hejaz stamps Storrs planned to advertise the Sharif's rebellion. He was also more and more interested in learning from Storrs all he could of Arabia, his knowledge of which, so Storrs says, did not at that time extend beyond the Suez canal. This last remark is not true, but Storrs was probably thinking of Arabia proper, since at that time Lawrence's knowledge was limited to Syria, Palestine, Sinai, the fringe of the Syrian desert and the country a little beyond the Euphrates. Lawrence had wanted to visit the little-known and vast "real" desert areas, and had failed to do so because of lack of means and opportunity, though from laziness he had neglected the German invitation to ride farther East. There was a moment during the war when, riding with Auda, Lawrence caught a distant glimpse of the sand-dunes of the Great Nefud, remembered how Palgrave, the Blunts and Gertrude Bell had been there, and said he was disappointed that Auda refused to enter it. Clearly, these talks with Storrs aroused for the first time Lawrence's interest in the Hejaz; and Storrs consequently sent him all the information that came in about the tribes and topography of the area. As we shall see, it was Storrs, and not Lawrence or Hogarth, who really originated the idea of provoking and exploiting a Hashemite rebellion against the Turkish government.[1]

Storrs recollects that Lawrence was below average height, slight but strongly built, with a high forehead, yellow hair, and straight nose.[2] A confidential French report of mid-1917 may be compared: "Aged 27"—in fact, then 29—"short and slight, determined clean-shaved jaw, very high forehead, light hair always ruffled, very blue eyes lit up by intensity of thought, he makes a strong impression of energy and intelligence."[3] Gertrude Bell, who came out to Cairo in November, 1915, mentions Lawrence (and describes him as "exceedingly intelligent"), who with Hogarth had met her and brought her to the hotel where they were staying.[4] This over-development of the intellect at the expense of more vital impulses—as if indeed he were an exemplar of that over-conscious mind and purely mechanistic will denounced by his great namesake, D. H. Lawrence—certainly accounts for that coldness of feeling as well as for the falsity, the "pose" of his attitude to life. His response to the news that his brother Frank had been killed (in May, 1915) is typical:

"Frank's death was as you say a shock, because it was so unexpected. I don't think one can regret it overmuch, because it is a very good way to take, after all."[5]

There is a nonchalance—perhaps an affected nonchalance, one never knows with Lawrence—about that, which is repelling. The same word "shock" but this time "a great shock," was the response to the death of his brother, Will, but, as that is all that is quoted from the letter (the rest being omitted), there may have been some real grief and humanity expressed. His epitaph on Hogarth (whose death he said hit him very hard): " Also much of his goodness lay in himself; and has gone into death with him. That makes it feel wasteful,"[6] is as trite in thought as it is sententiously studied in expression. And the almost blind mechanistic will to power, which wills merely to assert itself and not for any real purpose and so when gratified leads to nothing but emptiness and a taste of ashes—that will to power and its results, Lawrence's nemesis in life, are perfectly exemplified in one of these Cairo letters:

" Our particular job goes well. We all pulled together hard for a month to twist ' them ' from what we thought was a wrong line they were taking—and we seem to have succeeded completely: so that we to-day have got all we want for the moment, and therefore feel absolutely bored."[7]

Meanwhile, as Lawrence in Cairo under Storrs's guidance was learning all he could about the Hejaz with his special ability to pick up a subject rapidly, an attempt must be made to put before the reader at least the elements of this complex Arabian situation. Perhaps one reason why the public has preferred to listen to romantic tales of " Arabian Knights " instead of looking for the facts, is that the romance might be enjoyed without effort while the facts are so complex and minute, not to say tedious, that all but enthusiasts are apt to grow discouraged. What discourages rather than surprises an enquirer is to find that a situation so complicated was met by a series of organisations so cumbersome, so unco-ordinated, so leisurely and so smug. The adoption of what is euphemistically called " a forward policy " in the Middle East does not seem to have resulted in much tangible gain, while it is unnecessary to dwell on the losses, humiliations and hostilities which have resulted.

What is Arabia? Is it the million square miles of mostly desert land of the peninsula, or does it include the more fertile and settled areas such as modern Irak, Syria, Lebanon, and Palestine, with their diverse populations and religious sects? It is scarcely possible to speak of an " Arab race " when the ethnologists report three racial groups in Arabia proper alone. There were differences also between the settled and the nomad populations, and between rival sects. At the time of the 1914-1918 war the whole area still formed part of the Turkish empire, divided into vilayets and sanjaks, with Turkish garrisons at certain points, though the more distant and wilder tribes were more or less independent, except for rare punitive raids. The nomad tribes lived chiefly as Gertrude Bell says, " by stealing each other's washing," which is misleading, as they washed their clothes but once a year—but what she means is that the camels, sheep, goats stolen on tribal raids from Tribe B by Tribe A were stolen back again at the first opportunity. War was a ritual of robbery with violence. " The Bedouins," says the Sieur de Joinville in the 13th century, " live out of doors in tents with their wives and children. . . . They wrap their heads in towels *dont laides gens et hisdeuses sont à regarder*." And speaking of their plundering the camp of their nominal rulers, " the Saracens," he explains that " the use and custom of the Bedouins is always to fall upon the weaker side." Tenacious holders of old customs, the Bedouins whether of Arabia or Africa had not changed at all in that respect between the 13th and the 20th centuries.

In the main Arabian area were at least ten " states " or chieftains' spheres of influence with no fixed frontiers, yet roughly defined areas, expanding or contracting whenever a " strong man " arose or fell, a situation something between that of the Merovingian kings of France and that of the American Indians, with the succession usually decided by assassination. Starting inland from the head of the Persian Gulf were, as stated by a contemporary authority:

1. The Muntafik, ruled by Ibn Sadun, who were pro-Turk and in the pay of the Germans.
2. Kuwait, ruled by Ibn Saba, paid by the British Government in India.
3. Bahrein, ruled by Ibn Kalifa, in the pay of India.
4. Oman, a heretic people, ruled by Ibn Said and paid by India.
5. Hadramaut, ruled by Ibn Auda, in the pay of India.
6. Yemen, ruled by a holy man (a " poisonous blighter," according to Lawrence), the Iman, Ibn Mohammed Hamid, in the pay of the Turks.
7. Asir, ruled by the immensely corpulent half-negro Ibn Ali el Idrissi, in the pay of the British in Egypt.
8. The Shammar tribes of the Nefud, ruled by Ibn Rashid. Their capital at Hail was occupied by a Turkish garrison, and they

were very useful to the Turks in supplying Medina and the posts on the Hejaz railway.

9. Nejd, with its capital at Riadh, ruled by the great leader of the Wahabis (extreme puritans), Abdul Aziz Ibn Saud, the lately deceased king of Saudi Arabia. He received (for little more than his neutrality during the war) a subsidy said to have been £160,000 a year.

10. The Hejaz, area of the holy cities Mecca and Medina, with ports on the Red Sea at Jidda, Rabegh, Al Wejh, Yenbo. It had a population of about 600,000, about three-quarters of them Bedouins, and lived on the pilgrimage trade, a certain amount of camel breeding and Turkish subsidies. The ruler, the Emir Hussein Ibn Ali of the Hashemites, entitled to be called " Sharif " or " Sherif " as a relative of the prophet, lived up till 1909 for nearly thirty years in forced residence at Constantinople, never certain that his next day might not be the last. He had four sons, Ali, Abdulla, Feisal and Said.

Add to this the medley of mutually incompatible populations in Syria, the Jewish problem in Palestine, and Mesopotamia—and who will disagree with the proposition that, in taking on the main responsibility for this area, the British Government wasted a great deal of money and men to buy itself many vexatious troubles which have not yet ended? It was wonderful while they could pose as condescending patrons of " the Arab cause " (with Lawrence as the national hero) and " a national home for the Jews " (with Balfour as fatuous sponsor)*—Israel and the Arab League are the results. Many were the miscalculations, though perhaps the most serious was the minimising or misinterpreting of the wave of Oriental nationalisms which began with this century, under the menace of which we now exist. The effect of the Japanese victory over the Russians in 1904-5 can hardly be exaggerated. Lawrence's friend, Gertrude Bell, has recorded how in Lebanon the fanatical Moslems on hearing of the Japanese victories would come and shake their fists at the Christians, saying: " The Christians are suffering defeat! See now, we too will shortly drive you

---

* " Fatuous " because he should have known that " national home " would be interpreted to mean " national state."

out and seize your goods."[8] They call Lawrence a Crusader—but on whose side? Not on ours. Was it not a series of blunders to inflame these crude nationalisms for the sake of a little negligible military aid, to take over from the Turks the position of the power to be expelled, and to intrigue against the French instead of agreeing on a common policy?

It is anticipating, but, with this thumb-nail sketch of the complex situation in mind, this seems the moment to relate the remarkable series of British authorities who were supposed to deal with the situation in the Hejaz in its momentous military task of containing a few weak Turkish divisions:

1. The High Commissioner for Egypt (Sir Henry McMahon, succeeded in late 1916 by the Sirdar, Sir Reginald Wingate), advised by the Oriental Secretary (Sir) Ronald Storrs, and (later) the Arab Bureau, decided political relations with the Hejaz. Under the Foreign Office. In Cairo.

2. Supply and war material were controlled by the C.-in-C. the Egyptian Expeditionary Force—General Maxwell, succeeded by General Murray, succeeded by General Allenby. Under the War Office. In Cairo, then Ismailia.

3. The few troops sent to the Hejaz were controlled by the Sirdar, governor of the Sudan, Sir F. R. Wingate, succeeded in late 1916 by Sir Lee Stack, murdered after the war by Egyptian nationalists. Under the War Office. In Khartoum.

4. The Royal Navy, in this area commanded by Admiral Wemyss, who was under the orders of Delhi but was usually at Ismailia.

5. Delhi was running a war of its own in Mesopotamia.

From time to time superior but distant authorities in London issued orders and counter-orders or expressed hopes. More vexatiously, under the divers stresses of war, hopes of oil, and idealism, they authorised statements and promises hard to reconcile with a secret treaty (Sykes-Picot) of which the authorities in Egypt knew nothing definite until its English author arrived in Cairo asking boisterously: " What do you think of my treaty? "[9]

Leaving this imposing muddle to the amazement of future historians, let us turn back to the relations between the Hejaz and Great

SAME PICTURE—DIFFERENT CAPTION

Above: " Lawrence, Hogarth and Alan
Dawnay at Cairo " as reproduced in *The
Letters of T. E. Lawrence.*

Right: the same photograph as it appeared
in Lowell Thomas's book *With Lawrence
in Arabia* but with the caption " Colonel
Lawrence conferring with one of his
advisers at the Arab Bureau in Cairo."
Hogarth was, in fact, the Director of the
Arab Bureau in Cairo and thus Lawrence's
chief. In civilian life he was Keeper of the
Ashmolean Museum, Oxford, and had
encouraged T. E. Lawrence's undergraduate leanings towards archaeology.

Britain. Even before the war, in April 1914, to be precise, the Hashemites had made approaches to the British in Egypt. Sharif Abdulla, Hussein's second son (the recently murdered king of Trans-jordania), visited Cairo, and asked to speak to one of Lord Kitchener's staff. After much pleasant literary and historical conversation (for Abdulla was a man of great charm and highly cultured), he came to the point—would England give his father a dozen machine-guns? Asked why, he said "for defence" against the Turks—"defence," in modern politics, being a mystic and diplomatic word meaning much the same as "offence." Sir Ronald Storrs, the British representative, replied immediately that no arms could be supplied for use against a friendly power.[10]

Even before the war with Turkey, and still more after it was declared, there needed no messenger from Jove to point out the dangers of Turkish capture or destruction of the Suez Canal, or, after the alliance with Germany, the danger of German mines in the Red Sea. (Submarines were also feared, but seem rather unlikely at that time.) The advantages of securing an alliance with Sharif Hussein were actually rather political than military, and, in fact, his greatest service to England was performed in November, 1914, when he refused to endorse the Turkish proclamation of a Holy War. Now, it is probable that the conversation between Abdulla and Storrs in April, 1914, was known only to them and to Kitchener. At any rate, after the outbreak of the war with Germany, nothing was done about the Hejaz, and when Storrs sent in a memorandum suggesting that consultation with Mecca might result in an alliance, he was ignored. He then wrote a private letter to Kitchener in England, which brought telegraphic response on the 24th September, instructing Storrs to send a secret messenger from Kitchener to Abdulla to ask if Abdulla and his father would fight for or against England in a Turkish war.[11]

The messenger, who was not Lawrence in disguise but a native, brought back the reply that, if assistance were given, Abdulla and his father would not help the Turks. On the 31st October, 1914, Kitchener cabled the following ambiguous words: "If Arab nation" (where was it?) "assist England in this war, England will guarantee that no intervention takes place in Arabia" (meaning what?) "and will give Arabs every assistance against external foreign aggression." That seems to promise more than its sender was able to perform. In any case, the report from Mecca on the 10th December was that, although the Sharif was friendly he must await a pretext for breaking with the Turks.[12]

Unless Kitchener ran down to Oxford or a little later to the map-room in Whitehall to consult the young archæologist, it is impossible to agree with those who assert that " Lawrence planned the Arab revolt." All these preliminaries, which led to the rebellion, occurred before Lawrence ever reached Cairo, as did Hussein's refusal to endorse the Holy War. In other words, the rebellion of Sharif Hussein against the Turkish government would certainly have occurred if Lawrence had never existed. Obviously the prime mover on the British side in these tortuous manœuvres was Storrs. It was he who reminded Kitchener, immediately after the outbreak of war, of Abdulla's over-tures, and he who directed most of the secret negotiations. In the autumn of 1916, Abdulla told Storrs plainly: " It was your letter and your messages which began this thing with us; and you know it from the beginning, and before the beginning."[13] The main value of Storrs and Lawrence to each other was the natural sympathy of two æsthetes surrounded by a hostile crowd of officers interested only in their physical comforts.[14] Storrs, with his unique knowledge of the Hejaz intrigues, often told Lawrence things about them just to see his reactions.[15] It seems most improbable that Storrs had any idea then that Lawrence might take a practical part in a rebellion which was not yet begun, but Lawrence did succeed in impressing Storrs with his skill as a technician, teaching him how to use the Playfair Cipher, discoursing on the three-colour process, and generally demonstrating his " amazing knowledge." Yet, at the same time, Storrs speaks of him patronisingly as " little Lawrence, my supercerebral companion."[16]

Meanwhile, the slow, devious negotiations had been going on with Hussein, who, in July, 1915, began to disclose inordinate ambitions. As the price of his " revolt," he required the gift of " an area bounded on the north by latitude 37 from Mersina to Persia; on the west by the Red Sea and the Mediterranean; on the south and east by the Indian Ocean, the Persian Gulf and the frontier of Persia."[17] In fact, he demanded all Arabic-speaking South-west Asia with the exception of Aden not to mention the numerous non-Arabic-speaking minorities.[18] These are the demands for " Arab independence " sent to Hussein by the Arab secret societies of Damascus through

Feisal in May, 1915.[19] But when Hussein asked for " Arab independence," did he not really mean the establishment of his own rule and
dynasty over this area, irrespective of all other possessors and claimants?
McMahon replied, expressing gratification " at the Sharif's declaration
that British and Arab aims were identical "—a daring statement—but
prudently added that " discussion of boundaries in detail was premature."[20] But by October, 1915, the realisation began to penetrate that
the attack on Gallipoli had failed, which would release Turkish troops
for an attack on the Suez Canal; and the High Commissioner changed
ground. On the 24th October, 1915, McMahon wrote the Sharif the
astonishing news that his extravagant claim was accepted, with certain
exceptions, notably " the districts of Syria lying to the west of the
districts of Damascus, Homs, Hama and Aleppo." Reference was
made " to existing treaties with Arab chiefs," and the claims of France
were specifically safeguarded.[21] Lloyd George, from whom I derive
these facts, for some reason forgot to mention that he hoped to annex
most of Mesopotamia, or, as it was officially worded, " the Turkish
Vilayets of Basra and Baghdad would probably be subjected to British
control."[22] This premature allotment of as yet unconquered territories
cannot have greatly pleased Sharif Hussein or his sons, since he particularly wanted Syria (in which he included Palestine) and what is now
called Irak, while Abdulla wanted then to be king of Irak, and Feisal
of " Magna Syria," as it might be called.

In May, 1916, came the secret Sykes-Picot agreement which shared
out the territories of the (still as yet unconquered) Turks among the
powers of the Entente. Russia was to have the Dardanelles, Constantinople and a large area round Erzerum and Trebizond; England
was to have the Vilayets of Basra and Baghdad and " control " a large
" Arab State B " appended; France was to have Cilicia, a large
part of upper Mesopotamia and the coastal regions of Syria (including
Alexandretta), down nearly to Acre, with Mosul included in a large
" Arab State A " under French control; Italy (and not Greece) was to
have Smyrna, some of southern Anatolia and a " sphere of influence "
marked " C." Palestine was to have a condominium of England,
France and Russia. The concessions to the Italians were added later
because the original agreement was concluded without their knowledge, which made them very angry. Nothing was allotted to Serbia,
Montenegro or Belgium. Hussein knew nothing of this agree-

ment until the Bolsheviks discovered a copy of the agreement in the archives of the previous government and most unsportingly made it public.

It is impossible to deny that all this shows a lack of co-ordination. Perhaps with a view to cleaning up the chaos on the Eastern scene, an "Arab Bureau" was set up in February, 1916, for "the study and development of British policy in Arab affairs and the collection of information." There is a splendid vagueness about this which conceals the real objects of the Arab Bureau in much the same way as the declared military policy in the Middle East concealed ambitions which are revealed in the Sykes-Picot agreement.* The foundation of the Arab Bureau dates from the return to Cairo from London of Hogarth, who became its Director under the supervision of Clayton, but, as he also became Chief Political Officer to the Palestine Force towards the end of 1917, presumably Hogarth thereafter was in control at Cairo. Lawrence was one of those who found jobs in this Bureau, which did not however include Newcombe and Woolley, who were at the front, nor Gertrude Bell who, after giving them the benefit of her knowledge of desert tribes, had moved on to Baghdad by way of India. Some doggerel lines by Hogarth give us the Arab Bureau officers' names— Clayton, Symes, Cornwallis, Dawnay, Mackintosh, Fielding, Macindoe, Wordie and:

> "Lawrence licentiate to dream and to dare
> And Yours Very Faithfully, *bon à tout faire*."[24]

Unless the word "dare" was introduced merely for the sake of the rhyme, its use would indicate 1917 or late 1916 as the date of composition, since up till then Lawrence had not "dared" anything in particular. Part at least of his work for the Arab Bureau was connected with the publication of *The Arab Bulletin*, which was printed in Cairo from 6th June, 1916, to 6th December, 1918, and is claimed by Lawrence to have been originally suggested by him.[25] Only a few copies of each number were printed for circulation among officials, and all were considered and marked "Strictly Secret." Most of Lawrence's contributions have been published.

---

* "... to occupy the head of the Persian Gulf, thus guarding the oilfields, protecting the many Arab allies of Great Britain in those regions, and preventing the enemy from establishing naval bases on the flank of the British communications with India; the second was to keep open these same communications by the Red Sea and the Suez Canal."[23] Much the same in the Official War History but they unaccountably forgot the oilfields.

Not long after, the withdrawal from Gallipoli marked the collapse of the attempt on the Dardanelles, another and peculiarly humiliating disaster occurred on the Persian Gulf front, where the incompetent General Townshend contrived to get his army besieged in Kut-el-Amara, while all efforts to relieve him failed. By April, 1916, Townshend was faced with unconditional surrender, and, in a desperate effort to save his men from the horrors of Turkish prisoner-of-war camps, he persuaded the Cabinet to authorise him to offer a payment of a million gold pounds (raised to two millions) and the surrender of his forty guns on condition that " his force should be allowed to go free on parole."[26] The professional officers disliked the suggestion as dishonourable, and Sir Percy Cox (Chief Political Officer in Irak) felt so strongly disapproving that he " explicitly disassociated himself from the negotiations on such a basis," and they were " in consequence entrusted to others."[27] Those chosen were Aubrey Herbert, M.P., Colonel Beach, and Captain T. E. Lawrence. The choice of Aubrey Herbert was a natural one. His position as Member of Parliament gave him authority and made him a natural emissary of the Cabinet; he was a Turkophile, spoke Turkish well, had many friends in Constantinople and is said to have been personally acquainted with the Turkish commander, Khalil Pasha. Colonel Beach was an officer in the Mesopotamia Army. But the reasons for choosing Lawrence are not clear. He was a virulent Turkophobe, and if his pre-war antics in and about Jerablus had been known to the Turkish Commander, they would not have been a recommendation. Lawrence's version of the reasons for his selection are as follows. Since he had " arranged " for the surrender of Erzerum (for which statement no proof has yet been produced while all the printed evidence is wholly against it), " the War Office thought I could do the same thing over Mespot, and accordingly wired out to Clayton."[28] Both Hart and Graves repeat this tale and Hart adds that Lawrence wished to find out whether the Arab tribes on the Turkish lines of communication could be induced to revolt.[29] The idea, we are told, was that this revolt would " cut off the Turks " and eventually force them to surrender, while beleaguered Kut was supplied by eight airplanes. In view of the ancient Bedouin tradition of always abandoning the losing side, the moment for securing Bedouin aid seems ill-chosen. Nor are we told what British authority in Basra Lawrence approached with this suggestion, only that " he found it was hopeless."[30] Lawrence himself mentions "two Generals" who, however, did not know his mission.[31]

Gertrude Bell, who was in Basra, wrote on the 9th April, 1916: "This week has been greatly enlivened by the appearance of Mr. Lawrence, sent out as liaison officer from Egypt. We have had great talks and made vast schemes for the government of the universe."[32] On the 4th May she writes that Aubrey Herbert was helping to arrange the exchange of prisoners, "his knowledge of Turkish being very useful,"[33] and Lawrence was undoubtedly with him, was taken blindfold into the Turkish lines, and was present at Herbert's interview with Khalil Pasha.[34] Lawrence sent in a note to *The Arab Bulletin* on reported disaffection to the Turks among Arabs and Kurds in that area. Graves has a typical Lawrence story to the effect that "the Turk" (presumably Khalil Pasha) remarked that as both nations were "Empire builders," there was nothing that need stand between them. Whereupon Aubrey Herbert (who was "with" Lawrence) said: "Only a million dead Armenians."[35] Now as Townshend's surrender had to be unconditional, they were wholly dependent on Khalil Pasha's goodwill for the humane treatment of the British prisoners and the non-Turkish population. There is no need to stress the improbability, not to say absurdity, of imputing such a provocative remark to a responsible representative of the British Government at such a crisis, especially when he was a Turkophile.

Besides Gertrude Bell, another acquaintance of Lawrence saw him in Basra at this time—Hubert Young (at that time a Political Officer, seconded from his regiment), who has left two accounts, one published in Lawrence's lifetime and the other, much franker, after his death. According to Sir Hubert, it was Lawrence who came out "with Herbert," and seemed to him to be "thoroughly spoilt, and posing in a way that was quite unlike what I remembered of him at Carchemish." Young was much offended by Lawrence's expression of contempt for the regular army, and their former friendship was not renewed. In fact, Lawrence seems to have got on bad terms with all the military in Baghdad and to have made himself much disliked.[36]

In addition to the motives already assigned for this excursion, Captain Hart says that Lawrence was "ostensibly" sent to improve the Mesopotamian Army's map-making and to teach them how to compile maps from air photographs![37] and Graves says that Lawrence was to explain to the staff (" on behalf of the High Commissioner of Egypt ") that there was no intention of supporting Sharif Hussein's claim to the Caliphate.[38]* Fear of the results of such a claim was one of the reasons or excuses for the dislike of co-operating with Hussein shown by the Indian Government and the A. T. Wilson faction. Perhaps we should note that Hussein (contrary to British wishes) proclaimed himself " Malik " or king in October, 1916, but not Caliph until 1924—six months after which he was expelled from his kingdom by Ibn Saud and the victorious Wahabis.

Is it possible to make anything sensible and coherent out of all this farrago? It can only be by inference. The Herbert mission is, of course, genuine and historic, but why Lawrence? Well, there can be no doubt that liaison and some common policy between " Egypt " and " India " were badly needed, and Hogarth (who always pushed Lawrence whenever he had a chance) might easily have suggested the advantages of coming to an understanding, though a man so vain as Lawrence was a poor choice as emissary. Clearly, Lawrence poured out his arguments to Gertrude Bell and partly at least won her over, but failed with the soldiers, who would not stand his airs and insolence, and snubbed him. Hence his fury with " regular army " officers, which Young so much resented when he met Lawrence in the political officers' mess a few days after his return from Kut. Thus, just as Lawrence's anti-French activities in Syria derived from some personal pique against them in Lebanon, as Woolley hints, so his vindictive antagonism to " the Mespot gang " had the same origin. They would not support Arab nationalism, as he says himself in *Seven Pillars*,[40] and snubbed *him*.

One more item—on his return journey, Lawrence travelled on the same ship as General Webb-Gilman who had been sent out by the War Office as an investigator.[41] Talking with this officer, Lawrence produced a report which criticised almost every department of the Mesopotamian expedition. It is not hard to criticise a military disaster. This report has never been printed, and possibly no longer exists, but evidently there was one which severely criticised the unsympathetic " Mespot gang " from the stones used by its lithographers to the High Command's conduct of the campaign.[42] It is said that the

* "We now declare once more that the Government of Great Britain would welcome the reversion of the caliphate to a true Arab born of the blessed stock of the Prophet." Sir Henry McMahon to Sharif Hussein, 30th August, 1915.[39]

report was "hurriedly bowdlerised" before it was seen by General Murray, perhaps as much on Lawrence's behalf as to spare the general's sensitive nerves.

In his pointed, not to say sardonic, essay on Lawrence, Sir Andrew Macphail has remarked that, in the 1918 war fiction of the United States, a type of soldier hero was evolved who "must refuse to salute his officers, must be careless in his dress; contemptuous of rules, regulations and orders; smart, impudent or insolent in his answers; and he cannot exist without the comic element."[43] It was, no doubt, the natural protest of the uniformed civilian against the routine and ritual of a profession which was not his. However that may be, it is curious to see how closely Lawrence conformed to the type, at any rate in the published narratives of himself and his friends.* In 1916, he had certainly aroused the hostility of superior officers not only in Basra, but much more seriously for him, in his own area. Liddell Hart tells us that Lawrence annoyed the staff by altering the style of their reports and correcting them over the telephone, thereby deliberately provoking the Army authorities to find him a job where he could not be a cause of trouble.[44] Graves says, "it was decided to get rid of him," and that "he discovered that he was about to be put in a position where he could not do much more to help the Arab Revolt"—though what in fact he had done for the Arab Revolt previous to October, 1916, has yet to be demonstrated.

There was another aspect of Lawrence's position in 1916 which must have been in the minds of his superior officers and accounts for much of the disapproval of him, while it is entirely ignored by himself and his friends. Why shouldn't Lawrence see some active service? If not a hard-and-fast rule, it was at any rate the custom for staff officers to alternate between service in the field and service at headquarters or in offices. Newcombe, for instance, had gone off to France; Woolley went to the Turkish front and eventually got captured. Why should Lawrence be an exception? 1916—especially after the first battle of the Somme—was the beginning of a period of a prolonged hunt for man-power, though possibly a little before the newspaper campaign against "Cuthberts"—men supposedly sheltered

* Captain S. H. Brodie reports that Lawrence once walked through the Cairo railway station, without giving or returning salutes, wearing a badgeless cap, serge jacket, slacks, a red tie, patent leather shoes, with a star on one shoulder strap and a star and crown on the other, and without a belt.

in Government offices with or without uniform. In spite of his desire
" to root out the Turks," and the impressive self-training in high
strategy Lawrence afterwards made so much of, he had not hitherto
been employed as a fighting soldier.

Is it not possible then that this, and not his supposed sympathies
with the Arabs, was the real reason for military disapproval in Baghdad
and Ismailia, and that the various true or invented stories of his clashes
with authority were the response of his wounded vanity to coldness,
hints and sneers which he failed to interpret correctly? Hence his
transfer by Hogarth to the Arab Bureau (which was under the Foreign
Office) and the mission to Basra and Kut. Lawrence certainly expected
to continue at his Cairo desk when he returned from that mission,[45]
and, when he returned from his first and unofficial visit with Storrs
to the Hejaz in October 1916, he explained that the nature of his
duties in Cairo did not include field work.[46] Nevertheless, when he
returned to Cairo, he was told by Clayton that he must return to
Feisal. He did not like this prospect and said he was unsuited for the
job, as he hated soldiering and any responsibility.[47] But he had to go.
And a fortunate chance for him, since the alternative would have been
most probably that he would have been posted for active service, and
that, as he had no unit and no military training, would have meant
at best going to an Officer Cadet unit, training for the Western Front.

Meanwhile, although eight elaborate letters had been exchanged
between the Sharif and McMahon, resulting in an agreement, nothing
in the way of action had occurred, although the last letter of the series
was written in January, 1916. Such action as had occurred was naval,
including two landings at Akaba without casualties, one (February,
1915) by the French cruiser *Desaix*, and the other (April, 1916) by a
British cruiser, whose landing party of 50 men destroyed mines and
two small vessels brought over land, and took 12 prisoners. On each
occasion the garrison fled. A British naval blockade of the Hejaz
ports was declared on the 15th November, 1915. Long after the war,
Hussein asserted that he had asked for the blockade " in order to put
indirect pressure on the merchants and other townsfolk who were
politically lukewarm."[48] While this seems fully consonant with
benevolent Government procedure, General Brémond implies that
it was done by the British to put pressure on the Sharif to act. The
blockade, he says, " brought about a state of famine, from which the

Hejaz rebellion resulted."⁴⁹   However that may be, two other events precipitated the rebellion.   One was Jemel Pasha's execution of Arab nationalists in Damascus, the news of which is said to have affected Sharif Feisal so much that he tore off his head-dress and trampled on it, with a cry for vengeance.⁵⁰   The other was the Stotzingen mission of Germans, sent to set up a radio station to communicate with the Germans in East Africa and to undertake propaganda activities, accompanied by a force of 3,500 Turks who were to march on Mecca and thence to the Yemen.⁵¹   This forced the Sharif to act.

Sir Ronald Storrs, who had had so much to do with the protracted negotiations, now paid a visit to the Hejaz.   This was in consequence of a telegram from Abdulla (23rd May, 1916) urgently demanding an interview; and accordingly, five days later, he started off with Hogarth and Cornwallis, not knowing (though perhaps suspecting something of) what was happening. Amid all the heroics and arguments and propaganda which have derived from the Hejaz rebellion, Storrs's remarks have the merit of common sense and frankness.   He thought the Sharif asked for too much and the British Government gave him too much, while, for various reasons unforeseen or impossible to control, the British finally committed themselves much more deeply with aid and promises than anyone had conceived possible in September, 1914.⁵²   To which might be added that the exaggerations both of the Arab contribution to the war and of Lawrence's military genius have made the whole episode ridiculous.

The delegation was received by the Sharif's youngest son, Said, who confirmed what they had heard off Jidda, that a rebellion was definitely to begin on the 10th June.   Letters from Hussein and Abdulla asked that the British should at once " start operations in Syria," and asked for 500 more rifles and 4 machine guns.   Said asked for £70,000, and Storrs told him that he had £10,000 in gold with him and an authorisation for another £50,000 to be sent if the revolt had really occurred.   In answer to Storrs's natural questions as to what they intended to do, Said answered with a certain amount of boastfulness that they would kill the Turks if they would not surrender, and would destroy the Hejaz railway north to Medain Salih.⁵³ Brave words!

In parenthesis, the following facts give some idea of how primitive these Hashemite " Princes " were under their veneer of culture.   On the 6th June, Storrs saw that Said was looking with interest and admiration at his (Storrs's) gold wrist-watch, and he duly fastened it on Said's wrist. On the 13th December, 1916, Storrs again met Said, and asked about the watch, pushing up the Arab's sleeve to see if he still wore it. Said had to confess that it had been taken from him by his brother Abdulla, who had just acquired a new wife![54]

According to the Official War History, the revolt started on the 5th June, 1916 (the day Kitchener died), and, according to Abdulla, " on June 10th, 1916, the ninth day of Sha'ban." The first refers to the unsuccessful attempts on Medina by Ali and Feisal; the second to Hussein's proclamation. But the uprising was real enough. The garrisons of Mecca and of Jidda (British warship here) soon surrendered. In addition to the arms and money which had been lavishly sent to Sharif Hussein before his uprising, he was now supplied from the British in the Sudan with " 3,000 rifles, ammunition, and large supplies of barley, rice, flour and coffee," two mountain batteries and six machine guns manned by Egyptian Moslems and commanded by one of General Wingate's Egyptian officers, Sayed Ali. Most of the Turkish Mecca garrison had gone to Taif to escape the summer heats. With the help of these Egyptian guns, which frightened the Turkish commander by bombarding his house, Abdulla was lucky enough to obtain the surrender of 1,500 or more good troops and 10 guns. The French officer, Brémond, thought that " the commander who had surrendered such fine troops had failed in his duty." At the end of September, the Sharifian forces had captured prisoners estimated as high as 5,000, but they had failed to make any impression on the Medina troops and their commander, Fakri Pasha. The British governor of the Red Sea province of the Sudan, Lt.-Col. E. C. Wilson, was sent to Jidda as military adviser and head of the British mission to Sharif Hussein. " The appointment was not made public, lest the fact that British officers were directing operations in the Hejaz should create anti-Christian propaganda in Moslem countries and reflect adversely on the Sharif."[55]

Unfortunately the rebellion continued to make no impression on the garrison of Medina. The " Arabs " were almost invariably unsuccessful in attacking towns and fortified places, and Abdulla's success at Taif was due chiefly to the accident of a nervous Turkish commander. In June, 4,000 Harb tribesmen failed to take Jidda, which surrendered two days later to the Royal Navy.[56] It should be mentioned that not all the Hejaz tribesmen were on the Sharif's side. One of the most important chieftains of the Harb had a personal vendetta with Hussein, and some of the Harb sheiks remained with the Turks in Medina until the end of the war.[57] In August the sheik of the Billi at Wejh refused point-blank to support the Sharifians when approached to that end by Colonel Parker.[58]

The failure at Medina was the cause of the trouble. At the outset, in June, Ali and Feisal had cut the railway line in three places; but it was easily repaired, and they could not prevent the arrival of reinforcements and supplies from Jemel in Damascus to Fakri. Ali and Feisal retreated, the latter 45 miles to Bir Abbas between Medina and Rabegh. It was clear that Fakri's hope was to recapture Mecca, and that he would probably advance by way of Rabegh, since in summer the direct trail inland had insufficient water along its 250 miles. There was water at Rabegh; and out of this situation developed an endless wrangle between the too numerous commanders and advisers as to whether a European brigade should or should not be sent to defend Rabegh. The Sharif was of little assistance, since he changed his mind frequently, inclining to ask for the troops when he thought of what the Turks would do to him if they caught him, and inclining to refuse them when he reflected that, in the manner of allies, the European troops might stay on permanently. The matter was settled at last by Colonel Wilson's suggestion that the troops should not be sent until the Sharif asked for them in writing; which he never did. Meanwhile, the tribesmen with Ali and Feisal were in a very nervous state—since the Turks had artillery and planes while they had none, and the noise of artillery fire frightened them. At all events, they retreated in great haste in late October, after what Feisal reported as " violent fighting," though Colonel Parker, who was at Rabegh, reported that they had in fact fled from a force of 80 Turkish camelry.[59]

Antonius says that at the end of June the Sharifian forces enrolled amounted to between 30,000 and 40,000 but with only 10,000 rifles. At the end of January there were 70,000 enrolled and 28,000 rifles.[60] Copying the delicacy of King Abdulla in his memoirs, Antonius says nothing about money and supplies. According to the official French reports, the Royal Navy, by the end of July, 1916, had landed £528,000 in gold, 22,000 additional rifles and 14 guns.[61] And, in a personal interview with Sharif Hussein at Jidda on the 11th December, 1916, Storrs had to point out that there were no signs of an army, in spite of nearly 60,000 rifles having been sent to the Hejaz by the British Government.[62]

At the end of October, 1916, Sharif Hussein had contributed to the confusion and revealed his personal ambitions by having himself proclaimed Malik el Arab, King of the Arabs. This was particularly agreeable news for Storrs who, during a visit in September, had gone to much trouble to point out to Abdulla (Hussein's Foreign Minister) how ill-judged such a step would be, the offence it would give other Arab rulers, and how much Hussein's British friends would deplore such a step. Believing that Abdulla had been convinced by his eloquence, Sir Ronald telegraphed that he had got the matter postponed until his Government had time to consider it, only to be greeted on his arrival at Suez by the news of the proclamation. When later Storrs, "without mincing words," denounced the Malik to his face for this duplicity, Hussein replied with a rhymed proverb: "The blows of a friend are as the eating of almonds, the stones flung by him as pomegranates." Further, in diplomatic conversations Hussein had a habit in Jidda of referring to alleged statements in British official letters, the originals of which he said were in Mecca, thereby demonstrating, as Sir Ronald points out, the great advantage of keeping State papers away from infidel eyes.[63]

The Army List shows that Lawrence reverted from " staff captain " to " captain " on the 20th March, 1916, which is, of course, the time when he went to Basra, but when Colonel Brémond saw him towards the end of 1916, Lawrence was still wearing his red tabs as a staff officer. It was natural to assume that this was also the date of his transfer from the War Office to the Foreign Office, but Lawrence places the transfer in mid-October, at the time when he asked Storrs " point-blank " to take him with him on his next voyage to Jidda.[64] Lawrence is so vague about dates that we are lucky to have extracts from Storrs's journal, which shows that they left Cairo on the 12th October, 1916, Storrs returning in consequence of an urgent telegram from Abdulla. We have already seen that at this time Storrs referred to " little Lawrence, my supercerebral companion," and, in quoting from his journal, he later apologised because Lawrence's name at that time appeared so infrequently.[65] Quite so. It will be noted that

Lawrence had no official mission, and merely elected to spend a leave on this journey with Storrs.

But if Lawrence had no official message to deliver, Storrs had one, and not an easy one, as it announced a reversal of policy. In a business interview with Abdulla on the 16th October, at which Colonel Wilson and Lawrence were present, Storrs had to announce that the promised brigade would not be sent, that the planes were to be withdrawn, that he was not allowed to express any military opinion and had not brought the £10,000 Abdulla sought.[66] The accounts of this interview by Storrs, Abdulla and Lawrence stress wildly different aspects. Wilson conveyed their bad news by reading a telegram, whereupon a conversation occurred between Storrs and Abdulla which had to be translated by Storrs, as the others could only partly follow Abdulla's high Arabic ; which makes it hard to see how Lawrence was able to discuss with Abdulla the military situation, as he claims. King Abdulla says that, after a second reading of the telegram, he took leave, and meeting Colonel Brémond told him that, in view of this refusal, the Hejaz would have to make peace with Turkey. This is fully confirmed by Brémond, who dropped a hint of it to Storrs the next day. Storrs says he instantly tackled Abdulla, who asserted that his father had replied to Turkish peace feelers by saying that " the Arabs were now allies of Great Britain and could make no peace apart from her." But according to Abdulla's memoirs he said that he " would not depart a hair's breadth " from his decision (i.e. to make peace with Turkey unless his demands were accepted), though he agreed to give the British agents time by delaying his arrival in Mecca by twelve hours. On Abdulla's arrival at Mecca, his father announced that a telegram had just been received telling them that the supplies they needed would be delivered immediately.[67]

It does not seem possible to reconcile Abdulla's account of his dignified withdrawal and ultimatum with the indisputable fact that he was so much impressed by Lawrence that he obtained from Hussein permission to send Ali a letter which enabled Lawrence to go to Bir Abbas and to meet Feisal. Lawrence has expressed a poor opinion of Abdulla, with which however both Storrs and Brémond disagree. But there was curious naïveté in the easy way Abdulla fell a victim to Lawrence's " playing for effect " and assumption of omniscience. Whenever Abdulla mentioned a district of the Turkish empire,

Lawrence, from his knowledge of the Turkish order of battle, was able to state at once exactly what troops were there, until at length Abdulla naïvely exclaimed: " Is this man God, to know everything ?"[68]

Storrs and Lawrence, after these interviews, left Abdulla and made their way by ship from Jidda to Rabegh, where Lawrence landed to meet Sharif Ali, and Storrs returned to Cairo. At 6 p.m. on the 21st October (1916), accompanied by a sheik of the Salim Harb and his son, Lawrence rode out of Rabegh on a gorgeously adorned camel which belonged to Sharif Ali. He was made to wear an Arab cloak and head-dress and to ride after dusk in order to conceal the fact that an unbeliever was travelling so near the sacred places. Or so he says. Riding inland at an angle to the coast, and covering about a hundred miles in a direct line, Lawrence reached Feisal's encampment at three in the afternoon of the 23rd. Between that time and 4 p.m. on the 24th, when he left, Lawrence had four interviews with Feisal. The first of these was short and sharp. He later dined with Feisal and argued for hours, finding him most unreasonable. Next morning they had another talk, but this ended amicably, and the last interview was quite smooth and satisfactory. In between these interviews, Lawrence walked about the camp, explored Hamra, and talked to as many of Feisal's men as he could. In the end, Lawrence promised to do his best to get Feisal what he wanted.[69]

Evidently Feisal was pleased with the assurances Lawrence had given him, since the guest was despatched with an escort of fourteen —instead of two—sheiks, and reached Yenbo on the 25th October, where he had to wait for a ship until the 1st of November. There he occupied himself with writing some of the reports on his observations, which afterwards appeared in *The Arab Bulletin*. A few days after his return to Cairo, Lawrence (as already noted) was told by Clayton that he had to return to Arabia and Feisal, in spite of his protests that he was unfitted for such military work, after all those books on strategy! He was back in Yenbo on the 2nd December.

CHAPTER THREE

THE FACTS of Lawrence's first contact with the Hejaz, his return to Cairo with a handful of articles for *The Arab Bulletin* and his being promptly sent back to the Hejaz by Clayton are simple enough. In *Seven Pillars* he has explained away his troubles in Cairo as wholly due to the stupidity and jealousy of his superior officers on the British Staff, and has expanded the meagre Hejaz experience of a few days into about ten thousand words of excited narrative with a luxury of detail and much literary skill. Our problem here is not to attempt an assessment of *Seven Pillars* as a " titanic " work of literary art, but to ask how far it is history, how implicitly it can be relied on for the facts. This is a problem which can never be really solved, because the principal witness is Lawrence himself. In the first part of this book, examples have been brought forward of Lawrence's methods of building up his legend. While trying to preserve a reputation for shrinking modesty, he circulated through his friends exaggerated or wholly invented stories always to his advantage, stories which eventually got into print and now form the principal basis of his reputation, and in almost every case they were stories which could only have originated with himself.

The difficulty is to find any adequate means of verifying Lawrence's statements, and one danger is that his unsupported testimony may be doubted when it is in fact as reasonably true as human tendency to error permits. It is the inevitable penalty for the many fanciful stories he unquestionably did tell about himself. How far, for example, are we justified in believing or questioning Lawrence's version of his relations with staff and general officers in Cairo, Ismailia and Basra? His standard of judgment was that those who shared Lawrence's views about " the Arabs " were heroes or at any rate " good men," while those who disagreed with him were ignorant, foolish and incompetent. Everybody accepts Lawrence's version without question, omitting to observe that, even if the officers in question had wished to reply to the insults rather than criticisms of an amateur, they were debarred by professional etiquette from doing so while they held their commissions. Even supposing Lawrence was right, it is difficult to believe the following tale, which can have emanated only from one of the two participants and in all probability hardly from Major-General Lynden-Bell.

"The chief of staff one day rang him up on the telephone.

"'Is that Captain Lawrence? Where exactly is the Turkish Forty-first Division now stationed?'

"Lawrence said, 'At So-and-So near Aleppo. The 131st, 132nd, 133rd regiments compose it. They are quartered in the villages So-and-So, So-and-So, and So-and-So.'

"'Have you those villages marked on the map?'

"'Yes.'

"'Have you noted them yet on the Dislocation files?'

"'No.'

"'Why not?'

"'Because they are better in my head until I can check the information.'

"'Yes, but you can't send your head along to Ismailia every time.' (Ismailia was a long way from Cairo.)

"'I wish to goodness I could,' said Lawrence, and rang off."[1]

The Turkish 41st Division undoubtedly was in Syria in October, 1916, though perhaps this omniscient young officer might have mentioned that at least one of its battalions had been sent to the Hejaz.[2] The Chief of Staff at that time was Major-General Lynden-Bell. Now, making all allowances for a greater slackness of discipline on the Cairo, as compared with the Western, Front, and for tolerance of a highbrow civilian in uniform, it is hard to believe that the hero of Graves's instructive little anecdote did not find himself next morning on the mat and—officially, this time—beltless. It is typical of the cunning way in which such stories were framed by Lawrence that there were no witnesses—even if Lynden-Bell had denied it, well, it was one man's word against another's. And now, who can deny it?

Take again Lawrence's highly spiced account of his first meeting with Feisal, the white figure " waiting tensely " (why?) to meet Lawrence, " very tall and pillar-like," with his " dropped eyelids " and " face like a mask." And more in the same vein, leading up to Feisal's " soft " enquiry: " How do you like our place here in Wadi Safra? " and Lawrence's reply: " Well; but it is far from Damascus." And then the melodrama: " The word had fallen like a sword into their midst. There was a quiver. Then everybody present stiffened where he sat, and held his breath for a silent minute . . . "³ And so forth. It is an impressive picture of the Hashemite Emir nervously awaiting this all-important emissary of the British Empire, whose words smite the assembled sheiks into quivering breathlessness. But is it true? Is it even probable?

Nobody can assert definitely that it is not a true account, for the simple reason that Lawrence is the only vocal witness to the scene, for if King Feisal left memoirs like his brother Abdulla, they have not been made available, except perhaps verbally to some extent through Mr. Antonius. But we may ask ourselves why Feisal was so eager to meet this unimportant officer of whom he had never before heard, and who was merely spending a few days' leave in the Hejaz with no official mission or authority? Why should the Emir be so stirred at the prospect of meeting this self-appointed Talthybius, this herald of the lightning, as to leave his seated guests while he stood " waiting tensely " at the doorway of the " long, low house? "⁴ It is more like a scene from an old-fashioned historical romance than a war record. It is natural to suppose that a messenger had been sent on ahead to announce Lawrence's arrival, but in what capacity? Actually, he was a junior member of the Arab Bureau hoping to pick up some scraps of intelligence, as is clearly shown by his telegram of the 17th October to Clayton.⁵ He had no official message or mission. Although Lawrence admits that he was merely on leave because the Staff wanted to get rid of him,⁶ he very soon tries to create a totally different impression of his great importance, both to Feisal and to his readers. In his account of the interview with Abdulla, when he is trying to get permission to visit Feisal, he makes Storrs urge (and Storrs has strangely forgotten to note the fact in his contemporary journal) " the vital importance of full and early information from a trained observer for the British Commander-in-Chief in

Egypt, and showing that his sending down me, his best qualified and most indispensable staff officer, proved the serious consideration being given to Arabian affairs by Sir Archibald Murray."[7] It is not easy to reconcile this graceful tribute to Lawrence from Lawrence so modestly recorded, with the fact that far from being " most indispensable," he had just been fired as a nuisance,[8] nor had he in any sense been sent by Murray. And the invocation of Murray's interest in Arabian affairs seems inconsistent when you consider that, according to Lawrence, General Murray " could not be entrusted with the Arabian affair ; for neither he nor his staff had the ethnological competence needed to deal with so curious a problem."[9]

The contemporary notes in the so-called *Secret Despatches* on the interviews with Feisal can hardly be reconciled with the romantic version cooked up in *Seven Pillars*. In that work, as in his post-war political propaganda, Lawrence desired to present—and with great literary skill built up—the effigy of Feisal as the warrior-prophet unerringly picked by the sagacious Lawrence and designed by Fate to lead " the Arabs " to the defeat of the Turks and the establishment of their independence and the winning of the World War. And Lawrence, of course, was instantly recognised by Feisal as the heaven-sent military genius to guide him. Hence the drama of their first meeting and such a build-up as: " His men told me how, after a long spell of fighting, in which he had to guard himself, and lead the charges, and control and encourage them he had collapsed physically and was carried away from his victory, unconscious, with the foam flecking his lips."[10] And yet Lawrence himself afterwards confessed that Feisal was no good as a military leader. There is also good reason to suppose that Lawrence was not as much in Feisal's confidence as he gave out, for otherwise he would not have reported so confidently that Feisal had been president of the Arab secret society before the war, when Feisal, as he told Antonius, " had not joined any such society."[11]

What is really interesting is to find that neither of the two heroes in fact thought very highly of the other. Storrs has expressed resentment at the " good-humoured tolerance " with which Feisal spoke of Lawrence after the war. More detailed and more striking are Liddell Hart's notes of a conversation with Lawrence shortly after Feisal's death in 1933. Lawrence opened up and said that Feisal was a timid man, who hated running into danger, but would do anything for

163

" Arab freedom." He always was influenced by his adviser of the moment, but was " all right so long as T. E. was his adviser! " Liddell Hart asked why, in that case, Lawrence had made out in his reports that Feisal was such an heroic leader, to which Lawrence replied that only in this way could the British be persuaded to support the Arabs as physical courage is a quality the typical British officer demands. Liddell Hart, whose book was either in the press or about to go to press, then very justifiably asked why he had not been told this important fact—if it was a fact—when writing his book, and received the reply that it might have been bad for Feisal's position while he was alive.[12] We may perhaps correlate this with a remark of Lawrence's friend, Sir Hubert Young, who thought Lawrence possessed the qualities that lead to success in statesmen, including the lack of scruple necessary in adapting the means to the end.[13]

This sort of thing is very different from the inevitable misprint, pen-slip or error on which the average carper fixes so gleefully. It is not a question of honest blunder but of intentional write-up and misrepresentation by Lawrence, the more to be noted since the instances are many and to be found in a book most sedulously laboured. And there is even reason to be wary of his reports, though they ought to have the authority of first-hand contemporary evidence.

The question naturally comes up—if Lawrence actually held the contemptuous opinion of Feisal expressed in his conversation with Captain Hart, why did he attach himself to Feisal rather than to Abdulla? Especially since, having regard to the good opinion of Abdulla expressed by all competent witnesses, Lawrence seems to have invented excuses for not liking him? Well, if we remember Sir Leonard Woolley's pointed remark that Lawrence had for a long time been " an enemy to France in the Levant and that sentiment was the key to many of his later acts,"[14] we at once get our clue. At the time of Lawrence's first visit to Feisal (October, 1916), King Hussein had not yet made his modest announcement of himself as " King of the Arabs," but whatever he did, there is not the slightest doubt that his two sons had their own ambitions, and that each, far from sinking them in the interests of a free Arabia, hoped to carve out a kingdom for himself, if not at first wholly independent then under the suzerainty of England. In 1916 Abdulla hoped to be King of Irak, while Feisal's thoughts were wholly turned towards Syria.

An official Arab candidate for the throne of Syria would be a great help to Lawrence's hopes that the " Arabs " would " rush right up to Damascus and biff the French out of all hope of Syria."[15]   And he exults over the thought that the French would be furious if they got through to Damascus.[16]   Lawrence was far from being the only British officer who wanted to " biff " the French out of Syria (New-combe is said to have been one, and Cornwallis another, according to Colonel Brémond), but none was so nearly outrageous as Lawrence or behaved in his insulting fashion, as if the French were England's enemy, instead of the ally whose sacrifices made victory possible on the only front which really mattered after the Russian collapse in 1917.   A semi-private war of intrigue against France in the Levant was thus super-added to the European war by Lawrence and the Arab Bureau.

A French mission had been sent to the Hejaz under command of Lt.-Col. (afterwards General) Brémond, an officer practised in Arabiç and an expert in " native " warfare.   In the long debate as to whether or not an Allied brigade should be sent to defend Rabegh (which the Hejaz forces were obviously incapable of doing), Brémond supported those who favoured the plan.   Lawrence thereupon wrote a violent note accusing Brémond of having his own motives, which were not military, and quoted (or invented) " words and acts" which " just gave plausible colour to my charge."[17]   The last words constitute an admission that Lawrence knew his charges were false, including as they did that Brémond was not concerned with the interests of the Arabs or with the importance of the revolt to the British.   At a later date, after describing a difference of opinion between himself and Brémond, Lawrence penned the sneer that Brémond was a realist in war as well as in love, like most of his countrymen.[18]   He did not, it seems, look at life dreamily like the British.[19]   And, indeed, those who have read General Brémond's book have to confess that he has the bad Gallic habit of lucidly presenting the facts and scrupulously quoting his authorities.   At an interview between Feisal and Brémond on the 17th February, 1917, Lawrence says he sat " spitefully smiling " at what he represents as Brémond's clumsy efforts to avoid giving the " quick-firing mountain guns " Feisal asked for.[20]   The implication is that out of ill-will to " the Arab cause," Brémond eluded the request. Brémond's note on the conversation, made at the time, records that

Feisal expressed " great confidence, without any precise reasons," and adds that Feisal asked for " auto-mitrailleuses " (machine-guns mounted on cars), saying they could operate along the railway. Brémond tried hard to get them, but the French War Ministry refused them. Lawrence, entirely wrapped up in his own schemes, never troubled to understand that France was too hard-pressed to send more than token material to a minor front of mainly political interest.[21]

In contrast to Lawrence's attitude of malicious insolence to the French representative and his unconcealed hatred for France, General Brémond says in his book:

" I was firmly persuaded that European civilisation could only exist through a Franco-British understanding—a conviction which underwent severe shocks but remained unshaken."[22]

Lawrence's friend, Sir Ronald Storrs, though suspected of Francophobia (which he strenuously denied), was at any rate more tactful. He describes General Brémond as " very *sympathique*." He adds that Brémond once told them after dinner that he had just heard that his only male relative not hitherto killed or wounded had become a casualty, saying that he was proud to drink to his allies and expressed his great pleasure at working with the English.[23] In view of the high, not to say extravagant praise given Lawrence as a great military strategist, may it be suggested that injecting private feuds with one's allies into a war is not really a sound military practice?

It is unfortunate that, when he wrote his interesting account of that conversation with Gilbert Clayton, Lawrence omitted to tell us what his instructions were. Since he went apparently as political and liaison officer, we may be fairly certain that he was not told to be an " Arabian Knight,"[24] or to rush up to Damascus and " biff the French out of all hope of Syria." There had hitherto been far too many military cooks of this Arabian broth, and what was needed was not so much a great strategist or even a good tactician but some strong-willed person on the spot to urge concerted action and to secure some sort of continuity. This complex diplomatic errand was more difficult than blowing up trains or joining Bedouin rushes, and probably few professional officers could have done it as successfully. Such a man would have fretted himself uselessly (as Hubert Young did as Quartermaster General to the 600 or so troops of the Hejaz Regular Army) over all sorts of unmilitary horrors and incompetencies which

Lawrence either didn't see or cared nothing about. It is impossible to say whether he was potentially a Great Captain—A. P. Wavell didn't think so[25]—among other reasons because he was never in a modern battle, but he certainly had gifts as a political wire-puller. The skill and pertinacity with which he worked to embroil England and France in Syria, and to obtain thrones for his Hashemite friends, are truly remarkable. Lawrence's main task was to persuade the Sharifians to use what military force they had in the interests of the British Empire, which doubtless he interpreted in his own way.

But there were, in the autumn of 1916, certain definite objectives which he was probably told to urge on the Sharifian commanders. One was the capture of Medina, which in those days Lawrence favoured —" Abdulla will talk about his future kingdom, but we shall tell him to take Medina "[26]—a point of view which he afterwards abandoned. " The Arabs " did not take Medina for exactly the same reason as the Spaniards failed to take Elizabethan England—they couldn't. But there was another important objective—Akaba. As early as the 6th July, 1916, the War Committee in London had ordered the occupation of Akaba, on the assumption that this would threaten the Turkish communications.[27] A more valid reason, and one which explains the alacrity with which the Royal Navy supported " the Arabs," is that Akaba was being used to launch mines on the Red Sea, and might possibly even be used by a submarine. The threat, at any rate, had raised marine insurance rates in the Red Sea from one-half to two per cent, and, as an immense amount of shipping went through the Canal, the holding of the Red Sea Arabian ports would be a valuable achievement. Hence the two naval raids on Akaba, but to hold the place, Wejh (still in the hands of the Turks) would first have to be taken. On the 14th December, 1916, General Wingate, George Lloyd (afterward Lord Lloyd) and Brémond met in Khartoum and decided that Akaba and Wejh must be occupied (in their view, as bases for operations against the railway), that Rabegh must be defended, but— contrary to the opinion in Cairo which Lawrence was then parroting— that Medina should *not* be taken until a junction had been effected between the armies of Egypt and Irak, because, if taken earlier, the capture would " cause a development of Pan-Arabism harmful to the Allies."[28]

Less than two weeks before that meeting of Allied leaders in the

Sudan, Lawrence had landed at Yenbo and set out at once to join Feisal. In the report made after his first and unofficial visit to Sharif Feisal, Lawrence had taken an optimistic view of the military value of the tribesmen, " a tough-looking crowd, all very dark coloured, and some negroid."[29] Commenting on the difficult nature of the country between Medina and Rabegh, he had described " the hill belt " as " a very paradise for snipers," and thought that each practicable road could be held by " a hundred or two of determined men," especially if they had light machine guns.[30] In *Seven Pillars* he specifies Lewis guns, as does Graves in his book.[31] The observation and reasoning look perfectly sound, except that Arabs could not correct Lewis gun stoppages, but at that time nobody seems to have grasped the peculiar rules and panics governing this desert skirmishing.

About midnight on the 2nd December, Lawrence and his escort were astonished to see that the valley of Nakhl Mubarak (far in rear of Feisal's supposed positions) was occupied by men, shouting and firing rifles, amid the smoke of camp fires and the rumblings of camels. These turned out to be Feisal and his men in a disorderly retreat—Said and his men had been surprised and routed, chiefly by their fear of the Turkish artillery. The Turks had got on so fast that they were now between Feisal and the sea, and might either turn inland to attack his rear or capture his base at Yenbo—from which Lawrence had just come. In the confusion, Feisal's spy system had collapsed, and he was receiving only wild and contradictory reports; he had therefore fallen back with about 4,000 tribesmen to try to defend the approaches to Yenbo, while he laboured to restore the shaken morale of his followers.[32]

Evidently they were in a very jumpy state of nerves, since Lawrence complains of three sleepless nights, and says there were constant alarms by day.[33] His presence in the camp had been explained by the statement that he was a Syrian officer who had deserted from the Turks, which was a handicap to him.[34] Obviously he was in British uniform. Feisal asked him one day if he would wear Arab clothes, and presented him with a magnificent white silk wedding garment embroidered with gold.[35] When he left the camp on the evening of the 4th December, to return to Yenbo, Feisal mounted him on his own camel, " a magnificent animal," which had cost thirty pounds.[36] Whether these wedding garments were gifts in the Arab fashion or really intended for daily wear is obviously a question impossible to answer, though it seems strange that such elaborate clothes should have been intended for life in camps.   Lawrence explains that Arab dress made him less conspicuous and was more comfortable than his own clothes.   Now the only one of these Englishmen who really could and did pass as an Arab was Leachman, who had dark eyes and, of course, let his beard grow; but Lawrence shaved and had blue eyes, and himself admitted he could not pass as an Arab.   Compare the one extant photograph of Leachman, dressed as a Bedouin, with the nine or ten carefully posed portraits of Lawrence in elaborate dresses and histrionic attitudes in Lowell Thomas's book.   The one man looks like an Arab, the other like an amateur actor in a series of posturings in fancy dress. When Lowell Thomas assured the world that his photographs were taken without Lawrence's knowledge,[37] he made exceedingly large drafts on human credulity—and the amazing thing is that almost everyone believed him.   Much of the Lawrence legend was built up on the wearing of this Arab costume in and out of season and on the " Prince of Mecca " nonsense.   Was the elaborate and ostentatious costume really any more genuine than the invented title?

Lawrence had barely settled down to sleep at Yenbo when Said and 800 beaten men poured into the little town, followed next day by news that Feisal also was defeated and retiring.   The story was put about, as a sort of humorous alibi, that Feisal's left wing had gone off the field and caused his retreat, their reason for going being only to make coffee.   Meanwhile the Royal Navy turned up at Yenbo, and, on the 12th December, Storrs arrived in answer to a distress call to meet King Hussein at Jidda.   Storrs had two conferences with Hussein, and a long discussion on the general situation with Wilson, Lloyd, Brémond and the Italian representative, Colonel Barnabi.   Lawrence remained at Yenbo, and was not called to any of these meetings. Storrs reached Yenbo on the 13th, and reports that the night before " there had been a regular panic ashore," and many notables, including Feisal, had slept on board H.M.S. *Hardinge*.   Lawrence had slept on *Suva*.   Later he was told that " old Dakhil Allah " claimed to have guided the Turks near to Yenbo that night, but they were intimidated by the searchlights of so many ships and turned back. Lawrence asserts that he believed the Turks lost the war that night.[38]

At 9.15 on the morning of the 13th December, there was a conference between Storrs on the one hand and Sharifs Feisal and Said on the other. In the confusion, Lawrence seems to have been totally forgotten—at any rate he is not mentioned as having been present. Meeting him for the first time, Storrs thought that Feisal looked like " the legendary noble Arab," but that his demeanour was that of " one chastened by failure." Feisal grumbled about not having been given artillery, whereupon Storrs took him up sharply, saying that the recent retreats had hardly been a testimony of Arab valour. Feisal several times promised that he would make the advance on Wejh if the British would guarantee to hold Yenbo and Rabegh for him. Storrs strongly urged him to put his trust in the Egyptian, Aziz-el-Masri Bey who, on Storrs's urging, had been given by King Hussein the empty dignity of Hejaz Minister of War. Lawrence is not even mentioned.[39]

Nothing much now happened for a time. Ali tried to advance, and then fled, which caused Feisal to fall back again in a bad temper. On the 2nd January, 1917, Lawrence went out with about thirty men and shot at some Turkish tents at dawn. Then Colonel Wilson came up to insist on the expedition to Wejh, even going to the extent of giving his personal guarantee that the Navy would hold Rabegh. King Hussein was persuaded to send Feisal a positive order to make the advance, and it was agreed that Abdulla should move to Wadi Ais, about a hundred kilometres north of Medina. Meanwhile, before starting, Lawrence contrived to have a quarrel with Colonel Brémond at Rabegh. He also quarrelled with Major Vickery, one of the regular officers who, like Newcombe, had been sent out as military advisers.[40]

In the course of a dramatic description of his row with Brémond, Lawrence asserts that Brémond assured him " on his honour as a staff officer, that for Feisal to leave Yenbo and go to Wejh was military suicide."[41] According to Lawrence's vague chronology, this interview took place " a few days " after the night of panic at Yenbo, say, within ten days after the 13th December. Yet it was on the next day, 14th December, that Brémond had his conference with Wingate and Lloyd, had agreed that Wejh must be occupied, and, since regular troops were not forthcoming, had agreed to confer with Wilson at Rabegh as to the best that could be done " with the means at our disposal."[42] As

Wilson thereupon immediately came to Yenbo to urge Feisal to move, it must have been in agreement with Brémond.

Further, in one of his diatribes, Lawrence makes the accusation: " Brémond had some excellent Schneider sixty-fives at Suez, with Algerian gunners, but he regarded them principally as his lever to move allied troops into Arabia. . . . In the end, happily, Brémond over-reached himself, after keeping the batteries idle for a year at Suez. Major Cousse, his successor, ordered them down to us, and by their help we entered Damascus."[43]

Let me invite the reader's attention to the following official telegram:

" Ier Bureau. E. No. 15.458 19.11.16. Commandant en Chef à Guerre. The two batteries of 65 for the Sharif have priority *e*. Propose immediately three mountain batteries of 80.

JOFFRE."[44]

The two batteries of 65s were not at Suez, and were not used by Brémond " as a lever " to introduce European troops into the Hejaz. They were refused by Paris, and were not sent out until October 1917, after repeated telegrams from Brémond asking for them specifically for Feisal.[45] The guns at Suez were 80's.

The long description of the march on Wejh is one of the admired set pieces of *Seven Pillars*, containing, as it does, the splendid rhetorical passage of the march to Owais. The " Everybody burst out singing " is a tribute to Siegfried Sassoon, and the " bouncing camels " to Doughty, but it is worth noting that the passage " The march became rather splendid and barbaric . . . " occurs first in *The Arab Bulletin* report, from which Lawrence transferred it with a few verbal alterations to his book.[46] Shorn of picturesque literary descriptions, the plan was that Feisal and Lawrence—joined on the way by Newcombe —and 10,000 tribesmen would reach Wejh at dawn on the 23rd January,* at the same time that *Hardinge* landed 400 Arabs supported by a landing party of 200 seamen and the guns of the ships. The Turkish garrison was estimated at about 800, but must have been fewer, since about 500 Turkish camelry bolted. Why then these 10,000 men with Feisal and Lawrence, when 1,000 would have been ample? " Feisal was anxious to prove to the tribes on his route the

* One account says, 24th, but 23rd is undoubtedly right

popularity and power of his father's cause."[47]   Somebody else to whom Lawrence's criticism of Brémond applied, namely, the crime of having his own motives which were not military.[48]

Nor indeed did the military motive of straining every fibre to keep one's word and to be exactly on time at the rendezvous seem to have had much weight with the " splendid and barbaric " forces of Feisal and Lawrence. In fact, it looks as if they never had any intention of keeping a rendezvous where once more the main action, and credit for the action, would be demonstrably due to the Royal Navy and not to " the Arabs "; which, for " motives not military " did not suit Lawrence and his schemes. At all events on Lawrence's own showing, " his army " lingered on the way in a very casual manner. On the 19th they were " so comfortable in the tents at Semna that they delayed their start until the early afternoon ";[49] " next day we rode easily "; and on the 21st they " slept late . . . to brace ourselves for the necessary hours of " *talk*.[50] When, on the 22nd, they were " already two days behind our promise to the Navy," it was New-combe who rode on ahead, allegedly to see " if the naval attack could not be delayed until the 25th."[51] If Lawrence didn't know it was then too late, he ought to have known; and the excuse that, while the roads were too muddy, the " army " was at the same time short of water is a curious one.

The true story of the capture of Wejh is such a strange mixture of farce and squalid horror that it is worth a brief notice, especially since the narrative by Major Bray gives us a glimpse of Arab fighting from one who was indeed a passionate advocate of " Arab independence," but in his narrative tried to record facts rather than to show off his literary and typographical genius in a " titanic " book. Vickery and Bray were the two British army officers who accompanied the 400 Bedouins when *Hardinge*, exact to the rendezvous, arrived off Wejh at dawn on the appointed day, only to find no Feisal and no Lawrence and no supporting tribesmen! What should the naval party do? They were anxious that the garrison should not escape, and to that extent reinforce Fakri in Medina; and so decided to attack without the help of their main land force.

The 400 Arabs, landed at a cove about two miles from Wejh, provided the two regular officers with some shocks. The first was that 200 tribesmen took cover under a cliff and refused to fight.

About 100 of the remainder made direct for the town, in spite of casualties from Turkish rifle fire, and rushed for the nearest house:

> " Having entered it and slain all whom they found there, they proceeded to loot it. Later, I saw the result. In the street, before its entrance, lay three dead Arabs, and a pool of congealed blood covered the grey flat stone. . . . The interior was in a state of indescribable confusion. Everything was smashed, even the legs of the chairs. The whole place was littered knee deep in kapok. Mattresses, pillows and cushions had been torn to shreds in the frantic search for the gold the Bedouins hoped might be concealed within."[52]

Another group of about 70 went off on their own out of Bray's sight, and " there were no Turks remaining by the evening in this area."[53] Meanwhile, as the main body of looters " proceeded to reduce the place by attrition, going from house to house, eating their way into the bowels of the town," the remaining 30 with Bray and a young sheik, named Salim, engaged the enemy defence which was, " luckily for us, extremely badly organised." Attack and defence were conducted by bobbing up and down in a sort of mutual sniping. Bray then made his way to the beach, with the idea of getting supporting fire from the ship's guns, and came on Vickery signalling with a heliograph—only to find that the range of the ship's guns was ineffective. Suddenly they noticed a body of men marching towards them, and thought they were Turks; but they turned out to be a landing party of 200 British seamen, coming up as to " a most enjoyable picnic," marching " in serried ranks," with their machine guns " conspicuously carried on stretchers about fifty yards to the flank," but without flank-guards or scouts. After a certain amount of discussion, the naval party " grudgingly " consented to take a little cover, to send out scouts and to place machine guns. As nothing much more had happened by night-fall, Bray tried to make some sort of outpost line, while the Navy in cheerful innocence bivouacked in no-man's land. Next morning a shell from *Fox* hit the mosque, where a small group of fanatics had been holding out and preventing the others from surrendering. " A huge gaping hole was blown in the wall, and fifteen very bewildered and dusty and begrimed men staggered out without their weapons, in token of surrender. Strangely enough, none had been killed . . . ."[54] And that is how Wejh was "captured by the Arabs."

When Lawrence came to discuss all this in his book, he made no apologies for the military misdemeanour of being two days late for a fight—"this desertion," as Bray hotly calls it. On the contrary, he belittles the taking of the town on the grounds that 19 Bedouins killed were too many casualties, for, as Graves points out, the Arabs were not like most conscripts used to being treated as cannon-fodder.[55] Lawrence thought the garrison should have been starved into surrender or that it didn't matter if they escaped to reinforce Medina. Also, by this time, the reckless destruction had added to the difficulties of the situation. But why were he and Feisal not there in time to prevent all this? In any case, it is clear that most of the casualties to the attackers occurred among the 100 who went straight ahead on their own (out of all control from Vickery and Bray) merely to loot the town—"here and there a black heap on the plains" marked their line of advance. Moreover, it is doubtful that much damage was done to the town by the naval guns, for their shells glanced off the hard rock and burst far inland.[56] The real damage to the town and all the murdering of the inhabitants had been wholly the work of the Bedouins, whose intense greed for booty Doughty had long before described.[57] It is unfair to blame the two British officers for not preventing the massacre, destruction and pillage, which Lawrence himself never prevented or indeed attempted to prevent. Lawrence tries to palliate the sack by saying that the inhabitants of Wejh had been warned to leave, but remained because they were mostly pro-Turkish Egyptians, a good reason for murdering them.

It seems clear from the evidence that, at this stage, Lawrence had not succeeded in getting any real power over Feisal into his hands, and was chiefly working to assert himself against possible rivals. The positive documentary evidence shows that the idea of occupying Wejh was not his, although Graves asserts: "Lawrence had decided that the next thing to be done was to attack Wejh, a big port . . . .",[58] He was not called in to any of the important consultations at this period; he was doing his best to discredit personal enemies, such as Vickery and Brémond; and he did not take Wejh. His part in the events which had taken place during the eight weeks since he landed may have been more than the evidence shows, but hardly seems to warrant Liddell Hart's favourable comparison of Lawrence with Napoleon Bonaparte and his career. Liddell Hart suggests that the march on Wejh and its consequences are comparable with the conquests of the Army of Italy in 1796, when "a young man of twenty-six had subtly persuaded the Directory to adopt an audacious plan which likewise began with a flank march along the coast." Observe the insinuation that it was Lawrence who planned the march on Wejh. Liddell Hart then points out that Napoleon and Lawrence were both born on the 15th August; that Napoleon was made a general of Division on the 16th November—the very day that Lawrence landed at Jidda; that on the 27th March, Napoleon took command of the Army of Italy and Lawrence blew up some rails of the Hejaz railway; and that on the 10th May, Napoleon stormed the bridge at Lodi and Lawrence started on the Akaba expedition! But, Liddell Hart warns, the comparison must not be taken too far, Napoleon never achieved wisdom and was ruled by ambition, an unreality which brought him down![59]

There is one more claim which falls into the period just after the capture of Wejh, and is perhaps worth brief notice. It is made by Lawrence—and others naturally have repeated it—that in January, 1917, or thereabouts, "Sir Archibald Murray realised with a sudden shock that more Turkish troops were fighting the Arabs than were fighting him . . ."[60] This is elsewhere supported by handsome statistics, claiming that at this time the numbers of the tribesmen enrolled were 70,000 with 28,000 rifles; that 6,000 Turkish prisoners had been taken by them, and that the Arab forces had "locked up" 14,000 Turks in Medina, 5,000 at Tebuk and had caused the garrison at Maan to be raised to over 7,000—making in all 26,000.[61]

The number of prisoners seems about right. At the end of September, they were already over 5,000, "of whom a number of Arab or Syrian blood volunteered for service against the Turks."[62] There cannot have been many trained soldiers available in the Hejaz itself, since, dating from the German reorganisation of 1908, no men had been called up in the Hejaz by the Turkish Government. So that the numbers of the Sharifians are delusive, consisting at this date of untrained men and Bedouins who absconded as soon as they were laden with loot. (The French Captain Raho, who was with Abdulla on the 13th January, 1917, when they captured Eshref Bey and his column with £20,000, reported that after the pillage upwards of 5,000 Bedouins deserted.[63] Lawrence does not even mention this French officer's presence, nor such a fact as that Raho led the decisive cavalry charge of Abdulla's men.) Thus the numbers even of these irregular troops were always fluctuating. The French official war history, under date January, gives Abdulla (with Captain Raho) 10,000; Feisal (with Colonel Newcombe and Captain Lawrence) 5,000; and Ali (with Lt. Lalou) 4,500; making about 20,000. But Feisal had 10,000 at Wejh.[64] English estimates ran the total up as high as 50,000.[65]

Antonius gets his figures of the Turks presumably from Wavell and the British Official War History, adding 1,000 to their 13,000 for Medina, and ignoring the fact that the 7,000 at Maan are distinctly given for the period " towards the end of the year," 1917. But, even if reduced to 20,000 for January, 1917, his estimates are higher either than the French or Murray's figures. The Turkish Hejaz expeditionary force (that is, the troops in and near Medina), plus 800 " railway troops," and a regiment of camelry, is given by the French in November, 1916, as 13,300.[66] On the 11th January, 1917, Colonel Wilson estimated Turkish reserves, including Maan, at 13,000.[67] In July, 1917, total from Maan to Medina, 13,555.[68] As Fakri surrendered over 8000 with Medina in January, 1919, and had suffered 1,000 casualties from influenza, and must have had others, it looks as if he had at least 10,000 in early 1917. But, strangely enough, the one person who suffered no shock and who evidently did not think that more Turks were fighting the Arabs than were fighting him was General Murray. Under date 13th December, 1916, he cabled the War Office: " Enemy can now bring 25,000 against me; in a month's time, 40,000; if he abandons Hejaz, another 12,000. Any further additions must come from Europe, Mesopotamia or Caucasus."[69] If Murray counted the Turks at Maan as being on his front (as he probably did), then the estimate of 13,000 more or less for the Hejaz seems about right. A general who had 25,000 on his front and who expected in a few weeks to have 40,000 as against 13,000, or even 20,000 in the Hejaz, can hardly be said to have " realised with a shock " that more Turks were fighting the Arabs than were fighting him.

CHAPTER FOUR

THE CONTINUED holding of Medina by the Turks is said to have been an error from the military point of view—they should have withdrawn their troops to a more active front and have given the town up. It was retained from motives of prestige, both religious and political; and this decision can hardly be attacked by those who retained the Ypres salient at so heavy a cost merely to show that they hadn't lost all Belgium. Obviously, the Egyptian command were afraid these troops might suddenly descend on their front, and there in fact were one or two alarms to that effect, while the Germans continually urged the step. But, if the suggestion is permitted, there were good reasons other than those of religion and prestige for holding the place. When Lawrence counted up the number of Turks "fighting" the Arabs, he forgot to mention that most of them would have been there anyhow as they had been all along as garrison troops, linking up, however tenuously, with their forces in the Yemen, and threatening Aden. He forgot also to point out that much of the effort of the Arab forces—say, 20,000 to 25,000 tribesmen, plus the little regular army of 600, gradually built up under Jaafar—that this effort was diverted to hanging round the outskirts of Medina and to attacks on that part of the Damascus-Medina railway which was of least importance strategically, namely, the section Maan-Tebuk-Medain Salih-Medina, because the main line of supply to the Turkish troops facing the real menace of the British Army was not by that section but by way of Deraa and the Yarmuk Valley, and to a much smaller extent by way of Amman and desert convoy. Moreover, while the containing of Medina thus entangled the forces of the Arab revolt, it also prevented the movement from spreading, not only among the pro-Turkish

Shammar of Ibn Rashid but among the tribes near Damascus which Feisal and Lawrence tried in vain to bring over to contribute something more effective than words.

Except for a few raids, which didn't all succeed in doing anything, the Turkish holding of Medina for over two years pinned the Arab action chiefly to the least important part of the Damascus-Medina railway, until Allenby's great break-through in September, 1918, provided them with sitting targets which nobody could miss, and the chance to race hysterically into towns which they claimed to have captured after the British had done the real fighting.

The occupation of Wejh—150 miles away—can hardly have had much effect on the decisions of the Medina commander. When Lawrence lay sick with boils and diarrhœa in Abdulla's camp (March, 1917), and indulged in that pretentious strategic reverie he has described at such length, his theory that Medina should not be taken actually played into the hands of the Turks—though the whole debate seems rather superfluous in face of the fact that the Arabs couldn't take Medina. The much-opposed Anglo-French brigade would have been needed for that. The real importance of occupying Wejh was that it provided a base for raids on the Hejaz railway.

But what are the facts about this Hejaz railway which plays so great a part in the legends of the " Arab Revolt," and which gave Lawrence such voluptuous satisfaction when, on the 28th March, 1917, he actually touched the metal of the rails for the first time?[1] It was part of a system of rail communication, with a base just opposite Constantinople, which was so long and so awkward that the surprising thing is that it worked at all. From Haidar Pasha on the Bosphorus to Rayak in Syria (about 900 miles) there ran a standard gauge railway, broken by unfinished tunnels through the Taurus and Amanus mountains, so that at these two breaks (20 and 5 miles respectively) everything had to come off the railway and go by road. Although the tunnels were pierced for narrow-gauge lines in 1917, the first through train was not run until September, 1918. As far as the junction of Muslimie, just north of Aleppo, this single line served the Mesopotamian, Palestine and Hejaz fronts, and if the Arabs could have put that key-point (Muslimie) out of commission by sabotage, that would have been of real importance ; needless to say they never, with all their secret societies, did the slightest damage there. From Rayak (north of Damascus) on, the railways were all 1.05 metres (3 feet 6 inches) except for the Jaffa-Jerusalem section, which was 1 metre. The rail distance from Damascus to Medina is 850 miles. At Deraa, the railway supplying Palestine branched off, and again real destruction there would have been important. South of Deraa, demolition of the line only concerned the Hejaz or such limited supplies as went overland to Palestine from Amman.[2]

This 850 miles of one-track, narrow-gauge railway from Damascus to Medina had been completed in 1906. The intention of the Turkish Government had been to carry it on the 250-odd miles to Mecca, but the Bedouin tribes (who lived by exploiting and robbing the camel caravans of pilgrims or by being paid blackmail not to rob them) rebelled. When Kazim Pasha, the President of the Railroad Commission, went out to inspect the proposed Medina-Mecca route, the Bedouins attacked and killed about a hundred of his escort, and sent him flying for his life back to Medina. One result of this abortive effort to continue the Hejaz railroad from Medina to Mecca is briefly mentioned (but insufficiently stressed) by the Official History and ignored by Lawrence. There had been stored in Medina, and still existed there in good condition in 1916, materials for the construction of 100 kilometres of rail.[3] Obviously, this greatly simplified Fakri Pasha's task of repairing the line, especially since even in peace time the Turks had been accustomed as a matter of routine to constant repair of Bedouin sabotage to the track. It will be noted that Brémond (though not, I think, the British) reports at Medina a Turkish railway repair battalion of 800, men skilled presumably at their job, so that until the spring of 1918 the much-vaunted demolition raids were rather a nuisance to the Turks than a serious menace. It was but a war-time intensification of a constant peace-time nuisance. Even when the great reserve of rail material at Medina was used up in April, 1918,[4] the Medina garrison was still fed and supplied by caravans, which had little difficulty in bribing their way through the Bedouin tribes supposed to be stopping them.[5] There are extant photographs of German officers in uniform entertained as honoured guests by the tribesmen of the Shammar.[6] And they, of course, were Ibn Rashid's followers, who controlled the northern approaches to Medina. In any case the rail communication with Medina, tenuous as it was, remained uncut until Colonel Dawnay was sent to do the job properly in April, 1918:

> " At a cost of 250 casualties, Medina was now definitely cut off from the north, for the great reserves of rails were at last used up. The line between Maan and Mudauwara remained a ruin for the rest of the war and is a ruin to-day."[7]

The rolling stock, the destruction of which has been celebrated with such gorgeous rhetoric, was in fact pathetically meagre. At the outbreak of the rebellion, the Hejaz railroad possessed only 30–50 effective locomotives. There were only 180 passenger cars, fewer than 1,300 freight cars and about 40 mobile water tanks. Trains were short, ranging from 13 to 20 cars, and each train had to bring with it four additional water tanks for the supply of stations and block-house guards. The greatest danger to the continued running of the line was the scarcity of fuel. The engines ran on wood, either brought down from the north or cut from desert acacia trees.[8] At a later date, Fakri was so hard pressed for fuel that he began tearing down the houses of Medina in order to burn the woodwork in the engines. This, then, was the railway which managed to survive so many attacks and thereby assisted Medina to hold out for the entire war.[9]

The Medina debate occupied the attention of both sides. On the Allied side, Wingate, Lloyd and Brémond had agreed (as we saw) that the capture of Medina was undesirable politically (i.e. because they thought it would stimulate Pan-Arabism), and Lawrence either was not told or chose to ignore this joint Anglo-French decision, attributing it entirely to Brémond's alleged unworthy motives. Lawrence's reasons are quaint and not very realistic: " We must not take Medina. The Turk was harmless there. In prison in Egypt he would cost us food and guards."[10] The absurdity about the prisoners has been often noted, and is not to be reconciled with Lawrence's loud praise that " Feisal offered a reward of a pound a head for prisoners, and had many carried in to him unhurt."[11] On the other side of the war fence, Liman von Sanders disagreed with the Turks about the advantage of holding Medina, and thought the garrison troops would be more useful if withdrawn—hence the scare at British Headquarters, Wilson's efforts to force Ali and Abdulla to attack

Fakri, and finally Dawnay's effective destruction of the line south of Maan.

"Lawrence the Train-Wrecker" is one Lowell Thomas caption, under which we are told that Lawrence and his "associates"—Feisal, Ali, Abdulla and Said—blew up "twenty-five Turkish trains, tore up fifteen thousand rails and destroyed fifty-seven bridges and culverts."[12] It would perhaps not be impossible to divine whence those statistics derived, but I have not come across any confirmation of them in any of the official records I have seen. I do not myself think that the four Hashemite princes in person ever touched a rail or harmed a passenger car, but Lawrence most certainly handled explosives to destroy lengths of railroad track and to derail trainloads of soldiers and civilians. There is no doubt about it, and he is entitled to all the esteem and deference such bold feats deserve. But readers of the books by Lawrence and his friends—let alone the enthralled listeners to Mr. Thomas's lecture—were left with the impression, suggested rather than stated, that it was Lawrence who conceived the idea of sabotaging the railway, and that Lawrence was the chief if not sole saboteur, except for the aid of one or two English officers, such as Major Garland, Hornby, Newcombe and Davenport. Lawrence himself was briefly generous to their destructions, but his personal narrative of his own feats swamped theirs. A reader of his "pompous, professorial"[13] discourse or reverie on the high strategy of the war in the Hejaz might be pardoned, under that cataract of great names and impressive principles of war, for thinking that Lawrence was not only the chief exponent of the Hejaz railway cutting but almost the inventor of this form of attack, thus:

"We were to contain the enemy by the silent threat of a vast unknown desert, not disclosing ourselves till we attacked. The attack might be nominal, directed not against him, but against his stuff; so it would not seek either his strength or his weakness, but his most accessible material. In railway-cutting it would be usually an empty stretch of rail . . . ."[14]

Graves evidently assumed Lawrence to be the originator or at any rate prime mover since (with Lawrence's silent consent) he says that Lawrence did not "urge Abdulla to attack Medina, but suggested a series of pin-pricking raids against the railway, offering to set an example in these himself."[15]   True, Graves mentions Major Garland's lessons in dynamiting to Lawrence, and shows us Major Garland hastening off on his camel with detonators, fuses and explosives to blow up the railway.   This was in December, 1916, "shortly after which he died,"[16] though the official history shows him still actively at work in August, 1917, and Lowell Thomas met him in April, 1918.[17]   What is to be noted is that these Lawrence Bureau writers ignore all the attacks on the railway made by the French officers, giving the sole credit to Englishmen, and to Lawrence above all.

The idea of destroying the Hejaz lines and trains went back to the beginning of the uprising.   With the first deliveries of arms, sticks of dynamite were sent to Hussein who later returned them, explaining that none of his troops knew how to use dynamite.   Major Garland and Capitaine Raho were accordingly sent to give the Arabs training and to show examples.   The first recorded raid started out from Wejh on the 12th February (1917) ; reached Toweira, 120 miles north-west of Medina, on the 20th February, where Major Garland blew up a train, and his Arab assistant a bridge.   A few days later, Capitaine Raho (with the forces of Abdulla) also blew up a train, but the Bedouins with him were afraid to attack it and fled.[18]   On the 3rd-4th March a very successful attack was made by Colonel Newcombe 80 kilometres north of Medain Salih, where he destroyed 2,500 yards of line, 2 to 4 locomotives, and took 15 prisoners.[19]   Lawrence was instructed in the use of explosives by Major Garland, and made his first raid from Abdulla's camp under the guidance of Capitaine Raho (whom he patronisingly described as "hard-working and honest") on the 28th March, and the expedition is described at great length in *Seven Pillars*.[20]   What Lawrence omits to tell us is that, from April, 1917, on, the Frenchmen Capitaine Raho and Adjutant Prost made attacks on the line every week;[21] that the French Lieutenant Kernag raided the line on the 14th-17th May;[22] that the French Lieutenant Zamori blew up a 4-arch bridge on the 22nd June; that these and other French officers "made frequent raids" during the whole of 1917.[23]   Among these officers making frequent raids was one attached to Feisal, Adjutant Lamotte, described by Lawrence as Brémond's representative and shown by Lawrence as doing nothing but take a farewell photograph of Lawrence and his Bedouin friends as they set out to "win a new province."[24]   Similarly, frequent raids were made by Garland, Hornby, Davenport and Newcombe; until Dawnay turned up in 1918, and did the job thoroughly. We may claim that Lawrence was the most adventurous and wide-ranging of these demolition raiders, but in frankness must admit that what the others lacked was literary skill to write up their achievements, and that, while the Lawrence legend was being built up, their achievements or most of them were either ignored or by implication credited to him. The figures of rail destruction quoted above from Lowell Thomas and credited to Lawrence cannot be verified, but one of the facts recorded about Thomas's lecture is that a film caption told the audience that the other British officers had merely remained at the base, and had not helped Lawrence up country.[25] When Major Young protested, Lawrence said he would have it changed, but it never was.[26] If the constant attacks of others on the railroad line were even mentioned, it was but casually and as unimportant.

The build-up of the taking of Akaba is even more vociferous than that of the Hejaz railroad demolitions, and of course is almost impossible to check, since Lawrence is practically the only witness. But the preliminary drums beat loud. Akaba, Lowell Thomas tells us, was the most important strategic place north of Aden, with a large garrison " far more important " than any yet captured, except those " at Mecca and Jidda." (The Akaba garrison was 300; that of Taif, captured by Abdulla, much over 1,500.) " It was Lawrence's intention to capture Akaba and make it the base for an Arab invasion of Syria! This was a truly ambitious and portentous plan."[27] But, as we have seen, the capture of Akaba had been ordered by the London War Committee as early as July 6th, 1916, and plans for its occupation by an Anglo-French brigade had been frustrated only by King Hussein's suspicions of his allies. Graves beats the tom-tom as loudly as his American predecessor. " There was need for true epic action if Akaba was to be taken," he asserts, " for it was a feat beyond the scope of unheroic twentieth-century soldiering." Well . . . It hadn't been beyond small landing parties of British and French sailors. Akaba, Graves assures us, was " so strongly protected by the hills, elaborately fortified for miles back," that a division of Allied troops could not take it, while " Auda's men " could probably " rush them with the help of neighbouring clans of Howeitat."[28] Lawrence himself gave

out that Akaba was " another Gallipoli "—three hundred strong!
" The port of Akaba," he says, in a chapter heading, " was so naturally
strong that it could be taken only by surprise from inland."²⁹ Yet it
had been taken from the sea twice already during that war.

As for the " elaborate fortifications " for " miles back," they never
existed.

The force which left Wejh on the 9th May, 1917, was a small one,
but included Sharif Nasir of Medina and Nesib el Bekri, a Damascene
politician. The party carried four hundred-weight of gold. Just
outside Wejh they were joined by Auda. Marching due north, they
crossed the Hejaz railway at kilometre 810.5, and blew up some rails
with dynamite. By the 2nd June they had got as far north as Nebk,
near Kaf, where Auda, who had temporarily left them, rejoined with
his tribe of 200 tents. Then, in Lawrence's narrative and table of
movements, there is a blur of talk and a hiatus of about two weeks.
By the 18th of June, Sharif Nasir had collected about 700 men, 200 of
whom were left behind to guard the tribal tents. From the 20th to
the 28th of June, they were at Bair, where the Turks had tried hastily
to destroy all the wells. One of the wells was found undamaged, and
the others reopened. Demolitions were made on the railway, and
Turkish staffs of two stations were killed to show the Arabs who
had arrived. Lawrence from here rode north-east, and again raided
the railroad. The first fighting occurred on the 30th June at Fuweilah,
and soon became something more than military necessity demanded.
The Turks, coming on undefended Bedouin tents, murdered
an old man, six women and seven children. The Howeitat in revenge
massacred the whole Turkish garrison. On the 1st July, Sharif Nasir
and Auda, with 500 of the toughest of the desert tribesmen, occupied
a position at Abu el Lissan on the road from Maan to Akaba. A weak
battalion of the recently arrived 178th Turkish Regiment was
sent against them and sniped at all day by the Bedouins. After it
had wasted its artillery ammunition in futile shelling, this Turkish
force was suddenly charged in flank from a hidden valley by Auda
and 50 of his horsemen, while the remainder on camels charged
frontally downhill, Lawrence among them. He started firing his
revolver, shot his own camel through the back of the head, and was
thrown heavily. When he recovered from the shock, the action
was nearly over, all the Turkish soldiers being massacred except

for about 160, many of whom were wounded. The Bedouins had been rather fortunate in meeting a battalion of young soldiers.[30]

As the crow flies, they were now not much more than 50 miles from Akaba, but the way was over rugged mountains and through narrow twisting defiles where, as Sir Hubert Young says, there were ideal rear-guard positions, and one where "a company with two or three machine-guns could have stopped an army corps."[31] After the great distances they had travelled, they still had to press on under that terror of the Arabian summer, so graphically described by Doughty as "a scalding tempest of sun rays, which strikes up again, parching the eyeballs, from the glowing sand."[32] Lawrence, with his blue eyes and fair skin, must have suffered greatly, especially as he had not really recovered from his boils, on which Doughty's reflection that the Arab diet often led to "a leprous disposition of the blood,"[33] was very much to the point. Indeed, after two years of being protected in Cairo, without his knowledge, by the hygiene of a modern army, Lawrence was exposed to serious dangers by the food and water he was compelled to live on, and only toughness and resistance of constitution saved him from the collapse from sunstroke which befell Storrs when, just about this time, he made a desert expedition on the Irak side.[34]

But they pushed on, and profited greatly both by the element of surprise and their late victory. The small posts of Guweira and Ketheira surrendered, giving 240 prisoners. The garrison of Akaba, 300 strong, had abandoned their forward positions to be out of range of naval guns, and were discovered at Kadra, under siege by the local Bedouins who had joined the winning side after hearing the news of Abu el Lissal. This little force also surrendered, and 58 days after Sharif Nasir and Lawrence had left Wejh, they reached Akaba with 600 prisoners, including 20 officers and a German non-commissioned officer, who was much perplexed at being captured by a revolt of which he had apparently not heard.[35]

Their troubles were not yet over, for the food at Akaba is said to have been insufficient. Lawrence determined to make his way at once to Egypt to ask for supplies, and may perhaps have foreseen the advantages of personally bringing the news that Akaba was taken and giving it in his own words. He set out with a small escort on the old Egyptian pilgrim road; and in *Seven Pillars* Lawrence says that at 3 p.m. on the 8th July,* 49 hours after leaving Akaba, the party had covered the 257 kilometres to Shatt, on the side of the Canal opposite to Suez. The various stories—of the obstructionist naval authority, the profane sergeant telephonist, the helpful naval man, the funny joke of refusing to show his pass on the train—may be passed over without regret; and the fact recorded that on Lawrence's announcing his news, *Dufferin* was sent off with food and 16,000 pounds.[36] The Arab Bureau made the most of this success of Hogarth's protégé, a success which they attributed entirely to him. It is said that he was recommended for the Victoria Cross. Why? He was, in fact, promoted Major and made a Companion of the Bath, which is a military as well as civilian distinction, limited (at any rate at that time) to 705 military companions. I cannot find any record of what decorations, if any, were given to Sharif Nasir and Auda, but the French War Office, doubtless approached by the right people, suggested to Colonel Brémond that he should recommend Lawrence for the Croix de Guerre, which was eventually presented to him by Captain Pisani, whom Lawrence has contemptuously represented as always on the look out for decorations for himself.[37]

It was the capture of Akaba which first brought Lawrence out of the obscurity of the Arab Bureau, and in view of the extensive claims made by himself and his friends, certain questions arise which are worth discussing, even if definite conclusions are hard to reach. Was Lawrence the originator of the "strategy of occupying Akaba?" Was Lawrence the originator of the idea of taking it from inland with the Howeitat? Was Lawrence the commander of the expedition which set out from Wejh with Nasir, and was he "the general" who really planned and directed their operations? Finally, what was Lawrence doing in that blurred-out period between the 3rd and 19th June, and why did he refuse to give any but ambiguous information about that period?

I do not find it anywhere proved that Lawrence, from Cairo in July, 1916, "subtly persuaded" the War Committee in London to include the occupation of Akaba in their orders, any more than he originated the "Alexandretta strategy" and "arranged" for the surrender of Erzerum. Unless evidence is forthcoming, there is no

---

* So dated in *Seven Pillars* and in Liddell Hart, but Lawrence's original (suppressed) report says July 9th. So the journey really took 73 hours. Baedeker (1912) gives the distance as about 60 camel hours.

proof whatever that he had anything to do with the planning of any of them. The decision of Wingate, Lloyd and Brémond to occupy Akaba[38] has been mentioned already, as also the fact that the earlier plans were frustrated by Hussein's refusal to allow the landing of European troops. The Hashemites were extremely suspicious of their British allies, and were even disagreeably impressed when General Maude captured Baghdad in March, 1917. King Hussein publicly lamented the " loss " of the city, which had been " the cradle of Caliphs and the source of light which had enlightened the world," and Abdulla complained that the English were not keeping to their promises about Arab territories.[39] Feisal, in telegraphing the news of the occupation of Wejh, omitted all mention of the Royal Navy, and said Wejh had been captured by his troops![40] Therefore, if indeed Lawrence " subtly persuaded " Feisal that Akaba ought to be taken without British aid, he had no difficult task. Whether he had " persuaded " the War Committee in London in July, 1916, is another matter.

I have already mentioned Lawrence's *Seven Pillars* description of the interview between himself and Brémond, in which Brémond is falsely said to have refused Feisal the mountain 65's and Lawrence sat smiling with spite after having told Brémond that he had known Akaba before the war and that Brémond's scheme (it was agreed on by the other commanders) of attack by a composite brigade was " technically impossible."* This interview is dated by the editor between the 3rd and 18th February, 1917; and in Lawrence's own record he was at Wejh on the 25th January, and again at " Wejh, etc." from the 6th to the 19th February. Now Colonel Brémond's official, contemporary reports show that he had at that time two interviews with Feisal. The first was on the 31st January, 1917, when Lawrence was in Cairo ;[41] Brémond saw Feisal on that occasion, not with Lawrence but with Newcombe, who said he knew Akaba well as he had made a topographical survey there. Feisal said there were only 150 police troops in the town, and that he engaged to take it himself.[42] Obviously, Lawrence must have heard about this interview from Feisal and Newcombe after his return from Cairo, and pretended in his book that he had been present. On this (31st January) occasion, there is no note of any discussion of the 65's. That discussion occurred

---

* After the place had twice been taken, without casualties, by small naval landing parties !

in a private interview between Brémond and Feisal on the 1st April, 1917, when Lawrence was at Abu Markha[43] and therefore could not have been present. Of course Lawrence heard of it afterwards from Feisal, and, in writing his book, telescoped the two interviews into one, and pretended that he had been present. Incidentally, on the 16th February, Brémond, who had left Wejh some time before, was on board the *Saint Brieuc* off Akaba, which appeared to him at that time entirely deserted.[44] Unless some contemporary and objective evidence can be found, the presumption is unavoidable that the Lawrence-Brémond interview described in *Seven Pillars* is wholly fictitious, and based by Lawrence on what he heard from Newcombe and Feisal about the interviews they had with Brémond where these topics undoubtedly were discussed. It should be added that the whole description of Lawrence's alleged interview with Brémond and Feisal, with its highly-coloured story of Brémond's discomfiture, was cut from *Revolt in the Desert*, so that Brémond never saw it and had therefore no chance to give his denial.

The other questions I have asked are so much entangled one with another that they have to be taken together, and no really definite answer can be given, only a probability suggested. Let us look first at the claims made for Lawrence in the capture of Akaba. If I begin with Lowell Thomas, it is not because I don't know that Lawrence pretended he scarcely knew him, while the Lawrence Bureau abused or ignored him; but, as I shall show clearly later on, Lawrence's immense popularity was created by Lowell Thomas, and it is from him that the whole legend stems, carefully though secretly nurtured by Lawrence himself. I have already quoted Thomas on Lawrence's "ambitious and portentous plan" (which wasn't his plan) to capture Akaba. According to Thomas, the force which set out from Wejh was "headed by Sharif Nasir," but, "as usual, Lawrence went along to advise the Arab commander; he always made it a point to act through one of the native leaders . . . ."[45] If we turn to Graves, we find that Nasir "was the guide," and Lawrence, instead of advising him, "took counsel together" with Auda on how to capture Akaba.[46] In *Seven Pillars*, Nasir has the ambiguous part of "leader." "Sharif Nasir led us; his lucent goodness . . . made him the only leader . . . for forlorn hopes."[47] "Nasir gave the marching signal . . . ."[48] "When Nasir, without my prompting, had halted . . . ."[49] "Nasir and I mustered the Aegyl," i.e. the camel-men.[50] He " led " them and it is not clear whether he was the real commander, or a figurehead for Lawrence and Auda, or the Mecca aristocrat sent along to see them safely through tribes who were at feud with Auda and knew not Lawrence. In Liddell Hart, " it was a small party that Nasir led forth that afternoon."[51] They all agree, however, either by direct statement or by insinuation, that the real commander was Lawrence, and how ably " he handled Feisal's army, in spite of his complete lack of military training and experience."[52]

Another person on this expedition rather brushed aside was a political character, Nesib el Bekri, who was there to represent Feisal to the Syrian villagers.[53] Why to the Syrian villagers on an expedition to Akaba, which is far from Syria? In *Seven Pillars*, Nesib grows over-ambitious and sets out for Damascus, not for Akaba; while Lawrence " planned to go off " by himself to Syria as soon as Nesib had gone.[54] Then there is a hiatus filled with invectives against the allegedly falsified promises of McMahon to " the Arabs," and the abrupt beginning of a new paragraph: " When I returned, it was June the sixteenth, and Nasir was still labouring, in his tent."[55] What happened during those two weeks to Lawrence? Hints are scattered by his panegyrists, but a great mystery is observed. Why? In this context I must quote again the curious words, written and signed, which Lawrence sent to Graves (you may read them paraphrased in his book[56]).

" You may make public, if you like, that my reticence upon this northward raid is deliberate, and based on private reasons: and record your opinion that I have found mystification, and perhaps statements deliberately misleading or contradictory, the best way to hide the truth of what really occurred, if anything did occur."[57]

Passing lightly over the cynical arrogance of that statement, may we not ask where was the need for " mystification " over this " northward raid " and what was the purpose of hiding the truth? *Seven Pillars* is an uninhibited book—little that in any way concerns the author is by him considered uninteresting or to be concealed. Why the exception here? Why, " if anything did occur " on this raid (and it can later be shown that certain things did occur), why, just here, secrecy, hints, mystification?

It seems as if this is the moment to take a look at the Arab view of these transactions. Mr. Antonius devoted several years of research to his book, travelled and enquired in Arabia, knew and had the confidence of Feisal. While he is no more infallible than any other "authority," he undoubtedly gives us the Arab, probably King Feisal's, version. Auda, who is described at some length, is said by Antonius to have "sent a thrill through the camp" on his arrival, and it is added that he and Feisal soon came to an understanding:

"Auda . . . gave Feisal a sweeping promise that, for his part, his only feud now was with the Turks; and in the same breath, *he proposed an attack on Akaba which, he boasted, he and his tribesmen could capture unaided.*"[58]

As this proposal was in harmony with Feisal's own plans, he at once agreed, and Auda thereupon arranged to collect his followers (he was sheik of 200 tents of the Howeitat) and to "storm the Turkish posts guarding Akaba." It so happened that just at this time, Feisal was sending off a political mission "to preach insurrection" in Syria; and chose Nesib el Bekri as his political emissary. Feisal's own cousin, Sharif Nasir, was "to lead the expedition as his personal representative."[59]

So far no mention of Lawrence, but at this point "Lawrence asked to be allowed to go, offering his services as an emissary to the Arab leaders in Damascus."[60] Thus, according to the Arab account, Lawrence did not plan the Akaba raid, but Auda spontaneously suggested it to Feisal, and Lawrence merely went along on his own suggestion as a volunteer, not to lead the fighting men but to carry Feisal's instructions to Damascus. Antonius then gives an account of Lawrence's movements and the people he met, which corresponds very closely with Lawrence's suppressed report to the Arab Bureau, which was first published by David Garnett in the *Letters* after Antonius's book appeared. Evidently, Antonius's sources of information were good. In any case there was nothing here that needed concealment when the war was over. Lawrence started out on the 4th June with two men to the Wald Ali country where however he failed to end the feud between the Bishr and the Howeitat. On the 8th June, near Tudmor, he met Sheik Dhami of the Kawakiba Anaizeh, and went with him and 35 men to dynamite a small girder bridge near Ras Baalbek, the effect of which on traffic was very small, though the noise of the explosions was a great propaganda weapon! On 13th June, near Damascus, in the home of friends of Feisal's, Lawrence met Ali Riza Pasha Rehabi, the general in command at Damascus, one of those members of the secret societies who talked much and did little until Allenby's men were just about to enter the town. Lawrence then rode south to Nebk, meeting other sheiks on the way. Nasir was sent to Hussein el Atrash of the Druses with a ten-point political programme, quoted in full by Lawrence in his suppressed report. On the 19th, Auda and Nasir started for Akaba.[61] The Akaba fights are described very briefly in this suppressed report, which then harks back to political matters, and ventures the opinion that, with sufficient material assistance, dispositions of Arab forces could be made by the end of August, as marked on the sketch map which Lawrence attached, showing a formidable array of revolters from Sidon to Jerusalem and from Damascus to Maan—very few indeed of whom ever did anything to help before October, 1918.

But though the report was too optimistic, that was no reason for suppressing it. Lawrence wrote other unjustifiably optimistic reports which were not suppressed. When Liddell Hart questioned Lawrence about its existence, Lawrence gave him, not the report, but an extract from a letter which Lawrence asserted he had sent to a friend who asked to see the report " a few weeks later."

> " I handed it to Clayton whose eyebrows went high (some of it was comic, some scurrilous, some betrayed horrible secrets) and who sat on it. I don't think anyone in the Savoy ever saw it, whole. It certainly never went to H.C. or W.O. or F.O., and I am too tender-hearted to ask after it now.* It was an MS. document of three pages, and compressed two months' march into it: rather dull except to one who knew Syrian politics . . . It's all ancient history now."[62]

Very interesting. To whom was that letter written, and where is the original? Or was Lawrence, with his " phenomenal memory," quoting it verbatim from memory—after 16 years? The report itself is certainly rather dull, but there is nothing comic and nothing scurri-

---

* Yet the words in *Seven Pillars*: " In my report . . I had stressed the strategic importance of the eastern tribes of Syria "[63] imply that Allenby saw the suppressed report. But, if so, what about the alleged " comic " and " scurrilous " passages which raised Clayton's eyebrows ?

lous in it, nor has it any " horrible secrets." Even if there were secrets, was it the business of the Arab Bureau to conceal them from their masters, the High Commissioner, the War Office and the Foreign Office? What is meant by Lawrence's phrase, that he was " too tenderhearted to ask after it now? " It is as obvious a put-off as his telling Hart that one reason he wrote nothing about this Damascus journey was that he kept no notes, when full notes existed in this report, and he had been allowed access to all his reports. But the report does show very definitely that what Antonius says is true— Lawrence went on the Akaba expedition not as military commander but as Feisal's envoy to Damascus and the intervening tribes, trying to arrange an uprising in August or thereabouts. It also implies that Lawrence was in a subordinate position, since in the opening he himself describes Nasir as " O.C. Expedition," i.e. Officer Commanding Expedition. This (suppressed) report is dated Cairo, 10th July, 1917, obviously written the day he arrived and containing his full report, as it goes down to his arrival at Shatt on the 9th. But later on, in August, the Arab Bureau published another and very different report, describing at length and with picturesque phrases the purely military operations from June 18th on. From which it looks as if the original political report was suppressed by the Arab Bureau, and a military one substituted for reasons best known to them. Clearly, it was on the second report that Lawrence's supposed military conduct of the expedition was based.

An echo of all this came later from the Iraki officers of Abdulla's army in November, 1917, when Colonel Wilson was sent to urge them to capture Medina, as at that time the Arab Bureau changed its mind and wanted the town taken. Various excuses were made to Wilson, but there was one objection " never mentioned to the English, but a constant theme of Sharifians," and this was their objection to Colonel Wilson having any part in the operations. " If we fail," the Irakis said, " it will be said that the fault was ours; and if there is a success, all the merits will go to the English."[64]

In conclusion, let me call the reader's attention to the remarks of Antonius:

" His (Lawrence's) summing up is that ' Akaba had been taken on my plan by my effort '—a claim that will perplex the historian.

... The Arab evidence is that the plan was first suggested to Feisal*
by Auda at their first meeting at Wejh; that Lawrence was not
made privy to it until Feisal had given his consent; and that it
was carried into execution by Auda and his Howeitat tribesmen
independently of all outside help. . . . Sharif Nasir and Lawrence
had accompanied the expedition and taken some part in the fighting,
but neither as leaders nor advisers. . . ."[65]

I may add that the official citation for Lawrence's C.B. makes no
mention of Akaba, but was awarded to him and two other officers,
whose names precede his, for unspecified " valiant services rendered in
connection with Military Operations in the Field."

* But of course it had been suggested to Feisal long before by Brémond and Newcombe.

CHAPTER FIVE

THUS AMBIGUOUSLY the problem of Akaba was solved, and the place taken into the hands of those who were friendly to the British, or at least would probably remain so while they were fed and given gold and their ally seemed successful. (Incidentally, almost the first task Lawrence had to carry out on returning from Cairo was to cajole and threaten back his hero, Auda, who, dissatisfied with his rewards, was making overtures to the Turks!) And why not, when he found the credit for his achievement given to the political officer? Those who, like Wingate and Brémond, had believed that an Anglo-French brigade ought to have been landed at Akaba, may or may not have been right. They argued that such a nucleus of trained soldiers with artillery would have rallied the Bedouins and given confidence to the Sharifian irregulars, thus making the " Arab revolt " really of use in drawing off or containing important numbers of the enemy. But there were good arguments against, and those military leaders who had thought Akaba was worth a brigade could hardly criticise when they got it in exchange for supplies and four hundredweight of gold.

It was perhaps a stroke of luck for Lawrence that, a week before he returned to Egypt from this expedition, there had been a change of command, and Allenby had succeeded Murray and Maxwell. Unlike them, Allenby knew nothing about the Middle East, his former service having been in Africa, and in France as a cavalry commander and a not too successful Army commander. Allenby was interested in English literature, in music and ornithology, and was a Fellow of the Zoological Society.[1] Lawrence says he first saw the General on the station platform at Ismailia, where, through Admiral Wemyss' flag officer, Lawrence got permission for *Dufferin* to sail at once to Akaba with supplies. In a later interview, Lawrence says he succeeded in impressing Allenby sufficiently for the General to promise to do all he could to help him. Lawrence, on his side, promised to contain the enemy by rousing the Arabs, if he were given arms and supplies and 200,000 sovereigns.[2]

Lawrence speaks of Allenby with adulation. Allenby was " clean-judging," he was " morally so great that the comprehension of our littleness came slow to him."[3] Allenby had " splendour of will,"[4] " calm drive and human understanding,"[5] and as " a reader of Milton, had an acute sense of style."[6] " What he could do was enough for his very greediest servant ";[7] the " campaign of September, 1918, was perhaps the most scientifically perfect in English history,"[8] and indeed " the victory had been the logical fruit solely of his genius."[9] The Field-Marshal—in his public utterances—said that Lawrence interested him as much as any figure in the Great War;[10] he was a brilliant war leader[11] and " the mainspring of the Arab movement,"[12] " the shy and retiring scholar—archæologist-philosopher—was swept by the tide of war into a position undreamt of "; " praise or blame was regarded with indifference by Lawrence " and " himself an Emir, he wore the robes of that rank, and kept up a suitable degree of state."[13] It seems unfortunate that Allenby's public commendations of Lawrence should be so much at variance with his private judgment, as recorded by Lord Wavell and General Barrow. In *Seven Pillars*, Lawrence remarks that Allenby could not decide how much of Lawrence was " genuine performer and how much charlatan "; and Lord Wavell informs us that Allenby never solved the problem, " but always suspected a strong streak of the charlatan in Lawrence."[14] To General Barrow, Lord Allenby was even more explicit:

" I was talking with Allenby in his study in his London house. He tapped *The Seven Pillars of Wisdom* in his bookshelf and said: ' Lawrence goes for you in his book, George.' I replied to the effect that I was not taking any notice of it, and he said, ' No, that would be a mug's game. Besides, we know Lawrence. He thinks himself a hell of a soldier, and loves posturing in the limelight.' "[15]

We will not pause to enquire why Lord Allenby publicly praised so lavishly a man he thought privately had a strong strain of the charlatan and loved posturing in the limelight, but merely remark that Allenby's promise of support in July, 1917, gave Lawrence the opportunity his starved ambition hungered for. Here was his chance, and he fought for it like a wild cat. It was no longer a question of being Dr. Hogarth's protégé in the Arab Bureau (though, of course, that was always useful), but of having direct access to a Commander-in-Chief, fresh from the war, with all the ensuing prestige. Premising that "Akaba had been taken on his plan by his effort"[16]—a sweeping assertion which, as we have seen, there is every reason to doubt—Lawrence modestly asked General Clayton to be given the command of the forces in Arabia, which was refused, for the reason that an officer junior to the others could not be given the command.[17] But the arrangements agreed to between them certainly improved Lawrence's status, whatever might be the case with others. Feisal's forces were to be brought up to Akaba, detached from the Hejaz, and Feisal ranked as an Army Commander under Allenby, with Lawrence as Political Officer. Lawrence then tried to get all stores, supplies and officers with Ali and Abdulla cut off from them and diverted to Feisal and himself; and again failed. But he was allowed to have for base commandant Joyce, who, being strongly anti-French and no intriguer, would not interfere with plans, and would devote most of his attention to building up the Regular Arab Army of 600 being raised and trained by Jaafar and Maulud. With his fund of 200,000 to 500,000 sovereigns and this plan, which brought Feisal a long step nearer Syria, how could Lawrence fail to be well received by the anxious candidate for its throne?

Lawrence claimed the war in the Hejaz was won at Wejh; at Akaba he considered it ended.[18] This was a convenient assumption now that Lawrence had left the area, but what of Ali and Abdulla whom Clayton had refused to abandon at Lawrence's request? Well, they had the not very entertaining task of blockading or containing the Medina garrison, and of preventing them from re-joining the Turks in Palestine; which was after all a genuine excuse for British military and political support. There were even one or two abortive attempts to capture the place, which failed for the obvious reason that the Arabs were not good enough. For the rest, the Hejaz " war " went on very much like Lawrence's " war," with blowings up of trains by Davenport and Raho and others, destructions of rails, and local actions of Bedouins. If their successes went unrecorded, it was because there was no picturesque reporter, and partly because they received fewer supplies, less money, and were refused the artillery Abdulla constantly pressed for. In addition, it appears that the only recruits (of deserters and prisoner of war volunteers) they received for their " regular armies " were those rejected by Jaafar for Feisal's " army." Some of these Syrians and Irakis were animated by " motives not military " and were much more interested in forming political committees on Soviet lines than in fighting the Turks, whom they described as " our Moslem brethren." The committee in Ali's army was dominated by a violent Anglophobe, called Jemil, and the committee itself expressed a near adoration for the Germans, and made no pretence of concealing its pro-Turkish feelings, its contempt for the English and hatred for the Bedouins.[19] Only when old Hussein heard of them—for Ali was apparently too sick to bother—were these scandals abruptly quelled.

The Arabs, we are told,[20] in these operations killed, captured and above all " contained " many thousands of the enemy; but a disinterested enquirer, looking over the facts and figures as more or less truthfully revealed in post-war official publications, asks himself who contained whom? and were the results commensurate with the expense of men and money?[21]

In August, 1917—a month after the taking of Akaba—Lord Wavell estimates that " as a rough estimate of available rifles," the Turks on the Palestine and Irak fronts had 71,000 and the British about 180,000. Who was " containing "? A year later, just before Allenby's " great victory," Wavell estimates the British at 200,000 and the Turks at about 60,000 " ragged, hungry, ill-equipped " men.[22]

In the same way one cannot help asking if the Arab war (" a sideshow of a side-show ") was militarily worth either its cost or its damaging political consequences? Obviously those in control thought so at the time or they would not have authorised it. Yet Allenby seems to have had his doubts, since in October, 1917, he sent for Lawrence and demanded to know what was the purpose of his blowing up trains? Were they not simply a melodramatic advertisement for Feisal's political ambitions? Indeed the whole objection to the "Arab war" as expounded by Lawrence after Akaba, is simply that it was a political demonstration, that militarily its aid was negligible, while time and again it failed to achieve what Lawrence promised. And one cannot escape the conviction that much of the "history" of the Arab war was simply political propaganda designed to prove that "the Arabs" had captured certain areas and towns (and therefore were obliged under "British promises" to be ruled by Lawrence's friend Feisal independently though perhaps not unsubsidised), though in fact all the real work was done by English, Scottish, Anzac and Indian troops. And there is a noteworthy ambivalence in Lawrence's own propaganda, for while asserting as a *boutade* that this war was more like peace (as indeed, from the point of view of the Western front, it was), and seriously that it was "like a general strike,"* Lawrence and his friends claim for him the achievements of a great military genius. Nobody denies the value of propaganda and guerrillas in warfare, but it is unhistoric to suggest that Lawrence discovered them. And great generals do not make their reputations by directing a general strike.

Another difficulty which confronts the enquirer is the discrepancy between different reports of the same occurrence. An example will show the strange contradictions better than pages of explanation. It is agreed that in October, 1917, the Turks gathered a small force to attack the 500-600 "Arab regulars" then in Wadi Musa under Jaafar and Maulud. What happened? Lawrence, tells us that the Turks fell "foxed and fogged" into a prepared trap over which "Maulud presided beautifully," i.e. he exterminated them. "He opened his centre and, with the greatest of humour, let in the Turks until they broke their faces against the vertical cliffs of the Arab refuge," whereupon Maulud attacked the "puzzled and hurt" Turks on both flanks, causing them heavy losses, while they never again dared to attack "a prepared Arab position."[23] Lawrence, of course, gives no date, but his editor puts "12 Oct., 1917," at the top of the page. Similarly, Lawrence gives us none of the facts needed for the understanding of this military action—he gives no estimate of the numbers on either side, what was the purpose of their movements or why the Turks did so idiotic a thing or what their losses were.

* Except that there was no "strike" within the large area controlled by the Turks.

Neither does he tell us how and why the Arabs " prepared a position "
in Wadi Musa, or why the Turks attacked it.

Turn now to the British Official History. The Turkish force (it
says) consisted of 4 weak battalions, the 7th Cavalry Regiment and
4 guns. The Arabs had 2 companies of camel corps, 2 of mule-
mounted infantry, 2 mountain guns, 4 machine guns. They numbered 350 " regulars " and 250 Bedouins. Jaafar was at a place called
Elji, against which the Turks advanced; shelled and bombed it;
carried the outer defences; but were taken in flank by the Bedouins
and retired, leaving a few prisoners. The date is given as 27th
October, and the following comment is made: " The ill-trained Arab
camel-men behaved badly, but the mounted infantry under Maulud
Pasha, a veteran cavalry officer of the Turkish service, was steady
enough." Yet it was the flank attack of the Bedouins which caused
the retreat.[24]

That at any rate gives some idea of what may have happened,
which is very seldom the case with Lawrence's flowery descriptions.
Obviously both refer to the same action, but how differently! Neither
seems to have had access to the report (possibly of the Arab commander)
which Brémond quotes. According to him, Jemal Kutchuk, with
" considerable forces and 3 airplanes," attacked the Arabs in Wadi
Musa, completely defeated them and recaptured the " fôret d'Aiche."
Now this " forest " was made up of those dwarf desert acacia trees
which furnished the fuel for the railway, and, when we realise that
the Arabs had occupied that area, we instantly see the reason for the
Turkish action. The cut wood had been transported by a Decauville
railway, which the official history says was destroyed by the Arabs
early in October, 1917. But, Brémond continues, on the night of
22-23rd October, " Mouloud efendi " (obviously the Maulud Pasha
of the English), with 300 Arab " regulars," made a night attack on
the Turkish camp, killed 400, captured 300, with the loss of only
40 killed. " It was a magnificent success, which does the greatest
honour to the leader and his troops."[25] Here there is no question of
a Bedouin flank movement or of the humorous Maulud leading the
Turks into an extremely funny death-trap.

If we follow the diary of dates given by Lawrence at the end of
Seven Pillars, we can see that, for some time after Akaba, the political
side of his appointment was uppermost, and he spent most of his

time at Cairo and Alexandria and on board ship. His hasty journey
to Guweira to bring Auda back to his allegiance has been mentioned,
though why this was not the task of his sponsor and "lord" Feisal
is nowhere explained. And it was not until the 7th September (1917)
that Lawrence initiated or resumed his train-wrecking. The section of
the railway chosen for the attack was near the station of Mudowwara,
which is about 100 kilometres from Maan and nearly 600 from Medina.
The advantage of this point of attack (only about 100 kilometres from
Akaba in a direct line) is obvious when you realise that Medina still
held such large quantities of pre-war railway material, so that the
greater the distance from that centre was the break, the longer it
took to repair.

Doubtless, it is a modern sentimentality, unfortified by the high
principles of "manuals of chivalry", which regards the wrecking of
trains—whether carrying soldiers or civilians or both—as among the
more inglorious forms of modern warfare. One does not altogether
visualise Sir Sagramors le Desirous and Sir Gawain upsetting an enemy
market-cart in a ditch and leaving the wreck of humanity and goods
to the tender mercies of the local villeins. Not until the 19th September
did Major Lawrence and his men succeed in their daring new plan.
The expedition was accompanied by two sergeant-instructors who
had been trying to teach the Arab patriots how to handle Lewis guns
and Stokes trench-mortars. Following the explosion which derailed
the train, there was a deathly silence, broken by rifle and machine-gun
fire which swept the Turkish soldiers from the tops of the carriages
like bales of cotton. When the survivors fled to cover, they were
rendered harmless by Stokes mortars, and the Bedouins rushed to
pillage the train. A bridge had been destroyed and the first car,
filled with Turkish sick, had fallen into the hole. All but a few had
been killed, and the explosion had hurled the dead and dying into a
bleeding heap at the splintered end of the coach. When Lawrence
looked in on this successful result of his activities as "Emir Dynamite,"
one of the dying casualties moaned out the word "typhus"—"so
I wedged shut the door and left them there alone."[26]

Turning from them, Lawrence became aware of the pillage of the
train by screaming, half-naked Arabs. There were also thirty or forty
terrified women survivors of the wreck, who rushed to Lawrence—
evidently the commander from his rich garments—and clutched at

him, howling for mercy. Lawrence assured them that "all was going well," but they would not leave their clutching until he was delivered from this fulsome importunity by "some husbands." The Turks brushed the women aside and fell at the conqueror's feet in a state of terror, expecting instant death—a most absurd and unpleasant sight—and there was nothing Lawrence could think of to do but kick them away as well as he could with bare feet, and break free. There were some Austrian soldiers and officers who asked to surrender, and were told by Lawrence that they would be all right. However, they were all murdered, except two or three, by Lawrence's own bodyguard before he could or did interfere.[27] How much of this is true, and how much write-up? His official report merely says that about 70 Turks were killed, and 30 wounded, many of whom died. There were 90 prisoners, of whom 68 survived to reach Akaba. An Austrian second lieutenant was killed.[28]

The lurid details of the wrecked train and its pillage may or may not have been invented for literary purposes, but what cannot have been invented is the unconscious cruelty and savagery of the eye-witness who could describe such scenes with such callousness to suffering and such contemptuous disdain for women's and men's fear of Bedouin brutalities. Sir Andrew Macphail, who has pointed this out, felt that Lawrence had been infected by the savagery of his associates. It may indeed be so, though even as a schoolboy, one of his friends thought him "ruthless,"[29] and the descriptions of his behaviour in pre-war Turkey would indicate considerable natural truculence. On the other hand, we find rhetorical statements, verging on cant, such as that in his suppressed introduction to *Seven Pillars*: "All our subject provinces to me were not worth one dead Englishman."[30] There is always something suspect in respect for human life limited by blatant nationalism—and that limitation was not recognised by the old professional army Lawrence affected to disdain. And, on the other hand, it is impossible to deny that he seems to enjoy the idea, if not the reality, of brutal cruelties, as when he praises that "silent, laughing, masterful man," his friend Meinertzhagen, because he "took as blithe a pleasure in deceiving his enemy (or his friend) by some unscrupulous jest as in *spattering the brains of a cornered mob of Germans with his African knob-kerri*."[31] The British and the old British Army have many and grievous faults, but that sort of brutality and delight in it were very seldom among them.

It is noteworthy that, a few days after these Mudowwara horrors, Lawrence wrote to a correspondent (" a Friend ") to boast of this exploit, as " the last stunt " on which he had " potted " a train with two engines, and had " killed superior numbers." He goes on to say that he won't " last out this game much longer," his nerves were going and his temper wearing thin. He feels the " show " is making too great demands on him, and that he is becoming self-centred. He winds up: " This killing and maiming of Turks is horrible. When you charge in at the finish and find them all over the place in bits, and still alive many of them, and know that you have done hundreds in the same way before and must do hundreds more if you can . . . " and there the officious censor has cut the sentence short. Even in this apparent mood of remorse, Lawrence cannot help exaggerating his exploits, for, apart from the rail destructions with Raho and on the way north during the Akaba expedition, this was in fact his first personal attack on the line and the first train-wreck of which he was guilty. It is perhaps hardly worth noting that in this letter he mentions that in the pillage he " got a good Baluch prayer rug," which, by the time the story reached Graves, had become a gift " with a charming letter " from the Lady Ayesha, " a friend and hostess of Feisal's," in gratitude to Lawrence for saving her from the wreck, and Lawrence afterwards sent the identical carpet and story to Lady Allenby.[32]

Lawrence tells us in *Seven Pillars* of a second train-wrecking near kilometre 500 on the 6th October (1917), when he was accompanied by the French captain, Pisani. Lawrence was only 100 yards from the line when he blew the charge; and then Pisani led the Arabs to the attack. A Turkish colonel fired at Lawrence, giving him a flesh wound in the hip, which caused Lawrence to laugh at his thinking that the killing of an individual would help to win the war.[33] In his report, Lawrence says " some civilians were released,"[34] which in *Seven Pillars* becomes " we kicked northward some dozen civilians."[35] In the report it is stated that a Kaimakam, General Staff, " fired at us with a Mauser pistol, but a Bedouin blazed into him at twenty yards."[36] In Pisani's report at the French War Office,[37] it is stated that Major Lawrence was only 100 metres from the line when he fired

the charge, that there was a " fusillade " for twenty-five minutes, that
Pisani then rushed forward with ten Arabs, and was fired at with a
revolver by a Turkish officer who was killed by a Bedouin.[38] Curious
coincidence! Either there were two Turkish officers firing at each of
the Europeans, or one of the Europeans has claimed the experience of
the other.

Having blown two trains, and thus become a master of the art,
Lawrence now trained " pupils " to spread the destruction, while
being careful not to cut the line so seriously that Medina might have
to surrender. But was all this explosive zeal necessary, and was it for
this that Allenby had promised support and sovereigns? The suppressed report on Akaba had promised tribal risings, and though there
were the obvious difficulties that these could happen only once and,
if a failure occurred on the British side, would lead to hideous Turkish
reprisals, still that rather than sabotage was what had gained Allenby's
support. At all events, when he summoned Lawrence to G.H.Q. at
Ismailia (October 13th, 1917), Allenby, as we have seen, chaffed him
about his melodramatic train-wreckings, which indeed might well
seem inadequate action from the forces of an Army Commander.
Piqued in his vanity by Allenby's chaff, Lawrence made a wild proposal—he would take a select party and raid far to the north 400 miles
from Akaba and destroy one of the bridges on the main railway line
of supply through the Yarmuk valley to the Turkish front in Palestine.
Lawrence's account of this must be read to be believed—the Turkish
Army was to be isolated from its base for two weeks by his stroke,
" no coherent unit of von Kress's army would survive its retreat to
Damascus," whereupon " the Arabs " would take over when the
British were " nearly exhausted," and would " carry their wave
forward into the great capital," a fantastic delusion. Allenby at once
asked for this serviceable aid to be rendered between the 5th and 8th
November, 1917.[39]

The only criticism to be made of this grandiose scheme is the
bleak fact that it failed, and it cannot be said that Allenby's advance
on and capture of Jerusalem owed much or indeed anything to the
assistance of Major Lawrence and " the Arabs." They doubtless
reached the Yarmuk valley, for which Lawrence has been enormously
praised, but they failed to make the slightest interruption to the main
line of Turkish rail communication, which fact has been passed over.

We have two contemporary reports by Lawrence on this unsuccessful expedition from which such useful results had been promised; and they leave one wondering what protector enabled him to get away with such things. The *Arab Bulletin* report, published 16th December, 1917, and presumably read by Allenby, airily says: "On November 5th we camped at Kseir-el-Hallabat, and on the 7th failed to rush the bridge at Tell-el-Shehab, and returned to Kseir."[40] But why did they fail? Another and earlier report to Joyce says nonchalantly: "Tell-el-Shehab is a splendid bridge to destroy, but those Serahin threw away all my explosives when the firing began and so I can do nothing. I am very sick at losing it so stupidly."[41] According to *Seven Pillars* the raid failed because one of the Indian machine-gunners (a regular) dropped his rifle, which gave the alarm to the Turkish sentry, whereupon the raiders fled precipitately to the hills.[42]

Two British officers had started out with Lawrence and his men on this expedition. One was Captain Lloyd, M.P. (afterwards Lord Lloyd), who rode with them to el Jefer to see them fairly started and then returned—a valuable and influential friend. The other officer was Lieutenant Wood, R.E., who went as far as the Yarmuk bridge, but left the retreating party on the 9th November, as Lawrence had then fallen back on the expedient of blowing up a bridge near Minifir (which is about half-way between Deraa and Amman), a repetition of what had been done earlier on the Auda expedition to Akaba. In the destruction of the train, Lawrence was hit by pieces of the exploded boiler and painfully but not seriously hurt. They learned afterwards that the commander of the Turkish Eighth Army Corps, Mehmed Jemel Pasha, was on the train; but they failed either to harm or to capture him. Thence, in dismal weather, the party returned to their oasis hide-out at Azrak (on a line with Amman, but far out in the desert), where their Arab commander, Sharif Ali Ibn el Hussein, was visited by parties of Bedouins under their sheiks. The visit of one of these, a bandit named Talal el Hareidhin, suggested to Lawrence a ride back to the Deraa area in his company, which rounded out this whole abortive expedition with a disaster to Lawrence personally of the most painful and humiliating kind.

Was there really any practical object served by this ride? With Allenby's battle towards Jerusalem still in progress, Lawrence must have felt that, after his glowing promises, he could not merely sit in tents out of the rain at Azrak. He had at all costs to seem to do something. But a reconnaisance of Deraa itself was futile, for by this time even Lawrence must have realised that neither the Bedouins nor the " Arab army " nor both together were capable of storming a town held by the Turks. All this bravura of desert heroes and flaring about on camels had resulted in what? The wrecking of a train with a few Turkish casualties. Contrast this with the bitter fighting of the real soldiers—say that of the Yeomanry Mounted Division for twelve days in " one of the roughest and bleakest areas of the Judæan hills," during which " they had been fighting continually, day and night, not only against a vigorous and determined enemy but against difficulties of a roadless mountain country. Exposed to constant rain and cold, without tents, blankets or greatcoats, often short of food, and opposed at all times by greatly superior forces of the enemy." They lost 41 per cent. of their effectives, and Allenby came personally to tell them that if they had not held on for those critical days, " the whole army would have been compelled to give up the hold it had secured on the mountain passes, and that, if this had occurred, it would have taken three months' hard fighting and thousands of casualties before we should have been able to capture Jerusalem."[43] And this was the action of only one unit during part of the offensive, yet surely enough to show up this Arab nonsense and Lawrence's pretentious theorising about winning wars without fighting or having casualties; though in a military journal he did describe the Arab campaign as a " side-show of a side-show ". Of course, you can fight without casualties, if you confine yourself to tip-and-run and hasty demolitions and ambuscades of small isolated enemy units, while somebody else holds up the enemy's real fighting force and does all the dirty work.

At any rate, after riding with Talal and two of his guards, Halim and Faris, as far north of Deraa as Mezerib on the Palestine railway, Lawrence walked right into the town of Deraa with no more disguise than Halim's old clothes (instead of his own silk garments and gold ornaments) and accompanied only by the old man, Faris. As they walked through the town, they were stopped by Turkish soldiers, who brushed Faris aside but told Lawrence that he was wanted by the Bey. In the evening it turned out that the Bey was a pederast, who had seen from the window what he probably supposed was a young Circassian—Lawrence's curious arrested development still made him look much younger than he was. It was a horrible predicament, for, if he had been discovered to be a British officer not in uniform, his status would obviously have been that of a spy, and his fate that of death by torture. When Lawrence repulsed the Bey's more intimate advances, he was hit in the face with slippers and then savagely flogged. According to the rather lurid narrative in *Seven Pillars*, Lawrence endured set after set of lashings, remembering even to cry out in anguish in Arabic. When he was completely broken, his tormentors seemed satisfied, and desisted. Later, when the Bey called for him again, they threw water on him, wiped his face, and carried him, retching and crying for mercy, to where the Bey lay in bed. According to this version, the Bey turned from him in loathing " as a thing too torn and bloody for his bed." Lawrence was therefore taken away to an outer room, where his wounds were dressed and he was told that the door to the next room was unlocked. At dawn he managed to escape.[44]

But is that the whole truth? There exists a letter from him to Charlotte Shaw, in which he confesses that he had failed to put down the whole truth, although he had striven hard to force himself to do so. The truth was (he admits in this letter) that he had not been able to endure, and, to escape further torture of flogging, had yielded to the Bey's pederasty and so secured respite and ultimate escape.[45]

But the story, at once so pitiful and so nauseous, has been doubted by some who have been perhaps unable to endure the thought of this degradation of their hero. Now, as we have constantly had to note, Lawrence could very seldom resist making small episodes into a startling tale, and would even invent them. May this not be the case with the Deraa flogging? The whole of the *Seven Pillars* is so over-written in its self-conscious striving to be " titanic " that there may indeed be a heightening of the situation and a working up of lurid details. There is no way of saying, and the narrative may (for once) be exactly true: and there is decisive evidence (as we shall see later) that Lawrence had at some time suffered such a flogging.[46]

In 1933 Lawrence told Liddell Hart that he was still able to ride after the outrage.[47] But he had continued to walk until he fainted away during his 1911 dysentery or typhoid. And St. John Philby has given a glimpse of how Lawrence liked to display his endurance.

In winter they had to travel on an engine, and, while everyone else stood "cowering as near the boiler as possible against the icy wind and driving rain," Lawrence stood on the footplate for two or three hours enduring, for no particular reason except to impress his companions, the bitter fury of cold and wet.[48]   It therefore seems quite possible that, after a punishment which would have disabled a man less wirily tenacious, Lawrence was able to walk and even to ride without betraying his secret.   Yet there are one or two details left unexplained.   The wounds were bandaged by "an Armenian dresser"[49] before he escaped; but was the bandage never changed? Lawrence could not have changed it himself, the secret would hardly have been safe with an Arab, and an Army doctor would have ordered him into hospital.   He must therefore have taken the risks of infection in a climate where the least scratch is likely to fester.   Again, in an Eastern village, everything is known.   Halim (one of the Arabs with Lawrence) had gone into Deraa and, from the lack of rumour, knew that the truth of Lawrence's identity was undiscovered.[50]   But how was it that Halim did not learn that his British officer friend had been flogged?   Perhaps the fact was known all along to a select few, whose natural sympathy for so tragic a disaster would go far to explain the particular favour with which Lawrence was treated.   But this is mere speculation.   There is no evidence.   If Lawrence himself revealed his misfortune, it would surely have been only to Hogarth.   On the other hand, when you consider how all-powerful the motive of vanity was with Lawrence, it seems equally possible that at the time he concealed the flogging, even though in the end his romantic exhibitionism craved the partial and literary confession in *Seven Pillars*, completed afterwards by the letter to Mrs. Shaw.

CHAPTER SIX

Aᴀfter three years of preparations and three months of fighting, the British forces based on Egypt had gradually advanced and, by the 8th December, 1917, had captured Jerusalem—at a cost. The fighting had been severe, through very difficult mountain country and under bad weather conditions. The figures of casualties in the Official History give those of the Turks for the months of November and December (61 days) and of the British for the 6 weeks from the 27th October to the 15th December (49 days), so are not strictly and exactly comparable. The British casualty reports for their period show losses of 18,928, of whom 16,862 were British, 1,138 Australians and New Zealanders, and 928 Indian. The killed were 2,509, and the missing 1,721, though how many of the latter were prisoners is not stated. For their longer period, the Turks reported losses of 28,443, of whom 3,518 were killed and 15,460 missing. The number of Turkish prisoners reported by the British was over 12,000 so that of the missing over 3,000 were either killed and never identified or managed to escape into concealment.[1] If you consider that the Turks started the war with about 700,000 men, that the heaviest losses of their best troops were at the Dardanelles and in the Caucasus, that there was another British Army fighting in Irak, and that this loss of 28,000 was due to continuous fighting, you will see how exaggerated are the claims that the " Arab Revolt " and Lawrence's military activities (whatever they may have been) had a decisive or even considerable effect on the war. The total number of prisoners accounted for in the 660 pages of Seven Pillars (before Allenby's September, 1918, break-through delivered them a mob of disordered fugitives to kill or capture almost at will) is just over 1,000, of whom 600 were taken on what one cannot help thinking was really Auda's expedition to and capture of Akaba. After the first 5,000 prisoners* taken in the surprise of 1916 (at least half of them due to Abdulla's lucky coup at Taif), the casualties inflicted by " the Arabs " were very small until Allenby's September, 1918, victory.

Trains most certainly were blown up and Turks in them killed or mangled, three or four desert convoys were captured, railway posts were attacked and destroyed, successful little actions like Abu el Lissal, Tafileh and Maulud's night attack near Petra occurred, Faki Pasha and his garrison were more or less held to Medina, but to claim that these spasmodic and comparatively trifling efforts had any serious bearing on the war with Turkey, let alone on the greater war beyond, is as absurd as the comparison of the Arab rebellion to the " running sore " of Napoleon's war in Spain. The Emperor at the height of the struggle had 350,000 men in Spain, and at a minimum his losses averaged 100 a day for 6 years. His marshals had to fight the (frequently defeated) regular armies of Spain and Wellington's undefeated Anglo-Portuguese, as well as innumerable guerrilla fighters, both Portuguese and Spanish, with such leaders as Trant, Robert Wilson, Don Julian Sanchez, Mina, Porlier, Temprano, El Empecinado. There was no question of these partisans joining whichever side won, no need to bring them out with " horsemen of St. George " (i.e. gold sovereigns), no need to allow their leaders to take lucky dips of a handful of gold for each successful feat, or of scattering as soon as plunder was seized. The Spanish guerrilla warfare was horribly savage but not venal, and it was both heroically brave and effective. As soon as a French army moved, it was cut off from its base, and letter-carriers without armed guards failed to get through—Masséna once had to send a whole battalion with General Foy to make sure that envoy and letter got through to the Emperor. On the other hand, Wellington received so many captured letters that he was constantly informed of the enemy's plans, and grew so conscience-stricken at intercepting so many of King Joseph's private letters when the King's children were ill that he sent a trumpeter under a white flag to tell the King they had recovered. There was no Arab rising in the rear of the Turkish Army in Palestine —which on a big enough scale with determined leaders would really

---

* According to *Military Operations* (Vol. 2, p. 429) the *total* of all Turkish prisoners for the whole area between Tafileh and Medina up till August 1918, was 6,000.

have accomplished something—but only raids of a few score men, rail and telegraph wire cuttings.

Indisputably, guerrilla warfare can cause immense vexation and loss to the regular forces of an occupying power, especially when as widespread and determined as was the case in Spain in 1808-13. If the Arabs had risen and, in spite of all efforts at suppression, had continued guerrilla warfare over all the area claimed by Feisal at the Peace Conference, they would indeed have been a valuable aid to their British allies. But the revolt was limited to the Hejaz (which was too far off and too worthless, except for sentimental religious reasons, to be worth the Turkish effort of recovery) and to desert areas close to the British Army, from which small raids could be made with comparative impunity. Beyond those areas, where there was real danger to be faced and real damage to be done, the Arabs did nothing but talk and conspire. Their "movement" spread only because Allenby advanced; and the world is still told that Allenby advanced because their movement spread. The Arab guerrillas were not an essential part of the British 1914-18 campaigns in the Middle East as they were of Wellington's in the Peninsula. Nor did Wellington ever make the mistake of thinking a war can be won by guerrillas alone —even the Boers couldn't do that. In his panegyric of Lawrence's alleged strategic genius and achievements, Liddell Hart argues that Wellington's early victories had been " profitable because they drew the French towards him in Portugal " and so helped the Spanish guerrillas " to tighten their grip on other parts," but that his 1812 victories caused the French to concentrate and thereby the war was prolonged. The decisive factor was not the guerrillas but Napoleon's 1812 withdrawal of good French troops and the cessation of reinforcements. And as to great victories prolonging the war—well, from Roliça to Salamanca was four years all but a few weeks; only eleven months after Salamanca came Vittoria which threw out of Spain all the French armies except Suchet's in Catalonia. Was that " prolonging the war "?

The line between guerrilla warfare and banditry is always hard to draw (with Lawrence's Bedouin friends particularly so), and, if prolonged, guerrilla warfare always tends to lapse into that endless class warfare of criminals against society which compels every state to maintain a regular army of police which checks but cannot exterminate it. Strange indeed is the fact that one of the most orderly countries in the world should, as a legacy of its foreign wars, have bequeathed so much banditry to other countries.

Though the various forces of " the Arabs " had some military importance, their strength has been greatly exaggerated, and their real significance was political. Possibly on Lawrence's advice, Feisal was being groomed as the native candidate for the throne of Syria—he would keep out the French and be amenable to English influence. Feisal had with him about 12,000 armed tribesmen and his small, slow-moving " regular army " of 600; yet in 1917 Feisal had been grandly appointed an Army Commander (Allenby's own rank in France), though no British general under Allenby held that rank. While commanding very much larger numbers of regular soldiers, Bulfin, Chauvel and Chetwode ranked only as Corps Commanders. Everything was done to render Feisal independent of his father, Hussein; and it is easy to see why. If Feisal could be installed after the war as " native king " of Syria, in place of the French, he would play the same game of collaboration with the English that he did eventually in Irak. There is evidence that Allenby placed no real reliance on his " Army Commander " and the " Prince of Mecca " as a flank guard. As already recorded, when he believed that the enemy was about to bring Fakri and the Medina garrison back for service in the field, Allenby at once sent Colonel Wilson to persuade Ali and Abdulla to take action which would have pinned Fakri and his men to Medina. When that failed and Lawrence and Feisal showed that they either could not or would not *effectively* cut the Hejaz railway, Allenby sent Colonel Dawnay, who did the work so thoroughly that the railway remained derelict for many years.*

The political basis of the Foreign Office exaggeration of the " Arab effort " and of Lawrence of Arabia can be traced clearly at the Peace Conference. All readers of Lawrence's narrative will remember how he stresses continually that the Arab " victories " were obtained with very few casualties. If you believe him, the casualties of the whole Akaba expedition amounted only to " two killed and several wounded."[2] Yet at the Peace Conference, Feisal presented a statement (possibly written by Lawrence) which claimed that " the Arab

* For a succinct and objective account of Colonel Dawnay's operations, see *Military Operations*, Vol. 2, pp. 406-7.

army" had "lost heavily, some 20,000 men having been killed."³ It would be interesting to see the casualty lists and to learn at what actions these losses were incurred. Later on, President Wilson (evidently believing the propaganda thrust on him) said in Allenby's presence that Feisal "from first to last had probably had 100,000 men,"⁴ and all Allenby said was that "he never had so many at one time"! Whereupon Wilson went on to say that "nevertheless, from first to last, France would have to count on having 100,000 troops against her."⁵

This predominantly political importance of "the Arab war" is the obvious explanation of why Allenby so lightly brushed aside Lawrence's failure either to cut the Yarmuk valley bridge or to secure, as he had promised, any effective support from "the tribes" in that or any other area. It will be remembered that, long before Allenby came out to Palestine, Hogarth or the Arab Bureau had arranged to transfer Lawrence from the War Office to the Foreign Office to save him from the wrath of the "regulars" he had offended; so that, from Allenby's point of view, Lawrence was not a soldier but a Foreign Office official in costume. Lawrence himself tells us that Allenby was so pleased with his own victory and capture of Jerusalem that he easily allowed Lawrence to pass over his failure.⁶ After several days at Azrak, Lawrence had returned in leisurely style to Akaba, whence in early December he was flown to Allenby's headquarters north of Gaza. On the 8th December, Jerusalem was captured, and Mark Sykes, with his "catholic" imagination,⁷ planned elaborately Allenby's official entry on the 11th. Why Lawrence was invited to be one of the small group of staff officers (instead of Newcombe or Joyce or Davenport) attending Allenby has never been explained, but attend he undoubtedly did, dressed in borrowed uniform, supposedly as Staff Major to Clayton, Political Officer in Palestine and military supervisor of the Arab Bureau.

It is comforting to learn that Lawrence felt his entry into Jerusalem was "the supreme moment of the war."⁸ According to the Official History, Lawrence walked with Clayton and Monsieur Georges Picot, the civil representative of the French Government;⁹ but, according to Lord Wavell's recollections, Lawrence walked with him and was greatly amused by his borrowed uniform and temporary appointment.¹⁰ Lord Wavell praises him for barely mentioning his ride to the Yarmuk bridge and his " unlucky failure " there.

But what was M. Georges Picot doing there, " permitted by Allenby "[11]—such are Lawrence's gracious words—to accompany the victors? He was merely the High Commissioner for France, as Sir Mark Sykes for England, appointed to carry out that part of the Sykes-Picot agreement relating to Palestine—namely the setting up of an international civil administration at Jerusalem, in accordance with Clause 3 of the agreement. Russia not being represented owing to the revolution, the task remained for France and England. Allenby evaded this obligation by setting up a " provisional " military government and appointing as " military governor " of Jerusalem a Foreign Office official, Ronald Storrs.

As Picot and Storrs had just arrived from France together, it seems unlikely that Picot and his government were deceived, especially since Storrs' military administration continued after the Armistice until the 1st July, 1920.[12] The contention of British officials in the Middle East was that " the defection of Russia " had cancelled the Sykes-Picot agreement. According to General Brémond, he was with George Lloyd when the news came through of the murder of Czar Nicholas II, whereupon Lloyd remarked: " That lets us out, but in any event we should never have allowed the Russians to establish themselves in Constantinople." And yet, as Brémond reflects, there was a signed treaty—but a different mentality from the legalistic French.[13] On the 15th December, Storrs had warned Sykes that Picot was not at all pleased with the position in Palestine.[14] Five days later, Storrs found Picot " bitter," because Allenby had not presented " the notables " to the French civil representative as he had to the French and Italian military representatives, because no French guard had been mounted at the Holy Sepulchre, and because no progress had been made in setting up the Anglo-French civil administration.[15] All the way out from France, Picot had been accepted as French High Commissioner for Palestine—by Italians, Greeks and the British Navy—but not by Allenby, who presumably acted under instructions.

Lawrence has dramatised this situation in a lively but spiteful description of an alleged " scene " between Allenby and Picot, the object of which is to ridicule Picot and the French attempts to carry out the terms of the Sykes-Picot agreement. It is characteristic of

Lawrence and his group that nobody could profess a loftier morality and a more exacting scrupulosity in keeping to the uttermost the promises they said he had been ordered to make to " the Arabs," whereas they are cheerfully exultant and derisive whenever they succeed in breaking promises made to the French. At the Peace Conference, Lord Curzon described the agreement authorised by his predecessor as " a sort of fancy sketch to suit a situation that had not then arisen, and which it was thought extremely unlikely would ever arise."[16] Passing lightly over the implied defeatism as well as the frivolity of a government which in war-time wasted its time and that of its allies in drawing up and signing " fancy sketches," one cannot avoid noting that, when this extremely unlikely situation began to come true, their first thought was how to evade the agreement by avoiding the Palestine condominium—i.e., they intended to keep Palestine for themselves. According to Lawrence, the bicker between Allenby and Picot occurred at the luncheon after the Jerusalem entrance ceremony. On the face of it this seems an unlikely place to be chosen for a diplomatic conversation, but Picot was so outraged by the pointed insult to the civil representative of France in not introducing him to the " notables," that he may have chosen to make a protest by implication before the military representatives of Italy and France. Where Lawrence strains credulity is in making a senior diplomat, who had negotiated treaties, fall into the common French journalists' trifling blunder of calling the former Foreign Secretary " Sir Grey,"—hastily corrected by Picot to " Sir Edward Grey "—the less probable since at that time Sir Edward had been for 18 months Lord Grey, a fact of which Lawrence's narrative seems quite unaware.[17] Whether or no this " scene " occurred as Lawrence asserts, the fact is that during the week following the capture of Jerusalem a quarrel of interests was started which, in Lloyd George's words, " after the victory · · · almost provoked an open rupture between the British and French governments."[18]

Lawrence's table of movements shows that he did not return to Akaba until the 25th December, after more than three weeks' absence. He then had before him just over nine months of service before he left for England. But there were considerable gaps of time, when he left Feisal's forces and was in Egypt or in Palestine or at sea. On the 21st February he puts himself at Beersheeba, with visits to Cairo and Jerusalem; he was at Akaba on the 4th March but at sea again on the 6th, and did not return to Akaba until the 15th March—a period of 22 days. On the 27th April he was at sea again, and then shuttling between Cairo, Jerusalem and G.H.Q., until the 21st May when he returned to Akaba—a period of 26 days. Three weeks later, on the 10th June, he was again at sea and shuttling between Cairo, Alexandria and G.H.Q., with a voyage down the Red Sea to Jidda on a diplomatic mission (in which he failed) to Hussein, and he did not return to Akaba until the 28th July—a period of 48 days. Thus, during the last 9-10 months of the war, Lawrence was absent from the Arab forces and Feisal for periods amounting to 13-14 weeks, or about one-third of the time. It is surely a peculiar sort of " general "[19] who during a war spends one-third of his time away from his troops; and the visits to Cairo, where the Arab Bureau still had its headquarters, were much more frequent than the visits to G.H.Q. Lawrence during this period was eleven times in Cairo and three times at G.H.Q., which suggests a possible ratio between his political and military activities.

Nevertheless, on his return from Jerusalem, Lawrence brought orders from Allenby that Feisal's forces were to move up from the Akaba area to Tafileh, which is to the south of the Dead Sea. The reason for this move is obvious. Allenby's advance had brought his forces almost level with Amman, so that much of the Hejaz Railway, with Turkish forces he then estimated or over-estimated at about 20,000, lay to his flank and rear. He could not make the further advance—to Damascus and Aleppo!—which Lloyd George was urging on him, and leave this force behind to attack his rear. Theoretically it was possible for the Turks to bring back Fakri from Medina, to collect the various railway posts and to concentrate on Maan for an attack or destructive raid on Allenby's communications—and intelligence indicated that the enemy was actually planning something of the sort, though from the arm-chair viewpoint one would think that the great distances involved, the difficulty of the terrain and the observation of Ali and Abdulla would give plenty of warning. But Allenby evidently was worried about it, and determined not to attempt the forward move (for which he was to be given additional Indian divisions) until the Hejaz railway forces were dealt with. Hence Colonel Wilson's unsuccessful attempt to persuade Ali and Abdulla to attack Medina in December, 1917, and hence Allenby's insistence in his letters to the war cabinet that, after the capture of Jericho, his next move must be the destruction of the Hejaz railway.[20] The bringing forward of Feisal's forces (or part of them) was to use them as a flank guard or at any rate a screen of scouts, while later in the year Allenby possibly hoped that they would be able to carry out Lawrence's promises and raise the local Bedouins to aid his attack on Amman.

When Allenby ordered the move to Tafileh, Lawrence as usual went beyond him by suggesting that they might join forces with him at the north end of the Dead Sea and move their headquarters from Akaba to the Jordan Valley—which suggestion, it is hardly necessary to say, was never carried out.[21]

The winter of 1917-18 was very cold and snowy in the mountainous regions over which Feisal's forces had now to operate in accordance with Allenby's orders. Just before the New Year, 1918, Sharif Nasir attacked and captured the station of Jurf (between Maan and Hesa) with 200 prisoners. He then made a march through snow and took Tafileh and its garrison. This result had been accomplished by Beni Sakr Bedouins and one mountain gun. About the middle of January, Lawrence and Said turned up, bringing about 100 of Jaafar's "regulars" and two more mountain guns. Whereupon Hamid Fakri Bey with "three weak battalions," 100 cavalry and 2 mountain howitzers started out on the 23rd January to attack them. This led to an engagement grandly described by Lawrence as "the Battle of Seil el-Hasa" (others call it Tafileh), in which the Turks were defeated and Hamid Fakri Bey was killed. The accounts of this battle are all by Lawrence and consist of: A preliminary despatch (undated), published in *The Arab Bulletin* for 11th February, 1918; another despatch, dated "Tafila, January 26th"; an article in the *Army Quarterly* for April, 1921; and the elaborate account in *Seven Pillars*, which is also reproduced in *Revolt in the Desert*. The description occupies about 3,000 words in *Seven Pillars*, but I shall endeavour to summarise the essential.

The Sharifians were unprepared, and Lawrence says he judged Said's position a bad one, and persuaded him to send up 2 machine-guns to support an outpost line of 30 Howeitat and 30 peasants. They drove back the Turkish cavalry, but lost a machine-gun and 5 crew killed, and when Lawrence arrived he could only order a retreat to be covered by the horsemen. On his way up he had told his bodyguard to occupy the south-western ridge of the Tafileh valley, sending urgently to Said to bring up all available men and machine-guns, including 2 fusils-mitrailleuses manned by Pisani's French Mohammedans. This new position held up the Turkish advance. An Arab regular officer, Rasim Bey, with 80 horses, worked round one Turkish flank; about a hundred villagers crept to within 200 yards of the other flank; Lawrence's guns fired 22 rounds of shrapnel, and he launched " a frontal attack of 18 men, 2 Vickers and 2 large Hotchkiss."[22] The villagers killed the machine-gunners, the horsemen charged, and Lawrence advanced the infantry with their banners in the centre.[23]

In his second report on the battle, Lawrence says he paced the distance between the first and second ridges occupied, and found the range to be 3,100 yards. He says they " replied with Vickers and Hotchkiss " machine-gun fire, and in *Seven Pillars* says that knowing the range they elevated their Vickers, "blessing their long old-fashioned sights," and " bothered their exposed lines with hits and ricochets." The effective range of 1914-18 machine-guns was up to 1,750 yards; the most extreme range 2,900. That distance, 2,900 yards, is the extreme limit of a Vickers sighting. British rifles were sighted from 200-2,000 yards. A machine-gun action at 3,000 yards is an innovation. Or is this the " bitter parody " which Lawrence afterwards claimed?[24]

The Arab losses are given by Lawrence as 25 killed and 40 wounded. Estimates of the Turkish losses vary. According to Lawrence, Hamid Fakri Bey was "the general commanding" the Turkish 48th Division;[25] according to the Turks, he was a Lt.-Colonel.[26] Lawrence says 500 Turks were killed and 250 taken prisoner.[27] Brémond reports 400 killed and 300 prisoners.[28] *Military Operations* says 200 prisoners and perhaps 300 killed,[29] and Antonius confirms *Military Operations*.[30] You would think they might at least have been able to count the prisoners and agree on a total. The Turkish account says the whole of their force numbered 600, that it was defeated and Hamid Bey killed, and that 21 officers and 420 men returned to Kerak, which makes total casualties of 159.[31]

For his services on this occasion, Lawrence received the Distinguished Service Order. Lord Wavell recommends Lawrence's account of the engagement as " one of the best descriptions of a battle ever penned."[32] Maps of the battle, with turning movements and symmetrical advances worthy of Aldershot, will be found in *Military Operations* and Captain Hart's book. By a curious coincidence, there is a documentary puzzle here as over the occupation of Akaba. It will be recalled that in the Akaba case Lawrence afterwards confessed that his original report had been suppressed from publication in *The Arab Bulletin* and from the knowledge of the War Office and Foreign Office, while his claims to have conceived and directed the expedition are denied by Antonius on the authority of Arab sources, including apparently King Feisal. In the Tafileh case we are told by Graves—and Lawrence did not object—that the report was " a parody, like the battle itself,"[33] which statement is echoed by Captain Hart.[34] Lawrence himself bears this out—the report was " meanly written for effect," it was full of " quaint smiles and mock simplicities," and so forth.[35]

This is a curious confession—or boast. Now, there are parodies of style and parodies of content and of both, but no one unwarned would ever have suspected any of these forms of parody in Lawrence's two reports, which are no different in style or content from all his other reports. And even when warned, none but the obsequious Lawrence worshipper has ever discovered the parody unless it lies in the absurd story of a machine-gun duel at 3,100 yards. The *Seven Pillars* account, written years later, is different, and may perhaps be a parody or perhaps merely self-conscious and pretentious. Undoubtedly to quote Clausewitz, Foch and Masséna in the account of a " battle " in which the " General " launches a " frontal attack " of 18 men,[36] either shows an attempt at humour or a prodigious lack of it. But, it may be asked, what right has any officer who, on his own showing, has just assumed responsibility for 65 casualties to be funny about it on paper ?

Lawrence did not remain for long on the scene of his triumph. Tafileh turned out to be cold, snowy and dirty. Inaction and propinquity started tedious quarrels among his followers, and he looked around for an excuse to get away from them. It occurred to him that he could go down to Akaba and collect the gold sovereigns which would be needed for the Bedouin patriots in the spring offensive. True, he might have sent a chit to Joyce asking him to arrange to have the gold sent up, but he decided that it would be " more virtuous " to go down than to suffer the filth and promiscuity of Tafileh.[37] *Où la vertu va-t-elle se nicher?*

After spending three pleasant days with Dawnay and Joyce at Akaba, Lawrence received the gold. It was packed in thirty bags each weighing 22 pounds and containing 1,000 sovereigns, about the equivalent (in paper money) of a year's pay for 1,000 British cannon-fodder tommies. After enduring quite unspeakable hardships on the way up, Lawrence handed all the gold over to Said, explaining that he was to pay out any money that was needed, intending of course that most of it should be kept in hand, as it would not be wanted for some time. Lawrence then rode off on reconnaissance, in spite of the cold weather, and listened to the distant thud of the British and Turkish guns as Allenby's men fought their way to the capture of Jericho. He returned to Tafileh on the 19th February, and learned that he had committed yet another of his blunders in entrusting so much money to the weak-minded Said. The older sheiks had over-persuaded Said to let them get their hands on the money, allegedly for the payment of men who were on the rolls, but had in fact done nothing, and consequently every sovereign had gone, and with them the indispensable funds for future action. Lawrence decided that he must throw up his post; and, after dismissing his bodyguard, set off for G.H.Q., to confess that he had lost the 30,000 gold pounds entrusted to him.[38]

It is a curious fact that though Hogarth was the effective Director of the Arab Bureau at Cairo (Clayton being up at G.H.Q.), and must have seen Lawrence on each of his numerous visits, very little is said about him in *Seven Pillars*. Indeed, he is not mentioned for 443 pages of that great work until this contretemps when a remarkable coincidence, or perhaps a telephone message, found him waiting for his distressed protégé on the station platform. Lawrence poured out to Hogarth the story of his latest blunder and his distresses—he had made a mess of things, his judgment was sick, he wanted a smaller part elsewhere, he was tired to death of free will and longed for irresponsibility, he had been riding 1,000 miles a month on camels and had been forced to fly in dangerous aeroplanes, in his last five actions he had been wounded, and he now had to force himself when under fire, he had been hungry most of the time, he felt the Arab war was a fraud on his part, he had suffered from frost and dirt, his will was gone and he was afraid to be alone.[39]

Here was a come-down for the uncrowned king of Arabia, a dismal change in comparison with "quips from Clausewitz"[40] in the clamour of battle, and Hogarth must have been somewhat dismayed by this sudden change of his protégé from the successor of Saladin to a querulous neurotic with a bunch of real and imaginary distresses. It was a peculiar situation, for after all Lawrence had wanted the war. Hogarth must have reflected that little was to be gained by taking a neurotic to the army doctors of those days—who were capable of assuring a collapsing patient that he looked as if he hadn't a nerve in his body—and that such a tale would not go down very well with the Commander-in-Chief, who always lives on the legend that everyone in his command is as keen as mustard, if not keener. Hogarth made a wise and fatherly decision—he took Lawrence to have lunch with Clayton where, with witnesses present, Lawrence was most unlikely to repeat his confession.

Hogarth may also have warned him not to say anything about the wasted gold. At any rate Lawrence did not mention it, and listened to Clayton's talk of General Smuts' visit and of the reinforcements which were to come for the great spring offensive which was to knock Turkey out of the war. This lunch apparently occurred on the 21st February, 1918, exactly one calendar month before the great German break-through on the Somme dismissed all these strategic pipe dreams to oblivion. Lawrence later saw Allenby, and asserted that, given 700 transport camels, Feisal's forces would capture Maan—which they never did capture, until, under pressure of Allenby's September advance, the town was abandoned by Turks and Germans.

But what of Tafileh? In this change of plans it had become unimportant, and Said was abandoned to his fate. Two Turkish columns attacked the town and Said was defeated in engagements described by Liman von Sanders as "violent but successful." But, as the authors of *Military Operations* remark, perhaps with not wholly unintentional irony, "as Major Lawrence had quitted Tafila . . . little is known of the engagements which followed."[41]

But it so happens that the French adjutant Trabelsi, who had been present at the "battle" of Tafileh with 26 men, remained with Said, who sent the French troops out with 300 Bedouins. On the

3rd they ran into a force of 3,000 Turks and some Austro-Germans, artillery and three planes. At the first shell-burst the Bedouins fled, but Trabelsi and his men held out until evening, when all their ammunition was gone, and they retired, bringing pay-books from dead Germans and 7 captured horses. Next day, Said with 4,000 men came out to fight, but at night the searchlights frightened the Bedouins, who fled and plundered Tafileh. On the 5th February, Said set fire to Tafileh and retreated.[42]

The citation for the award of the Distinguished Service Order to Lawrence runs thus :

> " For conspicuous gallantry and devotion to duty in an engagement. He showed splendid leadership and skill and was largely responsible for the success of the action in which 300 prisoners, two field guns and twenty-three machine guns were captured.

It will be seen that the award was made on the basis of the report which Lawrence himself described as a " bitter parody."

Let us end this chapter by briefly disposing of another Lawrence story that has grown deep roots—that the enemy offered a reward ranging (according to the teller) from £5,000 to £50,000 for the capture of the great guerrilla leader, Lawrence. No evidence for this is forthcoming beyond Lawrence's assertion, and not one of the persons in Arabia at the time claims to have seen this notice. According to one version Lawrence seated himself directly underneath one of the reward notices, but was not recognised. Later, with a smile he said that was an exaggeration. By whom was this large reward offered ? Either by Jemel Pasha or Liman von Sanders, neither of whom in his war memoirs even mentions the person on whose head he is alleged to have placed this large, not to say unique, price. To whom was it addressed ? The Bedouins and most of the poorer Arabs could not read. And where ? In the desert ? If so, who would read it ? If in the towns, who was going to win the reward ? But the unresolved mystery is how the two enemy leaders came to offer so substantial a reward for a person of whom either they had never heard or whom they did not consider sufficiently important to mention in their books.

CHAPTER SEVEN

WHEN, AFTER an absence of three weeks, Lawrence returned to Akaba on the 15th March (1918), his situation was different from that in which he had been on leaving. Whether or not his main difficulty was (as he claimed) that he felt he was defrauding the Arabs is very doubtful, for after all the Bedouins at least were quite content, and only praying that the unexampled prosperity of the war might last for ever. As for the comparatively few politically-minded Arabs—many of them seem to have been far more hostile to the English than to the Turks; and if there is any evidence that Lawrence was ever ordered by any competent authority to make false promises to "the Arabs" or to Feisal, I have not been able to find it. Sykes and Picot, and not Lawrence, were sent to King Hussein to explain away (if they could) the incompatibilities between their agreement and his ambitions. In any case, Lawrence had taken up once more his responsibilities—whatever they were—and returned with the rank of Lieutenant-Colonel, the D.S.O. and an "independent credit" of 300,000 pounds.[1] The 700 camels followed a little later. Such were the advantages of wasting nearly 30,000 gold pounds of public money.

This began the epoch of Lawrence's splendour as an Anglo-Semitic chieftain, and perhaps a few lines should be devoted to this topic.

His private bodyguard, if it had ever really been dismissed, was at once re-formed on a larger scale, consisting of twenty to forty youths between 16 and 25, dressed in the beautiful coloured garments worn by the Bedouins and Aegyl, delicate pastel shades which in 1941 inspired the British tommies to nickname the Bedouin Desert Patrol "Glubb's Girls."[2] His headman, Abdulla abu Saleh, was "a great swell," wearing a " flowered cassock, light-blue Zouave jacket with black braid, and *aba* of soft sheep's wool." Saleh had long corkscrew curls shining with hair oil, and his red and white saddle trappings hung almost to the ground.[3] The bodyguard were quite aware of their reflected importance, and apt to be insolent to the other British officers.[4] What they were paid is nowhere stated, but " gold was nothing accounted of in the days of Lawrence."[5] In those days every tribesman had sovereigns knotted into his clothes, the coast towns were glutted with English gold (as Lawrence himself reported) and the rupee was down to 10-12 to the pound.[6] Brémond saw a Bedouin give a sovereign for a box of matches, and haughtily refuse change.

Lawrence himself had a set of the finest camels available, and his bodyguard were mounted on the best camels that money could buy. His own clothes were most beautiful and expensive. His over-shirt and loose trousers were of pure white silk. On his shoulders he wore a cloak of the softest wool embroidered with gold or silver threads. The souks of Cairo, Damascus, Baghdad, Najaf and even Hail were " ransacked for the finest and most costly products of Arab workmanship " for his adornment. His head-dress was caught up with a head-rope of plum-coloured silk threads bound at intervals with pure gold. Such a head-dress alone cost 50 golden sovereigns, of which 45 were melted down to make the ornaments and five more were paid for the workmanship to Lawrence's Cairo specialist in such work. In addition Lawrence wore a gold belt, in front of which was the curved golden dagger presented to him by Hussein.[7] King Hussein and Feisal undoubtedly were privileged to melt down some of the war-subsidy sovereigns received from the British tax-payer or captured from the enemy* to honour their uncrowned rival, but where did the gold of Lawrence's head-dress come from? He himself explained wearily that he " put all his pay into the show," but British officers were then paid in paper, not in gold.

The mention of this much-publicised gold dagger (which Lawrence afterwards sold in order to repair his cottage) brings up a problem. It is perhaps hardly necessary to say that I am not referring to the legend that the presentation of this dagger symbolised his elevation to the

---

* The dagger is said to have been made from " 150 captured Turkish sovereigns ", but the main source of the Hashemites' gold obviously was the lavish British subsidies. Where were " the Turkish sovereigns " captured ? And by whom ?

dignity of " Sharif." Since " Sharif " is applied only to a descendant of the Prophet this could hardly have been the case. The question is —did Lawrence go to Mecca to order it? It would seem so from a letter to H. R. Hedley, in which Lawrence gives a vague description of Mecca, and says it is " not really so difficult to go there if they know you." He then explains that the fanaticism of some Moslems would be offended by the visit of a non-Moslem and adds coyly: " So if anyone asks me if I've been there, I have to say ' no ' in public; but in private you can guess about it! It mustn't get into the papers. . . ."8 That letter was written in 1920. In 1927 another letter speaks of the dagger and says, " it was made in Mecca, in the third little turning to the left off the main bazaar, by an old Nedji goldsmith whose name I fancy was Gasein."9 And again, in a letter to Wavell in 1923, he says: " Yes, I've promised not to admit the Mecca jest. I did it because I wanted to choose my own gold dagger, and it was not serious for me. Hussein will never forgive it me."10 If we go by Lawrence's calendar of his movements, this Mecca visit could only have happened just after the occupation of Akaba when Lawrence went to Jidda, and had an interview with Hussein. The chronology in his main narrative is as usual vague, but the calendar fixes his stay in Jidda from the 22nd July to 1st August—ten days, certainly long enough both to see the king and to carry out this not very tactful whim.

About this time—early in 1918—the Sharifian forces in Arabia Petræa were taken out of the political control of the Arab Bureau and came under a staff unit of Allenby's headquarters, established in Cairo, and called for some reason "Hedgehog." This was made up of Colonel Alan Dawnay, Captain Barlow, Major Wordie and Captain Bennett. They were officially charged with " Hejaz operations," and set up in Cairo presumably to keep in touch with the Arab Bureau. Even more numerous were the officers with Feisal's small regular army, which now had a double importance. While the Bedouins with whom Lawrence acted were politically essential to Feisal who could not have existed without them, " they could not be depended upon to co-operate in any attack on a fortified place," and were generally useless even in attacks on the railway unless they had artillery support.11 Trained troops were essential, and this of course fitted in perfectly with political plans for the future of Feisal's Syrian kingdom. Even including non-combatants and numerous camp followers, this

" army " never exceeded 3,000, and 600 was about its real fighting
strength. Colonel Joyce commanded the British units, which were
made up of 5 armoured cars under Captain Gilman; a flight of airplanes under Captain Siddons; 2 ten-pounder guns on Talbot cars
under Lieutenant Brodie; 20 Indian machine gunners under Jemadar
Hassan Khan; a company of the Egyptian Camel Corps under
Bimbashi Peake; Transport Corps; Labour Corps (both Egyptian);
and personnel for the radio station at Akaba. The mountain 65's,
about which Lawrence fabricated such dark legends of Brémond's
imaginary " intrigues," had been despatched from France in October,
1917, and at last reached Akaba in February, 1918. These, along with
4 machine-guns and 10 automatic rifles, were manned by Algerian
gunners under Captain Pisani. The " Arab Regular Army " under
Jaafar Pasha was made up theoretically of a brigade of infantry, a
battalion each of Camel Corps and mule-mounted infantry, with
" about 8 guns." Joyce was chief military adviser to Feisal, and had
Major Maynard as second-in-command; Captain Hornby, R.E.,
demolition expert; Major Marshall and Captain Ramsay, medical
officers; and, at the Akaba base, Major Scott, Captain Goslett and
Lieutenant Wood.[12] It will be seen that Lawrence was one of a
considerable group of officers, though he passed himself into legend
as the only important one when he happened to meet two American
reporters, and, being a civilian, permitted himself to be exploited as
the professional soldiers could not and would not. His functions
were still mainly political, but of course he was also chief liaison
officer, sat in on military discussions, accompanied military expeditions or went off on his own with his " guard " and the Bedouins.
" Joyce and Maynard worked out and supervised all these independent
affairs, most of which were suggested or inspired by Lawrence," says
Young.[13] Young had been told by Lawrence that he had been brought
from India at Lawrence's suggestion to take Lawrence's place " in
case anything happened " to him; on which Young comments sar-
castically that there " was never any need or question of his being
replaced, for, even if a second Lawrence could miraculously have
been found, he would not have been needed."[14]
  The only expedition commanded by Feisal in person (after his
early reverses between Medina and the coast) was the attack on
Mudowwara in January, 1918, which Lawrence referred to as a great

expedition which ended unprofitably.[15] Thereafter, Feisal wisely sat back, preparing himself for his hoped-for role of Syrian monarch. Later in the spring, no greater success attended the plan that Lawrence should link up the local Bedouins with Allenby after the British had captured Amman, and that the regular Arab forces should occupy Maan. Colonel Dawnay had come up from Cairo to supervise the Arab movements. According to Brémond,[16] that "superior officer," Colonel Dawnay, never thought the Arabs could take Maan, and, as Lawrence heard that the British had failed also at Amman, there was nothing they could do but retire. There was, however, one possible operation and that was the complete and final destruction of the Hejaz railway between Maan and Medina. In spite of Lawrence's sneers that the British were "dense" about Medina, but that he could not be expected to teach them to be more imaginative,[17] the decision had been made that the line must be destroyed, and Dawnay had been sent to see that it was done. Now there may have been cogency in Lawrence's argument that the best policy was to attack the Maan-Medina section of the Hejaz railway, and leave it just but only just functioning. But, as the authors of *Military Operations* point out: "That in 1917 they ever consciously acted on this principle is improbable; at least it is not put forward in any contemporary appreciation."[18] Precisely so. You will find no mention of it in Lawrence's Arab Bureau reports—it is merely one of the many *ex-post-facto* discoveries put out after the war in *Seven Pillars*.

At the time when Allenby ordered Colonel Dawnay to make a permanent break in the line, he believed he would soon have reinforcements sufficient to launch an attack towards Damascus and even Aleppo. Possibly, if he had known that there was to be the great German victory of March, 1918, in France, with the panic withdrawal of his British divisions, he might not have been so insistent on the railway destruction.

Obviously, Allenby could not advance on Deraa and Damascus and leave to 13,000 Turks the opportunity to concentrate and raid his communications. Dawnay carried out his instructions thoroughly. Stations near Maan were attacked, and about 300 prisoners taken. Then, after the failure at Maan, Dawnay turned his column south, and succeeded in destroying "the whole line from Mudowwara up to Maan," with seven stations, though he failed again to take

Mudowwara. The railway material stored in Medina was at last (April, 1918) used up and that long section of line " remained a ruin for the rest of the war " and for years afterwards.[19]

The period between Dawnay's destruction of the railway and the opening of Allenby's final offensive covers the months from early April, 1918, until late September, during which time not very much happened except for re-organisation and planning. According to Lawrence's table of movements, he was (as already noted) either at Cairo or G.H.Q., or travelling during the period 27th April-21st May and between 10th June-28th July. Thus over ten weeks of the summer were occupied in conferences or rest periods. Some of these journeyings were made by ship, some across country and some by plane. After the war, Lawrence solemnly assured Captain Hart that he had flown " 2,000 hours " during the war, with " seven write-off crashes," which had broken his " collar-bone, wrist and several ribs," and left him with " a rib sticking into lung—so one lung useless and bleeds in heavy exercise."[20]   Now Lawrence was certainly badly smashed up in his Handley-Page accident near Rome in 1919, but what and where the other six crashes were is as difficult to discover as the sixty wounds he talked about. 2,000 operational hours are a lot of flying. Even in those distant days of slow 100-miles-an-hour planes, 2,000 hours would mean about 200,000 air miles and no less than 4 hours a day every day for 500 days. Now, it is certain that Lawrence went out on reconnaissance plane flights even in the Yenbo days, and was often in the air afterwards, either on trips to Cairo or G.H.Q., but is it possible that he flew so much? He himself dates his active service from 1st January, 1917, until the 7th October, 1918, when he reached Cairo on his way back to England. That makes 645 days, from which—if he is to fly 2,000 hours—we must conclude that he was in the air every day except 145 for 4 hours, although his record shows 180 days spent at Cairo, Alexandria and G.H.Q., and on board ship. And what about all the days spent in dashing over the desert on " racing camels " at " 100 miles a day ? " We seem here to be entering that realm of arithmetical romance which included the reading of 50,000 books from the Oxford Union Library.

Lawrence has told with dramatic emphasis how he more or less tricked Allenby into giving him 2,000 camels with which he promised firmly he would put a thousand men into Deraa whenever Allenby wanted.[21]—which he never did, for it was not until the night of the 27th September, when Deraa had been evacuated by all but a small rear-guard and a hospital train of wounded, that the Anaizeh tribesmen —not the Sharifians—broke first into the town. 2,000 camels were a princely gift, and Feisal and the other Arab leaders were understandably delighted—with 700 extra camels they had been able to operate 70 miles ahead of their base, with 2,000 they could pace the British to Damascus and even Aleppo, if the advance reached that far. The political motive is obvious. The one person who was unhappy about this was Young, who was being deprived of the British officers and Egyptian personnel who had looked after the original 700, and so had to find somehow " wild camel-men from Mecca " to take charge of the whole number. Nor did Young approve Lawrence's plan of " putting a thousand men into Deraa " by mounting 1,000 Arab " regulars " on 500 camels and making a sudden dash across the 300 miles to Deraa. Lawrence's " plan " not only omitted all supplies, but forgot the artillery without which the place could not possibly have been taken.[22] Young suggests, with the anguished irony of the man who has to deal with logistics, that Lawrence thought he could take 1,000 regulars to Deraa and back " with their supplies and ammunition tied on with bits of string, and a roll of apricot paste . . . snugly stowed in each of the thousand haversacks."[23] Of course, the whole " plan " was nothing but talk, and never came to anything.

Yet, before the end of March, Allenby must have realised that the German break-through in France meant the postponement of his offensive. By the end of April, he heard from Sir Henry Wilson that the British casualties in France since March 21st had amounted to 225,000; and he had sent off 60,000 of his best troops as reinforcements. Though he received his Indian reinforcements, his whole army had to be reorganised. Inevitably there was a period of waiting and of comparative inaction which affected Feisal's forces as well as the army. Perhaps the most important developments of the period of waiting were political. The propaganda sent out by Feisal and Lawrence had all along maintained that the cause of " Arab freedom " and of Hussein was identical with that of British arms with which they urged active collaboration. This was undoubtedly forthcoming, subject to the fact that the Bedouins were always liable to switch sides if they thought the fortunes of war were going against their temporary allies, though it must be admitted that the Shammar remained faithful to the Turks and Germans up till the end of the war. Even Feisal was not immune from these customs. During the early summer of 1918, there were times when the Germans looked like winning in France, and Feisal was perfectly well aware that the victor on that front would be the victor everywhere. Curiously enough, he waited until the second half of August, when German defeat was assured, before offering to betray the English and take his army to the assistance of the Turkish 4th Army, provided he received "certain assurances from the Turkish government about the formation of the Arab State."[24] Feisal even gave away the essential knowledge, which he must have got from Lawrence, that "the English were preparing a big attack on the coastal sector."[25] Fortunately for the British, the Turks doubted Feisal's good faith, and let the matter drift,[26] while Feisal himself must soon have realised his mistake. Lawrence has given his version of these negotiations, explaining that the Arabs must have some means of seeking agreement with Turkey, adding that his own fear was that England would make a separate peace and thus leave them in the lurch![27]

Arising out of this "Arab propaganda" is the ever-present problem of the alleged false promises to the Arabs which Lawrence made such tremendous play with after the war. It seems hopeless to try to get the facts, through sheer lack of evidence. Hubert Young, who was with Feisal's forces from early in 1918, and afterwards in the Middle Eastern Section of the Foreign Office, says it will never be known whether Lawrence was in fact let down by the British government or whether he promised the Arabs more than he should, adding that he would certainly have exceeded his instructions had he thought "true British interests" demanded it.[28] If he did make such promises, "the Arabs" were fools to believe him, for he certainly had nothing to show that he was authorised by Government to make pledges on its behalf. One might turn Young's phrase and say that, if he thought "Arab interests" were being served, Lawrence would probably not have hesitated to create and exploit a fictitious situation. As I have shown, he had not hesitated to gratify his anti-French and personal spite by writing a violent memorandum against Colonel Brémond, which he knew to be exaggerated and untrue.[29]

There was, however, during June of 1918, a genuine declaration of British intentions and promises which is another instance of the carelessness with which sweeping commitments were made under pressure of war needs, without foresight and without precision of language. Storrs has half-apologised for the McMahon correspondence by telling us that it was put into Arabic by his " little Persian agent, Ruhi," who was " a fair though not a profound Arabist," and checked by Storrs " often under high pressure."[30] That hardly seems a safe or satisfactory method of conducting international negotiations containing far-reaching pledges. This 1918 document was read once by a member of the Arab Bureau (name not given) to a delegation of " seven Arab leaders domiciled in Egypt."[31] This declaration said, among other things, that " His Majesty's Government recognise the complete and sovereign independence of the Arabs inhabiting . . . territories liberated from Turkish rule by the action of the Arabs themselves."[32]

That is an English translation of the Arabic version, but the original English version was seen by Sir Hubert Young at the Foreign Office, on which he remarks that " it at once became clear to me why the Arabs had made such superhuman efforts to win their race with the British cavalry into Deraa, Damascus and Aleppo," and " I understood, too, for the first time why I had so often been asked, after the fall of Damascus, who had really taken the city? Was it the British Army, or was it our Lord Feisal?"[33] Now, Lawrence of course knew about that document, for, in talking to Captain Hart, he referred to the " Cairo promise " that " the Arabs shall keep what they take."[34] In other words, the real object of Lawrence and the Arab army during the final offensive was not to furnish any real military assistance but to rush headlong for evacuated towns and get there first, after the resistance of the enemy had been broken by British troops. Lawrence gave away the political and not military action of the " Arab army " when he told Graves: "What mattered to me was getting the government of Damascus."[35] Hence the violent propaganda for priority of entry (especially into Damascus) which so much puzzled General Barrow, who looked at the operations purely from a soldier's point of view.

There has been printed a political survey by Lawrence (which never appeared in *The Arab Bulletin*), written on Arab Bureau paper, certainly in 1918, and probably in June, as a comment on and answer to this delegation of seven Arabs in Egypt, since they might interfere with his own policy of an Arabia split up into Sharifian kingdoms under English hegemony. According to Lawrence's paper, only the Sharifians had the right to this leadership, because they had conquered a country of 100,000 miles with their own hands! while these others would much prefer to see Syria conquered at the expense of English blood, and so forth, in sophistries too obvious to need refutation. The Sharif, he says, is the one factor in British hands which will enable the British to check " the new fanatical revival in central Arabia," meaning of course, Ibn Saud, who was far indeed from ever being held in check by poor old Hussein. So much for Lawrence's political prophecy. He also asserts in this memorandum that the Germans and " the financial interests that back the Mediterranean-Mesopotamian railway schemes " are trying to raise an Arab party against the Sharif, " because the Sharif is irrecoverably ours "—an interesting admission. They want to prevent the British from making themselves " founders' kin " to the " federated Arab states " which he considers " inevitable." But his last sentence is really the operative one:

> " The success or failure of the Sharifian invasion of Syria—a new operation and a new movement—is going to affect the other phase of European rivalry in the Levant, by determining whose candidate is going to gain control of the trade routes and commercial centres of Western Asia."[36]

Surely that disposes of Lawrence's claim that he was a conscience-stricken martyr to remorse because he had obeyed orders from some unspecified authority and had deceived " the Arabs "? England was to support the Sharif and in Syria his " more plastic son, Feisal "[37] in order to gain control of trade routes and commercial centres. To pose as an outraged martyr for " Arab freedom," with that cynical programme set down in his own hand in June, 1918, was impudent even for Lawrence. The wholly political object of tacking the " Sharifian army " on to the British advance in September, 1918, must now be abundantly clear to any reader.

If there was one person who had no particular illusions about the military value of the Arabs, it was, as Lawrence frankly admits, Allenby. He took no account of them as tactical units, and counted on them—as the Bruce on his camp followers at Bannockburn—only as a phantom force which might frighten the enemy. Again, as Lawrence records, Allenby's chief of staff repeatedly stated—so often and so pointedly that Lawrence got annoyed—that all G.H.Q. wanted or expected of him and his Arabs was "three men and a boy with pistols" outside Deraa on a given date. And that was about all G.H.Q. got. As everybody knows, what the General wished to do was to deceive the enemy into thinking that he intended to attack on his right when he intended to attack on his left. All sorts of extraordinary and ingenious devices for so deceiving the Turks were thought up, as zero day drew nearer; and they may be read of in the official history. Any chance of Fakri bringing his men out of Medina had been wiped out by Colonel Dawnay's demolitions, but to create the impression of acute concern for his right flank, Allenby, in August, 1918, sent Major Buxton and two companies of the Camel Brigade to destroy Mudowwara station and garrison, and to blow the main bridge at Amman. The first succeeded, the second failed. Lawrence did not accompany the Mudowwara raid, but went with them on the northern expedition until they were spotted by a Turkish plane outside Amman, and had to retire without accomplishing anything.

The small regular army in Feisal's area was made up of trained soldiers captured from the Turkish army. They had done well during Dawnay's demolition raids, capturing railway stations and over 300 prisoners, at a cost of 250 casualties, though they had failed to take Maan. This was between the 11th and 19th of April; but they were not very successful during June and July. Thus, Nuri Bey, one of their best officers, with 800 Sharifians and 1,000 Bedouins, 4 guns and 10 machine-guns, helped by English planes and armoured cars, was repulsed from Jerdun by the Turks who had only 400 men, 3 guns and 6 machine-guns.[38]

Meanwhile, in June, Lawrence had put forward another of his fallacious strategical plans, which in the event came near to wrecking the whole "Arab army". His responsibility if any for the British failures at Es Salt and Amman earlier in the year cannot be assessed. While it was his fallacious reports which had created the impression that the local tribes would assist, the blame for believing them must rest wholly on the General—if he did believe them. The ordering of two divisions to France in the middle of one of these actions is surely sufficient excuse for failure. This latest suggestion—for Lawrence flourished by making ingenious suggestions which seldom if ever had practical results—was both political and military. It was simply that Hussein should be asked to hand over to Feisal the regular units of Ali and Abdulla, which Lawrence " bravely " and gravely asserts would have raised them to 10,000 men in uniform. Part of these would keep Maan quiet, 1,000 on camels would attack Deraa-Damascus and 2,000-3,000 would join Allenby at Jericho. The raid on Deraa would compel the enemy to withdraw one or two divisions, and allow Allenby to advance at least as far as Nablus. Lawrence succeeded in getting letters to Hussein from Feisal, Wingate and Allenby, urging this step, which would undoubtedly have advertised to the Turks the pretended threat to their left. Otherwise the merits of the plan were small. There were, in fact, not anything near 10,000 men available, and a large withdrawal might easily have tempted Fakri to a raid on Mecca. Moreover, the Hashemites always went in suspicion of their Wahabite neighbour, the great Ibn Saud. To top his series of clever failures, Lawrence took the long journey to Jidda—and again failed: " I had no more success than I expected."[39] Why, then, waste time in going, except to amuse G.H.Q. with imaginary projects?

That the Grand Sharif or Malik had grave faults and overweening ambitions is undeniable, but he was certainly not the silly old ass Lawrence makes him out. The one Englishman who understood and liked Hussein and was liked by him was Sir Ronald Storrs, whose neat appreciation should be compared with Lawrence's clumsy attempts at contempt. With all his faults, absurdities, little tricks and longings to annex all his neighbours, the Sharif was an Arab gentleman, and cannot be brushed off merely as a vain old fool. If Lawrence had been doing his job as political officer, instead of trying to out-Clausewitz Napoleon—on paper—he would never have made the *démarche* or been snubbed by Hussein on the Jidda-Mecca telephone. Through Lawrence's clever propaganda—and it was very clever—British interest had been turned almost entirely on to Feisal, who now got all the pick of the money, supplies, recruits, artillery and other aid. Hussein had now nothing more to give the British, and more and more was to become a voice vainly calling for the fulfilment of McMahon's rash promises. Hussein was naturally annoyed by

Lawrence's demands, and suspected—not unreasonably—that Feisal, if he ever got to Damascus and established himself there, would do so as the emissary, not of his father, but of England. It was only exasperating a bad situation and courting refusal to ask Hussein to send his troops to Feisal and Allenby. The *démarche* created a situation where Hussein awaited the first opportunity to express his displeasure and if possible to clip Feisal's ambitions. There is so much affectation of fine feeling in Lawrence and his Bureau that, just for the record, it must be observed that Lawrence strenuously urged Wingate to threaten the Malik with a withdrawal of his subsidy if he did not agree to Lawrence's obviously fatuous plan—which Wingate, of course, refused to do. When Hussein saw a chance of asserting himself, he took it. A British decoration to Jaafar, in the citation for which Feisal was described as "Commander-in-Chief of the Northern Hashemite Army," brought a denial of this rank to Feisal* in the king's official newspaper, *The Qibla*. Whereupon Feisal and all the other officers resigned from the Army; but both Young and Brémond pass the affair over lightly, and Young says there was never any real fear that the resignations were serious.[40] Lawrence, who was really responsible for this mess, has given a very dramatic account of it, with the resignation of "our divisional officers and their staffs, with the regimental and battalion commanders"—in an effective army of 600![41] Lawrence claims to have solved the situation by a sort of Ems telegram in reverse, cutting out on his own responsibility the last and operative sentences of one of Hussein's telegrams. He ends the more or less imaginary scene with this dialogue:

FEISAL: The telegram has saved all our honour. I mean the honour of nearly all of us.

LAWRENCE (*demurely*): I cannot understand what you mean.

FEISAL: I offered to serve for this last march under your orders: why was that not enough?

LAWRENCE: Because it would not go with your honour.

FEISAL (*murmuring*): You prefer mine always before your own.[42]

Obviously, no one is in a position to deny—or to affirm—that

* Some accounts say that the officer denounced in the Qibla was not Feisal but Jaafar. It does not seem worth the trouble of verification.

such a dialogue took place and in those words, but did soldiers ever talk to each other like that outside the pages of 19th-century cloak and dagger novels?

Allenby's offensive was being planned for early October, but, in the middle of August, the date was suddenly advanced to the 19th September—"a fearful shock" to Joyce and Young, who were feverishly labouring to arrange supply and transport for the raid towards Deraa. The reason for advancing the date was the turn in the tide of events on the Western front and the beginnings of the final German defeat. Allenby had to hurry up if he was to do something decisive before the whole war ended. It was on the 1st September that Franchet d'Espérey began the attack on Bulgaria which knocked it out of the war in a month, a day before Allenby's Australians entered Damascus.

The instructions to the forces under Feisal were to rendezvous at the oasis of Azrak—about 60 miles from Deraa—with the idea of surrounding that town and railway junction and cutting their communications. The Sharifian regular "army" was on this occasion made up of 450 Sharifian Camel Corps with 20 Hotchkiss machine-guns; Pisani's French battery; two British armoured cars; 4 machine-guns with Gurkha crews; and some Egyptian demolition sappers. They were to be joined by Auda and his Howeitat, Talal with his peasant tribe, and a new ally, Nuri es Shalaan—not to be confused with Nuri Said, a very able officer who had been with Feisal since 1916. Though they were late in starting, they managed to reach El Umtaiye (near Deraa) on the 16th September, within the period set by Allenby. On the 17th, they destroyed 4 miles of railway line north of Deraa, and captured a redoubt with 200 prisoners. The station of Mezerib was destroyed, and further demolitions carried out during the 18th and 19th.[43] On the 20th, Lawrence returned to the base at Azrak, and there learnt of Allenby's break-through, with the capture to date of 7,000 prisoners and 100 guns. Lawrence flew back to G.H.Q. on the plane which had brought this news, to ask for air protection against the 9 German planes in Deraa which were demoralising the Arab forces by their attacks. He was lent two Bristol fighters, and a Handley-Page bomber—the size of which, it was thought, would favourably impress Arab opinion.[44] As a result of the intense pressure by the Arab army, "a few hundred troops

(Turkish), including some Germans, hurriedly despatched by rail from Haifa and Damascus, then occupied Deraa and kept the traffic moving."[45] By the 23rd September, " the Germans had restored communications between Deraa and Samakh, and also north of Deraa."[46]

But already, on the 24th September—only five days after the launching of the attack—the pressure of Allenby's rapid cavalry advance was being felt even as far north as Deraa. The 4th Turkish Army, which had not been attacked, began to retreat—the first contingent of about 300 reaching Mafraq (only about 25 miles south of Deraa) on the night of the 24th, when it was bombed by British planes. Feisal now called up the rather uncertain Bedouins of Nuri es Shalaan, which raised his nominal strength to somewhere about 4,000. The whole force then pressed forward, destroying rails as it went, until it reached Sheik Saad, which is about 15 miles north-west of Deraa. The Bedouins went into action; Talal occupied Ezra; and Auda captured a train with 200 prisoners at Ghazale. On the evening of the 27th September, Deraa was evacuated by the Turco-Germans under the imminent threat of the rapidly advancing 4th Cavalry Division of Allenby's army; the Anaizeh Bedouin got into the town and " spent the night in killing, in burning and looting the station and camps about it."[47]

Atrocities were committed on both sides. When Lawrence and the Sharifians reached the village of Tafas, which was the home of their ally, Talal, they found that all the inhabitants had been massacred, including the women and small children. Lawrence says that he particularly noticed a pregnant woman, who had been forced on to a saw-bayonet,[48] luridly elaborated in the *Seven Pillars* version with sadistic details.[49] Talal thereupon committed suicide by riding straight at the retreating Turks, who " riddled him with machine-gun bullets." The Sharifians and Bedouins found themselves no match for the Germans in the retreating columns of the 4th Turkish Army, and were forced to turn on the Turks, whom, " after a bitter struggle, we wiped out completely. We ordered ' no prisoners ' and the men obeyed, except that the reserve company took 250 men (including many German A.S.C.) alive. Later, however, they found " one of our men with a fractured thigh who had been afterwards pinned to the ground by two mortal thrusts of German bayonets. Then we turned our Hotchkiss on the prisoners and made an end of them."[50]

The spectacle of a British officer encouraging a mass slaughter of prisoners is deplorable. With all his talk of Saladin, Lawrence might then have called to mind the humanity of that hero when at Merj' Ayun, he refused to harm any of his Christian prisoners, though Richard I of England had treacherously murdered all the Saracen prisoners before Saladin's eyes.[51] One can at least report that Lord Winterton and Captain Pisani, in the name of their two countries, protested strongly to Nuri, and managed to save a great many prisoners.[52] Lawrence did not associate himself with this protest. How could he when he had approved the slaughter?

Patrols of the 4th British Cavalry Division made contact with the main body of Arabs early in the morning of the 28th September, though late on the night of the 27th, a few mounted Sharifians had ridden into the British bivouacs. At 9.30 that morning, their Commander, General Barrow, met Lawrence, who had delayed in order to shave and to change into clean clothes—after which he accused Barrow's column of wasting time in watering their horses!—and at their interview " behaved with histrionic nonchalance."[53] Why? General Barrow had served in France and, as he tells us, knew the obliterating destruction of massed artillery, but he confesses with some horror that he had seen no sight like Deraa that morning— " the whole place indescribably filthy, defiled and littered " with dead, dying and wounded Turks, some crying feebly for water, all who were conscious " gazing with eyes that begged for a little of the mercy it was hopeless for them to ask of the Arabs."[54]

While Lawrence thought only of posing—clean-shaved on his camel among the cavalry[55]—Barrow was looking with distaste on the spectacle of the Arabs looting a long ambulance train, " tearing off the clothing of the groaning and stricken Turks, regardless of gaping wounds and broken limbs, and cutting their victims' throats."[56] One of General Barrow's staff tells me that in addition, " nameless mutilations " were being inflicted on these helpless wounded. And let me interject that this Deraa atrocity was not an isolated case. On the 28th—the same day—the Australians came on the Maan garrison in retreat near Amman. The Turks offered to surrender, but only on condition that they were protected against the atrocities of

Lawrence's friends, the Beni Sakr. The Australian commander accepted their surrender, threatened to shoot the Arabs if they attacked the prisoners, and throughout the night Turks and Australians stood to arms side by side against the Bedouins! When the prisoners marched next day, the Australian commander allowed two battalions of Anatolian Turks to retain their arms and ammunition to protect themselves and the other prisoners from the Arabs.[57]

Thus General Barrow was not the only officer to take measures against the Arab methods of making war, and it is absurd to pretend that his angry reaction to the horrors of Deraa was only the petulance of a narrow-minded regular confronted with the superbly irregular military genius of Lawrence. Barrow asked Lawrence to get his Arabs out of Deraa—"this place is in a hell of a mess." Lawrence retorted that he couldn't, and that anyway the murders, robberies and tortures of Deraa were the Arabs' idea of war. "It's not our idea of war," said Barrow, "and if you can't remove them, I will." Lawrence replied: "If you attempt to do that, I shall take no responsibility for what happens." "That's all right," the General told him, "I'll take the responsibility." Barrow's men brushed the Arabs away without difficulty, and then posted sentries to guard the train of wounded.[58] Naturally, not a word of all this occurs in Lawrence's accounts; on the contrary, he loses no opportunity of sneering at Barrow, and passed statements by Graves which General Barrow describes as either "not in accordance with the facts," or "entirely suppositious."[59] It is only Barrow's word against Lawrence's? Good enough. But, on their records, which do you believe?

No military commander sets out with the primary intention of binding up the enemy's wounds and behaving chivalrously to prisoners —even if he has read "all the manuals of chivalry." His duty is to fight and to win, but in fighting and winning to spare when possible the vanquished, to bind up the wounds of the fallen. It is the little he can do to mitigate the vast brutality of war. Graves says that Lawrence's most original contribution lay in his theories of modern war—let us hope not in his practice of war. Barrow and the Australian Colonel Gregory were not modern intellectuals, but "Victorians," with an obsolete code of pity for the fallen. Arab chivalry had no time for such trifling; their own badly wounded men, on the rare occasions when they occurred, were finished off by a revolver shot in the head, even when they were beautiful camel drivers, while less serious wounds (Lawrence tells us) were treated by " spraying with piss "* by the youngest boys.[60] ?

From the time of the junction with the 4th Cavalry Division until the fall of Damascus, the energies of the Sharifians were concentrated on trying to out-race the advancing British and to be the first in Damascus, in order to keep to the letter if not the spirit of the Cairo declaration to the Seven. At all costs the Sharifians must try to get first into Damascus, however few, so as to claim that they had captured the great city, no matter how much they were outnumbered by the British, no matter how overwhelmingly more important the British military achievement compared with the Arabs' insignificant contribution, which in this phase of the battle at its most effective hardly went beyond Auda's night-long slaughter of helpless fugitives when the old man went on killing and plundering till the dawn.[61] Yet even here Lawrence's melodramatic " There passed the 4th Army "[62] is an exaggeration. The British patrols did indeed find " hundreds of dead " in the Jebel Mani, and yet from this supposedly annihilated column must have come the 1,600 prisoners swept up by the Australians on the 2nd October.[63]

Two roads led north from Damascus, one towards Homs and the other towards Baalbek and Beirut, through a deep gorge called the Barada. At 8 p.m. on the 30th September, the Australian Mounted Division was in position on the southern edge of this gorge, with the 5th and 4th British Cavalry Divisions coming up rapidly on their right, and the Arabs somewhere " to the north-east."[64] The Australians had been ordered to cross this gorge, ride round the town and cut the Homs road. They found they could not get down the steep side of the gorge in the dusk, and specific orders had been issued to them not to enter the city.[65] A long column of fugitive troops was trying to escape by this gorge, and the Australians turned them back by a machine-gun massacre of the head of the column, which sent the remainder fleeing back into the town. Why were the Australians forbidden to enter Damascus on the evening of the 30th September? Perhaps to avoid plunder of a supposedly friendly town, but more likely for political motives. At all events, the delay seemingly allowed

* If we may trust Richard Burton this repugnant behaviour was contrary to the religious laws of Islam and to the Bedouin treatment of wounds. See the notes to Burton's *Arabian Nights*, Vol. 3. p. 229 ; and vol. 5, p. 201 (American edition).

a few mounted Sharifians to get into the city—but they were quite unobserved among the other Bedouins, who for days had been riding about cracking off their rifles in the usual style; and so arose the claim that "the Arabs were the first to enter Damascus."⁶⁶

The 3rd Australian Light Horse marched at 5 a.m. on the 1st October, and so were the first disciplined Allied troops to enter Damascus. They were mobbed by "a population gone mad with joy,"⁶⁷ and had some difficulty in getting through the town to continue the pursuit. At 6.40 a.m., the advance guard of the 4th Australian Light Horse entered, and received the surrender of over 10,000 Turks, including many sick. Colonel Bouchier, their commander, "discovered 1,800 more sick in three other hospitals, in a state of appalling misery and destitution. In some cases those that had died had lain three days on the floors of the wards amidst the living. He then posted guards upon the principal public buildings and the consulates, which remained until the following afternoon when they were relieved by Sharifian troops."⁶⁸ Readers of *Seven Pillars* will recollect Lawrence's description of the hospitals and their plight, and how Chauvel refused to take them over. Even his friend Wavell protests against this, and declares, "Lawrence's story of the events in Damascus after the entry and of his dealings with Chauvel is not the whole truth, and is unjust to Chauvel."⁶⁹ It is natural that a man should be concentrated on his own task, but surely a degree of more than usual egotism was required to greet so blankly on the Damascus road the news that Bulgaria had surrendered, thereby cutting the great confederacy in half, with Franchet d'Espérey already within 250 miles of Constantinople. The news, Lawrence says, "came orphaned and as it were insignificant."⁷⁰

Lawrence has omitted to give us the hour of his entry into Damascus with Nuri and Major Stirling, and it is not given in Stirling's reminiscences which are rich in laudations.⁷¹ The official history says that Lawrence reached Damascus about 7.30 a.m., on the 1st October; possibly genuinely unaware that the Australians had preceded him. His part, as always, was a political one, and his intention was to make sure that everything was done to push aside Syrian native claims and French ambitions, and to instal Feisal as the British nominee of Arab "independence."

When Lawrence reached the Town Hall, he found that Jemel

Pasha had handed over the government to two Algerians, Mohammed Said and Abd el Kadir, who long before had tricked Lawrence, in spite of Brémond's warnings. In the Moslem world the name of Abd el Kadir, defender of Algeria (this was his grandson), was something like that of Louis Botha to the Boers. Lawrence's report complains that " Ali Riza, the intended governor, was missing."[72] And for a reason. He was that governor of Damascus, secretly a traitor to his salt, whom Lawrence had met with so mysteriously during the Akaba march. It was he, too, who fell over and upset into the dirt Barrow's breakfast table, when he came in and boasted of his treacheries to his Turkish masters. Barrow forgave the loss of his breakfast, but didn't much like the idea of an officer betraying his salt. The more Ali Riza asked to be sent to the Sharifians, the more Barrow suspected he might be a spy. To put him off, the general said the Bedouins would rob him. When at last it seemed safe to release him, and Ali Riza rushed off to Damascus, the Bedouins on the way did in fact strip him of his clothes, money and watch![73]

In Ali Riza's absence, Lawrence appointed as governor Shukri el Ayubi, he says with the support of the Algerians. But was this wholly true? Lawrence has to admit that there was a revolt supported by the Algerians and Damascenes. I have not been able to discover what really happened, so carefully has fact been smothered for political reasons. The contemporary newspapers had the streets of Damascus running with blood, and even Lawrence admits to " five killed and ten wounded."[74] Perhaps most of these were due to Kirkbride's ruthlessness; but he admits that Nuri was firing his machine-guns ceaselessly; that he even appealed to Chauvel for help; that the Druses left their booty and fled down side streets; that when Mohammed Said was captured, Lawrence could hardly forbear shooting him.[75] The silence of all English witnesses to this anti-Feisal, anti-British, uprising is remarkable. If the truth has been recorded, I have been too ignorant and clumsy to discover it. It is one of the many hushed-up scandals of history. On the 3rd October, Feisal arrived, and then was seen how circumstances alter cases. The reader will remember how the " military situation " in Jerusalem in 1917 wholly forbade General Allenby to implement the British promise to set up a joint Franco-British government in Palestine. Although an attempted military revolution in Damascus had just been quelled, Allenby at once deputed Feisal as governor. Let me quote an eye-witness, Sir Hubert Young:

> "General Allenby told Feisal . . . an Arab military administration would be set up in the whole area east of the Jordan from Akaba to Damascus. The military governors and civil officials throughout this area would be Arabs, and would work under direct orders from Feisal, who would himself be responsible to General Allenby so long as war conditions prevailed. . . . In deference to French claims, a French liaison officer would be appointed."[76]

Thus, while the military situation in Jerusalem—where at that time there had been no outbreak—still required and continued to require until 1920 the services of a British military governor, who was simply a Foreign Office official in uniform, the situation in Damascus—where the regular Arab forces had used "continuous barrages of machine-gun fire"[77] to beat down an anti-Feisal revolution—permitted the immediate appointment of an Arab administration. We must recollect that in the case of Palestine, Mr. Lloyd George, who did not "care a damn for the Jews or their past or their future," felt it would be "an outrage to let the Holy Places pass into the possession or under the protectorate of 'agnostic, atheistic France'."[78]

But at the same time Feisal was told that the Arab flag must come down from Beirut, where it had been raised the day before by Shukri and about a hundred horsemen who had ridden in ahead of the British.[79] Now this was a direct provocation to the French, an attempt to jockey them out of an area allotted by treaty—no doubt a bad treaty, but still a treaty—and it is fairly obvious that this irresponsible move originated with Lawrence. Until the arrival of Allenby and Feisal on the 3rd October, Lawrence had been virtually what government there was in Damascus—on which, needless to say, he has received a great many compliments. Nuri and Lawrence had put down the revolt against Feisal; when Ali Riza Pasha failed to turn up as planned (having as already recorded fallen first into the hands of Barrow and then of the Bedouins), Lawrence appointed Shukri to hold his place until he arrived, and on Riza's arrival, Shukri had left for Beirut. On the 7th October, Feisal admitted to the French representative that he assumed responsibility for sending Shukri to Beirut[80] but he could only have acted through Lawrence, since he was not in Damascus at the time, but either still at Azrak or on his way. The result of this move, as was no doubt calculated, was at once to create "an incident" when Allenby ordered the flag to be hauled down—there was "violent effervescence" in Damascus, and "an incipient mutiny" in Feisal's forces.[81] In a letter written in 1929 to Professor William Yale, Lawrence says that "Feisal had ordered his people to have nothing to do with littoral Syria south of the Tripoli gap," and asserts that "Shukri was sent to Beirut by Ali Riza Pasha."[82] Yet the French official note of the 7th October, 1918, shows Feisal admitting full responsibility for Shukri's action! Lawrence in this letter does not really deny his responsibility, but writes one of his artful word twisters:

"If Shukri told you I had urged him to Beirut, it was probably that he was getting frightened at the magnitude of his error, and wanted to make-believe that he had authority."[83]

One can hardly imagine a more feeble suggestion. Lawrence then expresses amazement at Yale's remark that "British political officers were working to create a situation in Syria which would make impossible . . . the Sykes-Picot treaty." In this letter, Lawrence says "the Sykes-Picot treaty was the Arab sheet-anchor," though, in his memorandum to the Cabinet written 4th November, 1918, he had said that "the geographical absurdities of the Sykes-Picot agreement will laugh it out of court," and thought it "would perhaps be as well if we spared ourselves a second effort on the same lines."[84] As to the behaviour of the British political officers in Syria, I limit myself to three examples. At the time of the Shukri-Beirut trouble, M. Coulondre, the French representative, received from General Clayton (who was about to leave) the assurance that Major Cornwallis (of the Arab Bureau, but then British liaison officer to Feisal) would warn Feisal that only Allenby had the right to appoint these Arab governors. When Clayton had gone, Cornwallis, according to Brémond, refused to carry out his orders.[85] On the 10th December, 1918, Georges Picot telegraphed from Damascus[86] that "the officers of the British Intelligence are carrying on an anti-French agitation" by falsifying the text of the Anglo-French declaration of the 26th September, 1918, and asserting " that the agreements of 1916 no longer subsist." On the 2nd January, 1919, Pontalis, the new French representative in Syria, telegraphed[87] that the English authorities had refused permission for a Francophile Lebanese delegation to go to London, and that the English postal censorship had received orders to hold up the correspondence of French officials dealing with the question! These are French secret official documents, not quasi-fictional heroics, and certainly support Professor Yale's contention. Of course, at the time those telegrams were sent, Lawrence was no longer in Damascus, but working in the same sense in London and at the Peace Conference. Thus, while some of the sympathy expressed for " Arab freedom " and " Arab self-determination " was doubtless sincere, these " causes " were in the main British camouflage for the more realistic purpose of excluding the French as far as possible from the Middle East and establishing British influence throughout that area.

PART THREE

CHAPTER ONE

"WHEN DAMASCUS fell," says Lawrence dramatically, "the Eastern war—probably the whole war—drew to an end."[1] This is typical of Lawrence's blatant propaganda, which succeeded so well because its blatancy harmonised with those to whom it was addressed. In spite of a few acknowledgments—which can always be triumphantly quoted—that other fronts existed, that his "war" was "a side-show of a side-show,"[2] even "a tussle in a turnip-field,"[3]—the whole trend and assertiveness of *Seven Pillars* (and extracts in *Revolt*) are designed to insinuate that the Eastern war was the really important one and that the important contribution to that war came from Lawrence and "the Arabs." There was a political as well as personal motive for this, as there was an obvious political motive for the systematic over-estimate of "the Arabs" in Antonius's book, which is essentially propaganda for "the Arabs" against the British, the French and the Jews. Similarly, in spite of its too sweepingly generous and patronising compliments to others—British and Arab—which ring as hollow as a hearty vote of thanks to the staff—the whole trend of *Seven Pillars* is to build up Lawrence as the hero of this over-estimated "Arab revolt." Hence his extreme annoyance with Herbert Read for pointing out that the book hasn't got a real hero.[4]

It is perfectly true that six weeks after the fall of Damascus, both the Eastern war and the World War ended; but they did not end because of the fall of Damascus, and they would have ended at the same time if Damascus had not fallen. The surrender of Bulgaria, on the 30th September, opened the way for an immediate invasion of European Turkey, under the threat of which the Turkish government capitulated and signed an armistice with Admiral Calthorpe. Much more important, and the key to the whole situation, was the fact that the German armies were unable to hold up the Allied advances in France and had been driven out of the Hindenburg Line in the latter part of September. So long as there was a hope that Germany could win in the West, the Eastern satellites held out, knowing that, in such an event, they would soon recover all lost territory. If the Germans had defeated and destroyed the armies of Foch, Haig and Pershing, the hold of Allenby and Feisal on Damascus and Jerusalem wouldn't have been worth a rotten apple. Those Allied victories on the Western front were not the sole cause of the satellites' collapse, but they took all the heart and hope out of them. And in fact it was on the 4th October, the day Lawrence left Damascus and the war, that the German government sent President Wilson its proposals for an armistice. The other Central Powers then knew it was useless to continue. Lloyd George's expensive policy of "knocking out the props," as he demagogically called his attempts to make a new empire from Turkish provinces, was really rather a cutting off of superfluities, and always took for granted that the Western (including Italian) fronts would be held.[5]

Why did Lawrence leave Damascus on the 4th October, so soon after its capture? There seems no reason to doubt his declaration that he was bored and exasperated by the Arabs;[6] and after nearly four years without home leave, he might most legitimately ask for it, though he had few or none of the usual motives which made ordinary men over-value such brief concessions of liberty. The suggestion that he left in order to hasten to the aid of the Western front need not be taken seriously, though Lawrence encouraged the tale.[7] If he had gone to the French front, in what capacity would he have served? As Anglo-Arabian liaison officer to his military hero, Marshal Foch? And he hurried so determinedly that, while leaving Damascus on the 4th October, he did not reach England until (so he says) the 11th of November. None of these arguments would have weighed with General Allenby, who, if anyone, would have been able to tell Lawrence that the war in the West was ending. Lawrence says he invoked a "year-old promise" from Allenby, and thus secured release,[8] but does not go into details.

The fact is that, since Feisal's "Arab army" had a political rather

248

than a military significance, the moment had now arrived for its British officers to disappear discreetly. At Deraa they had all, except Lawrence, gone over to Barrow in a body; and before they reached Damascus, Sir Hubert Young—the all-important Q of " the Arabs " —had, with the aid of Lawrence and telegrams, already re-transferred to the British army, with a soldier's sigh of relief at finding once more the soothing influences of " military precision and punctuality."[9] I have already quoted Lawrence's " What mattered to me was the government of Damascus," and it was to secure that object that he had been employed. " When I left Damascus on October the fourth, the Syrians " (surely the Sharifians?—the Syrians had rebelled) " had their *de facto* Government, which endured two years, without foreign advice, in an occupied country wasted by war, and against the will of important elements among the Allies."[10] Another example of Lawrence's propagandist skill, is that sentence. Feisal's government endured because it was supported by British subsidies and ultimately British arms—as witness that moment of panic during the Abd el Kadir rebellion, when Lawrence had been forced to ask General Chauvel for military help, though it had not been used.[11] This fact is passed over very lightly by the Bureau, as is the further fact that Abd el Kadir was murdered by Sharifian police on the 6th November.[12] When Allenby let Lawrence go on the 4th October, the reason was that, with the ending of the war, the scene of Lawrence's —and at times Feisal's—political activities would have to be transferred from the Middle East to Paris and London. The two of them would be pawns in Lloyd George's game of keeping the " agnostic, atheistic French " out of Palestine and as much of Syria as possible.

The last entry in Lawrence's calendar of war movements shows that he reached Cairo on the 8th October, 1918. From there he wrote a letter on the 14th, not to any of his long-neglected friends in England, but to Major Scott, who was still base commandant at Akaba. Lawrence reports that he was leaving Egypt but with no indication that he was hurrying back to Europe to fight on the Western front. On the contrary. The " old war," he says, is ending and he thinks his use is gone; he asks for his engraved British rifle to be sent to Cairo, with the modest reflection that " we have, I expect, changed history in the Near East."[13] His last reflection is a purely political one, of wondering how the Powers will deal with

" the Arabs." That was what he was being sent back by the Arab Bureau to try to influence.

Of course, Lawrence could not even be conveyed from Cairo to England without a fresh crop of stories. At that particular epoch, about three weeks were needed for officers on leave to make the journey, ten days of which had to be spent on a troop train between Taranto and Le Havre.[14] There was also a faster *wagon-lits* staff train on which (so Lawrence says) none could travel under the rank of full colonel. Lawrence put out the story that, because he " liked comfort," he wanted to travel on ths train, and therefore Allenby at once created him full colonel " special, temporary and acting,"[15] with which should be connected the saluting stories with which Lawrence entertained his friends and, at a later period, the ranks of the R.A.F. Now, the only special appointment to which Lawrence was ever gazetted was that of " Deputy Military Governor, Class X Special Appointment " in 1918,[16] though for what purpose is not stated. There is no evidence that he was ever even temporarily appointed full colonel, though he certainly claimed it, and it appears in the early Lowell Thomas version of the saluting story, which soon branched out into more stories. Lawrence was still claiming in 1933 that the full colonel, staff-train story was true, as recorded by Hart.[17]

Whether there is anything in the full colonel story or not, Lawrence certainly turns up as one in the story he told Lowell Thomas of the Railway Transport Officer who was a Lt.-Col.* when Lawrence returned to England after the war via Marseille. According to the common plan of these stories, Lawrence wears a raincoat over his badges of rank, is rudely spoken to on the assumption that he is a junior officer, displays his badges, and exacts an abject apology.[18] One can see how well such stories would always go with " other ranks." The full-colonelcy for the staff train also turns up in Graves's book in 1927, and immediately precedes an improved version of the saluting story, still more sympathetic to other ranks. Here " at a rest-camp "—place unspecified— a major is seen bullying two privates (" battle-wearied men ") for not saluting him, and makes them twice salute him without returning the salute. " ' One moment, Major,' said a voice behind him " . . . and we can almost guess who it is before

---

* In my experience R.T.O.'s dealing with movements of officers on leave were invariably captains.

Lawrence, " starred and crowned," emerges to compel the Major to return the salute of the privates.[19] Liddell Hart, who investigated a number of the stories which Lawrence had so incautiously approved in print, tackled him about this one. Having forgotten that he had told Lowell Thomas that the episode happened in Marseille, Lawrence now placed it in Taranto (he had to, after the staff-train story), but added modestly: " I understand that the major did not mean what I thought, in his action."[20] Well, the story as he told it admits of only one interpretation—the major was bullying two privates and Lawrence, the friend of the downtrodden, revenged them. This later proliferated into a third story, that in Oxford Street just after the war, a lieutenant-colonel, walking with a woman, " obviously a new acquaintance " (I like that touch), pulled him up for not saluting,* Lawrence as before wearing a badgeless raincoat, which he then took off and showed his badges. " The lieutenant-colonel grew red in the face. Lawrence said, ' You can go away ' . . . The woman went a third way."[21] The puerile snobbery of these stories is hardly excused by their absurdity, for, even if Lawrence had been given local rank by Allenby in Egypt, he was not entitled to it in England, and was consequently liable to arrest by the provost-marshal. When Hart laboriously tackled him on this Oxford Street yarn, Lawrence surpassed himself in evasion: " No, I was never in Oxford in uniform, I think." On which Hart reflects, " it would seem that his misunderstanding was feigned to suppress an incident."[22] It couldn't possibly be, of course, that the whole incident was feigned?

In any event, Graves cannot be accused of inventing the stories or blamed for publishing them, since he could only have heard them from Lawrence, and Lawrence read and passed his book. In April, 1919, on his Handley-Page flight to Egypt, Lawrence at some period before the crash had told Captain Henderson a telescoped version of these stories, with Regent Street for Oxford Street, and an assistant provost-marshal instead of a lieutenant-colonel, and no " obviously new " woman acquaintance. Like so many of Lawrence's stories, these have the advantage of no traceable witnesses.

The real purpose of Lawrence's return to England was obviously not to fight but to intrigue, and this is plainly demonstrated by the

---

* How likely that an officer walking with a woman " obviously a new acquaintance," would court publicity by exacting salutes, on leave, in London!

report on Arabian affairs (dated 4th November) which he sent in to the Government, and the telegram of enquiry despatched on the 18th November by the Secretary of State for India to Delhi and Baghdad. Here we come upon an extremely complicated subject and a controversy which lasted for years—indeed the complicated subject remains complicated after 35 years, and the controversy has become plural with no very hopeful signs of solution. Lawrence was out of it by 1922; but, for good or evil, the influence of his views long prevailed, though they would not have done so if they had not been originated by a considerable and powerful official clique.

Earlier in this book, attempts were made to prepare for an understanding of this situation and also to indicate its complexity by listing the different petty states of Arabia proper with their rulers, the different and mutually hostile British authorities (especially those of " Cairo " versus " Delhi and Simla ") who strove to deal with them, the complication arising out of French historical claims to Syria, the ambitions of King Hussein, the Jewish ambitions in Palestine, the British conquest of Irak and the oil-fields therein, the excited native nationalist political caucuses. On top of that you have to consider the extraordinary pell-mell of peoples in those ancient lands, not so much a mosaic or a melting-pot as a retort of unmixable liquids with mutually repellent chemical qualities—religious, as Moslem, Christian, Jew, Druse and weird sectarian survivals; racial, as Arabs, Turks, Assyrians, Kurds, Circassians, Armenians; linguistic, for there were large areas of " Arabia " where Arabic was not spoken or even understood. Consider, too, that all these varying strains of population had endured centuries of arbitrary Turkish rule—which was usually misrule—now suddenly abolished by the violence of war in miserable conditions of famine (especially in Syria), and yet however much they had hated Turkish rule, it was for most of them the only way of government they knew, for we must except the real nomad Arabs of the desert who were more or less independent since they and their lands were too poor to be worth more than anyone's casual exploitation. The view of the political committees of Syria and Palestine and Irak was unanimous that the enormous expenditure of European lives and money was well worth while if it led to the immediate transfer of complete sovereign power to those local committees, the immediate withdrawal of all the conquering troops, but the continuation of ample subsidies and supplies for an indefinite period. The British and French query: where do we come in? was howled down as base treachery to the self-determination of small nations.

Mr. Antonius, the special-pleading advocate of " the Arabs," describes the Sykes-Picot agreement as a " shocking document," and so it is from the point of view of an irresponsible doctrinaire *bombinans in vacuo*, but it was an attempt—however imperfect and self-seeking— at a practical solution. Antonius also makes a great point of the fact that the backward desert tribes were left to themselves, and only the politically more advanced and settled populations handed over to foreign tutelage. But it is impossible to impose settled government on primitive nomads (did the United States ever succeed with the redskins?), and it was precisely the settled population of " Arabia " which was far enough advanced for some government though not for complete self-government. In spite of off-stage and up-stage critics, there really was no panacea for immediately arranging all this satisfactorily, and nothing but trial and error remained. One factor which would have contributed greatly towards reasonable solutions would have been a close and cordial co-operation between the two great European powers involved. And this Lawrence and his friends had done their best to destroy.

The solution put forward by the Arab Bureau through Lawrence, and continuously urged by him with fanatical pertinacity and a fine disregard for all contrary opinion and evidence, had certain good points about it—especially good debating points—but also suffered from certain defects. According to the telegram from the India Office he had proposed:

" . . . formation of three Councils of Arab States outside Hejaz and its dependencies, viz.: (1) Lower Mesopotamia, (2) Upper Mesopotamia and (3) Syria, to be placed respectively under Abdulla, Said and Feisal, sons of King Hussein. Hussein himself would remain King of Hejaz and would ultimately be succeeded by his eldest son Ali."[23]

This simply meant handing over the whole of this immense area of the defeated Turkish Empire to members of one aristocratic family related to the Prophet, though not the only one entitled to the dignity of Grand Sharif of Mecca. Obviously, motives of self-interest and financial dependence would make them virtually guardians of British interests, commercial and otherwise, as set forth by Lawrence in his *Arab Bulletin* report, [24] until they felt strong enough to repudiate their benefactors. It ignored the claims of France, it brushed aside Ibn Saud, and, while half-accepting, half-sneering at the views of those trying to set up a colonial government in Mesopotamia, it overlooked their practical problems of organisation, revenue and so forth for the romantic political object of setting up " Arab government." In urging " sovereignty " for Feisal in Syria, Lawrence certainly mentions that he had " inherited " the old Turkish bureaucrats, " all of whose lower ranks, and many of whose upper ranks, are Arab."[25] If so, they don't seem to have been of much use, for Young notes that at Damascus, half his time was spent " in trying to help to organise the departments with which I must come in contact."[26] A gross miscalculation lies in the words Lawrence applied to Ibn Saud:

> " Ibn Saud is now striving to limit the puritan revival becoming too strong for him. If he is carried away by it, and attacks the Holy Places, orthodox Islam will deal with him, as with his ancestor. If he can control it he will remain Emir of Nedj after military failure has warned him to recognise the Sharif as his overlord."[27]

Every forecast there made was completely disproved by facts and time. Ibn Saud did not find Wahabism too strong for him; he not only smashed Abdulla and his " Arab regulars," but eventually occupied the Holy Places—orthodox Islam being unable to do anything about it—and instead of " recognising the Sharif as his overlord," ruled over the Sharif's former dominions as king! But, in spite of such errors of prophecy, the document achieved the object of all such propaganda—while pushing the views of its author, it told its readers exactly what they wanted to hear, namely that what " the Arabs wanted " was: Hussein as " overlord of all desert Arabia," which they (the British) didn't want to rule; Abdulla as " nominal " Arab king of Lower Mesopotamia, which they intended to have; Said as " nominal " ruler of the Mosul area supposed to go to France, but which they also wanted; and Feisal as " sovereign " ruler of Syria to keep out the French from the area so regrettably promised to France. The last item could not have been put more clearly or more tactfully:

"In Syria the Arab movement becomes really important, since its origin was to prevent the man-power and strategic advantages of the country falling into the hands of any continental power."[28] (i.e., France).

For cool cynicism that is hard to beat. But where in this dexterous neo-Machiavelli are we to find that anxious and tortured " man with a conscience," who could not endure the thought that he had been commanded to give " the Arabs " promises which had not been fulfilled, a situation which so much revolted his plain-dealing integrity that he felt compelled to throw his medals back at his King?

The influence of Lawrence in the highest political circles in England soon made itself felt in a move as clever as it was mischievous. On the 17th November, 1918, Feisal suddenly arrived in Beirut (when Picot was absent in Cairo) and was entertained publicly by General Bulfin at dinner as " His Royal Highness, the Emir Feisal, Commander-in-Chief of the Arab forces."[29] He had been invited to come to England with a small suite which included Nuri Said with the rank of brigadier, but was in fact taken on board a British cruiser and landed at Marseille; and there or at Lyons he was met by Lawrence. According to Lowell Thomas, Feisal was accompanied by " Lawrence's tent-mate, Major Marshall " (he was one of the doctors at the Akaba base), who was curious to see what the French would do with their uninvited guest. In a few hours Lawrence turned up and:

". . . with his usual tact, he avoided friction with the French by borrowing Marshall's Arabian head-dress, and attaching himself to Feisal's delegation as a member of the Emir's personal staff and not as a British officer."[30]

Mr. Thomas must have been fairly accurately informed by somebody, for he correctly gives the name of the ship which brought Feisal—H.M.S. *Gloucester*. Note that this account was published before Colonel Brémond's book, and that Graves—also pre-Brémond —passes over the whole episode in silence. Colonel Brémond had returned to France in December, 1917, not because of the Lawrence-inspired *démarche* of the British ambassador, but because of the French

War Office rule that officers on detachment after a certain time had to return to active service in the war. Brémond was at Ghent when he was suddenly called by telegram to Paris (morning of the 27th November, as he says with soldierly precision) and told at the Quai d'Orsay to go and meet Feisal and amuse him with various expeditions without allowing him to come to Paris until further orders. Then came the instructions concerning Lawrence:

" You must be quite candid with Lawrence, and point out that he is in a false position (*il fait fausse route*). If he is in France as a British colonel in British uniform, we welcome him. But we don't accept him as an Arab, and if he remains in fancy dress, he is not wanted here (*s'il reste déguisé, il n'a rien à faire chez nous*)."[31]

Feisal's party was at Lyons when Brémond caught up with it, accompanied by a Monsieur Bertrand, who had once been French consul at Jidda. To him Colonel Brémond confided his orders and, as Lawrence was *en costume oriental*, M. Bertrand passed on the instructions to Feisal, who said Lawrence would leave at once. Lawrence came and said that as he was expelled, he would leave immediately, and then at once returned his Croix de Guerre, which Brémond sent to the French Foreign Office.

After the appearance of Brémond's carefully documented book, Lawrence reversed himself. The story about borrowing Marshall's Arab head-dress was dropped, and Hart at Lawrence's instigation put in his book the following: " Contrary to Brémond's statement, he had not worn Arab dress, so that Brémond must either have suffered a lapse of memory or have introduced the excuse to cover up the French government's breach of courtesy."[32] Once more it is Lawrence's word against another's. But surely a breach of courtesy lies with uninvited guests, not with the involuntary host; and gate-crashers are not welcomed anywhere. If Lawrence wore only the Arab head-dress with khaki (as Lowell Thomas was told), then Brémond was justified, for such was the dress of Feisal's Arab officers, as may be seen from contemporary photographs. At one time Lawrence gave out (and his brother Professor Lawrence has repeated) a story that he tied his Croix de Guerre on to the neck of Hogarth's dog and sent it round Oxford.[33] Whatever Lawrence did or did not tie round the

14 Aug 1919

ROYAL OPERA HOUSE,
COVENT GARDEN.

PROPRIETORS   THE GRAND OPERA SYNDICATE. LTD.

Commencing Thursday Evening, August 14th, and Nightly at 8.30.
. . Matinees Wednesday, Thursday and Saturday at 2.30. . .

PERCY BURTON

(by arrangement with the Grand Opera Syndicate)
presents

LOWELL THOMAS

in

His Illustrated Travelogue of the British Campaigns:

AMERICA'S TRIBUTE TO BRITISH VALOUR

With Allenby in Palestine

including

THE CAPTURE OF JERUSALEM

and

THE LIBERATION OF HOLY ARABIA.

The motion pictures used in this travelogue were taken by Mr. Harry A. Chase and Captain Frank Hurley. Still photographs by Mr. Chase. Art work by Miss Augusta A. Heyder. Projection by Mr. Chase.

Business Manager (for Lowell Thomas and Percy Burton) W. T. Cunningham.

With authority from the Secretary of War and the Secretary of the Navy of the United States Government, Mr. Lowell Thomas, accompanied by Colonel W. C. Hayes and a staff of photographers, journeyed over sixty thousand miles gathering material for a series of travelogues. Mr. Lowell Thomas was attached to the Allied forces in Europe, Asia and Africa, and was with them from the Orkney Islands to the forbidden deserts of Holy Arabia, from New York to Jerusalem, from Rome to Khartoum, from Paris to Salonika, and from Cairo to Berlin. He was the first pilgrim to tour the Holy Land by airplane, and the first person to go into the holy land of the Mohammedans with a cinema camera. After the signing of the armistice he was the first to visit Kiel, Hamburg, Berlin and other parts of Germany, and bring back the pictorial story of the German Revolution.

By arrangement with Mr. Percy Burton, Mr. Thomas cancelled a number of his engagements in America in order to appear at Covent Garden Royal Opera House for a limited period, under the auspices of the English-Speaking Union.

His travelogue on Allenby's crusade in Palestine and the liberation of Holy Arabia, is not a tale of Jules Verne, but the story of the reality of the present, surpassing the dreams of the imagination of the past.

(Under the auspices of THE ENGLISH-SPEAKING UNION.)

. President: Rt. Hon. A. J. BALFOUR, O.M.
Hon. President: The AMERICAN AMBASSADOR to England.

Vice-Presidents:

Field-Marshal Sir DOUGLAS HAIG, O.M.
Rt. Hon. WINSTON CHURCHILL, M.P.
Earl CURZON of KEDLESTON, O.M.
The ARCHBISHOP of YORK.
Sir ROBERT S. S. BADEN POWELL, K.C.B.
Rt. Hon. Sir ROBERT BORDEN, K.C.M.G.
Viscount BURNHAM.

Rt. Hon. J. R. CLYNES, M.P.
The ARCHBISHOP of CANTERBURY.
BISHOP of LONDON, K.C.V.O.
Viscount BRYCE, O.M.
Earl of READING, G.C.B.
Rt. Hon. W. M. HUGHES.
Viscount NORTHCLIFFE, &c.

Programme for the first night of the Lowell Thomas travelogue at Covent Garden, August 14th, 1919. Preserved in the Enthoven Collection at the Victoria and Albert Museum neck of Hogarth's dog, it was not the Croix de Guerre,* for he himself admitted to Captain Hart that he had returned it to Colonel Brémond.[34]

All this was extremely petty political intrigue, but it certainly achieved two immediate successes; it forced Feisal on French official-dom, and it enabled Lawrence to be personally insolent to France. Feisal's position as delegate for the Hejaz at the Peace Conference could have been secured, as in fact it was eventually, by the insistence of the British delegation—after they had either forgotten all about him or showed that they had never heard of him, until Lawrence reminded them.[35] Yet there is reason to think that it was precisely this " clever " dumping of an uninvited Feisal into the chaos of immediate post-Armistice France which confirmed succeeding French governments in their conviction that Feisal was simply a British " stooge," and made them determined to get him out of Damascus on the first possible occasion. At the time the uninvited Feisal was courteously received, shown the battlefield of Verdun, given the Légion d'Honneur (*grand plaque*), a present of Lyons silks; and, after an intentionally long delay, received in Paris. On the 9th December, still escorted by Brémond, Feisal proceeded on his way to England, and at Boulogne was met from the ship by Lawrence in his white silk Arab robes, looking under the foggy sky " like a choir-boy "[36] as he crept deprecatingly down the gangway.

In London they stayed at the Carlton Hotel, where Lionel Curtis saw Lawrence dressed in khaki with an Arab head-dress, as Lowell Thomas says he was in France; and it was not until a month later that they returned to France—Lawrence officially as a member of the British delegation—and were put up in the Hôtel Majestic. While in England, Lawrence had served as Feisal's guide, and as his self-appointed interpreter. Dressed in his white Arab costume, he accom-panied Feisal, as interpreter, to a reception at Buckingham Palace, and at least one of the usual anecdotes has been recorded to call attention to the fact. He is said to have performed the same service for Feisal at the Peace Conference, with additional anecdotes which bear the hall-mark of their origin. One of them runs to the effect that, before the Council of Ten, Feisal, as previously arranged with Lawrence, merely

* It might have been the Légion d'Honneur though that should have been returned with the Croix de Guerre.

recited a chapter of the Koran, while Lawrence made the necessary speeches.[37] This seems rather risky, for Lawrence may not have been the only person at the Conference who could speak Arabic fluently and incorrectly, and someone might have understood. Lawrence —forgetting this story—told Graves that he addressed *the Conference* in English, French and Arabic.[38] Why address them in Arabic if they were so ignorant they didn't know the difference between politics and the Koran in that tongue? Mr. Churchill tells us that Lawrence also went about Paris acting as Feisal's interpreter, and that he personally saw Lawrence dressed in full Arab costume. He was obviously impressed by the vision that met his eyes and was moved to describe it with true Disraelian eloquence.[39] Mr. Lloyd George, describing the appearance of Feisal and Lawrence before the Peace Conference on the 6th February, remarks that both wore "flowing robes of dazzling white," but says nothing about the interpreting. But this elaborately built-up story of interpreting, which dates back to the war period, is rather shaken by a statement of General Liman von Sanders, the reorganiser of the Turkish Army and successor to von Falkenhayn on the Palestine front. He was in Constantinople and came to know Feisal well during the summer of 1914. They had a common interest in sport and often met each other. Of Feisal he wrote, "He was typically a great Arab noble. He had been brought up in the European manner and spoke English fluently."[40] Of course, the statement might be attributed to the malice of the enemy, but for the fact that, like Jemel Pasha, Liman von Sanders seems to have been unaware of Lawrence's existence; at least, neither of them mentions him. Of course, Feisal was perfectly within his rights in making use of an interpreter, even if he did speak English fluently. But if General von Sanders was right, and Feisal could speak English, then it adds another histrionic touch to the whole costume play.*

Considering that he had been expelled from France only a few weeks before because of his questionable Arab guise, Lawrence undoubtedly scored a personal triumph over the French he hated by returning as a British delegate, and then parading the Arab costume with impunity in the capital and before the Council of Ten. We will not stop to enquire why a British officer was told to dress as an

---

* There is evidence that long after the war Feisal could speak French.

Arab or how it came about that he acted apparently as a second delegate for the Hejaz (no other is mentioned except Feisal but it may have been Nuri); or, more cogently, whether his behaviour really advanced the cause of his protégé, Feisal, in his claim to the throne of Syria. And it would be a mere guessing at the inscrutable sources of motive to ask whether he wished more to advance Feisal's cause than to insult the French. One thing is clear—he must have had very powerful protection to be able to do this without being mistaken by the Parisians for another Raymond Duncan. If Hogarth and the Arab Bureau were the distant cause, Lloyd George was the near one. Liddell Hart assures us that Lawrence's gift of clear exposition was very much to Lloyd George's liking; the statement may be received with confidence since—as we have already noted— what Lawrence had expounded in London was exactly what Lloyd George wanted to hear: Palestine for England and Jewish home-makers, Irak and Mosul for England under Abdulla and Said, and France kept out of Syria by a native sovereign from another country, of the same Hashemite family, and not unfriendly to his island sponsors. Palestine, as we learned from Asquith's memoirs, had long been an object of Mr. Lloyd George's ambitions, and as far back as December, 1917, he had puzzled Allenby by telling him to conquer " the whole country between Dan and Beersheba,"[41] for though Allenby also had read the Bible and had actually captured Beersheba, Dan had disappeared in the cataclysm of time—represented perhaps by Banias. Lawrence had written to Lloyd George that the Arabs would not countenance an independent Jewish Palestine though they might support a British-controlled Jewish immigration.[42] One may have serious doubts that " the Arabs " ever approved any such thing, but here again was supposedly expert support for keeping " agnostic, atheistic France " out of Palestine. It is true that towards the end of his term, the Prime Minister's assiduous visits to the cultural centre of Le Touquet led to the belief that his moral objections to France were softening, but in 1919 religion and self-interest alike required the exclusion of France from Syria.

The Middle East, indeed, seems to have been one of Lloyd George's great preoccupations after the war, and he himself has unwittingly revealed the fact by printing an interesting little anecdote. Just after the war, Clemenceau came to London, and, as he and the Prime

Minister drove through the streets, the crowds demonstrated their admiration for the French Army by enthusiastic cheers for the French Prime Minister. At the end of their drive, Clemenceau turned in his hard profiteering French way and asked what it was Lloyd George (or might we say "England"?) "specially wanted from the French"? In his impulsive, warm-hearted Celtic way, the Prime Minister "instantly replied" that he "wanted Mosul attached to Irak, and Palestine from Dan to Beersheba under British control."[43] Mr. Lloyd George adds that this was instantly granted and that Clemenceau loyally kept his word. Apparently the British Prime Minister forgot to ask in return what France most wanted of England. And Clemenceau was so little pleased by the episode that it seems he allowed some time to pass before confessing to his colleagues how the Welsh wizard had taken him for a drive.

Nevertheless, the best summary of Peace Conference proceedings with reference to the Syrian section of the Turkish Treaty is Lloyd George's. But that summary occupies a hundred pages, and it is not for me to attempt to summarise that summary in a page—especially since it appears from Lloyd George's narrative that Lawrence was officially present at the Conference on only one occasion and no mention is made of his speaking. Indeed, from what the Prime Minister says it would seem that Feisal himself spoke, "with clarity, conciseness and dignity," and not through Lawrence as interpreter.[44] Among the modest assertions put forward by Sharif Feisal was that "the Arab army" had advanced 800 miles (so it had, with a little help from Allenby's flank guard), had captured 40,000 prisoners, and had raised 100,000 men of whom 20,000 were killed. As Mr. Lloyd George himself reflected, there is usually "something romantic about Oriental arithmetic." Moreover, Sharif Feisal continued, his father "did not risk his life and kingdom by joining in the War at its most critical time to further any personal ambitions."[45] It was just this self-effacing lack of ambition which had led Hussein to proclaim himself King of the Arabs, to claim for himself as King the vast area and different peoples south of a line drawn from Alexandretta to Diarbekir, and eventually to proclaim himself Caliph. Feisal was questioned closely by President Wilson, who apparently wanted to find out how far he would go, and among other questions asked if he would prefer one or several mandatories. Feisal tried to evade this, but the President insisted, and: " Emir Feisal said that personally he was afraid of partition. His principle was Arab unity. It was for this that the Arabs had fought."[46] Now, if it was true that at the Conference Feisal merely repeated the Koran while Lawrence made all the speeches,[47] then the minutes of the session (Feb. 6th, 1919), the only one at which Feisal and Lawrence are reported as present, are either entirely mistaken, or Lawrence himself denied his own solemn assertion on this topic on every other occasion. If he, when " making the speeches for Feisal," so emphatically came out for " Arab unity," why did he always elsewhere repudiate " the dream of a united Arabia " ? Why did he go on to say: " I never to my knowledge suggested it . . . the physical difficulties alone make it a plan too wild for me. . . . I have always been a realist and opportunist in tactics; and Arab unity is a madman's notion. . . . I am sure I never dreamed of uniting even Hejaz and Syria. My conception was of a number of small states."[48] The reader will draw his own deductions.

During this session of the 6th February, one of the delegates made a remark to the effect that the Arabs were a semi-civilised people. At this Feisal retorted: " I belong to a people who were civilised when every other country represented in this room was populated by barbarians." At this the Italian delegate dissented, and Feisal added: " Even before Rome came into existence."[49] Without going into the historical accuracy of this statement, we may trace how this haughty snub to the majesty of Rome was worked up by Lawrence into a jeer at the French. Probably everyone has heard and many have repeated—it has even crept into the Official War History—that, when Monsieur Pichon spoke of " the Crusading pedigree of France's claim to Syria," Feisal replied: " Pardon me, Monsieur Pichon, but which of us won the Crusades ?"[50] It has been ceaselessly used to deride French claims to Syria; and it was a mere invention of Lawrence's.

Look at the facts. In the Peace Conference the affairs of Arabia were discussed at two meetings, one on the 6th February, which we have just been considering, and one on the 20th March. At the first, Feisal (accompanied by Colonel Lawrence) made his statement, and had his dialogues with Orlando and Wilson; he was then followed by a missionary, Dr. Howard Bliss, who wanted a League of Nations commission to go to Syria; and by the Chairman of the National Syrian Committee, who was " strongly opposed to the inclusion of

Syria in an Arab state " and " fiercely contemptuous of the idea of
a ' highly civilised people ' like the Syrians being governed by the
Hejaz." Among other sharp invective, this Syrian leader denounced
Feisal for trying " to play the part of master in our country," and
added significantly that, in dismissing and appointing officials (including the Governor of the predominant Christian Lebanon), he " tries
to make people believe that he is acting under high and powerful
inspiration."[51] This speaker may have been hitting at Lawrence
when he referred to " the somewhat Bolshevist formula improvised
by the secretary of a foreign delegation (whose august chief and
prince already calls us his people) of : ' Let us massacre one another,
so long as we are free. It is only by killing each other that we shall
attain total independence.' "[52] The sentiments sound very characteristic of Lawrence but may have been some Arab's. That long
speech concluded the proceedings, and Monsieur Pichon did not say
anything; he made his speech, stating the case for French claims,
six weeks later, on the 20th March, when Feisal may have been
present but is not reported as saying anything. Nor did M.
Pichon make any reference to the Crusades. In summarising a
letter from Clemenceau to Lloyd George (5th February, 1919), he said:

" It had pointed out that there was no Government in the
world which had such a position as France in the regions claimed.
It had given an exposition of the historic rights of France from the
time of Louis XIV. M. Pichon continued by pointing out that
French intervention in Syria had been frequent, the last instance
being the case of the expedition organised in Syria and Lebanon
in 1860 which had resulted in the establishment of the status of
the Lebanon."[53]

After which he went on to speak of French schools in Syria, the
French-built railway, and so forth. There is no record of any inter-
ruption to the speech, and his claims go back no further than Louis
XIV, who had been recognised by the Sultan as Protector of the
Latin Church in Syria.

The session of the 20th March produced some melancholy examples
of high political thought. Thus Mr. Lloyd George indignantly and
virtuously exclaimed that " the whole " of the Sykes-Picot agreement
was based " on a letter from Sir Henry McMahon to King Hussein,"

while M. Pichon indignantly replied that at the time the French had never heard of it, and anyway had made no promises to King Hussein. President Wilson referred, as if it were a personal discovery, to the idea of " government by consent of the governed "; but he did not reveal how this consent was to be achieved from a population of Mohammedans, Christians and Jews, Kurds, Arabs, refugee Armenians and Circassians, Turkmans, Greeks, Maronites, Druses and so forth. Was this a case for pedantic self-determination of nations? What M. Pichon failed to explain is why he wanted to pick up such a hornets' nest with his bare hands. They wound up by agreeing to send out a Commission of Enquiry, which was to investigate Palestine and Irak as well as Syria.

The Commission, which included two missionaries, was accompanied by Lord Allenby's military secretary; it did not go to Mosul or Baghdad, and confined itself to finding reasons against a French mandate for Syria. Some of these are worth recording. It will be remembered that M. Pichon had made rather a point of the education given by French schools in Syria. The Commission discovered that French education is superficial and " inferior in character-building to the Anglo-Saxon "—i.e. no compulsory " Scripture " and ball games. It leads, they said gloomily, to familiarity with " that kind of French literature which is irreligious and immoral "; and indeed the Moslems reported to them that when their women received a French education, " they tend to become uncontrollable."[54] There may be more in this than meets the eye. Some time before the Commission arrived, the French had landed 20,000 troops, and Sir Richard Burton has testified to the effect on the ladies of the harem caused by the arrival of European military in countries where too many of the males subscribe to the deviationist penchants of Saladin, Hafiz and Abu-Nawas.[55] Even more to be preserved and mused over is the Commission's telegram of the 10th July, 1919, which runs thus:

" Emir Feisal despite limitation of education has become unique outstanding figure capable of rendering greatest service for world peace. He is heart of Moslem world, with enormous prestige and popularity, confirmed believer in Anglo-Saxon race; and great lover of Christians. Could do more than any other to reconcile

Christians and Islam and longs to do so. Even talks seriously of American college for women at Mecca."[56]

Lawrence had done his propaganda work well and truly when his preachments and expensive costume had achieved such results. Even he at his most brilliant and most cynical could hardly have composed a telegram to equal the production of these solemn buffoons. The spectacle of a campus of shameless ones in shorts under the pious noses of old Hussein and the fanatical Moslem pilgrims at Mecca is funnier even than that of the ladies of the harem driven to nymphomania by reading *Salammbô* and *La Vie Parisienne*.

CHAPTER TWO

THE DISPUTE over Syria and the other ex-Turkish provinces was far indeed from being settled by the Conference meeting of the 20th March (1919) and the setting up of this impartial Commission. Meanwhile, nothing whatever was done by the British Government to come to some arrangement with the French. Mr. Lloyd George throws the blame on Lord Milner, who (he says) was in a state of "nervous lassitude," so that almost as soon as he reached Paris to take up the problem of Syria, he discovered that important colonial business called him back to London—business which he was never able to particularise. It is conceivable that, at the end of a long life of public service, a man should grow old and tired; but what seems extraordinary is that he was not given the alternative of carrying out his duties or resigning. And since Milner afterwards dealt ably enough with the problems arising from a serious revolt against the British in Egypt, it rather looks as if Lloyd George were merely making excuses. But there is no doubt that this ignoring of the situation exacerbated the tension between French and British and the various Arab groups, especially since Milner had made promises to Clemenceau which he had failed to keep. That the French Government was annoyed is surely natural, while they, like Hussein and Feisal, had a suspicion that they were being double-crossed. After all, in his elaborate defensive Note of the 18th October, 1919, Lloyd George himself says:

"You will observe that the acceptance of the Agreement by Great Britain was made conditional upon the Arabs obtaining the four towns of Damascus, Homs, Hama and Aleppo. If that condition is not fulfilled, the whole Agreement clearly falls to the ground."[1]

That he could go on to claim that the Arabs had done so by "remaining in the War until the end" seems as fanciful as his proposition that they "played an indispensable part in the overthrow of Turkey."[2] It is not extraordinary that the French Government was unconvinced, and so able a lawyer as Mr. Lloyd George would probably have found little difficulty in refuting his own Note. In any case the French Government held him to the Sykes-Picot Agreement, and even he could find no way out. Feisal was told that he must go to Paris and make what arrangements he could, which resulted in his being temporarily installed in Damascus as French puppet ruler of inland Syria. Then Clemenceau fell, and while French financial interests were pressing for an unwise alliance with the Turks (Ottoman Loan), the Kemalists arose and drove their troops out of Cilicia. Encouraged by this, a gathering of Arabs in Damascus proclaimed the independence of Syria with Feisal as King. General Gouraud on the one side, and Feisal on the other, now put forth mutual accusations of "stirring up trouble," and French demands and actions became more and more drastic until Gouraud's ultimatum of the 14th July, 1920, which led to a battle in which many Arab sheiks were killed. Damascus was occupied and Feisal fled.[3] Such were the deplorable results of the bright idea of "rushing up to Damascus" in order "to biff the French out of all hope of Syria." Strangely enough, what intrigue failed to do after World War I was accomplished after World War II by British arms, which expelled the French officials, and left Syria to the happiness of a native military dictator. Those who think that the French Government of Syria between the wars was but a series of repressive acts and exploitations should read the last chapter of Mr. Robin Fedden's *Syria*, from which I will make one brief excerpt:

"It is no exaggeration to say that Syria in twenty years advanced in many respects further than it had done in several hundreds, and this in spite of the weakness of French capital, the sterling wall that surrounded the country, and the disastrous effects of the world slump which intervened just at the moment when new schemes were getting under way. Two things alone are vastly significant of the post-war achievement: the land under cultivation increased by fifty per cent, and the population rose from two to three and a half millions."[4]

On different lines an equally good case could be made for the British in Irak. But the active political minorities did not want order and prosperity for their countries, they wanted power for themselves. Emancipated slaves do not value freedom; they crave dominion over slaves of their own.

It was through something more than a coincidence that this Middle Eastern imbroglio was the direct cause of the fall of Lloyd George's Government, the destruction of the Liberal Party, and his exclusion from power for the rest of his life. After the Russian Government published the Sykes-Picot agreement, a region C in Anatolia, including Smyrna, had been hastily and tentatively allotted to Italy, and in the chaos of the Conference eventually fell to the Oxonian's friend, Hellas. The reconstituted Turkish Government wanted to throw the Greeks out, and the French Government—still furious over the "biffing out of Syria" policy—came to a secret agreement with the Turks which made easy the expulsion of the Hellenes; and that was the end of Mr. George. It was a signal triumph for the policy of the Arab Bureau. In the light of these facts, Lawrence's public propaganda and his confidential reports to the Government must be read. If in his first report he had described the Middle East as "our Monroe area" in the hope doubtless of provoking an anti-French declaration, he trimmed when he discovered that a majority of the British Cabinet was disinclined to go to war with France about it. Lawrence then invented a new slogan: "My own ambition is that the Arabs should be our first brown dominion, and not our last brown colony."[5] Clever propaganda, but had it any basis in reality? In fact it was a smart absurdity. Moreover, Lawrence's confidential advice to the Foreign Office contained such wild wishful thinking as this:

"Above all things in our interest a conflict between French and Arabs is to be prevented. If the Arabs came off badly, first clash, the affair might fizzle out, but they hold the initiative, and a preliminary success would unite all Moslem Syria against the

French in arms. Such action will probably force us back to the Baghdad and Jerusalem lines as a measure of security . . . "6

The event disproved this broad hint that kicking out Feisal would have such serious repercussions. In the same spirit, Lawrence tried to disparage Ibn Saud, who, as some officials in Irak were constantly and unsuccessfully trying to explain, through and against the propaganda of the Cairo Arab Bureau, was the real warrior leader of the desert Arabs through his control of the Wahabi movement. Which Lawrence countered thus:

" A Wahabi-like Moslem edition of Bolshevism is possible, and would harm us almost as much in Mesopotamia as in Persia."7

There was a paragraph in one of these memoranda which must have caused Lord Curzon to raise his eyebrows.

" I think Feisal will accept these terms, if I explain them to him. He has the Zionist proposals behind him, though I suggest that H.M.G.* remain ignorant of them! "8

How did Lawrence reconcile these confidential promptings of *Realpolitik* with his public pose as the heroic and self-sacrificing defender of " Arab freedom "? In the post-war chaos it seems to have been unnecessary, and of course very few were aware that the hero who so indignantly denounced the British Government for failing to keep its word to the Arabs had previously supplied confidential, though not very reliable, information to enable that Government to exploit the situation to its own advantage. In 1919, Lawrence was little known outside the small circle of specialists in Arabian affairs, though Mr. Lowell Thomas tells me Lawrence, on account of his Arab costume, did receive some publicity in American reports on the Peace Conference. In 1919 the Secretary of State for War was Mr. Winston Churchill, and somebody—he does not say who —called his attention to Lawrence, saying he was a " wonderful young man " whose exploits were " an epic." The then Secretary of State for War goes on to confess that up till that moment he had been " only dimly conscious of the part played in Allenby's campaigns by the Arab revolt in the desert."

The result of his investigations was that Lawrence was asked to

* His Majesty's Government.

lunch, and Mr. Churchill heard the story of Lawrence's returning his decorations to King George V. Mr. Churchill instantly rebuked this action as "monstrous," which was exactly what Lawrence wanted, for it enabled him to assert that the Arabs had been sacrificed to the demands of France in Syria, and their betrayal would be a dark stain on our history.[9] Apparently in studying the papers, Mr. Churchill did not stop to enquire just how it was that Lawrence's friend Feisal, a younger son of the Sharif-King of Mecca, always was identical with "the Arabs."

Nobody will be surprised to learn that there are at least two versions of this story of the returned decorations—the King's and the Bureau's. According to Lawrence, he made his statement to the King, not at the public investiture but at a private audience. The King at the private audience asked for "souvenirs," and Lawrence sent him a rifle captured from the Essex Regiment at the Dardanelles, given by Enver Pasha to Feisal, and by Feisal to Lawrence.[10] He said, moreover, that he had told the King his part in the Arab revolt was "dishonourable to himself and to his country and government," that "by orders" (of whom?) he had "fed the Arabs with false hopes." He went on to say: "I explained that I was probably going to fight them by fair means or foul, till they had conceded to the Arabs what in my opinion was a proper settlement of their claims."[11] This is taken from Lawrence's own statement to Graves, and what can the words about going to fight "them" mean, if not his "country and government" in the preceding sentence?

It so happened that the King ordered Lord Wigram to make a note immediately of what had happened.

From this we learn that the King's recollection of the incident—dictated at the time, and not remembered afterwards as was Lawrence's version—was not quite the same. The King heard Lawrence refuse the decorations because of promises made to Feisal (who had authorised promises to Feisal?), adding that, since these promises had not been kept, Lawrence might find himself "fighting against the British."[12] This statement was issued by King George's private secretary, Lord Stamfordham. But we can bring other evidence to disprove Lawrence's version. In 1931 the Duke of Windsor (then Prince of Wales) told Mr. Ralph H. Isham that Lawrence's action had "definitely caused the King embarrassment" because the refusal was not at the private audience, but " at the moment of presentation "—which lack of consideration for his father so much angered the prince that he refused ever to meet Lawrence.[13] Yet Lawrence denied to Liddell Hart that he had said he would " fight the British " and Professor Lawrence brushes aside the evidence of the King and the prince, and asserts: " In reality, it was in the preceding private audience with the King that he asked to be excused," and that Lawrence said he would have to fight the French, not the British.[14] We have Lawrence's own admission to Graves that he said he would fight the British; and is it credible that the King could have been mistaken as to the words spoken on the occasion of so rare a discourtesy?[15]

And was the return of the decorations genuine, a real renunciation and cancellation of the honours, or was it one more case of Lawrence's claiming the credit for an action he had not really performed? If he officially and completely denuded himself of his honours, how did it happen that when Winston Churchill sent him in 1921 to negotiate a treaty with Hussein, the patent began thus:

> " Our most trusty and well-beloved Thomas Edward Lawrence Esquire, Lieutenant-Colonel in Our Army, Companion of Our Most Honourable Order of the Bath, Companion of Our Distinguished Service Order . . . "[16]

If Lawrence had effectively resigned his honours, why were they cited in this patent? If he had not resigned them, why did he and his friends claim for him the *réclame* of having done so?

At the suggestion of the editor of *The Times*, Geoffrey Dawson, Lawrence was elected Fellow of All Souls College, Oxford—some say in February, but it was November, 1919. This was rather an honour than a living, for, although the fellowship was valid for seven years, the stipend began with a miserable £200 a year for three years, thereafter dropping to a token £50 a year. According to Sir Charles Oman (who, in spite of Lawrence's denigration, had in fact voted for his young colleague), All Souls was " a sort of week-end club " for well-known Oxonians of large private means or high salaries residing in London.[17] The purpose of this lavish award from Oxford was to enable Lawrence " to write a book about the Middle East." For, in the midst of his political interests, he had by no means lost sight of his literary and artistic ambitions. He still continued to talk of setting up a printing press, and of his intention of writing a " titanic book " about his experiences.

Indeed, at this time, Lawrence's literary ambitions led him at least to talk about writing yet another book. Readers of *Seven Pillars* will remember his remarks about Um Keis, the site of that Gadara which Meleager described as " Attic," because of the cultured Hellenized society which frequented the place in the 1st century B.C. Lawrence felt it was enshrined with memories of Menippus and of Meleager (whom, however, he considered " immoral "), and he seems to have made the common mistake of identifying that Gadara with the " Gadara " of the swine in the New Testament, since he says that, if he had destroyed the bridge there (which he didn't do), the deed would " enrol me in the Gadarene school."[18] Meleager and Menippus did not rush violently down a steep place into the sea, and the miracle of the possessed swine did not happen at Um Keis. But there is no doubt that Lawrence talked about writing a book to be called *Background of Christ*, and we can well believe that his indolence recoiled from the tremendous task of research involved—if only because the Hellenizing writers named by Lawrence were dead long before Jesus was born, and their influence on the Prophet of Nazareth didn't exist. Are we supposed to take seriously the following anecdote or was it put out as one more example of funny leg-pulling?

" Lawrence was talking to the Regius Professor of Divinity about the influence of the Syrian Greek philosophers on early Christianity, and especially of the importance of the University of Gadara close to the Lake of Galilee. He mentioned that St. James had quoted one of the Gadarene philosophers (I think Mnasalces) in his Epistle. He went on to speak of Meleager and the other Syrian-Greek contributors to the Greek Anthology, and of their poems in Syrian of which he intended to publish an English translation and which were as good as (or better than) their poems in Greek."[19]

Well, there wasn't a university at Gadara—it was a summer resort of the cultured wealthy—and Mnasalces lived in the 3rd-4th century B.C. and had nothing to do with Gadara, and was certainly not quoted in the epistle attributed to St. James. What is meant by " their poems in Syrian "? If Syriac is meant, it is a blunder, for the oldest known

Syriac inscription is dated A.D. 77—long after the death of the poets and philosophers in question—and, anyway, Syriac literature is almost wholly Christian. If it means Aramæan, where are the texts? In the 1st century B.C. in Syria, Aramæan (or Aramaic) was the language of the conquered, and the likelihood of its being used by the cultured Hellenizers of Gadara as a literary language is about as probable as that Walter Pater would write an essay on Signorelli in the dialect of Dorsetshire. Menippus was a Cynic, and his lost works, like the lost prose of Meleager, were said to " overflow with laughter." Philodemus was an Epicurean, whose treatises turned up in the Herculanean papyri. How they can be said in any way to have influenced Jesus or early Christianity baffles conjecture. If Lawrence's remarks have been correctly reported, he was either trying to pull the leg of a very ignorant professor or displaying a very spurious erudition.

Lawrence seemingly spent much of the year 1919 in London or abroad. He was in Paris when he heard that his father had died of influenza and pneumonia at Oxford on the 8th April, 1919,[20] and Lawrence at once flew to England. It is said that he stayed only a few hours, and then returned at once to Paris where he embarked on one of a flight of fifty Handley-Page planes which were being flown from England to Cairo. A friend of Lawrence's, Captain T. Henderson, was in command of one of the squadrons, and relates that he was rung up by an unnamed Peace Conference official, and, in spite of his protests, told that he must take a staff officer who wanted to go quickly to Egypt. The inadequate official reason given for the exceptional privilege of this flight was that the officer— who turned out to be Lawrence—merely wanted to collect his kit, while Lawrence himself gave out that he wished to collect certain papers he required for the writing of his war book.[21] Unfortunately —or as will appear later, perhaps fortunately for Lawrence—there was something wrong with these planes, which crashed all over France and Italy; and so many delays and accidents happened that even the leading planes took three months to fly from Northern France to Egypt. Lawrence's plane crashed near Rome, both pilots being killed, while he was badly injured, breaking ribs and his collar-bone and suffering slight concussion, the only one of the

WITH GENERAL ALLENBY at Covent Garden Theatre.

A Remarkable Film Lecture Telling the Strange Story of Colonel Thomas Lawrence, the Leader of the Arab Army

Colonel Thomas Lawrence (on Left) with Mr. Lowell Thomas

Colonel Lawrence is here seen at the entrance to his tent with Mr. Lowell Thomas, the American journalist, who at Covent Garden is telling the story of the Arab campaign

Colonel Thomas Lawrence

When war broke out Thomas Lawrence was a young archæological student engaged in work on ancient Mesopotamian cities. His knowledge of Arabia was first made use of in the map department at Cairo, and finally we find him as leader of the whole Arab Army in its fight from Mecca to Damascus. He wore this Arab style of dress throughout the campaign, and gained the confidence of chiefs and followers alike. A price was set upon his head but Colonel Lawrence won through to Damascus at the head of a devoted army

Mr. Lowell Thomas's wonderful pictures of the operations in Palestine, at Covent Garden, have revealed to many what a really big cavalry "shbiw" means, and what it entails in the way of general organisation and detail, writes a military correspondent. Few laymen, at any rate in England, ever get the chance of seeing large bodies of cavalry massed for operations of war or of peace. In India, where there is elbow room and space, and where cavalry both on manœuvres and in the almost unending warfare on the N.-W. Frontier get more practice than any other cavalry in the world, we have, upon occasion, seen something of it. Ever since the times of what were called the "Kitchener tests," those of us who have served in India have had a taste of what the handling of large masses of Horse means. But even in India, when we perhaps had the equivalent of a cavalry division on manœuvres, it was a ceremonial parade compared to what this tremendous cavalry operation which Field-Marshal Lord Allenby conducted in Palestine connoted. These pictures, perhaps, brought home to the layman what it meant; they perhaps made him think of what it meant in terms of fodder, in terms of sore backs, and in terms of horse-shoes, quite apart from the little matter of the feeding and watering of both the horse and the man on his back. Good cavalry are supposed to be able to exist on the smell of an oil-rag; they are supposed to be able to fend for themselves if put to it.

Sometimes this thing is politely called "foraging," but people have also another name for it. Fending for yourself is possible when only a comparatively small body is involved; it is a different pair of shoes, however, when something very like a whole cavalry corps is on the warpath, as was the case in Palestine. Allenby started his service with the Inniskillings; he has been a cavalry soldier all his days, and the cavalry spirit has been breathed into him since the time when he first learnt how to "carry swords."

No one but a cavalry leader of such brilliance would have dared to conceive an operation of this magnitude over such country. Allenby, however, knew the quality of the cavalry he had under him—hunting yeomen from the "shires" and the "provinces." Anzacs who were bred in the saddle, Sikhs, Punjabis, Pathans, Gukkars from the Salt Range, natural horsemen, and, above all, horse-masters, every man Jack of them, and he took it on and knew that his Horse would not fail him. The most astounding fact to the cavalry soldier, who happens to know what it all meant, was the low percentage of casualties in horse-flesh—on an all-round reckoning, less than 25 per cent. If the percentage had been 50 per cent, it would still have been a magnificent performance. As Mr. Lowell Thomas rightly adjudged, it is the most astonishing cavalry achievement in the whole history of war, ancient or modern.

Copyrighted in the U.S.A.　　　　　　　　　Drawn by D. Macpherson
The Palestine Film Lecture at Covent Garden

A large number of well-known personalities gathered on the opening night last week to hear Mr. Lowell Thomas's film lecture on the Palestine campaign. The lecturer showed pictures of Arab and other cavalry columns in motion which were quite unfamiliar to the man in the street

The lecture was called " With Allenby in Palestine " but the publicity centred on Lawrence. Bottom left is an artist's impression of the scene

[Reproduced by permission of the Sphere]

numerous plane accidents he claimed to have suffered for which there is any outside evidence.

David Garnett long ago pointed out that this story of collecting kit and papers was obviously " not the whole story,"[22] but he refrained from printing whatever it was he had learned. If we turn to Lord Wavell's reminiscences, we discover that in the spring of 1919 he was on Allenby's staff in Egypt, and was shown by his chief a Foreign Office telegram saying that Lawrence had been " lost " from the Peace Conference, that " the fiddle-stringed French were persuaded that he was on his way to Damascus to aid Feisal in a revolt against them," and that Lawrence was " on no account to be allowed to proceed to Syria."[23] But did even this telegram reveal the whole story? After all, Feisal was still in Paris when Lawrence's plane crashed, and he did not return to Damascus until May, while the Foreign Office would hardly have considered Lawrence " lost " if the telegram had been sent after the crash, seeing that Lawrence had been visited by Sir Rennell Rodd, the British Ambassador in Rome, and taken into the Embassy to be nursed. And though Lawrence and his political friends were as anti-French as ever, this would not seem to be the moment for Feisal to start an anti-French fight since real efforts were being made to come to an agreement. As early as the 8th March, 1919, Lord Milner had written:

" . . . although I am aware that I have almost every other Government authority, military and diplomatic, against me, I am totally opposed to the idea of trying to diddle the French out of Syria."*[24]

And Milner had gone on to suggest an interview between Feisal and Clemenceau. Late in February, Allenby had even said to M. Picot in Damascus that he wanted Feisal back in Syria, at least for a time, counting upon his authority " to check the movement towards xenophobia and panarabism."[25]

Looking unhopefully through the tedious and verbose documents relating to the 1919 Conference, I was interested to come on a passage which seems to explain this movement of Lawrence's in the most unlikely place—the minutes of the daily meetings of the Commis-

---

* The cool cynicism of British officials implied by Milner's remark is more than equalled by Lloyd George's in printing it in a book where he uses all his lawyer's skill in arguing that there was no British intrigue against the French in Syria !

sioners Plenipotentiary of the United States. On Thursday, March 20th, 1919, there were present Mr. Lansing, Mr. White, General Bliss, etc., and the following is recorded:

> " (5) Memorandum No. 168 was read in which General Churchill submitted a proposal that Captain William Yale accept an invitation tendered to him by Colonel Lawrence to accompany the British Forces on an expedition which they are planning for the month of May against the tribes of the Nejd."[26]

Deciding that they had been sent to Paris, not to make war but to make peace, the American Commissioners refused permission. But the document is surely suggestive. The " tribes of the Nejd " were, of course, Ibn Saud's Wahabis; and though there were no British forces to attack them, there did exist the British-trained, British-equipped troops of Abdulla, who precisely at this time was being urged by Hussein to make yet another attempt to seize and hold the disputed border oasis of Khurma. Four previous attempts had been made and had been beaten off by the inhabitants; and Ibn Saud had warned that he would deal severely with another attack. Hussein had been demanding that the British Government should allot him the place. If not, he was going to take it.

The scene now shifts to the Foreign Office in mid-March, where, under the presidency of Lord Curzon, was collected " an imposing array of generals, admirals, Under Secretaries of State," with Hubert Young as secretary. The discreet pages of Sir Hubert will be searched in vain for any mention of this meeting, but a detailed account has fortunately been left by St. John Philby, the only person present who had any first-hand knowledge of Ibn Saud and his formidable Wahabis. Lord Curzon summed up the situation in his inimitable way:

> " The position is that we have promised both parties to settle this dispute between them. Hussein is now pressing for a settlement as he is entitled to do. The arguments on both sides have been fully considered, and Mr. Philby has stated the case for Ibn Saud as ably as Ibn Saud could have wished. There is indeed room for differences of opinion on the merits of the case, but the matter is pressing and it is a question rather of policy than of the merits of the case. Now in all these Arabian problems our policy is a Hussein policy, and

we need not argue the grounds on which it is based. But it is something more than a question of policy. It is a matter of expediency also. We must be satisfied that our man, if we decide in his favour as we would like to do, will win if it comes to a fight. Otherwise the consequences may be very serious indeed."[27]

The numerous military experts present were all quite sure that the Hejaz forces would win, and Philby's prediction that, in spite of the threat to stop his subsidy, Ibn Saud would instantly march on Khurma, was dismissed. Hussein, being given the word from London, then entrusted the attack to Abdulla, who has left in his memoirs a rather confused account of what happened. But surely this Hashemite attack on Nejd must be the expedition to which Lawrence referred in his request to the Americans? And, whether he was secretly ordered to join Abdulla or whether he went off on his own responsibility, this plan for the Hejaz forces to take Khurma was surely the reason for his attempt to fly to Egypt in April? If the plane had not crashed, Lawrence would have had plenty of time to get to Abdulla long before the end of May. But for the plane-crash, Lawrence might have perished and would certainly have lost his military reputation in the disaster which overtook Abdulla's forces at a place called Turaba, before they ever reached Khurma. On the night of the 25th-26th May, the Wahabi forces swept into the village with a fury and ferocity which give some idea of the horror of the original Arab attacks on the civilised world. Abdulla and his staff just managed to escape on horseback, but " the rest of his army was annihilated,"[28] and the Wahabis left the bodies of the slain unburied, a fearful insult among Moslems. Among those massacred was the French officer, Raho, who for some reason had been left in the Hejaz. Practically all the 60-70 Sharifian regular officers were slain, and it is said that only about a hundred of Abdulla's army escaped.[29] According to Brémond, Abdulla also lost 12 guns, 20 machine-guns, 400 horses and mules, and 1,500 camels.[30] Now, this humiliating miscalculation of the British Government was indisputably based on wrong advice tendered by Lawrence and the Arab Bureau, who absurdly over-estimated the military value of the Hejaz forces, and under-estimated that of Ibn Saud and the Wahabis. One would suppose that so startling a demonstration of Lawrence's incompetence as an adviser would lead to some self-questioning on his part and some diminution of his occult influence. Not at all. When Philby was sent out by Curzon (unnecessarily as it proved) to try to stop Ibn Saud's falsely reported march on Mecca, he and Lawrence met at Allenby's table, and Lawrence continued to back his Hashemites—"Lady Allenby used to get positively nervous at the vigorous arguments bandied across her on the respective merits of the Arabian protagonists."[31] And at that time—June, 1919—Lawrence was within a few weeks of being carried to world-wide fame by one of the most successful advertising stunts in this century of uninhibited propaganda.

CHAPTER THREE

UP TILL the late summer of 1919, Lawrence was hardly known to the British public, if at all. He did not appear in *Who's Who* until the edition for 1920. As we have seen, even the 1919 Secretary of State for War had never heard of him. On the other hand, he was certainly becoming known in official and political circles, and his voice—which was to a great extent the voice of the Arab Bureau—had received undue respect and attention. He had been heard by the Eastern Committee of the Cabinet (which was afterwards replaced by the Interdepartmental Conference on Middle Eastern Affairs),[1] but then so was Philby; and Young of course was present as secretary at all meetings. It was certainly an honour for a young man, but far from unique. More exceptional was the fact that he had been allowed to appear in Arab dress before a meeting of the Council of Ten at Paris; and this, as already noted, did give him a little publicity, as a few of the American correspondents wrote about him.[2] He had also met or was meeting many influential people in London, and evidently he had friends who were pushing him sedulously—recollect that so important a figure in modern English history as Mr. Churchill was told that he ought to meet Lawrence whose exploits were 'an epic'.[3] Gertrude Bell at that time was then much better known than Lawrence, and her letters refer more than once to the newspaper space given her. Yet within a few months of August, 1919, Lawrence's name was known to millions, an immense popular reputation had been created for him as " the uncrowned King of Arabia," a " Prince of Mecca," and the pre-eminent British war hero of 1914-18.

The story of how this vast renown was created is of crucial importance in the life-story of Lawrence, and it has even some historical interest as showing how heroes were made in the first quarter of the 20th century. Lawrence has been called a king-maker, and with some show of reason, since Feisal and even Abdulla to some extent might be said to owe their thrones to his propaganda, but the man who made the king-maker and gave him his popular influence was Lowell Thomas. Strangely enough, the part played by Mr. Lowell Thomas in the creation of the Lawrence of Arabia legend has been almost entirely overlooked by his biographers. Thus, Graves and David Garnett pass over the four years' world publicity of the Chase-Thomas film-lecture with a few condescending lines; and in his 482 pages on Lawrence,[4] Liddell Hart does not even mention the Americans' names. The Lawrence Bureau attitude, strongly encouraged by Lawrence himself after he had fully profited by the lecture, was to be rather shocked and annoyed about it as a distressingly vulgar episode which could not be avoided and for which Lawrence was not in the least responsible, so that it was decorous and gentlemanly to snub Lowell Thomas. But, as I shall show, it was Lawrence who invited Chase and Thomas to come to Akaba and who persuaded Allenby to let them come; Lawrence was fully cognisant all along of their intentions, and collaborated in the production of the film, the lecture and the Thomas book. The Thomas lecture and the innumerable newspaper reports resulting from it created the Lawrence of Arabia legend by putting into public circulation many of the episodes, stories and anecdotes we have been investigating. Lowell Thomas made Lawrence front-page news for life, and, even when Thomas was not responsible for circulating the stories which Lawrence had been putting out since he was a lad, it was easy enough for Lawrence's friends and flatterers to get a wide reception for them once the notoriety was secured.

Even during his arduous campaigns, Lawrence had never made the blunder of under-estimating himself. We have already seen that after the capture of Akaba—of which such contradictory versions are given—Lawrence claimed to General Clayton that the whole plan and action had been his and modestly asked for command of British operations in Arabia. Similarly, when newcomers appeared on the scene, Lawrence turned on them all the eloquence and winning charm of manner to which we have so many testimonies. Parenthetically, those who did not share Lawrence's high opinion of himself usually did not last long in Arabia. True, in spite of that diplomatic *démarche* of the British Ambassador in Paris (inspired by Lawrence's "spiteful report"), Brémond had stayed on until it was time for him to return to the war; but Vickery vanished, Bray (who was a personal friend of Mark Sykes and had intervened at the Foreign Office on behalf of Hussein's rebellion in July, 1916[5]) somehow slid towards oblivion, Newcombe moved to another front, and his reminiscences of Lawrence halt significantly at December, 1914; even Young, who retained some critical faculty, is treated with marked displeasure in *Seven Pillars*, but could not so easily be got rid of since Lawrence himself had asked for this officer. When Young arrived at Akaba, Lawrence had assured him that there was "plenty of honour and glory to be picked up without any great difficulty," and then had proceeded to tell so many thrilling stories of his own deeds that Young ironically did not know "whether to be more alarmed or excited at the prospect of what lay before" him.[6]

Young, a regular soldier, seemingly bore up in spite of this spate of propaganda, but it is interesting to note the reaction of another officer, Major Buxton of the Camel Corps. In a letter written from Rumm, he says:

"Lawrence has started all this Arab movement. . . . He is known to every Arab in this country for his personal bravery and train-wrecking exploits. I don't know whether it is his intrepidity, disinterestedness and mysteriousness which appeal to the Arab most, or his success in finding them rich trains to blow up and loot. . . . His influence is astounding not only on the misbeguided natives, but also I think on his brother officers and seniors. Out here he lives entirely with the Arabs, wears their clothes, eats only their food, and bears all the burdens of the lowliest of them. He always travels in spotless white, and in fact reminds one of a Prince of Mecca more than anything. . . ."[7]

On the face of it, this looks unimpeachable evidence of Lawrence's feats, coming as it does from an honourable soldier. But, if we look at the Official History of the War, we shall discover that Major Buxton reached Akaba from the Palestine front for the first time on the 30th July, 1918,[8] while his letter was written on the 4th of August of the same year.⁹ Thus all these important discoveries were made by this officer within the space of five days at the utmost; and since it is obviously impossible that in so short a time he could personally have witnessed what he relates, we can only conclude that he was merely passing on to his correspondent the very favourable opinions of Lawrence which somebody had passed on to him. Much of what he says is inaccurate or exaggerated. Thus, as the evidence adduced earlier in this book shows, it is simply not true that Lawrence " started all this Arab movement," though undoubtedly he tried to make people think he had. And while it is true that he eventually became known throughout the Middle East, that was only " after the event, from the publicity which he received in books, newspapers and cinemas."¹⁰ The origin of all which was the Lowell Thomas film-lecture we are investigating.

Before the United States entered the war in April of 1917, Mr. Thomas had been an instructor on the faculty of Princeton, which, it will be remembered, was the University of President Wilson. Eager to get at the enemy, Mr. Thomas applied to the authorities at Washington for military employment. There it was pointed out to him that the very considerable British contribution to the war had been reported in the United States with piteous incompleteness, and he was told to go out and cover British operations on all fronts, pick up interesting news, and come back and tell it snappily to the home folks. The idea was, as Mr. Thomas explains with a most pleasing candour, by beating the drum loudly enough, to work up a hundred per cent enthusiasm for a war which America across the wide Atlantic still viewed with a certain aloofness.¹¹ Unluckily, the drab butchery of the Western Front did not lend itself either to thrilling photography or to eloquent narrative. There, Chase and Thomas found only mud and blood, wounds and death, monotony and devastation, where the discomforts of trench warfare were only varied by gigantic and endless battles in which you couldn't hear yourself think. For the newspaper-fed civilians of those days war was still " romance," culminating in charges of cavalry dressed in full ceremonial uniform, our side triumphantly sweeping " them " into defeat and surrender —in short, popular war had to be, as *Seven Pillars of Wisdom* announces itself, A Triumph. Where was " romance " to be found in this colossal turmoil of artillery barrages, this racket of machine-guns, this endless deadlock of slaughter? Mr. Thomas was more and more discouraged, and with reason—the world was not yet ripe for Ernie Pyle. At length Mr. Thomas, in something approaching despair, applied to John Buchan, afterwards Lord Tweedsmuir; and he, grasping at once the prosaic horror of the situation, arranged that Mr. Thomas should be accredited to General Allenby.[12]

Thus, towards the end of February, 1918, in consequence of Buchan's help, Mr. Thomas arrived in recently captured Jerusalem. Wandering in the streets one day, he suddenly was aware of a clean-shaved, magnificently robed Bedouin with a curved gold dagger, looking, as Mr. Thomas coined the phrase, "every inch a king," or perhaps "a Caliph in disguise," or, since it was in Jerusalem, "one of the younger apostles returned to life," complete with dagger.

Unable to find the exact information he craved from the passers-by and merchants of the bazaar, Mr. Thomas went direct to Ronald Storrs whom he somewhat unfairly describes as "the British successor to Pontius Pilate," and put a plain, homely, American question: "Who is this blue-eyed, fair-haired fellow wandering about the bazaars wearing the carved sword of a prince of——?" The sentence was not even completed when Storrs suddenly threw open a door and disclosed "the Bedouin prince," wholly "absorbed in a ponderous tome on archæology," with the thrilling announcement: "I want you to meet Colonel Lawrence, the Uncrowned King of Arabia."[13] As was natural, one might say inevitable, the young Princeton scholar instantly made friends with the riper Oxonian.

During these heart-to-heart talks, Lawrence would always squat on the floor; and the first time he did so "blushed in his peculiar way," and remarked negligently that he had now lived for so long in the desert that he found chairs uncomfortable.[14] From these talks, Mr. Thomas learned that his bazaar hero, this "Prince of Mecca," had "virtually become the ruler of the Holy Land of the Mohammedans, and commander-in-chief of many thousands of Bedouins mounted on racing camels and fleet Arabian horses."[15]

As a young man straight from a mining camp in the Rockies, Mr. Thomas had been particularly "intrigued" with the idea that Allenby might "liberate the Holy City." And then, quite by accident, without one word of prompting from any human being, he had stumbled on this Lawrence epic, and instantly felt that he was on to "one of the greatest scoops in history."[16] What more natural, more inevitable than that he should follow up this story? But difficulties cropped up, which of course made him only the more anxious to pick up his news and pictures. Allenby, he heard, did not like reporters; and did not want the Moslem world to know that there were European officers in "the Arab forces"—a fact which must surely have been known throughout the Middle East since December, 1916, at latest. But, now Lawrence himself, in his generous and disinterested way, came to the rescue, and helped to get Allenby's permission for Thomas to go to him in the desert "for the Damascus campaign".[17] (Note the Damascus campaign.) Following this intercession on the part of Lawrence, Allenby lunched with Mr. Thomas and the Duke of Connaught, and graciously announced that if Mr. Thomas was interested in what was going on in Arabia, why "he would be glad to have me join King Hussein's army and afterwards tell the world a little of what the Arabs had done towards helping win the Great War."[18] But, such was the stress on that fighting front, that none of the usual transport facilities for war correspondents could be granted; and the two young Americans lost a great deal of time through having to proceed 1,500 miles up the Nile, then across the desert to Port Sudan, and at last by overcrowded tramp steamer to Akaba.[19]

When did Thomas and Chase reach Akaba, how long were they with Lawrence and what did they personally see? Unluckily, the members of the Lawrence Bureau have not been lavish with dates, and Lawrence himself was never anxious to give information about the visit of these enthusiastic Americans. He liked to pretend that the Lowell Thomas lecture and book had been produced virtually without his knowledge or consent, and definitely without his aid and approval. In 1927, Lawrence asserted that he did not know when Thomas reached Akaba, because he was "up country" when he arrived, spent "perhaps three days" with him at Akaba, and was again "up country" when the Americans left. Ten to fourteen days, he thought, covered their whole stay.[20] The Duke of Connaught, with whom Mr. Thomas lunched, was at Jerusalem in March, 1918.[21]

Young mentions condescendingly the arrival at Guweira of an American maker of cinema films at a date after 7th April, and adds that he " had perforce to content himself for the present with listening to the stories which were told him by the various British officers,"[22] which seems the obvious source of some of Mr. Thomas's tales, though many of them clearly came from Lawrence himself. According to Lawrence's table of movements, he was at Guweira on the 30th-31st March, on the 13th April, and at Akaba on the 26th April; after which he was away in Egypt until the 21st May.

The photographs of Lawrence by Mr. Chase in Thomas's *With Lawrence in Arabia* are carefully posed studies, and were taken either in Jerusalem, Cairo or possibly Guweira. But the fact is that Lawrence personally did not take the two Americans " up country," they never saw him on the Damascus campaign and indeed witnessed few if any of the alleged exploits Mr. Thomas has recorded so graphically. But Feisal did take the Americans up to Waheida, a place not far from Maan, and there gave them a dinner on an improvised table at which they sat on boxes—not having lived so long in the desert that they " preferred to squat." They were then sent on a war-time Cook's tour to Petra under the guard of two of Feisal's men, with Hassan Khalil, a fierce-looking interpreter, with " flashing eyes and fierce moustache."[23] He wore a red head-dress, multi-coloured robes, and carried two daggers and a pearl-handled revolver. This wild and romantic son of the desert introduced himself to the two Americans as Charley Kelley, " machine-operator in a tobacco factory " in New York; and fairly shattered them with such Arabian Knight's remarks as: " Say, cul, will youse slip me de can opener ? "[24] Under his guidance they safely visited Petra, where Mr. Chase took some admirable photographs. Petra—if you will look at the map—is to the west and north of the then supposedly heavily Turkish-occupied Maan, which suggested that camel rides in the country out of range of the Turkish posts may not have been so thrillingly dangerous after all. Sharif Feisal would hardly have risked the awful responsibility of losing two American journalists.

Mr. Thomas had barely completed his first-hand study of the war theatres when the Armistice upset all his plans, and he then went to Germany to study the Revolution. Consequently, his lecture, *With Lawrence in Arabia*, was not delivered until the 9th March, 1919, at the Century Theatre, New York. As a matter of fact, there were five lectures, but Mr. Thomas discovered that his audience was not in the least interested in the ordinary war fronts, but only in Allenby's campaign and above all in the Arabs. " Because the Allenby and Lawrence shows were full of sweeping cavalry, Arabs, camels, veiled women, Holy cities, they caught on and attracted great crowds."[25] What could be more honest than that statement? But Mr. Thomas fails to give the credit due to Chase's photography and his own eloquence—which was virtually unfettered since his proclaimed object was propaganda and picturesque reporting, not the drab factual pedantry of history and biography.

The Allenby-Lawrence lectures were so great a success that Mr. Thomas moved from the Century Theatre to Madison Square Gardens, after which he had arranged for a year's tour across America. On his last night in New York, his show was seen by a British impresario, Percy Burton, who invited Mr. Thomas to bring it to England. The lecturer explained that he had American engagements, but added that he intended to take August off and would come to England (he said jokingly) if he received an invitation from the King and was given either Drury Lane or Covent Garden.[26] It is perhaps not without significance that both conditions were met. Mr. Thomas opened his film-lecture at Covent Garden on the 14th August, 1919. Burton with his subtle devices had filled the theatre with the finest first-night audience seen in London since before the war.[27] And Mr. Thomas did not fail his hero and (secret) collaborator. From Sir Thomas Beecham he had borrowed an opera set, the Moonlight-on-the-Nile scene from " Joseph and his Brethren," and hired the band of the Welsh Guards to provide a " half-hour of atmospheric music to get the audience in the right mood." Then there was a prologue, which most fittingly included a Dance of the Seven Veils. Even this was not considered sufficient psychological preparation, so Mrs. Thomas—who was a musician—composed a musical setting for the Mohammedan call to prayer, which was sung off-stage by an Irish tenor.[28]

And then came the film and the lecture. Unluckily, the lecture was never written down, and each time it was given it was a fresh creation, following of course the same general lines, and built round the accompanying motion pictures. Mr. Thomas tells me that the films have now so much shrunk with age that they can no longer be shown, and that the scrap-books he owns of contemporary reviews contain none which give a summary of his lecture, while all these very numerous notices dwell on the same topics—the film and the anecdotes. And, as Mr. Thomas says he has now forgotten his lecture, it cannot be reconstructed except by doubtful inference from the tone and matter of his book. Lecture and book (which sold approximately 200,000 copies in the English edition) were the first means of introducing Lawrence to large audiences, and so strong was the original impression created that for the whole of his life Lawrence was seen through this golden mist of spurious glamour. I must repeat that Lowell Thomas personally saw few, if any, of the exploits he relates with such sensational emphasis; he had to rely on what he was told by Lawrence, by Lawrence's associates and by the Arab Bureau. Yet he clearly went to great pains to interview as many of them as possible, and his book includes notices of Newcombe, Wilson, Cornwallis, Dawnay, Hogarth, Joyce, Stirling, Young, Marshall, and even the demolition experts Garland and Hornby. He also certainly met some of the Arab chieftains who figure with so much bravura in the pages of *Seven Pillars*.

I must also repeat that Lowell Thomas was sent out to find news to make propaganda, not to collect material for history. He seems to have been given what must have looked like the impossible task of discovering a contemporary British hero who would be acceptable to the American public. He succeeded in doing this, and in discovering him for the British, too. Up till that time, the most successfully publicised British war hero was Rupert Brooke, a tribute to the high prestige of authors at the beginning of this century. What was now wanted was a success story, and who could give it better than an American, for whom success is a national duty? The technique was hardly understood at all in England, where advertising seldom rose above a flat monotony of uninventive mendacity—" Ponsonby's Pickles *are* the Best." With the aid of moonlight on the Nile, the atmospheric music of the military band, the Dance of the Seven Veils and the Irish tenor, the tale of the " Prince of Mecca " became a triumph. Triumph was so successfully sounded as the keynote that Lawrence adopted " *A Triumph* " as the sub-title of his own book.

The result at Covent Garden was startling. The whole theatre was sold out from the first night, and the show eventually had to be transferred in turn to the Albert Hall, the Philharmonic Hall and the Queen's Hall. It ran for just under six months and then set off on a tour of the English-speaking world. The film, of course, remained the same, but as Mr. Thomas was constantly picking up new hints he was able to vary his extempore talk, which was actually delivered some two thousand times. In London the show was patronised by Allenby and Feisal, and among others involved in its action, who are recorded as having seen it, were Generals Chetwode and Bartholomew, Colonels Joyce, Dawnay and Cornwallis. It was seen by Mr. Lloyd George, most of the Cabinet, and many members of both Houses of Parliament. In Australia, distinguished members of the audience mounted the platform after the performance to congratulate the lecturer on his just tribute to their merits and it is related that " Brigadier General Fighting Charlie Cox " was roused to such enthusiasm on the edge of the platform that he fell into the orchestra stalls, breaking his leg.[29]

Behind the success and aiding it was a strong if secret political motive. This irresponsible panegyric was just what the Government sorely needed to try to pass off its enormous expenditure and casualties in the Middle East, and to gain popular support for its policy of " Brown Dominions " and trying " to diddle France out of Syria." Mr. Lloyd George was so much pleased that he sent Mr. Thomas a message through Lord Riddell asking him to write and publish the story of " the Arabs " immediately. Lord Northcliffe, John Buchan, and Walter Duranty agreed that Mr. Thomas's " story " was " one of the greatest scoops in history." This favourable verdict was endorsed by Lord Burnham and Major Astor at a public reception given for Lowell Thomas by the London newspaper proprietors at the Criterion Hotel. Clearly, the whole splendid epic had been lifted out of the squalid surroundings of mere history and literature to the serene and opulent heights of popular journalism.[30]

The effects of the Chase-Thomas film-lecture on far less exalted personages was also striking. From many testimonies we may select that of Lawrence's favourite painter and sculptor, Mr. Eric H. Kennington. This eminent artist records that his first acquaintance with Lawrence was through Lowell Thomas's film shown at the Albert Hall. He was tremendously impressed by the photography and glamour.[31] And beyond and below these were the unknown million of British admirers of whose dazzlement nothing has been recorded, though it can be inferred from the indisputable fact that for the rest of his life Lawrence was front page news. Of course, they were children in the sway of a conscious or unconscious master of mob psychology. Every American entertainer tries to lull his audience by getting an early laugh out of them at his expense. Mr. Thomas began: " It never had occurred to me that the British people might be interested in the story of their own campaigns told through the nose of a Yankee." Is there a radio or advertising man in the world who does not envy Mr. Thomas that gambit ? All that he was going to show and tell the British was " their own campaigns," and the moment he had them genially laughing from the height of their superiority at the funny little American, he had got the grip on them he needed. Anyone who has seen a Japanese judo expert throwing hundredweights of London policemen about a stage will realise what Lowell Thomas did mentally and emotionally with those naïve British audiences.

While it is now impossible to reconstruct this hero-making lecture, something of its nature may perhaps be inferred from the book which followed it up and which Mr. Lloyd George so warmly encouraged. Mr. Thomas evidently acted on the sound journalistic principle that while he might not be a high authority on Arabia and its affairs, he knew more about them than most of his audience or readers. He doubtless calculated that what little they thought they knew came from hazy memories of the Arabian Nights and the Bible, a reading of sensational novels of " The Sheik " kind, and the newspapers. Snappy slogans and picturesque anecdotes would obviously be more effective than laborious expositions of tedious fact. " Arabian Knights " as a title for Lawrence and his associates seems a little daring and open to ridicule, but evidently was found acceptable in the general enthusiasm. " Shereef " or " Sharif " was plainly ridiculous as a title or description for an Anglo-Irishman since it is restricted to descendants of the Prophet, but possibly most people didn't know this; and, after all, that gold dagger must have meant something. Lawrence told Graves that the title of " Prince of Mecca was conferred on me by Lowell Thomas," but it appeared in his *Who's Who* record for 1921 and it was certainly used in August, 1918 (months before

Mr. Thomas began lecturing) in the letter written by Major Buxton, so there seems a strong probability that Lawrence conferred it on himself.

Quite apart from these catchy honorifics, Mr. Thomas had some impressive stories to tell his readers and, no doubt, the listeners to his lecture. Lawrence, he says, had 200,000 men available under his command, including those " Knights of the Black Tents," the Bedouins, whose chivalrous conduct at Deraa and elsewhere we have had occasion to note. He asserts boldly that " to accompany Lawrence and his bodyguard on an expedition was a fantastic experience," which may be so, but, his brilliant description reflects his imaginative powers.

> " First rode the young shereef, an incongruous picture with his Anglo-Saxon face, gorgeous head-dress and beautiful robes. Likely enough, if the party were moving at a walking pace, he would be reading and smiling to himself over the brilliant satire of Aristophanes in the original. Then in a long irregular column his Bedouin ' sons ' followed in their rainbow-coloured garments, swaying to the rhythm of the camel-gait."[32]

But, in spite of the attractions of Aristophanes " in the original," Lawrence was also capable of stern action. Thus, after the capture of Akaba, he " jumped on his racing camel " and " rode her continuously for 22 hours across the Sinai Peninsula to Port Tewfik," a world record for a desert journey of at least 150 miles. Arrived there " he sat in a bath for three hours with a procession of Berberine boys serving him cool drinks."[33] We may also recall the occasion when Lawrence interrupted a conversation about Hittite civilisation as a link between Babylon and Crete to confess that " one of the most thrilling sights " he had ever seen was " a trainload of Turkish soldiers ascending skywards " after a train demolition.[34] Another time he told how after a train-wrecking some of the surviving Turks tried to attack him; but, before they had gone " six paces," Lawrence " whipped out his long-barrelled Colt from the folds of his abba and used it so effectively that they turned and fled."[*][35] But if they were able to fly, he must surely have missed the lot? Lawrence always carried with him "a heavy American-frontier model weapon."[36]

* This sounds like Lawrence's final work-up of the Turkish officer who shot at Pisani.

What audience could resist so glamorous a hero? Especially when they learned that he had risen from the lower orders, " a shy young Oxford undergraduate," " a twenty-eight years old scholar and poet," a " studious archæologist," to be " the leader of a hundred thrilling raids, creator of kings, commander of an army, and world's champion train-wrecker."[37]

And then the veiled women. It is true that Lawrence in his anti-feminist way has told us that there was " nothing female about the Arab movement but the camels," and of the merry jests practised by his light-hearted bodyguard who often caused a female camel on the march to bolt " by thrusting a stick into its rump." Everyone knows that Arabia abounds with veiled women, and they had to be brought in somehow, for you can't sell even a new brand of tomato ketchup without feminine attractions. Women are ingeniously brought into the epic (with coy photographs) as introduction to the story that when Colonel Lawrence was not conducting " major military operations " or " planting tulips " (explosives, not his bodyguard), he " would disguise himself as an outcast Arab woman and slip through the enemy lines. . . . Time and again he penetrated hundreds of miles into enemy territory, where he obtained much of the data which finally enabled Field-Marshal Allenby's forces to overwhelm the Turks in the most dazzling and brilliant cavalry operation in history."[38] There were no Turkish lines in Arabia Petræa, but only isolated posts along the Hejaz railway, and, as long as he kept away from them and had reliable guides from Feisal, Lawrence was perfectly safe among the tribes; what little information he brought back was political rather than military, and often misleading at that. Similarly, although he in fact was not present at the variously-reported action of Maulud's forces in October, 1917, Lawrence, according to this narrative " slipped through the Turkish lines in disguise and returned with a copy of the Turkish *communiqué* of the battle,"[39] a useless feat of daring as they could have read it in the newspapers. When Lawrence and " the Arabs " triumphantly entered Damascus (far ahead of everyone else, of course), " howling dervishes ran in front of him, dancing and sticking knives into their flesh, while behind him came his flying column of picturesque Arabian Knights."[40] After all this, one is not surprised to learn that for Mr. Thomas in the end Lawrence appeared as a mixture or coalition of Marco Polo and General Gordon.[41] He was a soldier who had been " cited for nearly every decoration that the British and French Governments had to offer."[42]

In spite of all disclaimers and attempts to ignore or to snub Lowell Thomas out of the way, Lawrence's immense popular reputation was wholly due to his successful propaganda which at the time was politically gratifying to the Lloyd George Government and supported by them. How otherwise would Lawrence have been heard of outside specialist circles? Contributions to *The World's Work* and *The Army Quarterly* and (anonymously) to *The Round Table* would not have done it. He had to have an impresario, a fugleman, and Lowell Thomas did the job with resounding success—in fact, he overdid it, to the life-long delight but occasional embarrassment of his hero. But the reputation once made on this scale and in this image could not be altered, and inevitably for a generation every estimate of Lawrence was unconsciously influenced by Thomas's episodes and anecdotes and his optimistic over-valuation. Graves and Hart, for instance, tone down what to English ears sounds Thomas's blatant note, but as a matter of fact they contain just as many anecdotes that strain credulity. But the influence spread beyond them to other writers who joined in the chorus. What is one to say to a passage like this?

" Take the heart of St. Francis or Lincoln, join it to the mind of Leonardo da Vinci and the driving will of Stonewall Jackson; set them in the body of an anchorite or a Stefánsson; add the artful resource of all men of wiles from Odysseus to Sven Hedin and the tongue of a Shakespearian Conrad; stir all this into a wild old desert people on the warpath, and then you might get—*Revolt in the Desert*. But to get the *Seven Pillars of Wisdom*, you are bound to bring in Lawrence himself; for without him there is no troubled Hamlet to this great play."[43]

Well, that no doubt was the recipe for the seething cauldron of the Lawrence Bureau, but too many cooks and ingredients spoiled the broth. As a writer, Lawrence was another if not better Shakespeare (they claim); as a soldier, a definitely better Napoleon;[44] and as a character? But the reader will already have guessed. At Oxford he had once sat up all night discussing with a friend the principles on which they should base their lives, and Lawrence " considered that Christ had lived the most perfect life and he decided to model his on it."[45]

Moreover, other recorders of the Arab War somehow took on this *splendide mendax* style of writing. Thus, Mr. S. C. Rolls (one who was afterwards with Lawrence in Arabia) describes how his armoured car detachment rescued some captive and very hungry British seamen from the Senussi in the Libyan desert. "I tore open my locker and tipped out my emergency rations of bully beef, and in their ravenous haste to get at the contents they ripped the tins open with their teeth."[46] Admirers should make the experiment.

Readers of *Seven Pillars* will remember the neurotic outburst: "There was a craving to be famous; and a horror of being known to like being known. Contempt for my passion for distinction made me refuse every offered honour," etc.[47] He didn't refuse honours; he accepted all he could get until the moment when refusal was louder than acceptance. The first sentence is true, and explains but does not justify his treatment of Lowell Thomas. He collaborated with Lowell Thomas in the production of the lecture, went—as he hoped secretly—several times to bask in it; but when once Mr. Thomas had served his purpose, Lawrence personally and through the books he inspired tried to pretend that he had nothing to do with the lecture, hardly knew Lowell Thomas, and was deeply hurt in the tenderest part of his honour by this self-assertive fellow! But, after all, Lowell Thomas was not pushing himself, and if his lecture contained "crudities," who gave them to him? "In 1919," says Mr. Thomas, "he would spend the whole afternoon with me, going over the details of the campaign, helping me in endless ways with the story."[48] Yet the reader is again referred to the "Publisher's Note" at the beginning of Mr. Thomas's book.*[49]

This is exactly the same technique that Lawrence followed with Graves, passing every word of the book, and then persuading Graves to put in a sentence making it look as if Lawrence had not collaborated.[50] Lowell Thomas, perhaps unwittingly, showed that the disclaimer in his book was false when he wrote his contribution to *T. E. Lawrence by his Friends*. There he confesses that he consulted Lawrence in London in 1919 about setting down the lecture story on paper. Lawrence, who in November accepted a fellowship at All Souls in order to write a book about his Middle East experiences,

* See pages 107-8.

told Mr. Thomas that he himself did not intend to write a book, and had "not the slightest objection" to Thomas's "doing a bit of writing about him." Moreover, Lawrence gave active help, and "regularly" walked out to Richmond Park to discuss the book, and it was on one of these visits that he made his cynical remark about history not being made up of truth, so why worry?[51]

We need not rely solely on Mr. Thomas's already quoted testimony to Lawrence's collaboration in the Lowell Thomas book.* In a chapter about the Bedouins, Thomas mentions that after a sheik had done something, Lawrence would allow him to thrust his hand into a bag of sovereigns, and keep all he could hold.[52] This same story was told by Lawrence in a letter to Edward Garnett in 1927, where he boasts that the sheiks thought it the last word in splendour but was economical since it never cost more than a hundred and twenty pounds—in addition to the subsidies.[53] Moreover, in another chapter, Lowell Thomas reproduces almost word for word passages from a set of instructions on how to behave to Arabs which Lawrence contributed to *The Arab Bulletin* for the 20th August, 1917. One of these passages is ten or twelve lines long.[54] How could Thomas have these passages if Lawrence or the Arab Bureau had not given them?

Mr. Thomas showed a remarkable complaisance in playing up to Lawrence's peculiar quirk or craving for notoriety while wishing the world to believe that he hated it. How was it possible to reconcile with this contempt for vulgar publicity the undeniable fact that Lawrence was willingly one of the most photographed men of his time, and was always offering himself as a model to painters and sculptors? Apparently at the time of the lecture, people accepted the modesty story along with all the others. But when awkward questions came along, Mr. Thomas invented what he himself frankly calls "a cock-and-bull story."[55] Lawrence, he maintained, had been "tricked" into being photographed. "While I distracted T. E. with a conversation about Hittite archæology, his pet subject, Chase sat near us, pretending to fiddle with a high-speed camera of the sort used by tabloid photographers in America."[56] It is incredible that such a feeble story could be believed by anyone who had even glanced

* See page 108.

at the posed and posturing photographs in Thomas's book. Equally incredible is Mr. Thomas's reflection: " I could see no other explanation that would not place T. E. in a false light."[57] Mr. Thomas should have said " in his true light." The falsity lay with the man who posed for Chase's publicity photographs and then pretended to be so shrinkingly modest that this silly story had to be made up. Mr. Thomas assures me that Lawrence was always particularly anxious that " I should give full credit—in fact more than that—to Joyce, Dawnay, Feisal, Abu Tyi and others."[58]

By way of giving himself written alibis, Lawrence sent a note to Lowell Thomas: " I saw your show last night and thank God the lights were out ";[59] and when Burton the impresario asked him to be interviewed, he wrote: " It is unpleasant to see one's name in print and—in spite of the nice way Lowell Thomas does it—I much wish he had left me out of his Palestine show."[60] But it was Lawrence who had persuaded Allenby to let Thomas go to Arabia to start with, Lawrence who had posed for all the photographs, and Lawrence who collaborated in the lecture! It was Lawrence, too, who with " his eyes snapping with glee," told Mr. Thomas that his lecture " had made life impossible for him in London. Wherever he went he was stopped in the streets."[61] As late as 1926, Professor Namier met Lawrence in Air Force uniform, and Lawrence said that he had been walking all afternoon about the British Museum where all the attendants had at one time known him; but he had remained unrecognised till he asked about someone he missed there. On which the Professor comments somewhat caustically that it was obviously useless for him to disguise himself if no one recognised him.[62]

He used to call on or write to the publishers and alter his entry in *Who's Who*, not just adding as everybody does, but cutting out and altering.[63] Thus in 1921 his entry read:

" Lawrence, Thomas Edward, Lieutenant-Colonel, C.B. 1917; D.S.O. 1918; Prince of Mecca, Archæologist, Arabic Scholar, Research Fellow of All Souls College, Oxford, 1919. Educ. Jesus College, Oxford (scholar), 1st class Modern History School, 1910. Magdalen College, Oxford (Senior Demy B.A., 1911). Went to the East, 1914; 2nd Lt., 1914; Colonel, 1917. Organised the forces of the King of the Hejaz against the Turks, 1917. Chevalier

Legion of Honour; Croix de Guerre with Palms; C.B.: on staff of Prince Feisal. Attended Peace Conference, 1919."[64]

In August, 1922, Lawrence wrote to Bernard Shaw that " next year, *Who's Who* will not have me in it."[65] But, with various suppressions and alterations, his *Who's Who* entry continued until 1930, when the reader is referred to " Shaw, Thomas Edward," and so went on until his death. In the 1922 version, he dropped the Prince of Mecca and the mention of his decorations, but added: " Adviser on Arab affairs, Mid.-East Div. Colonial Office since 1921." In 1928, he added his publications, but in 1923 he corrected his military record, and instead of " staff of Prince Feisal," put himself on the staff of Wingate for 1917 and of Allenby for 1918. I don't quote the 1920 entry, because there is reason to believe it may have been made without his corrections.[66]

It can scarcely be said that Lawrence showed much gratitude to Lowell Thomas for the immense free advertising he received. Mr. Thomas writes a little wistfully about their later relations and his mistake in taking Lawrence at his word and leaving him severely alone, thinking Thomas had lost interest in him.[67] I fear Mr. Thomas rather flatters himself. As soon as the lecture had closed down in England, Lawrence was only too anxious to repudiate him and to give the impression that he had hardly known him and had no share in producing lecture or book. Thus Lawrence in one letter refers to " a Mr. Lowell Thomas,"[68] and complains that he has been made " a kind of matinée idol by him." This was in March, 1920, and a month earlier he had written to Colonel Newcombe:

" In the history of the world (cheap edition), I'm a sublimated Aladdin, the thousand and second Knight, a *Strand Magazine* strummer. In the eyes of ' those who know,' I failed badly in attempting a piece of work which a little more resolution would have pushed through, or left untouched."[69]

If he really believed that, why did he proceed to write a very long and elaborate book about his actions in Arabia, and describe it as " A Triumph "? To Hogarth, wanting to find an excuse for publishing his own book, after he had said he would not profit by his war reputation, he wrote: " Yet Lowell Thomas lurks still in the background, and if his book is the fulsome thing I expect, he will force

the truth out of me. It might be better to get my blow in first."[70]
But Lawrence had told Thomas that he didn't intend to write a book
about himself, although when he said that he had already started to
write it! If Mr. Thomas had been aware of the facts he would probably not have undertaken the task or have spent so many afternoons
collecting Lawrence's veracious reminiscences and anecdotes. The
final repudiation appeared in Graves's book, and may fittingly close
this chapter on the making of a hero's fame:

> "The advertising of his Arabian adventure, both by the Press
> and by Mr. Lowell Thomas's cinema lecture-tour, proved most
> unwelcome to him."[71]

But once again, Lawrence had arranged it all himself! What need
was there to persuade Allenby to allow Chase and Thomas to go to
Arabia, what need to pose for endless photographs and to prime
Thomas with examples of the self-advertising anecdotes Lawrence had
been telling about himself from boyhood? When Allenby gave the
permission he could not have supposed that the reporting of the Arab
rebellion would become twisted into making a liaison officer with
Feisal the colossus of the whole Middle Eastern front, and of the
World War. Once done, it was eagerly backed up by the " great "
for political reasons. Mr. Raymond Savage, with evident sincerity,
says that if " T. E. had courted publicity," Mr. Savage, as his literary
agent, would have been able to give him " as much as he could
possibly desire."[72] But Lawrence had been already cleverly and un-
deservedly " put across " to the great public as *the* hero of World
War I. Lowell Thomas, let me repeat, had made him front-page
news for life. What the newspapers don't want is any form of
concealed advertising; what they do want is any sensational-
sounding information about a public figure which is being kept
secret. Lawrence was always most careful to foster the illusion
that he was frantically avoiding publicity, which naturally created the
suspicion that he had something of great public interest to conceal.
Perhaps the last word on this may be left to his friend, Bernard Shaw,
who undeniably was an expert on this particular subject:

> "When he was in the middle of the stage, with ten limelights
> blazing on him, everybody pointed to him and said: ' See! He is
> hiding. He hates publicity.' "[73]

CHAPTER FOUR

Acccoording to a letter written on that day from Oxford, Lawrence was demobilised on the 1st of September, 1919,[1] and not " in July," as he told Liddell Hart,[2] or the " 31st July," as he told Robert Graves.[3] The discrepancy is not of the slightest importance except that it illustrates so well Lawrence's modest confession " that he never forgot anything he's read in a book and that, without an effort, he could recall any date."[4] At least one of his readers fervently wishes that he hadn't kept them nearly all to himself. Like everyone else in that situation of abrupt return to civilian status, he was faced with the problem of what to do with the life suddenly handed back to him after years of servitude.

On the face of it, he seemed more fortunate than most temporary officers just released. Lowell Thomas had made him the hit of the season in London, and was rapidly building him up as the national hero. An Oxford College had given him rooms (very hard to find at the time) and a small subsidy to write a book. But early in the next year he had discovered at least one of the inconveniences attached to great popularity. He wrote that he loved it though he couldn't afford it: he felt that popular heroes who were poor suffered greatly at the hands of well-intentioned admirers.[5] This brings up the topic of Lawrence's finances, which is another of his *ténébreuses affaires*. It is impossible to reconcile the different statements he made about his money affairs, and very likely this was done intentionally.

At all events on demobilisation, his army pay ceased and (as already pointed out) he claimed that he received only a small gratuity. His statement that during the war he put all his pay " into the show " probably means no more than that, like most other young officers, he spent it. His only known earned income at that time was the £200 a year from All Souls, and that in a period of inflation. Yet on that same day (1st September, 1919), he bought a little more than five acres of land at Pole Hill, Chingford, Essex, where he vaguely planned to build his medieval " hall " and to work at a new Kelmscott Press with his friend, Richards.[6] The same letter says that he was so short of ready money at the time that he was not able to go on and buy a hedge at Chingford he wanted, but adds that he expects about £300 within six weeks. This may have been the war gratuity, of which he said he received only £110.

At that time he had written a large part of his war book, and certainly then hoped to make money out of it.[7] Moreover, he evidently expected to inherit some of Sir Thomas Chapman's estate, unless it was mere boasting which led him to write to F. N. Doubleday: " My father was kind to me, and spent none of the capital he received from his father . . . and unless I marry non-supporting wives or have children, all will be well with me."[8] It is hopeless to try to reconcile this rentier's letter with his sturdy working-man's statement to the Socialist M.P., Thurtle, that he (Lawrence) was " almost entirely self-made," as his father had " five sons, and only £300 a year."[9] Although he received no money under his father's will, Lawrence also wrote to Mrs. Shaw stating definitely that he had received money from Ireland.[10] On the other hand, it would appear that he expected more than he actually received, for this seems the only interpretation of his letter to Mr. Kennington in 1921, where Lawrence says: " A lump of money I was expecting has not (probably will not) come."[11] Yet one can seldom trust him, for in this same letter he uses as another excuse for non-payment a story that his " house in Epping has been burnt down."[12] It was not a house but a hut, and it did not belong to Lawrence though it stood on his land; it belonged to Mr. Richards, and " Lawrence had nothing whatever to do with it, nor did he live with me there."[13]

All this is very confused, but one fact stands out clearly—during the period 1919-22, Lawrence overspent hopelessly and got heavily into debt. He could not resist doing things " in a lordly way," any more than he could resist his impulses of generosity. When he had money, he must spend it, and this led him to make reckless debts and commitments which he could not afford. It was generous but unwise. If he had really been the well-off Irish squireen Arabian hero he posed as, what could have been a better use of superfluous money than to come to the aid of Charles Doughty, who was in temporary financial difficulties? Lawrence arranged that the manuscript of Doughty's long poem, *The Dawn in Britain*, should be bought for the British Museum for £400, and David Garnett thinks that Lawrence had contributed most of the money. But Lawrence was quite unable to afford such a gift, while not long after Doughty inherited a life income of £2,000 a year. Again, there were few writers of the time more deserving of financial aid than Robert Graves. Lawrence gave him £50 in addition to the £200 (thousand dollars) he received from *The World's Work.*[14] It is characteristic of his vanity that in writing to Sir Edward Marsh, Lawrence turned the dollars into pounds, and claimed that he had been paid £1,000—nearly five thousand dollars at that period! Of course, if he had really been a wealthy young aristocrat, he could have devised no worthier way of spending money than on men of genius like Doughty and Graves; and the same may be said of his plan to patronise living artists by commissioning them to paint portraits to illustrate his projected book. But these grandiose gestures were far beyond his means. When he wrote that one of his reasons for joining the R.A.F. was that he was " broke," he was stating a plain but painful fact; for even as late as January, 1927, his bank overdraft is given as £7,000. It was magnificent, but it was absurd. You can't play Harun Al Rashid in modern London on four or even thirty pounds a week and a bit of land in Essex.

Some glimpses of Lawrence during the short period of his residence at All Souls are given by Robert Graves, who was then at Oxford as an ex-officer undergraduate. This was an unhappy period for serious Oxonians, when the university was thronged with rowdy and recalcitrant soldier-undergraduates, who, released from years of military discipline and war service, amused themselves by a puerile lawlessness and disregard for university rules. Although Lawrence was a Fellow of All Souls and over thirty, this was just the sort of attitude to please a man of his strangely arrested development, and he carried out, or more often (as one would expect) talked of carrying out, various student rags. Graves says he did tie a Hejaz flag to one of the College pinnacles, and did ring the station bell of Tell Shahm out of the window at night—not very awful adventures for an Arabian Knight. For the rest, he contented himself with talking about a plan to plant mushrooms on the College lawn; and talking about a plan to steal the Magdalen deer and pen them in All Souls' inner quadrangle; and talking of a plan to buy a peacock and call it Nathaniel, " after Lord Curzon with whom Lawrence had had a row and who was Vice-Chancellor " (surely " Chancellor " is meant?) and a Fellow of All Souls.

This perhaps is the moment to investigate Lawrence's Curzon story, which was so widely spread and believed—perhaps still is. At first Lawrence was proud of the fact that he had met Lord Curzon. He was in uniform and at the Carlton Hotel (so it may have been immediately after his interview with the Eastern Committee in November, 1918), when Dr. Altounyan saw him enter, proudly and happily announcing that he had just had half an hour with Curzon.[15] But evidently Curzon was not attracted into the ranks of the Lawrence-worshippers.   One can well imagine that his finicky tastes and prejudices would have been offended by the Barnum performances at Covent Garden.   And there were more serious annoyances.   Lawrence had posed as the expert on Arab forces, and his remarks on Ibn Saud in his memorandum[16] had been proved hopelessly wrong by the utter defeat of the Sharifians in Nejd.   But, though Lawrence's report was probably the basis of the blunder of " backing the wrong horse,"[17] the responsibility was also shared by the admirals and generals who had believed him.   There was something else to annoy Curzon.   In June, 1919, a letter in excellent English was sent to General Clayton by Feisal giving advice about the English occupation of Mesopotamia. Young believed Lawrence had written it, and Lord Curzon thought it " an impertinence."[18]   There seems no probability that there was any " row " in the sense of an altercation—Curzon would not have allowed it, and had other means of expressing his displeasure.

At all events, by the middle of 1920, Lawrence was trying to make Curzon look ridiculous by one of his usual stories.   At that time, Professor Ernest Barker saw him in Oxford and Lawrence spoke with pleasure of having succeeded in reducing Lord Curzon to tears.[19]   A much expanded and " official " version is given in Robert Graves's book:

"A late member of the Foreign Office staff, who wishes to remain anonymous, has told me an even odder story of Lawrence and Lord Curzon. ' It was at the first meeting of the British Cabinet held to discuss the Middle-Eastern situation. Curzon made a well-turned speech in Lawrence's praise. I could see Lawrence squirming at the praise, which he seemed to think was misplaced, and at the patronage. Lawrence already knew most of the ministers present. It was a very long speech and when it ended, Curzon turned to Lawrence and asked him if he wished to say anything. Lawrence answered sharply, ' Yes, let's get to business. You people ' (imagine Curzon addressed as ' you people '!) ' don't understand yet the hole you have put us all into.' Then a remarkable thing happened. Curzon burst into tears, great drops running down his cheeks, to an accompaniment of slow sobs.

"It was horribly like a medieval miracle, the weeping of a church image. I felt dreadful; probably Lawrence did too. However, Lord Robert Cecil, who seemed to be hardened to such scenes, of which hitherto I only knew by hearsay, interposed roughly, ' Now, old man, none of that!' Curzon wiped his eyes, blew his nose in a silk pocket-handkerchief, and dried up. And business proceeded."[20]

There is a familiar ring about this story, something reminiscent of the Gryphon and the Mock Turtle in *Alice*. But who was this "Foreign Office official"? If we turn to the *Letters*, we find this edifying comment from Lawrence himself: "Graves sent me an advance copy of his book. I'm relieved to find only two things in it which hurt—one, the story of Lord Curzon crying—the Middle East Committee. That is the version Sir Eyre Crowe used to tell, and I do not think it quite fair either to Curzon or to me."[21]

Well, this dignified protest showed a proper delicacy of feeling, and we know from so many of his friends what a "lovely person" Lawrence was, and can imagine the shock to his exquisite sensibility when he opened the book and read the paragraph for the first time. But, as I have had to stress repeatedly, we have Graves's assurance that Lawrence read and passed every line of *Lawrence and the Arabs*, and even wrote parts of it. In the very limited and almost unprocurable *T. E. Lawrence to his Biographer Robert Graves*, we find[22] that " the late member of the F.O. staff" was no other than Lawrence himself, who gave Graves the whole story.[22]   Turning further in the same book we find a long extract from a letter written by Viscount Cecil (formerly Lord Robert Cecil) to Lord Curzon's daughter:

" ... my impression is that your father gave one of his inimitable surveys of the whole position to which Colonel Lawrence listened with the most marked attention, and spoke to me afterwards in the highest appreciation of your father's attitude. It is true that there was, I believe, some difference of opinion on policy between your father and certain other members of the Committee (of the Cabinet), of which I was one, but I feel quite certain that your father never burst into tears, and I am even more certain that I never have addressed him in the way described under any circumstances. You are quite at liberty to use this letter in any way you please.   Cecil."[23]

After this the Oxford story of the arm-chairs is rather flat. They were a present from an American financier who came in and asked Lawrence point-blank (Graves was present and heard him) if Lawrence thought that Middle Eastern conditions justified an investment in Mesopotamian oil. Lawrence said ' No '; and the chairs were a slight acknowledgment of his invaluable advice. But, as time went on, it became perfectly clear that this was another of his blunders, for the development of Mesopotamian oil-fields proceeded in spite of the troubles. When oil had been found there in large quantities, Lawrence tried to convince Graves that the American had not said " Mesopotamia " but " Hejaz."[24] In 1919 there was no question of looking for oil in Hejaz, though some of the British officers thought it might be there. The Hejaz was the Moslem holy land, and Hussein would have been very obstinate against giving any oil concessions. It was not until 1944 that Ibn Saud gave a concession to an American company to look for oil; and Abdulla, seeing a chance to discredit the great and successful rival of his family, immediately protested in the name of religion, " as a Hashemite prince," against this " contamination " of the Moslem Holy Land.[25]

Although Lawrence continued to use All Souls College as his address, he soon abandoned it as a regular place of residence, and found secret refuge in the attic of an office belonging to Sir Herbert

Baker, an architect, in Barton Street, Westminster. Why was this? How did it happen that a man who very soon was to make the singular claim that he had sought and found monastic seclusion in the noise and promiscuity of a barrackroom, should have been unable to live and to work tranquilly at his book in the calm and near monastic conditions of an Oxford College? According to Sir Charles Oman (himself a Fellow), All Souls was particularly quiet since many of the Fellows were present only during week-ends.[26] It was urged that Lawrence was ruthlessly pursued by the press and film companies, but they could easily have been dealt with (had he really wished) by a courteous reception and a frank declaration that he had no news for them. As he knew perfectly well, it was his pretence of hiding that made the reporters think he had something important he was concealing. There was more substance to his claim that he couldn't afford to be a celebrity,[27] but in an Oxford College that status would not be ruinous. A man can always sport his oak. He told Lowell Thomas that he lacked the three requisites of an All Souls Fellow— " to be a good dresser, to be adept at small conversation, and to be a good judge of port."[28] At a later date he wrote that he had tried to live with decent people—" All Souls and elsewhere "— and had failed. There may have been something in this, but it was all really camouflage. The real trouble was 2 Polstead Road, and the situation there was the root of his neurosis and the suffering that is apparent in *Seven Pillars* and his letters. He partly confessed it to Graves when he said: " I can't live at home: I don't know why: the place makes me utterly intolerable."[29]

Although Lawrence had been working on his book for some time and continued to do so, the story of the writing, printing and advertising of *Seven Pillars* is so complicated and spread over so long a period that it must be dealt with separately, even though this means separating it from the events of the same period of time. The reader must bear in mind that, as Lawrence progressed towards the nervous crisis of his life, he was under the additional mental and nervous strain of writing his book—a strain which can very easily be underestimated.

Lawrence had been only a week out of the Army—and hence free from the regulation which forbids soldiers writing letters to the Press—when he began a public propaganda for the Arab Bureau ideas by a letter to *The Times*. Lowell Thomas's lecture, which perhaps as a delicate tribute had opened on the eve of Lawrence's thirty-first birthday, had already made him in the eyes of the ordinary public not only the hero of the great Arab war but the great authority on Arabian affairs. I have already mentioned the swift deterioration of relations between Feisal and the French authorities, during his short-lived and inefficient Damascus government. Hussein, while receiving an English subsidy, constantly attacked France in his Mecca newspaper. Feisal, also receiving an English subsidy—which naturally aroused French suspicions of their puppet King—is said by Philby to have used some of it to subsidise " those elements in Mesopotamia and on its frontiers which could be trusted to make most trouble for us."[30] In May of 1920, there was a sudden and bloody uprising in Irak—British garrisons were massacred, an infantry battalion was ambushed, and Leachman was murdered. Forty thousand troops and an annual expenditure of thirty million pounds were needed " to preserve order," as Mr. Churchill puts it.

Two months later came the defeat and expulsion of Feisal from Syria. Lawrence at once jumped into the debate which followed these disasters with newspaper comments during August, 1920. The scandal of Irak became such an embarrassment to the Lloyd George government that they took Arabian affairs out of the hands of Curzon and Montagu, and entrusted them to Mr. Churchill. Coming fresh to the situation, Mr. Churchill found Lawrence installed in public opinion as the authority on Arabia, and apparently did not know the flimsy basis on which that reputation rested. He really had no choice but to invite Lawrence's collaboration. With the Irish tenor and the military band, the motion pictures of Allenby's cavalry and Lowell Thomas's talk, Lawrence was obviously pointed to as the only popular expert, whose acquiescence must be obtained to any settlement. If he remained outside, sending letters to the newspapers and continuing to stir up trouble, the public would be continuously uneasy.

Rather different accounts are given of the Cairo Conference which met in March, 1921, to try to clear up the Middle Eastern muddle. The Conference, Mr. Churchill says, brought together nearly all the Middle East experts. It lasted a whole month, and came to the decision to make amends to " the Arabs " by placing on the throne of Irak the

Emir Feisal, and keeping him there not by a large and expensive garrison, but by the threat of air bombardment from planes of the R.A.F., which were stationed at an aerodrome on the Euphrates.[31] At that time there were hopes in Europe that aerial bombardment of towns and civilians would be abandoned as a weapon of war by mutual agreement. It is unlikely that modern governments would have kept their word, even if such an agreement had been made, but the decision to control Irak by the threatened use of air power naturally put an end even to any tentative trial. David Garnett says that Trenchard, with Lawrence's support, established this "air control," which was an excellent training ground for the R.A.F., while it was far less costly than an army of occupation.[32] Possibly the real bill was postponed for presentation until twenty years later. It never occurs to some wise men that what they do, or threaten to do, to a weaker may some day be done to them by a stronger.

According to Mr. Churchill, the Conference, having reached its decisions after a month's discussion, submitted them to the Cabinet, and it took an anxious and difficult year of administration to implement the decisions.[33] According to Lawrence's accounts, as reported by Liddell Hart and Mr. Namier, the Conference was a mere farce and camouflage. The High Commissioners for Egypt, Palestine and Mesopotamia, with Governors and Generals from all the area to Aden and Somaliland, were brought together merely to act as obsequious rubber stamps on documentary decisions " prepared by us in London, over dinner tables at the Ship Restaurant in Whitehall."[34] In explaining to Captain Hart what happened, Lawrence dropped the "us" and asserted that he personally "settled not only the questions the Conference would consider, but the decision they would reach." Indeed Lawrence had these decisions printed before the delegation left London, and wished to distribute them before the Conference started, but to this Mr. Churchill for some reason objected.[35]

Two very minor episodes at the Conference have been very naturally overlooked, both by Mr. Churchill and by Lawrence. A member of the Iraki delegation, Lt.-Col. J. I. Eadie, was greatly surprised at being asked to act as interpreter between Lawrence and his old friend Jaafar, who had ceased to command " Feisal's army " and had eventually become Prime Minister of Irak. Lawrence had to explain that his Arabic was not good enough to cope with military technicalities, which is a little surprising considering his alleged success as a military leader of the Arabs. Later on, Colonel Eadie was asked by a senior British representative to read through a large number of Arabic telegrams of protest which had come in from Palestine. Eadie objected that this was Lawrence's job, and not his; but was told that Lawrence did not know enough Arabic to read them.[36]

There were several candidates for the throne of Irak beside Feisal, among them a " native son," Saiyid Talib; Ibn Saud; and Khazal Khan. At an earlier date, " a semi-official plebiscite " in Irak had shown no wish for Feisal.[37] According to Philby, Sir Percy Cox had promised that " starting with a representative provisional government " the Irakis would then go on " to free elections to a constituent assembly, which would determine the future constitution of the country, and, if so desired, choose the future head of State."[38] Now, all this had been determined and promised before the Cairo Conference, and if it had been carried out honestly, nobody could say truthfully that Irak had not been allowed to choose its own form of government. But such a representative body would not have chosen Feisal, and the determination had been reached to impose him on the country. According to Lawrence, Sir Percy Cox protested at Cairo against presenting Feisal as a *fait accompli*, and said, " he had promised the Baghdad Arabs that election of a king should be as free as elections in England." And Lawrence says that Mr. Churchill replied that so they should be, as in England electors have a choice between candidates which are selected by the parties and that an English election is not therefore free.[39] If that is true, Sir Percy was very easily satisfied; for this was how the election was carried out:

While the Conference was still sitting, Jaafar wrote to friends in Baghdad saying that all was going well for Feisal. Saiyid Talib (Minister of the Interior in the provisional government and a candidate for the throne) made a speech to a party in his own house, saying that the people of Irak did not want Feisal and would not tolerate his imposition on them. What happened may be told in Philby's words:

" Saiyid Talib had, by Sir Percy Cox's orders, been kidnapped while a guest in his house, and had been carried off in an armoured car to a launch waiting downstream to take him to Basra and internment in Ceylon."[40] The other candidates for the throne were simply ignored, and " Cox organised a plebiscite on the single question: Do you want Feisal to reign over you?"[41] As the alternative was the continuation of the undiluted foreign rule which the Irakis most wanted to be rid of, it is hardly surprising that 96½ per cent of those voting said 'Yes.' The analogy with the elections to a British Parliament is striking. Thus, a typical example would be for the Government to kidnap and exile the local candidate who was hostile to themselves, refuse to allow any independent candidates, and send down a supporter of themselves brought in from Northern Ireland with the single question to the voters: ' Will you have Mr. So-and-So to represent you in Parliament?' As the only alternative would be no representative at all, 96½ per cent of the constituents would vote: ' Yes.' " And Liddell Hart would obviously highly approve, since he wrote that " Feisal's election by the people was as free as elections in England."[42]

There was one arrangement hurriedly made after the Conference had ended which had not been settled over dinners at the Ship Inn, Whitehall. The Conference itself had been somewhat dismayed by a telegram conveying the unwelcome tidings that Sharif Abdulla with armed forces had arrived at Amman " for an attack on the French in Syria."[43] This was gallant, not to say rash on Abdulla's part, especially since his unfortunate affray with the Wahabis. Probably there was not much fear that Abdulla would drive the French out of Syria, but there were no British troops available to check him, and the real fear was that when he was defeated the French would pursue him and occupy Amman. According to Lawrence, it was he who suggested to Mr. Churchill that Abdulla should be installed (without even an English election) as head of a new kingdom to be called Transjordania under British hegemony.[44] At all events, Abdulla was summoned for an interview to Jerusalem, while Mr. Churchill made his way to Gaza, where he was met by the Palestine High Commissioner, Sir Herbert Samuel. And here for once we come on a Lawrence story which is mildly amusing and not solely devised to advertise his preeminence in something. Large Arab crowds at Gaza greeted the two statesmen with shouts of enthusiasm bordering on frenzy. The great men stood bowing and smiling their acknowledgment, though, according to Captain Coote, Lawrence whispered to him that they were shouting in Arabic, not with enthusiasm for the statesmen but for the murder of the Jews.[45] Lawrence added that he brought the Sharif to Jerusalem avoiding the city, and Mr. Churchill made his decision after half an hour's talk at Government House. It should be noted that Abdulla looked and was an aristocrat, and that like Lawrence himself he could be " charming, a brilliant talker with intellectual and literary taste."[46]

Although King Abdulla is not a precise writer and goes in a good deal for Oriental arithmetic, his account of this conference is interesting. He says that Lawrence met him, not at Amman,[47] but at Es Salt, whence they drove by car to Jerusalem. Arab notables came to greet Abdulla at Jericho, but a motor-cyclist brought a message to Lawrence saying that the car was not to stop for the crowds, which Abdulla thought " discourteous," and he was annoyed that Lawrence was powerless to alter it. Abdulla dined that night with Mr. Churchill, and next day there was a conference at which six people were present, one of whom was Lawrence. The Sharif was told that his brother was to be king of Irak and that he (Abdulla) must use his influence to persuade his father and his friends in Irak to accept this. When Abdulla jibbed at writing to the Irakis, he was told that his failure to do so might mean the loss of all, as Ibn Saud might reach Mecca within three days and England could do no more. He was offered the throne of the new country on condition of remaining in " full agreement with Great Britain," and carrying on " a policy of appeasing the French."[48] Now, Abdulla is two months wrong in his dates here. If Mr. Churchill made any reference to Ibn Saud, it looks as if Abdulla must have misunderstood him. The Wahabi leader was not then threatening Mecca, though later in the year he utterly discomfited the Arab Bureau policy of encircling him with Sharifian states (Irak, Hejaz, Transjordan) by completely defeating Ibn Rashid and the Shammar, capturing their capital, Hail, and driving a " solid wedge of Wahabi influence . . . far to the north between the Sharifian régimes."[49] And the use of the word " appeasing " by the translator is surely an anachronism. Yet the account is interesting, if only because it shows the insuperable difficulties of complete understanding between men of alien cultures, as well as the folly of abandoning French, the only language which is lucid and precise, as the language of diplomacy.

Thus was attained another of the " permanent " settlements in the Middle East, of which there have been and will be so many. By

April of 1921, Mr. Churchill and his staff were back in London, and they had scarcely settled down when there came the unwelcome news that the northern part of Transjordania was already in rebellion against its new sovereign. Mr. Churchill therefore sent Lawrence back to the Middle East with a double errand—he was to act as Chief British Resident in Transjordania, and " to induce King Hussein to give his approval to the general lines of British policy in the Middle East."[50] Philby's words put it politely. The impossible task given Lawrence by Mr. Churchill was to persuade Hussein—who still saw himself as monarch of all Arabia, somewhat on the lines of Abu Bakr—not only to agree to the limitation of his kingship to the Hejaz, but to agree to the British mandates for Irak and Palestine.[51] Antonius is very free with allegations of " breach of faith " against the British, but never troubles to tell us why the British people should have incurred the grievous casualties and heavy cost of the war against Turkey merely for the aggrandisement of Arab politicians. But he is right in saying that it was naïve in Mr. Churchill (or whoever was responsible) to imagine that Hussein at that time would agree to such a treaty, although years later, with Ibn Saud's Wahabis sweeping down on Mecca, Hussein begged, and in vain, to be allowed to sign it in exchange for British protection. In any case, even if there had been hope that a treaty might be arranged (another permanent settlement for six months), Lawrence was the wrong envoy. If Abdulla was cool to him, Hussein positively disliked him.

The disturbances in Transjordan do not appear to have been very urgent, or at any rate Lawrence did not particularly hurry himself to deal with them, since, after his failure with Hussein at Jidda, he went on to Aden, and then on his return spent some time with his mother and brothers in Jerusalem. The eldest of the Lawrence sons then proceeded as a missionary to China, where he was joined by his mother a year later, after Lawrence himself had enlisted in the R.A.F. Without giving away any details, Mr. Churchill suggests a splendid energy in Lawrence's work for Transjordania: saying that a vigorous assertion of his authority eventually restored complete calm.[52]

Order reigned in Warsaw. Unfortunately, very little has been recorded about Lawrence's actions at this period. Only a bare mention is made of the arrival of his family who had given up Polstead

Road and followed him to the Middle East. His panegyrists are not anxious to record his failure with Hussein, and may have felt that a mere Colonial Office Resident's job in a nook of the desert was rather a come-down for the uncrowned King of Arabia. And only two letters from Amman have been printed, one of them full of the usual anti-French venom, in which Lawrence thanks whatever gods he has he is not as other men are, Arabs and Frenchmen.[53] Yet even after he had taken in hand the dramatic clean-up hinted at, he had leisure to continue work on his book, and to make a visit to Cairo in October (1921), when he evidently had asked to be relieved since the offer of his post was made to his successor in the middle of that month.

The successor was St. John Philby, who had resigned from his post as British Adviser to the Baghdad Ministry of the Interior in protest against what he calls "rigging the elections" for Feisal. Philby was not one of the A. T. Wilson faction who wanted to turn Irak into a British colonial possession. He was in fact a "more uncompromising champion of Arab independence" than Lawrence himself; and Philby as Resident allowed Abdulla so much independence that the King got hopelessly into debt, and Transjordan had to be virtually taken over by the Palestine Government with a much sterner Resident (1924-39), Colonel Cox; which as Abdulla remarks sadly was "a difficult time" when "much patience and wisdom was necessary."[54] Perhaps it may be added that in August, 1922, Sir Percy Cox in Irak (Feisal being ill with appendicitis) was issuing a proclamation, arresting and deporting "agitators" and persuading over-critical Moslem holy men to leave the country "voluntarily." It was by no means so simple a situation as the self-determinists assumed. The split between Lawrence and Philby was that the former, following the Arab Bureau policy, initiated by Kitchener and Storrs, believed that Sharifian leadership was essential to the future of Arabia, while Philby believed that the real leader was Ibn Saud; and thirty years later he was able to claim with some reason that events had proved he was right and Lawrence (and Mr. Churchill) wrong.[55] I think I have read everything Philby wrote about Lawrence in book-form, and have found no bitterness there, on the contrary, a generous effort at appreciation. What Philby said in private or wrote about Lawrence in the newspapers, I don't know. But Lawrence was bitter against the man he had himself chosen to take over his post in Transjordania. Later he asserted Philby was resentful at Lawrence helping him to get two jobs, and was angry at the success of his policy in Arabia.[56]

It is not true that Lawrence got him two jobs or that Philby found anything "galling" at succeeding Lawrence (the out-going official is usually asked to suggest a successor) or that he was angry or bitter. And, with the Hashemite encirclement of Ibn Saud completely smashed by his conquest of the Hejaz, and Irak, Palestine and Syria only protected from Ibn Saud by British and French arms, Lawrence's claim that "his" policy was succeeding is rather fanciful. The Lawrence remarks on Philby are simply one untruth after another, for even Philby's books, though carelessly written, are far from uninteresting.

There is nothing unfriendly in Philby's remarks on the month he spent with Lawrence at Amman. True, he was astonished to find Lawrence living in a "hovel," which served him as home and office, with one Arab clerk. He was also surprised and amused by Lawrence's idea of handing over, which consisted in tearing up all papers except Lawrence's own secret copy of the Hussein-McMahon letters and a half-sheet of paper showing that in three months he had spent about £100,000 in gold, including "£10,000—lost, I forget how or where." (That "phenomenal memory" again!) At that time the total annual revenue of Transjordan was £100,000 a year, plus a subsidy of £80,000 to Abdulla. Thus, in a few months Lawrence had distributed in gold a sum approximately equal to the country's whole revenue. Lawrence carried all his possessions in a small suitcase, but always wore a stiff collar and dicky which were always clean, as they were made of celluloid. Philby pays tribute to Lawrence's competence as administrator: "He seemed to know everything and everybody ... a month with him was an exhilarating experience, but he did all the work."[57] It is to be hoped that the straitened British tax-payer remains content with this experiment in lightning king-making, for in exchange for benefits which are not easy to discover, he still retains the privilege of paying Transjordania an annual subsidy which is said now to have risen to three millions sterling.

Thus ended Lawrence's activities in the Middle East. Eleven years

had passed since he first arrived as an undergraduate in the summer of
1909. During that period he had been cast or had cast himself for
several parts. He had been student and æsthete, assistant-archæologist
and organiser of native labour for Hogarth and Woolley, a more or
less mysterious wanderer with Dahoum in the off seasons during
which, for some unexplained reason, he acquired a venomous grudge
against France. The Turks he had always disliked, and whatever his
propaganda feelings, he grew in time to hate his life as an " amateur
barbarian " among the Bedouins. But in fact he was, in that respect,
a very common type of chauvinist, liking no country and no people
but his own and—the German army. Where he differed entirely
from the pukka sahib or Blimp type was that he did not share their
Wog and Gippo attitude to Arabs. Yet he had enough racial prejudices to feel " hurt " that mere negroes " should possess exact
counterparts of all our bodies."[58] His accidental connection
with the Newcombe survey enabled him to begin the war an
immense stride ahead of most of his contemporaries, as a staff captain,
a rank which was attained by fighting soldiers on the Western Front
only after long experience of battle. The friendship and influence of
Hogarth, so important yet so occult, found and kept him in a perfectly safe post for two years in a Cairo untouched by war. When
the combing-out process of late 1916 (there were 50,000 casualties on
the first day of the first battle of the Somme) extruded him into the
Hejaz, he developed unsuspected gifts for intrigue and action, establishing an easy mastery over Feisal's rather weak character, and foster-
ing at once the raids and sabotage and the political influence of the
Hashemites. There will always be disagreement as to the military
value of " the Arab revolt," and still more as to the part played by
Lawrence in it. The outside evidence seems to show that he and his
friends grossly exaggerated his achievements and his importance, and
that he was not the isolated unique leader, but merely one of a number
of officers who lacked his personal associations with Feisal and the
Arab Bureau and his skill in despatch-writing. As it can be shown
that Lawrence " touched up " and highly improved with invented
stories every other phase of his life, there seems a very strong likelihood
that he did exactly the same thing for the period 1917-18. We have
only Lawrence's account of Tafileh; and only his account of the
whole Akaba expedition was known until Mr. Antonius published

the Arab version,[59] which put it in a very different light. Then the camera of Chase and the imaginative eloquence of Lowell Thomas made Lawrence the best-advertised Briton of his age. With this prestige and the power of immense notoriety, his powerful and pertinacious will, his ability in propaganda and wire-pulling, he succeeded in finding a throne for his friend Feisal, though not in " biffing the French out of Syria." He failed to secure the co-operation of Hussein, and fatally misjudged the power and character of Ibn Saud who easily crushed the projected Anglophile Hashemite hegemony.

CHAPTER FIVE

THE STORY of the production of *Seven Pillars of Wisdom* is long and complicated, and highly characteristic of Lawrence's pretentious egotism. To write a clear, straightforward account of the Arab war and of his own share in it did not suit him at all. While affecting a shrinking modesty and protesting how much was owing to others, he was all along casting himself for the leading part. Then the book had to be a literary masterpiece, a "titanic book," self-consciously and pretentiously planned as such, according to Lawrence's Oxonian ideas of what constituted a masterpiece, looking to literature, not to life. People influential in the literary world were enmeshed as advisers and approvers during the revision; and, according to Lawrence, Bernard Shaw improved every paragraph.[1] So we are left uncertain as to how much of the book was in fact rewritten by Shaw over Lawrence's rhetoric. The completed work then had to be illustrated by colour reproductions of specially commissioned portraits and pictures, and produced in accordance with Lawrence's notions of typography. By a series of brilliant manœuvres, he contrived to enjoy the reputation of having sacrificed his fortune to produce a book beautiful for the happy few, while arranging for a popular cut-down edition which sold in tens of thousands and repaid all his losses. After which, he gave all his royalties to charity; but, when the book was withdrawn in England, these royalties can only have continued from abroad.

Lawrence had considerable gifts as a rhetorical and propagandist writer, though he lacked spontaneity and naturalness and the "tact of omission." He was a persuasive and plausible advocate with a decided taste and ability for descriptive writing. He was not naturally an observer, but could force himself to note and to remember when he felt that it was called for, and must have kept elaborate notes during 1917-18. (His private 1911 diary of his walk is one of the most jejune travel productions ever printed.) It is Lawrence's perpetual conscious effort to write up to this artificial level which puts a strain on the admiration of his readers. At the same time Lawrence was clever enough to see that his contemporaries were mostly in reaction against his models and striving for what is loosely called "realism." And so in a work which is almost all murex-tinted, we come upon anti-purple patches of horror or nastiness or brutality or sadism. Let me repeat that Lawrence said himself he only wrote well when he was excited, and that it was exactly such repulsive things which excited him, for though they are far from being the only well-written passages in his long book, they are the best in point of view of vividness and gusto. It is necessary to remember this striving for complicated literary and typographical aims in order to understand why five or six years were occupied with the book. It is also necessary to remember that for much of that time he was in the ranks, and that the production of the book was carried out from a barrack-room.

Mention has already been made of Lawrence's statement that six and a half books of the original draft were written in Paris in 1919. Lawrence also explained that this part of his script was "nearly lost" in the plane crash at Rome.[2] At a much later date, Lawrence explained to Captain Hart his method of work at this early stage of his book. He said that he first wrote a draft from memory, and then "referred to his diaries and notes, and rewrote his narrative on the opposite page with the aid of this historical check."[3] What was gained by this topsy-turvy method of work is not explained. From Graves we learn that Lawrence—surely unfortunately?—destroyed, as he wrote, most of the notes he had made during the war.[4] Yet in a letter written to a fellow-soldier in September, 1920, Lawrence says that he was "too busy or too lazy to write down what happened properly," and asks if any of the others kept diaries.[5] It shows the curious amateurishness of that front or its laxity of discipline that they apparently did not know war diaries were forbidden in the Army.

At this point the anecdotes about *Seven Pillars* start to give out the familiar ring of the dramatic and the extraordinary. Just as the first script of Carlyle's *French Revolution* was destroyed by Froude's servant, so Lawrence lost the script of the greater part of his book in its first version. The first mention of this occurs in the postscript to a letter written to Charles Doughty on the 25th November, 1919, in which Lawrence says: " I lost the MS. of my own adventures in Arabia: it was stolen from me in the train."[6] This statement of the disaster was given in more detail to Graves for his book. From this we learn that the statement that six and a half of the present " books " only had been written may have been a mistake, since Graves's version assumes that the whole book had been written, and that in the theft eight of the present ten were lost. This had occurred while changing trains at Reading,[7] and was still further elaborated. The script had been carried in a bag similar to those used by bank messengers. Lawrence went to the refreshment room at Reading station and, dazed by the quality of the fare after the comparative luxury of the Arabian desert, forgot his bag; and when he telephoned from Oxford it had gone, and has not since been found.[8] Stories were then put about that the manuscript was hidden in the archives of a foreign power, or—less dramatically—that the thief had " probably " thrown it into the Thames. How anybody could discover the truth of either of these alternatives is not stated. And there seems no particular reason why the French government would want it, since it merely demonstrated what they had known all along—that British officers were secretly and openly doing all they could to make the French unpopular in Syria and to gain control of the country for themselves.

The news of this unlucky accident naturally caused consternation among the chosen few who had been allowed at that date to know that the great work was in progress. Dr. Hogarth who, it is said, had insisted that Lawrence should write the book, was most upset when he heard the sad news, and insisted that it must at once be re-written.[9] The most extraordinary measures of self-discipline were applied by Lawrence in order to comply with this requirement. He did not spare himself and wrote for hours at a stretch going without food, sleep and warmth.[10] He did not, however, remain unwashed, but took sixpenny hot baths in the Westminster public baths. The problem of dealing with used clothes did not escape his mind, and he informed Mr. Richards (gratuitously, one supposes, since few of us anxiously ask our friends how they get their washing done) that he put everything into an immense sack. When it was full, Lawrence took it in a taxi to the Savoy Hotel, stayed the night, and in the morning received everything back beautifully laundered. The economy of time and money is obvious. And then, as he informed Mr. Richards, a strange and tremendous experience befell him. That " phenomenal memory " forgot that all shops would be closed during the Easter holidays of 1920, so that he was totally without food for four days, during which period—and throughout most of the nights as well—he wrote incessantly, having forgotten also that many of the popular restaurants would be open. The new draft on which he worked with such concentrated and ascetic energy was " very nearly half a million words,"[11] and Lawrence informed Graves that on one occasion he wrote 34,000 words in 24 hours, but that his average was some four to five thousand words a day.[12] This did not leave him much time to take pains with his style, he added.

But at this point we begin to run into some of the usual difficulties with these *ex-post-facto* anecdotes of extraordinary prowess. If, in November of 1919, he had written the first draft of the whole ten books, had lost eight of them in Reading (as Graves and Hart relate) and, by the spring of 1920, had written a second draft of the eight books, how does it happen that at the time, 27th February, 1920, to be precise, Lawrence wrote to Mr. Richards:

" About the book-to-build-the-house. It is on paper in the first draft to the middle of Book VI; and there are seven books in all."[13]

A first draft is a first draft, and apparently in February, 1920, it was written in seven books, not in ten, and nothing whatever is said about the loss. Doubtless, Lawrence considered this re-writing from memory as still the first draft, though it is hard to see why he got stuck before the end or why he did not profit by the opportunity to improve his text. He apparently told Captain Hart that the whole book was done in February, 1920, yet he wrote Richards that he meant to finish by 30th September, and not in a London attic but in All Souls.[14] These statistics of re-writing solely from memory (the notes, it will be remembered, had been destroyed as the original draft proceeded) are prodigious, and calculated to raise envious admiration in all professional authors, journalists and even short-hand typists.   Sixty words a minute for fifteen minutes is, I believe, the test for an average stenographer merely copying, and I don't think that this could be kept up for ten hours.   It was certainly a terrific feat to remember and write down by hand, without getting writer's cramp, the text of this complicated prose work at the rate of 1,400 words an hour for 24 hours without a moment of rest.*   The story of the lost script was told first by Lowell Thomas (who staged it at Paddington) and then by the anonymous author of the Introduction to the American edition of *Revolt in the Desert*.   At this time it was not known that Lawrence himself had given out this information, which excuses the crisp comment of Sir Andrew Macphail:

> " One cannot say that no such theft occurred, although Lawrence makes no mention of it.   Only a fool would expect to be believed when he says that the author rewrote the book from memory."[15]

Now, of course, we know from Lawrence and from Captain Hart and Mr. Graves that Lawrence passed both stories.   Indeed, through Graves we have further testimony.   One privileged person who read both texts was Colonel Dawnay, and he reported that " one chapter at least that he read more carefully than others in the original seems to be the same, word for word and almost comma for comma, in the second version."[16]   Some might draw a deduction from this fact not so far distant from Macphail's, while others will content themselves with an awed wonder as to which of the two Arabian Colonels had the more " phenomenal memory."

This second version, remembered so miraculously and written down with such stupendous speed, was destroyed by Lawrence in 1922.   This is unlucky, for such a record-breaking manuscript should surely have been deposited either in the British Museum, the Smithsonian Institute or Madame Tussaud's.   A third text was completed by February, 1922 (soon after Lawrence returned from Amman), and eight copies were roughly printed off by the staff of the *Oxford Times*, as being cheaper than typing and a method more likely to

---

* In fairness I should add that Sir Walter Scott as an " apprentice " to his father, a Writer to the Signet, claims to have copied 120 folio pages within 24 hours.

ensure secrecy. But was secrecy all that Lawrence wanted? Of course it wasn't, what author does want it? He merely wished to discourage unauthorised readers, while having the book in a form less discouraging than a mountain of typescript, which he could show to a chosen few among the right people, and interest them personally in the book by a humble request for advice and correction. Whatever Lawrence's gifts as a practical and theoretical military strategist, there can be no doubt that he was a literary strategist of the highest order. He had observed that the usual method of advertising books was outworn. No use just writing your own book in your own way and letting a publisher solicit purchasers for an unlimited number. The obvious though exacting method was to start a curiosity in the work through the flattered commendations of the influential happy few, and then refuse to satisfy the resulting demand until it had reached an approximate maximum through deliberate frustration. Something of the sort had been done pre-1914 for Tagore, with a remarkable success which rather faded out when Tagore became an ardent admirer of Gandhi. Obviously a book by T. E. Lawrence could not in any event be given to the world as if it were the production of some vulgarian with absolutely nothing to recommend him but literary genius. Lawrence further showed his flair for success by choosing as his sponsors Bernard Shaw and Edward Garnett.

Meanwhile, the completion of his work and the setting up by the Oxford newspaper had taken time, and in 1922—dramatically on the 14th August, the eve of his 34th birthday—Lawrence had joined the ranks of the R.A.F. To avoid distracting the account of that psychological and material crisis by references to book-production, it will be taken up later and separately. Thus, Lawrence's letters to Shaw about his book were written not from the Colonial Office or an Oxford College, but from an Army hut of recruits. Lawrence had realised that if he could persuade Shaw on to his side, the reputation of his book with the official politico-literary world was safe.

By sheer accident—one of those fortunate accidents not uncommon in Lawrence's life—he had been introduced to Shaw in March, 1922, by the director of the Fitzwilliam Museum. On the strength of this old friendship, Lawrence in mid-August of that year wrote Shaw a very careful, deprecating letter asking the great man to read and to advise on his book.   Splendidly mendacious, this Oxford highbrow-æsthete tried to placate his Communist mentor (who on principle preferred economics to art) by asserting that his tastes were " daily-mailish," and feared that his book contained " enough piffle and romance and wooliness to make a realist sick."[17]   Writing almost at the same time to the literary Edward Garnett, Lawrence presented a totally different picture—he had collected a (somewhat exiguous) " shelf " of three books of a " Titanic " kind, " distinguished by greatness of spirit, ' sublimity,' " which were *The Brothers Karamazov*, *Thus Spake Zarathustra* and *Moby Dick*.   Lawrence had, he averred, the modest purpose of adding " an English fourth."[18]   From the *Daily Mail* to Dostoevsky is a long step, but Shaw hated Oxonian " culture," while Mrs. Garnett was the most gifted of all English translators of Russian novels.   Such are the advantages of keeping one's correspondence as well as one's friendships " separated by bulkheads."[19]

Before sending Shaw his book, Lawrence wrote another letter, in which among much humble self-depreciation, Lawrence, with that bluff frankness always to be associated with his character, tells Shaw that he (Shaw) is a " great man."   Then, while Lawrence was undergoing the unpleasant experience of a recruits' course possibly made especially nasty for his benefit, Shaw returned nothing but silence to the Great Book.   Miss Patch (Bernard Shaw's secretary) tells us that Shaw " flinched " from the chore, and for ten weeks could not summon up courage " to dip more than his toe in the ocean of words."[20]   Lawrence became anxious and wrote a cautious enquiry.   In reply Shaw was more than usually offensive.   He exhorted Lawrence to patience and told him not to shoot a second willing camel in the head; he said he had read only samples, and wondered how Lawrence would come out of a full reading.   He told him to consider General Gordon, saying that he was an unutterable scoundrel, and continued, " Have you ever considered the question as affecting yourself? "[21]

Here was a contretemps!   Shaw was obviously bored by the book, and shocked by Lawrence's sensational accounts of how he had to shoot his own men and so forth; and, however qualified by the reference to Gordon, the last sentence was clearly insulting. But Lawrence knew when he had to eat humble pie, and he wrote, plaintively asking for the return of his script. He added that his mother was a Gordon. Shaw having also mentioned Cæsar, Lawrence remarked guilelessly that Shaw's portrait of Cæsar was among the uncommon portraits of the great that showed any life, with the assurance that Cæsar's *Commentaries* were one of his pet books which he was even then re-reading. Shaw's reference to Cæsar was particularly nasty, since Cæsar had written of world-shaking events in a plain, lucid, unpretentious style, whereas . . . And now Lawrence revealed to his new correspondent that he was in the Air Force, explaining that he had no money and disliked work; but Edward Garnett was abridging the book, and if a publisher could be found to pay for it, Lawrence would again become a civilian. He added that a barrack-room was a poor home.[22]

What could be more obviously appealing and pathetic? But Shaw received a great many appealing letters, and this one might not have succeeded in spite of its pathos. But now Lawrence and his book found an enthusiastic and powerful ally. Strange to relate, Shaw was married; and his wife Charlotte read the book and became "ecstatic" over it. She thought the book was "a masterpiece," and Miss Patch draws the homely picture of her reading passages to Shaw as he sat ruminating over the fire.[23] Both Shaws were "quick with suggestions for improving the book," which Lawrence received very "meekly," for Shaw had capitulated to his domestic companion and had written Lawrence that his book was "great." They set to work so industriously that scarcely a paragraph was left untouched, a treatment Lawrence tried to pretend he found "bracing."[24]

It is not clear that Hogarth ever had anything to do with abridging *Seven Pillars*, except for Lawrence's purpose of letting Bernard Shaw know that Hogarth was one of Lawrence's friends. Garnett's abridgement was abandoned. Publication of the private limited edition was slow, and during that time the newspaper edition circulated among (at least) such commonplace members of the ordinary public as Charles Doughty, Siegfried Sassoon, Robert Graves, Granville Barker, and E. M. Forster. One of Lawrence's poses—which he ultimately came to believe himself—was that he had been producing finely printed books for many years. He had long talked of setting up a press with his old friend, Vyvyan Richards, but all that really happened was that Richards started the press, printed one small book.

and then handed over to Graves and Laura Riding.[25]   It was in accordance with this myth that Lawrence wrote to Henry Williamson[26] that he hated typewriting, as his long experience with "print" had given a profound respect for the details of typography. How could people fall for such myths? Lawrence hadn't printed anything by hand and had only overseen some of the *Arab Bulletin* and his monstrosity of a book. What he had done was to talk loftily about printing for years and to collect a number of Press books.

But it is the fact that the next phase in Lawrence's dealings with the love-child of his brain was the limited special edition for a highly select few. The type had already been chosen, independently by Lawrence and Mr. Richards, from the books in Lawrence's All Souls rooms. Their choice fell on the Caslon fount used in the Essex House Press edition (1899), collated by Janet E. Ashbee, of Bunyan's *Pilgrim's Progress*. A printer and assistant were found, and they worked in a small shop near Paddington, not indeed hand-setting, as required by William Morris, but making use of the linotype. Incredible pains were taken by the author-printer, not to say what he had to say, but to carry out his notions of fine printing. Every chapter had to begin with an ornamented capital (designed by Edward Wadsworth), so that the book had the appearance of a harmonious typographical unit in the manner approved by Morris. Naturally, there must be no "rivers," no space at the end of a chapter, and each chapter must end modestly at the bottom right-hand corner.[27]   To achieve this typographical exactitude, Lawrence, forgetting that he had a message to deliver, for purely typographical reasons re-wrote sentences, paragraphs and even pages, until the text fitted perfectly into the page. Some proofs passed between the printer and Lawrence as many as fourteen times.[28]

Here, in these "Procrustean games," as Mr. Richards calls them, was a singularly foolish frivolity. If a book, above all a war book, is not completely sincere and as exact as the author can achieve, what is the use of it? Was Lawrence writing a true account of the desert warfare, or merely producing a pretext for pretty printing; so that it didn't matter what he said if the page lay-out was satisfactory to his Oxford æstheticism? Only the best hand-made paper could be endured. The damping had to be exactly calculated to allow for the even stretching of the paper. Morris's "inking with a hand-ball" had to be abandoned, because the method would have taken too much time. Expensive illustrations were ordered and reproduced expensively. Further preciosities were ingeniously thought up. The reproduced portraits and illustrations at the end of the book were arranged in a different order in each copy, and for each copy there was a different expensive binding. Sangorski and Sutcliffe, MacLeish, Wood, Harrison, all the best London binders were employed and allowed to decorate as they wished and to choose the finest and most exotic leather that pleased their taste.[29]

The exact number of copies of this original edition was kept secret, because Lawrence " hated bibliophiles "—as is demonstrated by the simple, unostentatious way in which he issued his book. Naturally, the secret was only for the outer many. As a matter of fact 128 complete copies were sold in England at 30 guineas each. In America, George H. Doran printed 22 copies without plates, with two variant passages, and no introductory matter or appendices—all just for the sheer pleasure of disappointing the bibliophiles. Lawrence gave away 36 complete and 26 incomplete copies.[30] Although most of the copies were sold at thirty guineas, so much money had been spent on æsthetic trimmings that the actual cost to the author-publisher must have been more than three times as much, since he was left £7,000 in debt. And was the result worth the money? Obviously, we must go to the experts for an answer. Herbert Read thought it " an amateur's nightmare . . . a monstrous exhibition of all that a book should not be "; H. S. Ede, a Tate Gallery keeper who lived surrounded by masterpieces, thought it " so ugly "; and David Garnett, a director of the Nonesuch Press, admits it a " monstrosity."

But all this didn't matter, for Bernard Shaw was favourable and the subscriptions consequently dribbled in importantly. As they mounted, and the eagerly-hoped-for *succès de snobisme* became more nearly certain, an increasing severity of scrutiny was adopted towards late comers. With a remarkable sense of values, Charlotte Shaw had suggested that the book should have an introduction from Sir James Barrie. For this she had to be indirectly rebuked, and the widower in Thrums heavily snubbed. He was refused a copy because Lawrence despised him.[31] Another would-be subscriber was refused, apparently because she was a woman and Lawrence didn't like her manner.[32] No copy of the book was sent for review, which caused Bernard Shaw to wonder why he hadn't followed the same course of advertising. An unobservant man—it had long ago been the custom of Marie Corelli with her novels. As a further advertisement, the law was broken in at least three respects. No printer's name was attached. No free copies were sent to the British Museum and Bodleian Libraries—though in due course a manuscript was modestly presented to the latter. And no attempt was made to palliate such remarks as: "It's no bluidy good, sir, talking to them fookin water boogers.★"[33] But, even if the authorities had dared to interfere with a work by the national hero, it was no good then, since the whole edition had been distributed before they had a chance to tremble for their daughters' morals. And, of course, it has all been openly on sale since 1935.

What admirably thought-out propaganda all this was. The fusses about printing and binding and refusing subscribers and snooting reviewers were admirably calculated to stimulate the jaded snob public and to provoke that "susurrus" among the intelligentsia prescribed by one of the ablest of living literary strategists. When, after enormous delays, the book was at last distributed, each flattered recipient became a potential centre of further glory to the author and even of profit to himself—advertisements in newspapers offered as much as five pounds a week for the loan of a copy. Except that it didn't pay, *Seven Pillars* was really a bigger "unconventional" literary success than *Ulysses* and *Lady Chatterley's Lover*.

Lawrence told Liddell Hart that his intention had been not to publish his book at all, but that he had been persuaded by Gertrude Bell to issue a few copies for his friends.[34] Gertrude Bell did not "persuade" him to a limited publication, she merely suggested it by letter in August, 1923,[35] while his own letters show that long before that he had intended publication. In August, 1922, Lawrence wrote Edward Garnett that he had "dreamed again of publishing a little, and so getting cash in hand."[36] Then came the suggestion that Garnett should edit and cut the text for commercial publication—"if you get it to 150,000 and satisfy yourself, and then I take out 20,000 or so, that should do the trick."[37] That was early in October, 1922, but towards the end of the month, Lawrence was apologising for his waverings, saying he hated the idea of publishing, but would

★ Books "objected to" by various persons were suppressed for a single sentence such as this, which has been publicly circulated in Lawrence's book in England without a query since 1935.

have to publish some time and that "the motive will be money."[38] By the 6th November he had changed again, had missed an appointment with Edward Garnett, had failed to write because now he didn't want to publish "anything of the *Seven Pillars*," and evidently wanted to escape the drudgery of correcting Garnett's abridgement. Yet in December, Garnett was allowed to mention the book to Jonathan Cape, and Lawrence wrote his banker (to whom he was heavily in debt) that he had decided to sell an abridgement of "my Arabian narrative," which would "bring in some thousands (perhaps £6,000) next year."[39]

Lawrence used the newspaper publicity about his service in the ranks (January, 1923) as an excuse to cancel this arrangement; which naturally made Cape "furious."[40] Then Lawrence sketched for him the plan for a limited, privately-printed edition of 2,000 containing the illustrations he had so expensively collected.[41] On the day of his dismissal from the R.A.F., he cancelled that proposal, yet he obviously still yearned to have his book published and read. Only a few days later he thanked a sculptress for trying to discover what Shaw really thought of the book, and mentioned that at that time he had sent out copies to Hogarth, Shaw, Clutton-Brock, Garvin (editor of *The Observer* newspaper) and General Bartholomew.[42]

Obviously, publication was only postponed, not abandoned, and by August, 1923, he had hit on the idea of making the abridged edition subsidise his own extravagant production. In mid-December, 1923, this was decided upon by a council of Lawrence, Hogarth, Dawnay and Lionel Curtis. There were (at that time) to be 100 copies at 30 guineas. In March, 1925, Lawrence proposed that Cape should issue the abridgement—Lawrence's, not Garnett's—with an advance of £3,000, and a hoped-for £4,000 from America. All this careful planning and plotting should dispose of the myth that Lawrence was an artless and unbusiness-like person who rushed light-heartedly into publishing arrangements without calculation.

The abridgement, made by Lawrence himself in camp, was published as *Revolt in the Desert* in March, 1927, at least eight years after he had started to write the book; and was an immediate success. Yet even here, Lawrence could not refrain from exaggerating his success to guileless persons who would spread the tale. Thus, he wrote Sergeant-Major Banbury on the 29th April that his book was

" selling like apples," and that it was " over 40,000 in three weeks."[43] Yet it is quite clear that he had been given no figures at that time, and had guessed far too high. In a letter of 27th May he writes: " Your figure of 22,000 for the sale of Revolt astonishes me. At 30,000 the accumulated royalties will pay off the last of my debt to the Bank."[44]

There were three trustees for the book, and a clause in the agreement allowed the withdrawal of the book at any time they chose; and they chose to withdraw it in June, 1927. Lawrence thereupon wrote one of his ecstatically insincere letters protesting his delight at this " incredibly glorious news," which he declared showed " the most noble mind " of the trustees, quoted Dante, and urged them to continue to act " in the spirit of Don Quixote."[45] More realistically he admitted to Hogarth that " the alternative to stopping it, is a cheap edition," and explained to another friend that " the thing will not sell 100 copies next year," i.e., he was withdrawing the book in the spirit of Don Quixote because the library edition had stopped selling. He wanted to prevent Cape from issuing a cheap edition, because he said he had been sent to Karachi on account of the publicity attaching to him and his book, so, in an effort to get people to stop thinking of him as a legendary figure, he had collaborated with Graves in a biography.[46]

In that work (*Lawrence and the Arabs*), a story is told that when a Paris publisher asked for the French rights of *Revolt in the Desert*, Lawrence replied that he would give permission only if the book carried the note: " The profits of this book will be devoted to a fund for the victims of French cruelty in Syria "; and so, Graves exults, there could be no French translation so long as Lawrence controlled the book rights.[47] But there certainly was a French translation in Lawrence's lifetime, and it certainly bore no such insulting legend. He betrays himself in his *Letters* where he says that, after the withdrawal of the British edition, there will be left the American edition and " the French and German translations." Incidentally, General Brémond's book (published in 1931) was written after reading this French translation to correct some of Lawrence's mis-statements.[48] Here, as everywhere else, Graves is not to be blamed for putting out an easily refuted story. He wrote in all good faith, for he was simply putting down what Lawrence told him. Yet though Lawrence had passed the book for publication, he was always secretly telling others: "Do not take Graves' book as very true!"[49] He should know.

When we come to consider the financial aspects of this publication, there is both confusion and some suspicion of Oriental arithmetic. Graves was told that the cost of producing *Seven Pillars* was £13,000, and that after payment of the subscriptions Lawrence was still £10,000 out of pocket.[50] If that is exact, then Lawrence must have paid off about £3,000 from his own assets—perhaps partly from the sale of paintings and partly from money he told Mrs. Shaw he had received from Ireland, which he said he had used for his book. The balance of £7,000 was reduced to £4,000 by Cape's advance on *Revolt*, and the remainder of the debt was paid off by royalties. At this time, Lawrence's Chingford land was valued at £4,000. Presumably it was to that sum he was referring in a letter written to Graves in February of 1935, when he says that he had reserved enough money for him " to be at ease," but, owing to the fact that he had not fore-seen how the rate of interest would fall, he was short of the desired amount by £700.[51] In February, 1928, Lawrence wrote the editor of the *Daily Express* that " Revolt had made £17,000." In 1933 he told Liddell Hart that the total royalties were £24,000!

The statement that " Lawrence had not made a penny himself from either of these books "[52] is often repeated; and we have the evidence of his literary agent that Lawrence received nothing after his debts were paid, and that everything above that sum was given to Air Force charities.[53] This " not a penny for himself," however, seems rather ambiguous. Does it make any essential difference that you take money in order to make a lavish display and gratify your vanity as a writer-printer, or take money in order to achieve a modest security? Surely, it is as much " taking money " to pay off your debts, as it is if you used the same sum to buy an annuity? And, in any case, Lawrence on his own showing did " take money," because his royalties were either used to redeem the pledged title-deeds of his land or to give him the sum he thought he would need to live on when he left the army.[54] If he had not taken the royalties from *Revolt*, he would have had to sell his land, and use any other assets to try to pay his debts for *Seven Pillars*. If he had taken all the royalties his book earned and had really gone into retirement, nobody on this earth would have grudged him a penny—not even the French. Everybody would have been only too relieved to know that "Lawrence of Arabia" was no longer earning his rations by presenting arms to camp commandants, and could sink into the modest obscurity he said he longed for in vain. But that, as we shall see, did not fit in with the part for which he had cast himself. The truth is that he took for various purposes about £7,000 from a book from which he might have got more—and attentive readers of pages 472 and 529 of the *Letters* will suspect that may have included £400 for motor-bicycles, at any rate in Lawrence's intentions. In the former, he says (1925) that Brough has brought out a wonderful new model on which Lawrence was "going to blow £200 of Cape's."[55] In July, 1927, he wrote Hogarth to hold for him all the remaining complete copies of *Seven Pillars*: "One is to be a Brough, for me, in 1930, if I'm still inclined to ride after I get back."[56] Of course, the Shaws gave him a Brough cycle on his return from India, but Mr. Brough built for him eight motor-cycles, the last of which he did not live to receive. Lawrence told Captain Hart that Mr. Brough gave him each new model.[57] He told Graves that he "used to wheedle" a Brough-Superior every year from the makers and "ride it to death" to test and report on it. Well, if that was so, why did he write to his banker and to Hogarth about money to pay for them? But Lawrence always wants to have it both ways; in this case to buy his bicycle with money from his book and yet to claim the credit of taking "not a penny" from it.

One curious result of Lawrence's cunning literary strategy but dilatory tactics was that while an immense esoteric reputation was thereby created for his book, few people read it except in its expurgated, greatly cut-down form. The full text was not made ordinarily public until 1935, and by that time its market was diminishing. True, the national hero remained, but the Lowell Thomas "Prince of Mecca" was fading. Moreover, a flood of Western Front war books had rattled futilely over the public mind, and five years later that public was experiencing war on a scale and intensity infinitely beyond camel-riding and train-wrecking; people who lived through the Battle of France, the Battle of Britain, and the Battles of Russia could hardly be expected to thrill over the Battle of Tafileh. Of course, anyone can see that there are episodes and experiences—actual or implied—

in the book which the author would not want to make widely public in his lifetime. But Lawrence's curious vanity preferred notoriety to readers; he preferred to be known as the writer of a mysterious, unprocurable masterpiece rather than to have it read. It was more effective to come to the public indirectly, through the amusing bravura of Lowell Thomas, the inspired utterances of Hart and Graves, and the hysterical trumpetings of the newspapers. *Seven Pillars* is indeed a success story, but told as Lawrence tells it, in his rhetorical style and long-winded ramifications, it had to be diluted and showmanised for the general public. In addition to this straining for a "titanic" style, the book imposes on its readers the additional strain of watching the author's painful mental and spiritual contortions as he suffered the onslaught of a severe nervous breakdown. What Herbert Read called the "splendid ' copy '" and Lawrence himself the "Boy Scout" appeal of the book is spoiled by pretentiousness and an irrelevant self-torture, for the author's acute psychological sufferings arise from a cause totally unconnected with the Arab rebellion, though possibly brought to consciousness by its hardships, responsibilities and dangers.

At the same time that the reader has inflicted on him this extraneous neurosis, he is often irritated by Lawrence's cynical contempt and frivolity. Obviously Lawrence had a perfect right to give his book a meaningless Biblical title passed on from a destroyed work of his youth, and there was nothing to stop him from pulling about, cutting and adding to his laboriously composed and Shaw-aided text merely to gratify his amateurish typographical fads. But he cannot at the same time claim the merit of a serious recorder of an intensely-felt experience which he longed passionately to convey to others, for them to share and to take warning, not for self-glorification and the plugging of some political "cause." Something like six thousand words of fine writing are devoted to a two-days' camel-ride from the coast to Feisal's camp, which shows a singular contempt for his readers' patience. I cannot agree with those who think that Lawrence's style resembles Doughty's, though it is true that both write a self-consciously assumed and mannered prose—Doughty, a 19th-century pastiche of 16th-century English, and Lawrence, a 20th-century version of 19th-century æsthetic prose. Little unimportant details may stem from Doughty, such as "bouncing camels" and sheiks as "worshipful men of the desert," but the style of *Seven*

Pillars is not pseudo-Elizabethan. On the other hand, Doughty's influence may be to blame for the confused structure, the long-winded digressions, the ruthless translation into the chosen idiom of every detail jotted down as notes. Yet Lawrence was aware of the drawbacks to Doughty's style. He rightly regrets Doughty's use of foreign constructions, his archaic vocabulary and his use of hundreds of Arabic words which have perfectly good English equivalents. Lawrence's dictum: " Camel is a better word than thelul," should be noted and obeyed by all writers tempted into verbal local colour. On the other hand, Lawrence, like Doughty, sometimes forgets—or rather does not care—that his reader may not share his interest in endless descriptions of obscure desert features and persons. There is always a moment, too often several, in these books on the Arabian Desert when we are called on to thrill, Robinson Crusoe-like, to such a transcendent revelation as the spectacle of dried camel dung fretted by the drifting sand. And Lawrence's narrative is apt to be loaded with unknown or forgotten names, almost like those " begat " chapters in the Old Testament:

> " In the afternoon, Nuri Shaalan appeared, with Trad and Khalid, Faris, Durzi, and the Khaffaji. Auda abu Tayi arrived, with Mohammed el Deilann, also Fahad and Adhub, the Zebn leaders, with ibn Bani, the chief of the Serahin, and ibn Genj of the Serdiyeh . . . "[58]

On the other hand, there is certainly a considerable literary talent here, especially that talent for persuasive and plausible propaganda so noticeable in his *Arab Bulletins* and in his political reports and letters to the Press. Only a man widely conversant with literature, and in possession of a genuine gift for fitting words to thought and experience, could have worked out a style so high-flown and exacting and have maintained it through so long a book. This virtuosity in words, this meticulously mannered type of style had been much admired in the tardily æsthetic Oxford of Lawrence's youth. And is it too fanciful to see in him something of that Irish or Celtic love of playing with words, which has produced how many verbal preciosities down to the enormous word-bog of *Finnegan's Wake*? But, however that may be, Lawrence as a writer was also skilful in the art of using words so as to suggest or to imply something more or something less than is actually stated. This was often a useful defence, making it as hard to lay hold of his real meaning as to grasp a naked man smeared with grease. But that kind of verbal dodging is the virtue of a politician and intriguer, not of a writer. Almost the hardest and least often achieved triumph of the heart-breaking craft of words is to use them so that they will mean to the reader exactly what they meant to the writer. Suggestion is too easy. One example among many—Lawrence used the appeal to puritan prejudice of the word " clean " in the most unscrupulous way. Thus he warmly recommends his Farraj and Daud (who, on his own showing, were a couple of unwashed desert homosexuals) as " so clean." He praises " the sword "—i.e., the archaic symbol for War, with all its filth and degradation—as " clean." He tries to place Allenby above question or discussion by calling him " clean-judging." And elsewhere we hear that Lawrence admired a private soldier because he was " the rugged *clean* " type of Englishman, which leaves one musing over those dirty, slick English types one sees furtively bolting about all over the world.

May it be questioned whether a style so mannered, so literary and so inexact was really the most suitable for an honest war narrative? True, every personal war narrative is autobiography; but War is action, whatever it may involve of plans and preparations, and however much the neurotic intellectual who is writing may have been plagued by mental conflict and divided aims. Action does not ask a too sophisticated style, but rather a speech which is vigorous, direct, and unaffected, where the very existence of the sayer is forgotten in the vividness and meaning of the thing said. Is there a page of *Seven Pillars* in which we are allowed to forget Lawrence of Arabia? He might have written much better if he had not striven so painfully to write too well.

CHAPTER SIX

A CIRCUMSTANCE which has to be recorded is that Lawrence had no known love affairs. He was never married or engaged, and, from the sexual point of view, there are no women recorded in his life. He himself claimed that he had lived his life in complete sexual ignorance of women. More than once he spoke of his temperament as " cold," and indeed there is an absence of warmth of expression in all his letters, even the early ones. He told Robert Graves that he had never been able to fall in love, and that even as a boy he had never had much to do with women.[1] He allowed Graves to say in his biography that Lawrence did not like " children or dogs or camels in the usual sentimental way."[2] But there were certainly some children he liked, from his own youngest brother in boyhood to the young daughters of two of his Air Force officers in the later years. Moreover he certainly was on friendly terms with women, both before and after the war—Mrs. Rieder and Mrs. Fontana in Syria, and in later years Mrs. Clare Smith and Mrs. Charlotte Shaw. Graves thought that he liked practical, middle-aged women, the type that would make a good home.[3] By far the most intimate of these friendships was with Charlotte Shaw, and it was in his letters to her that he made the most revealing disclosures about himself. But she was much older than he was, and it is a natural inference that what he was looking for in these passionless relations, and what he found in Mrs. Shaw, was a substitute mother. One or two women, of no particular standing, have been ready to hint that " T. E." felt for them a warmer passion than these quasi-maternal relations, but those may safely be dismissed as yet more examples of the very common snobbish wish to be thought on terms of intimacy with the famous Lawrence of Arabia.

331

Yet if Lawrence was incapable of falling in love, he was obviously very much exposed to the accident of other people falling in love with him. He was forty-five when he wrote, after Christmas from camp, to Violet Astor, not without a touch of coquetry and possibly of romantic arithmetic, to complain that during the festive season he had received declarations of " carnal love from four women and two men."[4] The addition of two men is curious, but Professor Lawrence tells us that Lawrence's friendships were " comparable in intensity to sexual love," and were in fact his substitute for sex. Lawrence, he goes on, " rebelled unceasingly " against sex with a hatred which was " an irrational instinct which went far beyond reason's limits." I shall have occasion to refer again later on to this very revealing appreciation, and for the moment only record that the Professor adds that Lawrence may in childhood have been " endowed " with the idea of sex as sin, but that this thoroughly irrational attitude developed after the war. It was there all along, but became more vocal and uncompromising as Lawrence felt himself immune from retaliation and secure in his notoriety as national hero.

It was inevitable that a man who openly declared his hatred of women's sex, and indulged in friendships with men " comparable in intensity to sexual love," should have been suspected of homosexuality. Sir A. T. Wilson obviously hints at it in his *Journal of the Central Asian Society* notice of *Revolt in the Desert*. There is also a curious passage in E. M. Forster's notes on him, where he speaks of meeting Lawrence by chance at Queen's Hall in the company of men " whose faces I instinctively distrusted. All his friends will agree that he had some queer friends."[5] This is a bit mysterious, and perhaps was not meant to say what it seems to say. On the other hand, friends and relatives have been eager—perhaps too eager—in denying a suggestion which must have occurred to many people.

The reader will recollect the strong friendship in pre-war days between Lawrence and the Arab boy nicknamed Dahoum, otherwise Sheik Ahmed, and how greatly their living together aroused the suspicions of the Arab villagers. Sir Leonard Woolley, conceding that Dahoum was " remarkably handsome and not particularly intelligent," goes on to deny any homosexual relation. Lawrence, he says, had a " very strong vein of sentiment," but was in no sense " a pervert," indeed he had " a remarkably clean mind." He was, of course, interested in Greek homosexuality, of which his classical reading had made him tolerant, but the interest was not " morbid." Moreover, Lawrence never made " a smutty remark," and would have objected if one had been made.[6] The notion that all homosexuals have " filthy minds," but that Lawrence had not, is rather a dangerous argument to use to anyone who has read *The Mint*, which in parts is almost insane in its attack on female sex.

Mr. Lowell Thomas is naturally more splendidly sweeping. He states that anyone who has been in lengthy contact with " pathologues " knows that they will give away their secret eventually. He himself had met all types of them, and his father was a doctor. He had never found the faintest trace of the homosexual in Lawrence.[7] But the difficulty with these assertions on either side is that there is no real evidence for or against. Mohammed decreed the punishment of death for adultery, but added the proviso that there must be four witnesses who will swear to having taken the guilty ones in the very act, with the consequence that in the Moslem world a daily occurrence is visited with its penalty once in a blue moon.★ Norman Haire, with his thirty-five years' practice as " sexologist," points out that, in his experience, relatives and friends are the last persons to hear of or to suspect homosexual practices. The opinions of those who without any concrete evidence assert that Lawrence was a homosexual cancel out the opinions of those who thought he wasn't. So far as I can discover, there is no legal or medical evidence whatsoever.

The obvious course would be to leave it at that, but, though there is no evidence as to Lawrence's sexual actions, he has unconsciously left a record of his sexual sympathies. In his letters and other writings, he has left a good deal of evidence as to what sexually repelled him, what he tolerated, and what excited his preference and sympathy. And, although it would be easiest just to pass by, the service of truth demands that this indirect evidence should be cited. Lawrence's published pre-war letters are few, but most of them are addressed to staid elder women—his mother, his nurse, a woman missionary—or to his patron Hogarth, and therefore unlikely to contain any sexual information whatever. But significantly there is not one letter to a girl. Writing to a fellow student he refers sneeringly

★ There is a curious story of an Arab woman who—probably insane—insisted on accusing herself of adultery to Ibn Saud's Wahabis, who with great reluctance at last put her piously to death.

333

to odalisques as " upper housemaids," [8] but having the good fortune to visit Arles while Mistral's revival of the beautiful local costume was still effective, Lawrence writes briefly of the Arlésiennes as " glorious." [9]

The war brought a great change, and, when Lawrence came to write *Seven Pillars*, he abandoned his former reticence and wrote several passages of a highly sexual sort which were omitted from the public *Revolt in the Desert*. For some reason, that popular production also omitted the Dedication " To S. A." This is a rather unsuccessful attempt to write a poem in the free verse style introduced to England and America by the Imagists, and shows that Lawrence had not understood their aims. It is not surprising that when Robert Graves saw the poem in manuscript, his immediate impulse was to re-write it. But, from the point of view of our present enquiry, it has some interesting lines:

> " I loved you, so I drew these tides of men into my hands and wrote my will across the sky in stars to earn you Freedom; the seven pillared worthy house, that your eyes might be shining for me when we came. . . . Love, the way-weary, groped to your body, our brief wage, ours for the moment before earth's soft hand explored your shape. . . ." [10]

Whether we are to take these words literally or metaphorically, it is undeniable that the language and sentiment are erotic. " S. A.'s " eyes are to be shining for Lawrence, Love groped to this body, " our brief wage " before earth in its turn explored with its " soft hand " the shape of the beloved now dead. As usual when Lawrence had something to conceal, he told different stories about this dedication and its object. Presumably Graves was the first to be allowed to see it, and it was sent to him in the week following a conversation in which Lawrence had denied that he had ever been in love. [11] He later wrote Graves that this was " not altogether true," and explained that his dedication to S. A. had been " dictated " by one who " provided a disproportionate share of the motive for the Arabian adventure." [12] Graves goes on to say that in 1927 one of Lawrence's oldest friends had said that S. A. was " Sheik Achmed, an Arab with whom L. had a sort of blood-brotherhood before the war." [13] This old friend may have been Vyvyan Richards, who thinks that S. A. was

" Dahoum himself, whose real name was Sheik Achmed."[14] Dahoum is said to have died of typhus in Syria early in 1918, which agrees well enough, since Lawrence told Liddell Hart that S. A. had died " some time before " they reached Damascus.[15] And again that the " unhappy event " occurred " long before " they got to Damascus.[16] Possibly growing restive under questioning, Lawrence then tried to throw Captain Hart off by saying " S " was a person, and " A " a place.[17] Professor Lawrence, who at one time seemed to accept the identification with Dahoum, later changed his mind and thought the poem had " little personal significance."[18] Looking to the phrasing of the dedication, this seems unlikely, though of course nobody can say for certain that Dahoum was the person meant. On the other hand, if S. A. was not Dahoum, who was he or she? Taking this together with the many references to the boy in Lawrence's notes and letters and the absence of any erotic reference to girls, the inference seems clear that Dahoum was Lawrence's main pre-war interest and affection.

Quite early in the text of *Seven Pillars*, we come upon a paragraph which has caused a good deal of comment since it is such a downright if not defiant statement of Lawrence's disdain for heterosexual and sympathy with homosexual relations. Although he says elsewhere that between raids the married Arab men returned to their wives[19] (and in Moslem communities unmarried men are very exceptional), he here speaks only of " the public women " and how their " raddled meat " was not " palatable " to what he calls " a man of healthy parts." Such was the horror of " our youths " for such " sordid commerce " that they " began to slake one another's few needs in their own clean bodies," which process seemed " sexless and even pure." (Thus we see the meaning Lawrence attached to his favourite adjective " clean," and may remember that he always spoke of himself as " sexless.") He then dwells with sympathy and approval on a lurid vision of " friends quivering together in the yielding sand with intimate hot limbs in supreme embrace," which Lawrence says was " the sensual co-efficient of the mental passion, which was welding our souls and spirits in one flaming effort."[20] You would have to go a long way before finding in other respectable writers so outspoken a declaration of preference for homosexuality. We may link this with his gibe that there was " nothing female in the Arab movement, but the camels "[21]

—an interesting admission—and his comment on the "little vices and luxuries—coffee, fresh water, women."[22]

The Howeitat chieftain, Auda, who led the Akaba expedition, had acquired a "latest wife, a jolly girl," who "whisked away like a rabbit" when Lawrence entered their tent and began jeering at the Sheik for "being so old and yet so foolish like the rest of his race, who regard our comic reproductive processes not as an unhygienic pleasure, but as a main business of life."[23] Yet the "quivering" male "friends" were "clean" and "even pure." And, while expressing this unqualified disdain and even horror of Auda's young wife, Lawrence felt the greatest admiration for the young camel-drivers, between 16 and 25, who, he thought, were so "keen-looking, handsome, mannered, often foppish in habit," talking "a delicate and elastic Arabic," while elsewhere he remarks that these "white-handed Aegyl" were "too beautiful to be made into labourers."[24] This is surely carrying æsthetic appreciation a little far, in war time, and on a front of such importance?

One is tempted to ask how it was that so many quivering male lovers were recruited in the Arab army. Burton and Doughty agree that the practice of homosexuality did not exist among the Bedouins of their time. Doughty says that the desert tribes had "purified their bodies" from all excess except coffee-drinking, adding: "Marriage is easy for every man's youth; and there are no such rusty bonds in their wedlock, that any must bear an heavy countenance."[25] On the other hand, Burton's *Terminal Essay* is almost too lavish of detailed information about the existence of homosexuality among those Arabs and other Mid-Eastern peoples living outside the desert areas. Johann Burckhardt reported "unnatural propensities" as "very common" among the Druses, and Burton says much the same of the Damascenes, and considered that "the evil" was "deeply rooted" among the Kurds.[26] The Bedouins being thus exempted, we should have to look for these "male lovers" among the enlisted deserters from the Turkish army or Lawrence's own bodyguard. But since Lawrence had no command in the Arab army, and in any case could not from lack of training have manœuvred even a small number of regular troops, the probability seems that they must be looked for among the thirty or forty members of his own bodyguard, "the too beautiful ones " who, in their coloured robes, looked to him like a row of tulips.[27]

This inference is borne out by the affair of Farraj and Daud, two members of Lawrence's bodyguard to whose behaviour he devotes a disproportionately large space, especially for a book supposedly occupied with great historical events and the unfolding of profoundly original views on warfare—as if the Emperor in the Memorial of St. Helena had dwelt long and affectionately on the *jeunes ébats* of two drummer boys in the Young Guard. Lawrence introduces them as " an instance of the eastern boy and boy affection which the segregation of womenkind made inevitable." Such friendships, he thought, led to " manly loves," which were " of a depth and force beyond our flesh-steeped conceit." When these relationships were " innocent " they were " hot and unashamed," but when sexuality entered in they " passed into a give and take, unspiritual relation, like marriage."[28] It is a little surprising to read that a Christian-bred man like Lawrence thought of marriage as an " unspiritual " relation, seeing that for the largest body of Christians it is one of the sacraments, but it must be remembered that Lawrence looked upon marriage, in his peculiar way, merely as a kind of licensed prostitution.

Lawrence's description of Farraj, the " love-fellow " of Daud, is luscious, for the boy is described as " a beautiful soft-framed, girlish creature," who possessed an " innocent, smooth face " and " swimming " eyes. The couple came to volunteer for Lawrence's bodyguard, and when Sharif Nasir refused, the beautiful young Farraj knelt at the Sharif's feet in supplication, " all the woman in him evident in his longing." Lawrence at once accepted them, because they were so " clean " and " young," and they turn up frequently in the pages of his great volume. They " gave him great satisfaction," he says; they were " two imps," yet of an æsthetic sort, from their habit of " dancing along, barefooted, delicate as thoroughbreds."[29] Later they had to be punished, and this disciplinary measure was carried out in a very curious way. The boys were seated on rocks made intolerably hot by the fierce sun until they begged for mercy.[30] There is a marked contrast between Lawrence's sympathy for these boy lovers and their " fopperies " and quiverings, and his contempt for Sheik Auda's passion for his young wife. Such instances from *Seven Pillars* could easily be multiplied, but these should suffice to show that whatever Lawrence's actions the trend of his sexual preferences was anti-female and pro-male. A similar impression comes from the occasional mention of these topics in his *Letters*, a few examples of which may be given.

Intellectual women have naturally been offended by his repeated assertion that English literature would not have suffered if every woman who had produced original work never lived.[31] He thought women upset his friends.[32] In writing to a friend about the poetry of Charlotte Mew, he produced this curious judgment: " I'm frigid towards woman so that I can withstand her."[33] Yet there is nothing erotic, and not much that is obviously feminine, in her poems. But Lawrence not only disliked women who possessed literary gifts—he even objected to their acting as naked models for sculptors. " Do you really like naked women? They express so little," he wrote to Kennington; and at once proceeded to describe to him and to praise a clay-sketch for a war memorial, consisting of four or five " earth-bound, naked " (male) figures marching in step close together, carrying a huge weight.[34] " Women? " he wrote. " I like some women. I don't like their sex. It's as obvious as red hair: and as little fundamental, I fancy."[35] Less than three weeks later he repeated this with added absurdity:

" Surely the sex business isn't worth all this damned fuss? I've met only a handful of people who really cared a biscuit for it."[36]

We must surely agree with E. M. Forster that " T. E." must have had a lot of queer friends. And if the reader wants to see how really low Lawrence could drop in his vindictive attack on women, he should borrow a copy of *The Mint*. Lawrence always thought of ordinary sex relations as prostitution. He praised a correspondent for having written a " demolition " of David Garnett's novel *No Love* whose exciting of the spirit he regarded as prostitution.[37] He told Charlotte Shaw, to whom he felt he was able to unburden himself as to no other, that he hated and despised physical pleasures; so much so that he regarded sexual intercourse as degrading to a woman, although it might occasionally be compensated for by child-bearing! Yet, measured by his own experience and imagination, the experiences described in *Lady Chatterley's Lover* were mild. Nor did he believe that love affairs must necessarily be between persons of opposite sex; his own observations of life bore him out in this. And he saw no objection to the love experienced in the mind finding expression through the body.[38]

Footnote : I have not included in the body of this chapter any mention of or any quotation from the short piece on *Lady Chatterley's Lover* which appears on page 687 of the *Letters* under date 25th March, 1930 (i.e. soon after D. H. Lawrence's death) and is given as addressed to Henry Williamson. Mr. David Garnett describes it as "the best criticism I have seen of Lady Chatterley: one which shows complete sympathy and understanding of the author."[39] This is no doubt true, but the piece in question was written by Henry Williamson, and not by T. E. Lawrence. Mr. Williamson wrote it originally as a protest against the obituaries of D. H. Lawrence, but did not publish it. He was moving from one home to another when he sent in his T. E. Lawrence letters to the editor, and by accident included with them his own piece on Lady Chatterley. When the papers were returned he did no more than slit open the envelope without looking through the contents, and did not notice his mistake until the Letters were in print. He gave the story to a newspaper with specimens of the two hand-writings. Lawrence's hand-writing, like that of many neurotics, varied constantly—it is quite amazing to see the varieties in any collection of his hand-written letters. Occasionally his hand-writing resembles Williamson's so closely that anyone might be deceived. I have had the original of this Lady Chatterley note in my possession and have studied it with specimens of Lawrence's hand-writing. The hand-writing is certainly Williamson's. Moreover, the note is wholly in keeping with his line of thought and at variance with Lawrence's, and in Williamson's style.

339

CHAPTER SEVEN

WHEN LAWRENCE handed over to Abdulla and Philby at Amman and returned to England, the strong probability is that he had already decided on a sensational action which cut him off from all chance of further employment in the upper ranks of government servants. Lawrence was not a man to make sudden decisions on impulse. There was no spontaneity in him since he was so wholly an embodiment of will, one who acted out his life in predetermined parts, throwing off each persona (or mask) as he tired of it or as soon as it had satisfied his will-to-power. A romanticised version of how he worked out these conscious plannings of a future course may be found in the *Seven Pillars* account of Lawrence's meditations in Abdulla's camp. Of course they are highly coloured and worked up *ex-post-facto*, and make extravagant claims for the author, but the chapter illustrates Lawrence's habit of carefully working out the next role he meant to play. In Abdulla's camp, he was grooming himself for the part of the young hero of the " Arab revolt "; at Amman—strangely enough also as Abdulla's guest— he was pondering his next startling metamorphosis, into the ranks of the peace-time R.A.F. There is evidence that he had hinted at some such thing while on his 1919 flight out to Cairo.[1]

Lawrence's life did not end with enlistment, but his active career did; and the peace-time life of a private, whether in the ranks of the Army or the R.A.F. is so much a matter of routine and busy idleness that there remains little of importance to record of these last years. For a time Lawrence comforted himself with hopes of producing literary masterpieces, of a career as a great writer. Mr. Forster is probably right in thinking that Lawrence would rather have been a great writer than anything else. But he was such an amateur in his outlook, at one time believing that by taking thought he could produce a synthetic masterpiece designed to interest remotest posterity —whereas, common sense, if he had any, should have told him that posterity will do what we do, read what it wants to read and forget the rest; and at another time growing deeply discouraged because editors refused his contributions when they were sent in anonymously. Even literary journalism is a trade which has to be learned. It was a curious attitude in a man professing such contempt for the amateur motorist who did not thoroughly understand the engine he was driving—as if you have to be a vet. to ride a horse. But in journalism there is a technique of the day, which must either be accepted and applied—or out you go; an obvious if odious fact, which Lawrence either could not or would not admit.

Clearly, this spectacular disappearance into the limbo of the other ranks was the result of some exceptional stress. A man of Lawrence's gifts and education, of his remarkable strength of will, holding the unique place in the upper class public adulation which he had achieved by unscrupulous use of his gifts for intrigue and self-advertisement— such a man does not commit worldly hara-kiri without being impelled and harried by irresistible if intangible motives, whose real origin he may not necessarily have realised. Here evidently was a major crisis, the major crisis in his life; and if we could get a little closer to under-standing it than the contradictory and only partly true explanations given out by himself and echoed by the Lawrence Bureau, we should come closer to an understanding of this remarkable and too often disagreeable character. From the evidence collected in these pages, is it possible to deduce an explanation of his behaviour which fits the facts? If you remember that writers on Lawrence have deliberately omitted some facts, have fantastically embellished many, and have not been in possession of others here recorded, you will agree that the task of trying to interpret this crisis should not be shirked. I may add that if Bernard Shaw read Lawrence's letters to Mrs. Shaw, which he almost certainly did, then in writing his *Friends* tribute he either missed the clues afforded or deliberately ignored them. Lawrence had told Mrs. Shaw the truth as far as was possible for him, and had even wished that Graves should see the letters—a proposition she had rejected—but Shaw let the knowledge drop.

Lawrence's worldly position in the first half of 1922 looked—and but for the unescapable wounds of Fate was—unassailable and secure. His immense Lowell Thomas publicity had made him a popular figure of so much influence that the government had thought it prudent to associate him with its efforts to put some order into the Arabian chaos, though, unfortunately, he failed to persuade Hussein and threw up his Amman post almost as soon as he received it. The Colonial Office was paying him a salary which Lawrence variously and vaguely estimated at figures varying from £1,000 to £1,600 a year. Mr. Churchill, his chief, says £1,200; and that must be the fact. In addition, Lawrence had been receiving £200 a year for three years from All Souls. Considering that Lawrence was a bachelor with no known entanglements or dependants, that according to him he never smoked, never took wine (as a matter of fact, on rare occasions he did both), ate practically nothing, and, in England at all events, dressed plainly the question arises—On what did he spend his money? Well, as we have seen, he spent it on buying commissioned pictures (there is one recorded payment of £720 to Mr. Kennington alone) and in lavishly generous gifts of money. He did not enjoy this Colonial Office income for long, and very possibly it barely sufficed, in spite of his frugality, to pay off his early post-war overdraft. It is difficult to agree with Graves's opinion that Lawrence had "a sensible attitude towards money."[2] He certainly was free from the love of money either as power or pleasure, but he lacked common sense in handling it. But for his lordly gestures of extravagant patronage and pretentious publication, he would have been wholly solvent. Significantly, whatever sum he did give to Doughty was paid at a time (March, 1922) when, according to his later dramatised version of himself, he was already the starving ex-service officer often forced to humiliate himself by seeking the hospitality of friends (he specifically mentioned Mr. Lionel Curtis as one)[3] and eventually to enlist to keep body and soul together. Yet on his own showing this pathetic character had thrown up, for no reason whatever, an excellent job under a great political chief, and possessed, in spite of his over-draft, £4,000 worth of land, an expensive motor-bicycle, a gold wrist-watch and so forth, as well as the great potential asset of his book. Moreover, for years after he actually had enlisted, his credit remained good enough for him to lavish very large sums on the illustration, printing, and binding of his book.

Obviously, something here needs explaining. There is the popular idea that he was so patriotic that he insisted at all costs in serving the Empire; but where was the extreme patriotism of one who led the King to believe—even if he did not actually say—that he was ready to take up arms against his country in the cause of his Arab friends, and where was the patriotism of insisting on dawdling away the years on inferior jobs which thousands of men could do instead of employing his undoubted talents on far more difficult and responsible work only to be discharged by the few? His enlistment was not patriotic but selfish. The theory that he enlisted as a camouflage for important work as a secret agent is equally flimsy, and built out of ill-instructed popular sensationalism. True, Lawrence did make notes of his life as a recruit (afterwards called *The Mint*), which may have led the more suspicious of his comrades into the erroneous belief that he had been sent to spy on them. And there is some evidence that he may have been for a time connected in a very subordinate position with the intelligence service on the Afghan frontier. But nothing can be more certain than that he did not enlist with the connivance of the R.A.F. staff, which in 1922 did not want him, had to be ordered by high authority, to take him at all, and got rid of him as soon as possible.

As might be expected, Lawrence's own explanations hover in that realm of partial truth which was his special realm. In his curiously impudent letters to Air Vice-Marshal Swann (whom he had only met for a few minutes), Lawrence pretended that he had joined up only or mainly to write a book about the R.A.F.[4] For other reasons, only four days earlier, he had pretended to Bernard Shaw that *Seven Pillars* was the only book he would ever write.[5] In February, 1923, he wrote: "Did you understand that I enlisted not to write books, but because I was broke?"[6] On the 6th June of the same year, he complained to Hogarth that he was not sufficiently coarse-fibred for the life of politics and added: "When I joined the R.A.F., it was in the hope that some day I'd write a book about the very excellent subject that it was."[7] A very Hamlet—to write or not to write!

There was this much truth in his assertions and untruth in his denials that he undoubtedly did make notes for a book, which he completed years later in India. It is much the same with his other

343

"explanations." He was "broke" and had no "trade." He had
had a nervous breakdown and wanted a rest-cure. He was weary
of the world, and wished to retire to a military monastery. He
wanted to degrade himself and make himself "unfit for a responsible
position."[8] Then, again, he was mad. "This sort of thing" (i.e.,
life in the Tank Corps) "must be madness, and sometimes I wonder
how far mad I am, and if a mad-house would not be my next (and
merciful) stage."[9] On another occasion he was in the ranks because
he had failed to live with his own kind in such a place as All Souls,
and wanted to live among common men, although the communal
life was torture to him. His masochism, he explained, was "only
moral,"[10] but sometimes this moral masochism caused him to take
extreme views of himself, such as that he longed for people to look
down on him and to despise him, but was too shy to involve himself
in any scandal which would make him publicly disgraced and contemptible. In another mood he wrote at one time, "Honestly, I
couldn't tell you exactly why I joined up,"[11] and yet at another time
instructed his correspondent to "make clear that" Lawrence liked the
R.A.F., "liked the being cared for, the rails of conduct, the impossibility of doing irregular things."[12] Contrast that with his extravagant
mood of self-pity in the Tank Corps, where he speaks of brooding
all day, sleeping less than ever, refusing "every possible distraction,"
until, in a neurotic frenzy of self-pity, he "pulled out" his motor
cycle and "hurled it top-speed through these unfit roads for hour
after hour."[13]

I have already mentioned Lawrence's belief that he wrote best
when excited and have pointed out that if such were the case he was
usually most excited by scenes of brutality, violence and nastiness;
but there was one topic which occupied him just as much and quite
continuously—himself. The letters of March, April and May, 1923,
to Lionel Curtis have a high literary level and are entirely about
himself. Some of the citations in the preceding paragraph are taken
from them, and a study of them is recommended to those who think
that Lawrence could not write well, and to all those who may be
interested in trying to unravel the tangle of his neurosis which was
the real reason or unreason for his enlistment. I certainly would not
say that there is no truth in all this welter of his contradictions, in
some of which he was probably deliberately trying to mislead his

correspondent, while in others he luxuriated in the pleasures of dramatised self-pity. Thus, he was more or less " broke," he had been near
a " nervous breakdown," he had been too much the solitary individual
and intellectual, he now had a hankering after intimacy with common
men. But why the wish " to degrade " himself, and whence the
neurosis? What was behind such an extraordinary outburst as this:

> " . . . surely the world would be more clean if we were dead
> or mindless? We are all guilty alike, you know. You wouldn't
> exist, I wouldn't exist without this carnality. Everything with
> flesh in its mixture is the achievement of a moment when the lusty
> thought of Hut 12 has passed to action and conceived: and isn't
> it true that the fault of birth rests somewhat on the child? I believe
> it's we who led our parents on to bear us, and it's our unborn
> children who make our flesh itch. A filthy business all of it, and
> yet Hut 12 shows me the truth behind Freud. . . ."[14]

Guilt—that gives us the clue. Let us look back upon what we
have learned by this long enquiry about him and his circumstances.
He was, and knew that he was from an indeterminate but certainly
early date, the child of an irregular union between an Anglo-Irish
aristocrat and a girl of humble birth. Although there was the painful
but far from uncommon circumstance of a former wife and children,
this union—though unblessed by Church or State—was in all essentials
a life-long marriage, fruitful in five gifted sons. Unluckily, the social
and religious views of the protagonists, the prejudices of the age, and
the alarmed interests of distinguished relatives, all combined to insist
imperatively on the necessity for keeping the real relationship secret.
Thus Lawrence grew up to bear the intolerable burden for a sensitive
youth of a Guilty Secret, made no easier to bear from the fact that it
had to be borne in Oxford, the heart of censorious academic and
clerical respectability. Hence the solitude, the lack of society, the
absence of girls in his youth. The impact on a gifted, hyper-
susceptible, extremely vain youth of learning that Guilty Secret
must indeed have been shattering and heart-breaking.

From the point of view of our contemporary prejudices, this
treatment of the child was all wrong. The child must be told the
truth as early as possible or all kinds of psychological troubles may
develop. As Lawrence's arithmetic is so often " oriental," we may

justly doubt whether he grasped fully the situation before his teens; though even at that tender age he may very well have realised consciously—what he must already have registered sub-consciously—that something was very anomalous indeed in his parents' social position.

The arrest in Lawrence's physical development is officially attributed to the shock of his broken leg at school. It may be so, but what of his arrested mental development, noted by so many who knew him, and surely most remarkable in a man so highly endowed with intellect and will? Surely, the mental fixation in adolescence—if not the physical—was due to some overwhelming mental shock? And what could that be but knowledge of the Guilty Secret? Again, there is surely no stretching of probability if we connect the moment of full realisation with Lawrence's running away from home and joining up in the ranks of the Royal Artillery? Of course, there is always the possibility that the running away to join the army at seventeen is just another of Lawrence's stories, and there is certainly a difficulty in finding the six months of one version[15] and the eight months of another.[16] But just as, in his boastings, he turned his cycling kilometres into miles and his dollar earnings for a serial into pounds, so here he may have turned weeks into months—in which case all difficulty disappears. By a further but reasonable inference, the building of the bungalow for him in the Polstead Road garden can be connected with the epoch when he was presumably lured back from an escapade which threatened scandal. Why was the bungalow built for Lawrence, and Lawrence only? With the usual cunning, the seemingly simple and decisive reason given is that the house was too small for the growing family, which may indeed be true, but is it the whole truth? If so, why was it not for the eldest boy or, more practically, for two of the boys? But the whole situation becomes clear if we remember Lawrence's assertion that home life for him was intolerable, and realise the ferocity with which he blamed his parents for having children at all in their situation. Hence, in later life, the bitter antagonism to women as a sex, leading to a puritanical horror of normal sexual intercourse.

This impulse of refusal, of rejection, of wilful courting of plebeian degradation was linked with an irresistible and apparently contrary impulse to over-value himself and all he did and to persuade or to compel others to accept him at his own over-valuation. It is said—but I give this merely as common room gossip—that in the post-war days at Oxford, Lawrence made no attempt to maintain the Secret with his inmost group of friends, that indeed he would boast of it, saying he was born on Napoleon's birthday and that illegitimate children were often exceptionally gifted. Be that as it may, there can be no doubt that from his schoolboy days he practised—apparently with complete success—this compensatory telling of stories about himself, always in his own favour, and always to a greater or less degree an improvement of the reality, if they were not wholly invented. Lawrence was not singular in this, except that he did it so persistently, so cunningly and so successfully. Most men have a tendency to draw the long bow when relating their past deeds, but in general they do it so artlessly that few of their listeners are taken in. I have known at least two well-known writers who were incorrigible in producing picturesque anecdotes about themselves as supermen, transforming the most humdrum events and episodes into glittering tales of Araby, which showed in them a great aptitude for romantic fiction—to which indeed they would have done well to limit themselves. Lawrence, who was "a born actor and up to all sorts of tricks,"[17] as his friend and literary sponsor, Bernard Shaw, admits, also had this habit or faculty or weakness of dramatising himself in each of the many parts for which he cast himself in numberless little anecdotes. Where Lawrence excelled was in the skill with which he chose as his material, episodes to which there were no available witnesses but himself or which could not be verified without an absurd amount of trouble. Moreover, like every good novelist, he almost invariably started from fact and then proceeded to give it the embellishments of a polite and elegant imagination. But, as his stories usually started from a slight basis of fact, it is more than probable that he came firmly to believe in his embellished versions. As I shall show presently, in his later years he repeatedly asserted that he had been offered the great and responsible office of High Commissioner for Egypt, a story emphatically denied by men in public life who are in a position to know. Yet I am persuaded that Lawrence, however he may have started the tale, came in time to believe it. He himself admits that he early reached a point where perpetual blagueing and bluffing had rendered him uncertain where reality began and ended.

Take, for instance, the episode of the harmless exchange of shots between himself and a native during his first foot-tour of Syria, as recorded in his letter at the time. This becomes embellished into an encounter with a terrible Turk whom Lawrence skilfully disables by wounding the man's little finger at an impossible range, then binds up the wound and either dismisses the man with a kick or gives him money and swears eternal friendship. Who could find the Turk and verify? Similarly, the story of how he told Kitchener all about the Alexandretta strategy at some pre-war time was not put out until after Kitchener was dead. Even Hubert Young appears to have believed it in 1918, since he passed it on to Lowell Thomas. I should think it highly unlikely that Lawrence ever had a private interview with Kitchener, and the rest of the story is obviously faked up after he had heard rumours of the generals' debates on the subject in Cairo. There are no witnesses. In other cases, verification would be far too complicated for anyone to undertake—e.g., his tale to Mr. Richards that his bronze replica of Hypnos was picked up on an Italian rubbish heap and thought by the Museum experts to be an antique better than the original. Who was going to find out if the ships he had travelled on at that time touched at Italian ports (so far as I can discover, they did not), or where the rubbish heap was, or to question the Museum authorities, or finally to ask for a scientific test of the metal? Obviously no one; but what remains a mystery is that people believed and printed such tales. And obviously exactly the same process of touching up and heightening reality came into play when Lawrence related and officially reported the unwitnessed stories of his deeds in Arabia. Certainly there was a basis of truth and reality, but he was far from being the great leader he allowed or persuaded others to say he was. Take a simple matter of unimportant detail—did any English officer ever accompany Lawrence on one of his camel rides when he claimed that he had ridden 300 miles in three days? None, so far as I can discover; though several express amazement and admiration at his tales of fast camel-riding. Johann Burckhardt mentions as an astounding exception, a camel which once did 105 miles in a day. Burton thought 80 miles a very good day's journey and not to be maintained. Leachman averaged 60 miles a day on his fast Damascus-Baghdad ride. Of course, Lawrence undoubtedly had the pick of the best camels and rode very light and fast, but—100 miles a day for three days! Nobody can deny it, for there are no witnesses; but with Lawrence's proved record of exaggerations who will not feel sceptical?

There is one achievement which nobody can deny Lawrence, and that was his capacity to convince others that he was a remarkable man. Of course he was, but what was chiefly "remarkable" was his capacity for self-advertisement. He was a soldier among writers and a writer among soldiers. He succeeded in impressing such eminent and different persons as Sir Winston Churchill, Mr. E. M. Forster and Sir Lewis Namier. Unquestionably Lawrence was a determined and ambitious man, guerrilla fighter, and possibly administrator; but an immense legend was fabricated, largely by himself, from materials of uncertain substance. The tragedy of Lawrence's life is that the inner conflict started by the shock of discovering the "secret" was never resolved, so that his very gifts turned to self-destruction. His career and his strangely tortured psychology will always be of interest, if only as a problem involving so many unknown quantities. Perhaps when all the evidence is made public, the problem may be solved. Perhaps not. On the one hand, he cannot avoid embellishing all he does and simply must exhibit himself to the world as this astounding and triumphant character; and, on the other hand, he has an equally powerful "impulse of refusal," descending even to the wish "to degrade" himself. Christian egotists, who believe that the universe was designed for their personal salvation or damnation, pass readily from a conviction of supreme sanctity to the neurotic state of "greatest of sinners." Lawrence himself dramatised his neurosis as a war between the irreconcilable elements in the natures of his parents in himself. In a symbolical sense that was true, but the situation went beyond that. It was rather as if he had taken the whole of the Guilty Secret on himself, and had to punish the guilt of his parents in himself. When he is in the upward flight of a phase of comparative optimism and embellishment, it is as if he said to them: "See, in spite of the handicap and the wrong you did me, I am still able to triumph over all difficulties and win to fame and fortune far beyond yours." And then inexorably and, as it were, in the very moment of victory he passed to the phase of pessimism and self-disgust and voluntary "degradation," as if he now said to them sorrowfully or resentfully: " See, but for your guilt, I should be on top of the world, but your sin brings me down; because of you I must renounce what in spite of you I have won." Obviously he never formulated his neurosis in those terms, but he came near enough with his description of the war within himself and in the resentment against one woman carried over to all women in their sexual aspect. He could only be friends with a woman if all sex was tacitly but unmistakably ruled out. He could never forgive the fact that the baronet's son was the nurse-maid's child; and *vice-versa*.

It has been said that Lawrence had " no real self," that he was merely an actor who played many parts. But there was " a real self," which is fairly plainly shown both in *Seven Pillars* and in the letters to Lionel Curtis and Charlotte Shaw—an unhappy, wistful, tortured, hag-ridden self, floundering between heights and depths, aspiring to the rôle of a knight of the Round Table and tumbling with Hibernian awkwardness into grotesque and even terrible accidents and mis-fortunes—who can think of that flogging at Deraa without a shudder of pity for the victim? Yet he had the courage, the skill—the cunning, if you like—and the force of will and character to impose on the world his over-valued persona as reality, and to receive world-wide acclaim —for what? for the clever patter and pictures of a glib showman untroubled by the majesty of truth. And having triumph in his grasp he throws it all away, to escape the mother who now turned instinctively to the brilliant son for comfort. Let him be, as he dreamed, exalted like another Joseph to be ruler of Egypt, she could still follow and madden him with female efficiency and prayer. There was one place where neither she nor any woman could follow him—a barrack-room. And what a supreme punishment for the abhorred but inexorably shared Guilt—the baronet's son " gone for a soldier," the " Prince of Mecca " in the ranks! No wonder that, lacking the clue, the world was puzzled, and that the inventive powers of journalists flowered into ever more fatuous absurdities. Like the lady in the French farce, they stood aghast at this apparent repudia-tion of the only world they knew—" *Des enfants qui veulent travailler! C'est inouï!* " But of course he did not mean to repudiate the one thing he really cared for—his notoriety and above all his hoped-for literary notoriety. Love of literature, respect for all artists, especially poets, were wholly sincere in him; and doubtless he would rather have written *The Sphinx* than take Damascus.

If we look back over Lawrence's life, before he played this final trump card of enlistment, in his bitter game with Sin, we note previous examples of this " impulse of refusal " mixed in with his usual line of romantic over-valuation of self. The most striking is the earliest which we have been discussing—the rejection of the life of an Oxford scholar, which seemed opening before him, for the life of a private soldier. In spite of all the extravagant talk about his being a greater strategic genius than Hannibal and Napoleon, he had in him the makings of a soldier and a good officer—but you can't go through Sandhurst as a day-boy with scholarships. There is no evidence for it, but if the Artillery experience really happened, may there not have been a veiled reproach behind it? Perhaps the thought is too subtle for a schoolboy, but Lawrence was always a schoolboy and a very deep one. Whoever thought of the solution of a separate dwelling during term-time, and cycling tours during vacations, neatly solved the problem of reducing his family contacts to a minimum, especially as Lawrence added his pose of eating only a few scraps at any time, which could be invoked whenever he wanted to avoid a family meal.

Hogarth, who must have been aware of the situation, must also have felt that he had solved the problem rather well by finding Lawrence employment so far away as Carchemish; and indeed Lawrence seems to have been happy during that too-brief time. It is trifling but just worth noting that there seems to have been no real reason for taking his first trip wholly on foot and by rail—the money given him by his father would have sufficed to hire horses or mules if he had not spent so much of it on an over-expensive camera, and banked the rest. He had to demonstrate that he was forced to travel as a pauper, a Chapman of Killua! We see again the same ambivalence in the Carchemish days—sitting in the evenings with Woolley dressed up in a sixty-guinea jacket, and then wandering with Dahoum like a couple of Arab tramps. The unexpected start in the Army as a staff officer roused all his insolence, and but for Hogarth's protection he might easily have been dismissed by outraged regulars to the Western front in his full substantive rank of second-lieutenant. How brilliantly he turned to account his forcible exile to Arabia needs no demonstration, but as soon as he returned home the temporarily exorcised impulse of refusal came back. He took the first opportunity to get rid of his French decorations, and went out of his way to appear to resign his English honours—though actually he contrived to retain them. When he flew to Cairo, he demoted himself to second-lieutenant by cutting off the crown from his badges of rank. He is given the exceptional honour of rooms in All Souls, but hastens to " degrade " himself by retiring to a garret in Barton Street. He is appointed the actual ruler of Transjordan, and chooses to live in " a hovel," and almost immediately resigns—was it because the post was too good or not good enough? All Mr. Churchill's kindly efforts to help him by refusing his resignations and offering a choice of Colonial Office posts were pure joy to Lawrence but pure waste, gratifying as they did both aspects of his neurosis and enabling him when his resignation was at last accepted to wind up with the condescending remark:

" Thank the Lord for Winston coming round at last. I did so want not to quarrel with him. He's a most decent person."[18]

The last link in the chain of our evidence is provided by the very significant change of name on enlistment. Now this was the normal thing to do for the hero who had seen better days, into which character Lawrence was then busily transforming himself, but it happened not to be allowed in the R.A.F., which was only one of several things about his enlistment he didn't know. At the same time this was the perfect opportunity for him to repudiate and to abandon the borrowed name of " Lawrence," which, as he justly complained, was nominally his merely because of his father's whim when changing names, and an extra source of annoyance and embarrassment since it belonged by right to a contemporary author whom T. E. Lawrence warmly and sincerely admired. (He only began to find fault after D. H. in *Lady Chatterley's Lover* laughed at a certain " Colonel Florence.") Now, as Ross or Shaw, he could try to shake off the hateful reminder of Guilt. I believe—though I can't prove—that long before this Lawrence would have been very glad to throw off all pretence and acknowledge the situation, which, though awkward for a man in the limelight, didn't really amount to anything serious in the post-war moral chaos. Who would have thought the less of him except for a pack of old Oxonian aunts who, unluckily, were the characters most important to others who were not able to lean their elbows simultaneously on seven pillars of publicity? Not that Ross and Shaw intended that the deeds of Lawrence of Arabia should be forgotten along with the discarded name. On the contrary, as we have seen, he spent the leisure of years in planning and plotting the career of his veracious memoirs, and in encouraging the *vies romancées* and biographies of Thomas, Graves and Hart. But there are slight though unmistakable hints in both the later books of the real situation, and the facts that in Captain Hart's book the " Lawrence " was written with inverted commas on the title-page, and that " Ross " or " Shaw " encouraged his friends to address him merely as " T. E." need no stressing. Sometimes it became T. E. S. or Tes, but the student of Lawrence comes to feel at length a cold detestation for the self-important glee with which his servile adulators proclaim themselves the paladins and peers of " T. E." The fact that Lawrence went to so much trouble to maintain that his choice of " Shaw " was pure coincidence and had nothing to do with Bernard is fairly convincing evidence that the name was chosen to stress his intimacy with the Marxist of Mayfair.

Now that this point is reached and a frank explanation of Lawrence's action attempted, if not proved, little more remains to be said, since the story of the writing and production of *Seven Pillars*—the one important event of his post-enlistment life—has already been told. By way of epilogue, we have only to trace the curious little story of his first R.A.F. enlistment, his dismissal and enlistment in the Tank Corps, the desperate intrigue by which under threat of suicide he got himself reinstated, the routine of his later days broken mainly by a " spy story," and his death within a few weeks of his final discharge.

CHAPTER EIGHT

LAWRENCE'S ENLISTMENT in the ranks of the R.A.F. has been told in different and more or less romantic versions—of which not the least romantic was his own—and we are fortunate in having at least the main facts from first-hand witnesses. Perhaps the most striking fact that first comes up is that the Air Force did not want Lawrence, tried to refuse him and had him imposed upon them by high authority, managed to get rid of him, and after two years had him imposed a second time. Who was the " high authority "? In the second case, it was Stanley Baldwin coerced by Bernard Shaw and Buchan; in the first case, it has not been revealed or I have failed to discover it. But it must have been someone in a high position, since an Air Vice-Marshal writes that he was " *ordered* " (and underlines the word indignantly) to get Lawrence into the R.A.F.[1] Sir Oliver Swann goes on to say that he hated the business about which there was nothing open, and that he discouraged all communication with or from Lawrence.[2] In spite of which Lawrence as an A.C.2 persisted in writing the Air Vice-Marshal letters which are a strange compound of the impudent and the abject. So far as R.A.F. headquarters was concerned, Sir Oliver tells us that he and he alone dealt with Lawrence's entry and movements.[3]

What happened next was for long known only through hints in Lawrence's letters and romantic versions not worth mentioning, except for the fact that once more we find Lawrence at his old game of arranging and embellishing the truth. Fortunately, in 1951, an account of what really happened was published in the *Sunday Times* by the man who at the time was the chief interviewing officer at the London Recruiting Depot, and is now widely known as an author,

W. E. Johns. He begins by pointing out that the recruiting regulations were then so strict that nobody could get into the Air Force without his real identity being divulged. The practice in the old Regular Army was to accept any otherwise valid recruit without pressing him on the subject of his real name. It looks as if Lawrence may not have been aware that this old custom did not apply in the new Air Force. At all events, when he presented himself before Mr. Johns, in a high state of nerves,[4] under the name of John Hume Ross, the officer was warned by his sergeant-major that the new recruit seemed "a suspicious character." His photograph was not among those of men wanted by Scotland Yard, but he was told he must produce "a reference from his last employer, a moral character and his birth certificate." While Lawrence went off to get these, Johns found out from Somerset House that John Hume Ross did not exist, and, as Lawrence's references turned out to be forgeries, the sergeant-major "showed him the door."

"Ross" was soon back with an order for enlistment "signed by a very high authority," but now the R.A.F. doctors refused to pass him. Mr. Johns was asked by them to look at the "scars of flogging "* which "Ross" refused to explain—but there is no mention of any other wounds. The Commanding Officer, on Mr. Johns' report, then telephoned to the Air Ministry and returned with this rather sinister remark spoken "very seriously":

"Watch your step. This man is Lawrence of Arabia. Get him in, or you'll get your bowler hat."

The last phrase is here professional slang for "get dismissed." The doctors still refused to pass "Ross," and he had finally to be passed by "an outside doctor." Lawrence, after a talk, then left for Uxbridge Depot, leaving behind "the memory of a cold, clammy handshake." Everyone in the recruiting office now knew who "Ross" was, and Mr. Johns rang up the recruiting officer at Uxbridge to warn him who was coming:

"... for by this time Lawrence was making it clear that he had no time for junior officers. Lawrence himself soon saw to it that everyone knew who he was."[5]

* Strong evidence that the Deraa flogging story is true.

355

Now, if we put together the facts that from the start the Uxbridge R.A.F. officers knew who " Ross " was (which Lawrence, for the purposes of his own myth, later pretended was not the case) and that the R.A.F. did not want him, we have the obvious explanation of why Ross and his squad went through such a tough course of " fatigues " and military training. Lawrence kept a record of all this in *The Mint*, but echoes of his experiences and complaints are hinted at in his letters. He gratuitously informed Swann that the coarseness of life in the ranks worried him more than he had expected, but he hoped to get used to being at everyone's beck and call.[6] A few days later, in writing Edward Garnett, Lawrence says he put the critic's letter in his pocket when he went to feed the camp pigs, and read it on the roof of the sty, a situation which he contrasts bitterly with an offer of the editorship of a periodical to be called *Belles-Lettres*.[7] A month later, Lawrence still has not forgotten the indignity of the pig-sty, but, relieved from the stage of recruits' fatigues he now complains that they were drilling in the barrack square all day.[8] Apart from the pig-sty parade, I don't find that Lawrence was told to do anything that was not done by all war-time infantry recruits —both rankers and cadets—though he may have been given a bit of a run around, which was rather hard on a man of thirty-five.

Even after he was moved from Uxbridge to the more congenial surroundings of Farnborough, Lawrence still found much to complain of in his new life. One of Bernard Shaw's letters about *Seven Pillars* had asked what Lawrence had to do in the ranks of the R.A.F., and in replying he pulled out all the stops. On the morning after Christmas, Lawrence had been ordered to wash up for the sergeants' mess, where he found the plates covered with butter and tomato sauce and the washing water cold. In the afternoon he had motor-cycled to Oxford to consult his friend Dr. Hogarth on the abridgement of his great book. For three weeks, he complained, he had been used as an errand-boy, and also for all the other menial duties around the camp.[9] At this period, Lawrence was still planning the publication of his book, and it is evident that he was growing very restive at being treated as an ordinary A.C.2, with none of the small but highly valued alleviations of fatigues and parades which come to the old or specially employed or favoured aircraftman.

By a coincidence, on the very morning that Lawrence wrote that letter to Bernard Shaw, a London newspaper revealed that the uncrowned king of Arabia had joined the ranks of the R.A.F., " seeking peace " and " the opportunity to write a book."[10] The secret of the incognito had been kept from the public for just over four months. But how did the newspaper get the " story " of which it had apparently heard rumours on or about the 16th December, just before the newspaper silly season of Christmas? According to Lawrence, one of the officers recognised him, and sold the information " for thirty pounds "—and the officer was one he had known during the war.[11] It would indeed be a dramatic incident, if true, that a former disciple sold for thirty pieces of paper money a secret which Lawrence was so anxious to preserve that, when he enlisted, he took with him as a precaution against being recognised the official document appointing him plenipotentiary to Hussein, which in 1921 continued to name him C.B. and D.S.O. Now, as the officers had known Lawrence's identity all along, why did they wait so long to sate their lust of pelf by this Judas-like betrayal. Would an officer do such a thing, since the selling of even such a trifling piece of information would technically be a serious offence, not to mention the fact that in the mess it would be thought dishonourable? And would the news have been worth that much to a reporter? I doubt it. Sir Oliver Swann says that the discovery of Lawrence's presence in the ranks of the R.A.F. was " solely due to carelessness *at the Colonial Office* and to Lawrence's unfortunate love of drawing a veil of mystery about himself."[12] Was this publicity a gaffe or a private news-release? Real carelessness at the Colonial Office is surprising when you reflect that it would be hard to find a more reticent set of administrators than British civil servants charged with the least government secret. A curious fact is that this unnamed officer not only recognised Lawrence but was able to tell the newspaper one of the explanations of his enlistment which Lawrence was then giving privately to his friends—that he wanted " peace " and the " opportunity to write a book." How did the " officer " find that out?

Now, it was perfectly true that Lawrence had been making notes almost every evening for a book about his experiences in the R.A.F., which fact he had communicated to Sir Oliver Swann either as a threat or a promise. Whether it was this fact or the newspaper

comment or both or some unknown factor which caused the unnamed
"high authority" to reverse himself and to agree that Lawrence
should be dismissed is not definitely established, but the fact is that
the decision was made to turn him out. It is said that the official
explanation given Lawrence was that his recognition made it difficult
for the officers, while his friendship with an R.A.F. officer of high
rank, presumably Trenchard, also complicated matters.[13] These seem
inadequate reasons and rather unfair, especially since we know from
W. E. Johns that Lawrence had been known to the local officers all
along. The profound dislike for Lawrence and the cunning he had
used to get into the R.A.F. expressed by Sir Oliver Swann[14] may have
been a more potent motive. In any event, as one would expect, the
effect on Lawrence was that he set himself to the task of being reinstated
with all his tenacity of will and genius for intrigue.

In January, 1923, very soon after the dismissal, Lawrence made an
appeal in this sense to the Secretary to the Chief of Air Staff, rather—
the not very hopeful tone of the letter seems to imply—with the idea
of putting his request on record than with any real hopes that it
would be granted. His psychological and family problems still
remained exactly the same, and by the beginning of March (1923)
Lawrence was back in the ranks, of the Royal Tank Corps this time,
through the friendly influence of Sir Philip Chetwode among others.[15]
In the interval, he asserted, he had spent his time in trudging around
London.[16] He was posted to Wool in Dorsetshire, not far from the
home of the then living Thomas Hardy, and near land owned by
relatives of his father, where he rented and furnished a small cottage
called Clouds Hill for his leisure hours and eventual retirement.

Lawrence's life was henceforth more divided than ever between
the routine of peace-time soldiering in the all-pervading human
promiscuity of the barrack-room and his literary-æsthetic interests,
together with the many celebrities he so carefully cultivated. Such
was the impasse into which he had been driven by the complicated
motives of his family situation, his neurosis, and the vanity that he
tried to conceal behind his masks and subtleties. The writers who
have identified Lawrence and all his doings so completely with themselves that they start angrily at any fact which once recognised chips
their idol, like to maintain that he was really "perfectly happy"
during his dozen years of service in the ranks. There is something

to be said for this view if it is limited to Cranwell and the Cattewater period in the 1930's, when he had grown resigned to his fate, was occupied as an individual in testing speed-boats, and was favoured, not to say adored, by his C.O. and wife.[17]   The change is shown in the endless sequence of those photographs he courted which evolve from the lantern-jawed ugly pseudo-Arab of the Peace Conference to the round-faced, chubby, contented-looking little fellow in a turtle-necked sweater, standing on a projecting quay-pile in the wistful hope of looking as tall as the lanky Liddell Hart.   But a good many years were to pass before he reached that comparative felicity.

In one of Lawrence's unwanted letters from Uxbridge to Sir Oliver Swann he spoke pathetically of the fifteen wretched hours he spent daily,[18] and retrospectively lamented his five weeks there of daily fatigues, often till eight at night, and much of it heavy work too.[19]   At Wool he found the great improvement that most of these fatigues were done by duty-men and not by recruits, which again raises the query whether his squad at Uxbridge had not been severely tested in the hope that he might voluntarily get out.   Moreover, the Wool camp had more of the necessities of life, such as food and fuel, blankets and baths, and a library.[20]   In spite of this, Lawrence's remarks on the life at Wool are in general not very indicative of that happiness he is supposed to have found in the abnegation of the easy job.   He wrote Edward Garnett that he hated the Army and his fellow-soldiers with their animal outlook.[21]   He dramatically told Lionel Curtis that his aim was " mind-suicide," and that after seven years no one would be able to propose him for a responsible position[22] —rather overlooking the probability that, after his turning-down of Mr. Churchill's generous offers, nobody in an official position was likely to renew them.   Six months later he wrote Graves that he had attained " peace of mind " (had he?) by putting up with the unpleasantness of the life and allowing his mind to stagnate.[23]   And this culminated in a despairing cry to Kennington in November, 1923, that he hated the Army.[24]   How irresistible then must have been the compulsion neurosis which forced him to accept an environment so repugnant.

In August, 1924, he complained to Lady Sandwich that his lot was one-twentieth of an army hut, and said how much he disliked the noise and animal spirits, especially since he liked warmth and colour.[25] Even after he had got himself back into the R.A.F., he could write that (in December, 1927) he had lived five years in barracks and had never really got on with the men he had mixed with,[26] about which, however, he changed his mind four years later.[27] His unpublished letters from India have many complaints against life in the R.A.F. However much we allow for the moods of a hyper-susceptible man and the studied pathos of one who so deliberately created stylised portraits of himself, the conclusion seems obvious that he was not really resigned into comparative content until the 1930's, and even then deluded himself and his friends with nostalgic imaginations of great offices awaiting him, if only he deigned to accept them. In the many changes of his perpetual posing, he always remained intensely interested in himself—the eloquent letters wholly about himself to Lionel Curtis were written from Wool.

As was to be expected, he fostered a new growth of " stories " about his life in the ranks—there was even a revived and revised version of the saluting story, the victim this time being an unnamed major-general, who had the effrontery to want a copy of *Seven Pillars*, and to be rude to Lawrence of Arabia in his military disguise.[28] But these may now be taken for granted, and dismissed as inevitable. The first-hand testimonies as to his behaviour in the ranks are nevertheless contradictory. According to Mr. A. E. Chambers, who was in the same hut with Lawrence during his first R.A.F. period (this aircraftman acquired the Master's jargon so far as to describe him as " clean looking "), Lawrence was a " rear-rank soldier " who always fell in as an odd number so as not to have to move when the squad formed fours.[29] He hated drill, always tried to dodge fire picquet duty, and severely denounced the cook-house fatigue of peeling potatoes for two hours as a waste of technical time —sentiments shared by about 99.9 per cent. of all rankers, if indeed there are any so eccentric as to enjoy these grievous afflictions. At night, Lawrence was restless, having repeated nightmares of some unspecified " horrible experience " of war time; and would then get up and walk about the camp in the dark.[30] In view of this testimony, there seems a decidedly optimistic note in Captain Kirby's belief that Lawrence went through his second recruits' course (in the Tanks) of drill " with enthusiasm."[31] According to Mr. A. L.

Dixon, a corporal in the Tanks, Lawrence (then T. E. Shaw) was " not a happy man " during his first two or three months at Bovington Camp (Wool), as he hated the routine and the perpetual drills and guard duties.[32]

It was a great relief when, on completing his first sixteen weeks in the Tanks, he was given the " cushy " job of storeman and clerk to the quartermaster. In this store-room he worked on the proofs of *Seven Pillars*.[33] His real alleviations were in the letters of his friends, his escapes on his Brough motor-cycle (for the possession of which he was much more admired by the troops than for his Lawrence of Arabia reputation),[34] and above all by the hours he was able to spend in his cottage, which he gradually repaired and fitted up, with the aid of a pioneer-sergeant and money from the sale of his gold Arabian dagger to Mr. Curtis. There he gradually housed his books and pictures, his records and gramophone with its long straight horn, fibre needles, special sound-box, and dusting graphite.[35] As an economy measure he had a wide mantelshelf built at exactly the right height for him to use as a table to eat at standing; and there he entertained his soldier friends on a coarse diet of stuffed olives, salted almonds, baked beans and " T. E.'s own blend of China tea."[36] The China tea was probably that sent from Fortnum and Mason's by Charlotte Shaw, who also sent to Clouds Hill chocolates from Gunter's, and at Christmas peach-fed ham and *pâté de foie gras*.[37]

In confirmation of this austerity of diet, we learn from Graves that Lawrence lived mainly on bread and butter, and preferred water to any other drink. Exactly at the period when he was storeman at Bovington and eating as just described, Lawrence told Graves on one occasion that between Wednesday and Saturday he had taken only some chocolate, an orange and a cup of tea. Again, at the very time when he was carrying on these agapes of private soldiers at Clouds Hill, he assured Graves that eating was an intimate matter which should be done locked away in a little room.[38] He would sometimes condescend to eat a public apple, but was liable to affront coarse-grained sensual people by his combination of delicate asceticism and courteously fine Oxonian manners. Thus, being " extremely sensitive and kindly," he accepted an invitation to a dinner party, where he never once looked at his hostess or at any of the other guests, refused to shake hands with anyone, said nothing, and refused

to eat. The following dialogue is said to have taken place between
his hostess and himself:

' " Hors d'œuvre ? "
" No thank you."
" Soup ? "
" No thank you."
" Sherry ? "
" No thank you."
" Some water ? "
" No thank you."
" Fish ? "
" No thank you."
" But surely you're going to eat grouse ? "
" May I just have a little fried potato, please ? "
" But you *must* have some of this delicious bird, Mr.
Shaw."
" Really, no thank you."
" But don't you ever eat normal food ? "
" Frequently."
" What do you like as a rule ? "

' Shaw began to feel it was funny. He told the truth.

" Tea and wads."
" Whatever are wads, Mr. Shaw ? "

' He explained, sitting motionless in chair, hands clasped inertly
in lap.

" I'm sorry we haven't a canteen here, Mr. Shaw, since so
obviously you seem to prefer your own food." '39

Henry Williamson, who relates this tale with indignation, comments that the story as " the good woman tells it is, of course, a
self-criticism; which one day she may perceive."40 Now, for the
life of me, I can't see that. It seems to me that she kept her temper
admirably under gratuitous and ill-bred provocation.

Even his benefactions—which were genuine—were marred by a
too lordly lavishness or by patronage and the desire to snoot some-

body as much as by the wish to succour misfortune. Even his successful effort to get a cure for a lame sergeant by Sir Herbert Barker, which was worked through the Bernard Shaws, was mingled with a malicious pleasure in showing up the camp doctor. His compassion was as calculated as his flattery, and scoring off the R.A.M.C. as important as healing the sick.

It was during the Bovington Camp period that Lawrence began to make a little extra money by translating—which points up Graves's remark that " he has taken great care not to make a penny out of any of his writings."[41]   Lawrence talks of translating French books (plural), but the only one recorded is Adrien le Corbeau's *Le Gigantesque* which was published by Jonathan Cape as translated by J. H. Ross. Lawrence told Graves that he had other aliases besides Ross and Shaw, but did not say whether for literary or other purposes, and warned Graves not to mention the fact, if it was a fact.[42]   Obviously enough, through Mr. Cape and Edward Garnett he could have had plenty of French translating; and indeed he asserted that at different times he had done " a lot of translating."[43]

Either from a strain of indolence or from some pseudo-aristocratic prejudice, Lawrence always objected to working for money. He was quite ready to take a pension, he assured Bernard Shaw, but he loathed the idea of " earning money."[44]   That a man should talk such stuff and get away with it is the marvel, though no doubt Bernard Shaw as a Communist would have approved on principle, though in fact he himself was a tremendous worker. Lawrence carried his indolence so far that he sent out his *Seven Pillars* without an index, inventing one of his absurd excuses—that he had never used an index for any history book! Which merely shows that he had never done any serious literary work. Modern medical opinion has rather reversed itself on the subject of the effects of prolonged malaria which is (mysteriously) said to affect communities but not individuals: otherwise, the indolence might at least in part be traced to the disease. And, of course, the noise and promiscuity of a barrack-room are a wretched environment for any intellectual work—in fact, he must have done most of his literary work at this time in the Q.M.'s store.[45]   A service to literature at this period was Lawrence's recommendation to Cape of Roy Campbell's *The Flaming Terrapin*, the script of which Lawrence had seen in Augustus John's studio. At different times he wrote a few reviews, and also introductions to *Arabia Deserta* and Richard Garnett's *The Twilight of the Gods*.

Not much may be said about *The Mint*, which is still kept in an aura of pre-publication mystery and exclusiveness, dimmed by time and growing indifference. The script was given to the Garnetts, the copyright bequeathed to Lawrence's brother, but also vested, seemingly, in the Chief of Staff of the R.A.F.[46] Publication was promised for 1950, but in 1953 seems as remote as ever. The sub-rosa circulation and discussion of this work afforded Lawrence a hobby for years. In the *Letters* at least eighteen people are mentioned as having read it, and it was still being sent round in 1934. It is essentially a polished-up diary of Lawrence's experiences at Uxbridge, including the most lurid " obscenities " he could pick up, and some quite irrelevant attempts at fine writing. His hatred for women sexually is expressed there, as he might have put it, plangently. The book will never be publicly issued intact, and, even if it were, would probably disappoint most readers except those determined to worship everything " T. E." did.

There is talk of Lawrence's having compiled an anthology. Could this be the collection of mostly forgotten poems torn from the pages of issues of *The English Review* between February, 1913, and March, 1914, and preserved in the Clouds Hill library?[47]

If I seem to dwell overmuch on these literary occupations, it is because Lawrence had a genuine respect for literature and above all for poetry, on which he was duly rallied by his Communist friend Shaw, who thought that poetry was an end product of brandy and cigars. Lawrence with his over-conscious self-importance imagined that, by taking thought, he could add cubits to his mental stature and consciously make himself a " titanic " writer. Lawrence had picked up the itch for writing, but was not a writer. He had no creative ability, and was dependent on the hazards of his life for copy. By sheer will power, skill at intrigue, and their capacity for servile adulation of the Prince of Mecca, he imposed himself on his contemporaries as a literary genius. It was all artificial, and he knew and acknowledged that it was, yet his implacable conceit demanded the perpetual tribute of a worthless incense. What is the value of extorted praise and *un succès de snobisme*? But in the world of literature much will be forgiven him, *quia multum amavit*.

Lawrence thought that his " future biographer " would have great difficulty in explaining why he so greatly preferred the R.A.F. to the Army. The reason is simple enough—the R.A.F. tried to keep him out, and his maniacal will gave him no rest until he had got back. He admitted to John Buchan that he had gone into the Tanks only with the hope of returning to the R.A.F., and when, after infinite wire-pulling and the threat of suicide, he managed to get back, he admitted to Garnett that now he was in the R.A.F., he had ceased to care about it.[48]   Quite so—what mattered was not the life or the service, but getting the better of those who had thwarted him. As early as April, 1923, he had applied for help in that direction to his faithful patron Hogarth who on this occasion failed.[49]   Lawrence then emitted a cloud of pathos; he declared that whenever he saw an R.A.F. uniform in the street he felt a strange homesickness, though up till then the R.A.F. had not done much to earn such a sentimental yearning from him.[50]   Then Bernard Shaw wrote to Stanley Baldwin trying to get Lawrence a pension, an obviously futile effort, as it might have proved the thin end of a rather dangerous wedge. In March, 1924, Lawrence again wrote to the Air Council asking for reinstatement, and was again refused.[51]   Early in 1925 he began pulling more wires, writing to Lord Trenchard,[52] and thanking Sir Edward Marsh for seeing Churchill, who he thought might approach Sir Samuel Hoare, at that time Secretary of State for Air.[53]   But either Churchill did nothing or Hoare did not agree, for Lawrence was refused for the third time. He thereupon wrote a sentimental letter, saying he was homesick for the R.A.F.[54]   A month later he wrote Garnett in a truculent style: " I'm going to quit : but in my usual comic fashion I'm going to finish the reprint and square up with Cape before I hop it! "[55]   In case that seems ambiguous, he wrote in November, 1925, after his reinstatement : " I had made up my mind, in Bovington, to come to a natural end about Xmas."[56]

Edward Garnett, to whom the threat was made, communicated with Bernard Shaw, who wrote to inform the Prime Minister (Stanley Baldwin) of this planned suicide, threatening him with a dreadful scandal which would be worse after Lowell Thomas's book had made Lawrence such a hero.[57]   John Buchan also intervened, where-upon Baldwin weakly gave way, and ordered that Lawrence should be reinstated in the R.A.F., once more demonstrating the great principle of British government which is to yield to threats or violence what is refused to reason and justice. It was an error in the first place to allow Lawrence's wire-pulling to foist him on a service whose senior officers obviously did not want him in the ranks. But once in, it was unjust to expel him when he had done absolutely nothing unmilitary calling even for minor punishment, let alone a punishment so drastic, public and humiliating. To restore him to the R.A.F. was then only plain justice, but in the way Baldwin allowed it to be done, he merely added pusillanimity to the original error. This was probably Lawrence's most difficult intrigue—he was two years and four months in achieving success by frightening a Prime Minister with the threat that a private in the Tanks would commit suicide if not given what he demanded. One can but applaud him.

His first surviving letter from the Cadets' School at Cranwell, Lincolnshire, written to a private in the Tanks, lets us, for an unguarded moment, into the workshop of his legend-factory and shows how eagerly he cultivated small renown among private soldiers as he enjoyed lofty fame among writers, Oxonians, politicians and the public. He had been sent to an R.A.F. station at West Drayton (Nottinghamshire), and on arrival there was immediately accosted by a flight-sergeant with " Hullo, Ross," whereupon a " dynamo switchboard attendant " who " happened " to be passing behind the sergeant, said " Garn . . . that ain't Ross. I was at Bovington when he came up, and he's Colonel Lawrence." After which comes one of Lawrence's " delightfully humorous " scenes with a stage doctor, followed by an interview with a stage headquarters adjutant who didn't recognise him until Lawrence said: " If your name was Buggins and I called you Bill . . . " whereupon the H.Q. adjutant " yelled with joy, recognising my names for him, and gave me tea."[58] It was a bit of a coincidence that a sergeant who had known Lawrence at Uxbridge or Farnborough should have been moved to West Drayton and happen accidentally along to recognise him, but the coincidence becomes miraculous when a man who had served with Lawrence in the Tanks at Bovington has been transferred to the R.A.F. and happens along behind the sergeant to give the Lawrence of Arabia clue, while a super-coincidence makes the adjutant Lawrence's dear old friend Buggins. The childish vanity of the *procédé* is no more ridiculous than the gaping credulity of the stage-struck fans who took it all as gospel and spread it to the great man's greater glory. Of course it may be true—after all, Louis de Rouge-mont did actually ride an Australian turtle. In fact the C.O. at Cranwell was an old friend of Lawrence's, which is probably why he was sent there; but it would be too much of a good thing to have a similar experience at West Drayton, where he has staged all these affecting little scenes of welcome. The next day, Lawrence wrote to Mrs. Thomas Hardy that the R.A.F. was home to him,* even although he was surrounded by strangers.[59]

Nothing much happened to break the routine of his service days at Cranwell, except that in April, 1926, he broke his arm cranking up a stranger's car on the road, and bore that very painful mishap with stoical fortitude. By the beginning of January, 1927, he had been transferred to the station at Karachi, India. Nothing much was recorded by him of a voyage which took him over familiar seas and past ancient lands he knew, though he complained sharply to Sir Edward Marsh that the ship's accommodation was defective, and wrote a prose poem (headed " Leaves in the Wind "), describing with relish the nastiness of a stopped-up women's lavatory.[60] At first, he was " restless " in Karachi, and his racial superiority found Indians as despicable as he had found negroes in Arabia: " There's a suppressed meanness about them " (Indians) " which makes me regret their likeness in shape."[61] But the work in camp was " cushy " —a little over five hours' work a day for five days a week, with no duties after 1 p.m., and Thursdays and Sundays a whole holiday. In spite of which he neglected the opportunity to see a little of a country new to him (though as Karachi is a comparatively modern town, there was little interest apart from the people, whom he despised), and kept to the camp reading the old favourites among his books.[62]

It was while he was at Karachi that *Revolt in the Desert* and Mr. Graves's *Lawrence and the Arabs* were published, and Lawrence made his last stroke of vengeance on the Guilty by finally renouncing his reputed name and taking by deed poll the name of " Thomas Edward Shaw," which henceforth was legally his. The choice of the name is significant, and there is no reason for hastening to believe him when he says that its choice was purely the result of hazard. In the Shaws, Lawrence found substitute parents on whose interest in him he could

* He had been there six months, most of the time in the recruits' depot.

securely rest and to whom he could give what affection was in him—
" Lawrence's solicitude for both the Shaws certainly equalled that of
any son for his parents, and it was reciprocated by each of them."[63]
The more important of the couple to him was, of course, Charlotte
Shaw, to whom Lawrence wrote so many confidential letters for
eventual publication; but he also got to the point of suggesting
themes for Shaw to write on. He wanted a play about Venus and
Adonis (psycho-analysts!) and was insistent that Shaw should write
a biography of Sir Roger Casement, who was shot as a traitor when
he landed in Ireland from a German submarine after trying to recruit
Irish soldiers who were prisoners in Germany to fight England. There
was at first sympathy with Casement in English influential circles as a
" highly romantic " Irish patriot, until the government allowed it to
be known that among his papers was a diary describing " sex perver-
sions." That was the end of him. As a Communist, Shaw was
naturally not interested in romantic failures, but in successful tyrants;
and complains that Lawrence never would discuss Lenin, Stalin,
Mussolini, Ataturk and Hitler,[64] though, as a matter of fact, Lawrence
frequently asserted to other people that Lenin was the " greatest man "
of the 20th century, " greater than Napoleon." He claimed that he
had had a sharp difference of opinion with Mr. Churchill on this very
topic; and no doubt it would be difficult to decide which of the two
had caused more human bloodshed.

Though Lawrence remained as self-absorbed and self-important
as ever, sedulously cultivating his legend, and playing his latest part
with relish, the tone of his letters becomes calmer in these years. He
is no longer the tortured soul, and, though his threat of suicide was
probably never anything but stage thunder to frighten old Baldwin,
there is no longer in him the feeling of stress. Psychologists must
determine, if they can, whether this relaxation was due to the symbolical repudiation implied by the change of name and all that went
with it, or by his " home " life in the R.A.F., or by the self-imposed
imprisonment within the Karachi air station, or by the mere lapse of
time. At Karachi he completed his revision of *The Mint* and began
the negotiations for translating the *Odyssey*, on which he spent four
years and about which (the *Odyssey*) he said some rather silly things.
How, for instance, could " Homer " be a " book-worm "[65] at a time
when there were no written Greek books and when the Greeks

Clouds Hill

[*National Trust photograph*]

notoriously knew no language but their own? His prefatory note
to the translation is at once pretentious and unimpressive. He writes
for example, condescendingly of the *Journey to the Underworld* (the
" Nekuia ") without realising that its core is the old Babylonian epic
tale embroidered by later Greek Rhapsodists, whose additions have
been tentatively lopped off by Bérard, leaving a weirdly primitive
epic core. The " experts " have condemned Lawrence's translation,
but *les classiques, c'est le pain des professeurs*, and they will never do
justice to the work of an " outsider "—even an Oxonian—because
by their definition Homer is " untranslatable." " A pretty poem,
Mr. Pope, but you must not call it Homer." Lawrence's Greek was
perfectly adequate to his task, and his version, though perhaps a little
near the crib, is readable—the most important thing. But Lawrence
resented the time and toil exacted, and the work at last became a
labour of hate. " Homer," at any rate the " Homer " of the *Odyssey*,
who at one time had been for him " a greatest one," was now demoted
to " Wardour Street." But Lawrence got £600 for translating him.

In June of 1928, Lawrence was moved—or, as he claimed, arranged
with Air-Marshal Salmond to be moved—because he disliked his
superior officers,[66] to Miranshah Fort in Waziristan on the borders of
Afghanistan. This appears to have been a peaceful sort of place,
judging from Lawrence's references to its remoteness and silence.
There he translated a specimen book of the *Odyssey* for Bruce Rogers,
and there he remained for about six months (although the usual
period of service there was only two months) until he was suddenly
and dramatically returned to England, amid a fracas of journalists and
angry politicians. He was now accused of espionage, or rather of
having been employed on secret missions to Arabia and Afghanistan,
with a rumour that he had been arrested by the Afghans, for assisting
rebels to cross the frontier.[67] The absurdity of these stories is self-
evident. If Lawrence had really been employed on any secret missions
requiring sudden and indefinite absences the authorities would not
have put him into camps or forts in India, where a whole hut-full of
his comrades would instantly have known that he had left camp, and
the rest of the unit in a day or two. It would be ridiculous to expect
a number of men to keep such a secret, even if they had been ordered
to do so. Lawrence's actual duties were merely routine of a humdrum sort. He began as a sort of continuing orderly man, cutting up

bread for meals and so forth, then went to the engine repair section, where he was employed on clerical work and also as runner or messenger.[68] A former comrade of his at Karachi, Mr. T. Summel, recollects that Lawrence still kept up his habit of practical jokes by such witty devices as absconding with part of the guard's breakfasts and turning out the guard to present arms to the wrong person, so that they failed to be ready for the commanding officer—which was doubtless very funny to Lawrence but not to the guard commander.[69] Lawrence's repeated statements that he never went outside camp bounds[70] might be construed as camouflage for espionage, but they are confirmed by the camp adjutant.[71] At Miranshah the R.A.F. personnel were by orders kept inside their barbed-wire defences, and Lawrence was mainly employed in office work. By that time he had learned to use a typewriter, so typed office letters and orders.[72] There is no confirmation either that he reorganised the engine repair shop at Karachi, or took a large share in running the small camp at Miranshah as claimed for him. He lived the ordinary and far from strenuous life of a peace-time service man without doing anything astonishing and with far more leisure to do nothing than most civilian workers.

How then did these sentimental espionage stories get about, so that the (wholly unsympathetic) victims of the Russian " trials " of Trotskyists and Rightists " confessed " to nefarious dealings with the notorious British agent and so forth, Colonel Lawrence, in 1929 in London, when he was in India? The fact that he was so cited in itself seems a complete alibi. But the rumours were really due to Lawrence's incurable habit of building fantasies about himself and telling them as true stories to his comrades. It is noteworthy that if ever one of his service acquaintances was posted to Arabia, Lawrence quickly dropped him—he might find out too much. Lawrence's vanity led him to claim impossible experiences, such as his statement to James Hanley (who had been a seaman), that he (Lawrence) " once spent a month on the lower deck of a Q boat."[73] At what period of the war was Lawrence in the Royal Navy? The sole basis for this ridiculous lie was his acquaintance in the R.A.F. with Mr. A. E. Chambers, who had been a naval rating on Q ships during the war.[74] In a similar spirit he had written (June, 1927) to Sir Edward Marsh one of his pretentious letters about the " clash with Russia," which he felt was " bound to come."[75] He also said that he had " nearly gone " to Afghanistan which he considered the " most dangerous point."   And he went on self-importantly:

"The British attaché at Kabul is entitled to an airman clerk, and the depot would have put my name forward, if I'd been a bit nippier on a typewriter. I'll have to mug up typing: for from '14 to '18 I served a decent apprenticeship in semi secret-secret work, and Russia interests me greatly."[76]

The letter was meant for Mr. Churchill to see (Sir Edward Marsh was his secretary), containing as it does somewhat fulsome praise of "Winston's gorgeous letter." Mr. Churchill had evidently called his book *The World Crisis* a pot-boiler, on which Lawrence commented, "Some pot! and probably some boil too"—a phrase Mr. Churchill may have unconsciously recollected when he came to discourse to Congress of the chicken and its neck.

It is a fact that during his Karachi period Lawrence was called on to give what information he could to an R.A.F. survey party which was looking for landing grounds on the east coast of Arabia—which he had never visited except from afar during his sea trip and river journey to Kut. It is said that he requested that there should be no females in the party![77]   By Lawrence's habitual process this became transferred into a self-important statement to Captain Hart that he (Lawrence) had "spent eight months flying and driving over every yard of the North-West frontier between India and Afghanistan."[78] This feat was achieved in six months without his ever leaving the fort. To this may be added Mr. E. M. Forster's revelation that during a walk in Surrey, Lawrence insisted on giving him what he (Lawrence) asserted were the names, addresses and telephone numbers of two members of the Secret Service who thought the nation's safety depended on their incognito.[79] Forster does not say how or why Lawrence had been given this information, or whether he tried to verify it. Probably not, one would surmise. For supposing Mr. Forster had done so, and the information had turned out to be correct, what would Mr. Forster have gained but two blank denials and much suspicion and unwanted attentions from the police?

Here we are confronted by a variation on a familiar situation, in which Lawrence exaggerates an ordinary enough fact or two into a

" story " or series of " stories " (which he may ultimately have come to believe) told by him to his friends, circulated in gossip, and suddenly exploded upon an uncritical public with all the unscrupulous inventions of sensational propaganda—even to the " rumour " of his arrest in Afghanistan. The basis of the whole affair seems to be no more than his hope that he might get to be airman clerk at Kabul; that he had been a junior staff officer in Cairo; and that he had been present at a conference of an R.A.F. survey party. From this to knowing the names, addresses and telephone numbers of members of the British Secret Service in England and to eight months of driving and flying along the North-West frontier was a trifling effort for Lawrence's mythopœic mind. Of course, some of this development occurred after he left India, but the hints in the letter to Marsh are enough. Lawrence especially enjoyed telling sensational versions of such stories to his more credulous comrades, and how easily might they have passed them on to England by letter, leave or transfer. Or Lawrence's own letter would be enough. At any rate, there were the blaring newspaper headlines arousing the animosity of the friends of the U.S.S.R., to such a point that Lawrence suffered the fate of many popular heroes and passed from being flattered and fêted to being execrated and burned—fortunately only in effigy. Even the government must have rather looked down its nose on finding that its great romantic hero had once more turned out to be more of a nuisance and an embarrassment than an asset. They decided to bring him home at once, and thereby demonstrate that he was not labouring to overthrow King Amanulla and the Soviet Union in the disguise of an Arab sheik, talking Pushtu learned from the Greek dictionary he was using for translating Homer.[80] If this was reported by R.A.F. rankers, why not Lawrence's fanciful tales to them about himself and his secret service? But this was exactly what Lawrence wanted. Life in India was exile to him, and he longed to return to his motor-cycle rushing about the English roads, and to opportunities for seeing his English friends—exactly as all his comrades no doubt wished to return to their home interests. As far back as 1927, Lawrence had written wistfully to Mrs. Hardy of the years that must separate him from his return to England,[81] and with curious prescience had written to his friend Sergeant Banbury, mentioning that he would be in Karachi until 1929 or 1931, unless the Press transferred their attentions to him, as indeed happened in January, 1929.[82]

The whole episode is an instructive example of the abuse of what is called the " freedom of the Press," itself a tendentious phrase which tries to insinuate that nothing but newspapers come from printing presses. They might at least have taken the trouble to find out whether there was any truth in their assertions. For once, the offenders were not " the vile capitalist oppressors," but the Liberal *Daily News* and the Socialist *Daily Herald*.[83] The action of the authorities in bringing Lawrence home so precipitately has been much criticised as a feeble capitulation, but it is hard to see what else they could have done. It was a choice of evils, and they chose the less. Unfortunately, one cannot altogether praise either the plan or the execution of the plan for bringing him quietly into England without newspaper fracas—though it must be admitted that if the plan had succeeded amid complete silence, Lawrence for one would hardly have been pleased.

A radio message to his ship ordered him to avoid being interviewed " as far as possible."[84] This order appears to embody the view that a man may be interviewed against his will; and then, by way of reassuring the newspapers and the public that no mystery was connected with Lawrence's sudden return, the intelligent plan was formed of sending the R.A.F. commandant at Cattewater on board in civilian clothes to take off Lawrence, in uniform, on the guardship pinnace, through the boatloads of expectant reporters and photographers; and accompany him at once to London. Everything possible was done to create a maximum of fuss with a minimum of secrecy, in a journey which sounds like a parody of a detective story. By way of a brilliant idea for getting quietly to London, the smart Wing Commander motored his charge to Newton Abbot and boarded what he thought was an ordinary train for London, which was then attached to the section of the boat train carrying all the reporters they had been told to avoid.[85] No wonder Lawrence " chuckled."

From " knowledge " in his possession, the Labour M.P., Ernest Thurtle, reached the conclusion that Lawrence was a spy being used to foster British imperialism.[86] With this capacity for melodrama, Mr. Thurtle was naturally not reassured by the Dr. Watson methods used by the Air Force for Lawrence's home-coming and began asking House of Commons questions, which—whether he knew it or not—would inevitably have led to Lawrence's dismissal from the Air Force. To parry this, Lawrence arranged to meet Mr. Thurtle and his colleagues at the House, answered all their questions, and lent them copies of *Seven Pillars* and *The Mint*,[87] though how those works cleared him from the charge of espionage in Afghanistan is not explained. At any rate he succeeded in turning Mr. Thurtle into an admirer of his " almost devastating air of intelligence " and dazzled him with such views as this:

> " I think the planet is in a damnable condition, which no change of party, or social reform, will do more than palliate insignificantly. What is wanted is a new master species—birth control for us, to end the human race in fifty years—and then a clear field for some cleaner mammal. I suppose it must be a mammal."[88]

It is unfortunate that law-givers have " no time to read," or Mr. Thurtle might have realised that this was a clumsy parody of something published by D. H. Lawrence nearly ten years before, ending with his vision of " a world empty of people, just uninterrupted grass and a hare sitting up."[89] Luckily these attentions dried up the questions, though Lawrence claimed he was reprimanded for the offence of talking to M.P.s, and told that he would be discharged if he had any more talks with newspaper men.[90] Interesting admission! By way of warning, he was then posted to Cattewater (Mount Batten), where the C.O., Wing-Commander Sydney Smith, and his wife were Lawrence's humble admirers. It is typical of Lawrence's methods of ingratiating himself that he posed to Thurtle as " almost entirely self-made," one who had " gone up so fast " from a position where his father " had five sons, and only £300 a year."[91] Strictly speaking, it was true, and yet not exactly what a Socialist means by " self-made " —what would Mr. Thurtle's electors have said at a political meeting if he had proclaimed Oxford, Carchemish and a Staff appointment in December, 1914, as marks of a " self-made man "? The district would probably have speedily run short of dead cats. Hogarth said that Lawrence was quite ready to sacrifice the means to any end on which he had determined.[92] This applied in small as well as in large things; and the end worked for here was the silencing of Thurtle as a hostile and dangerous House of Commons critic. Yet in a sense quite different from that he intended, Lawrence might justly be called " a self-made man " for had he not " made " himself by a series of successful impersonations and a brilliantly organised propaganda? In this case Lawrence again succeeded so well that he soon had Thurtle working to carry into law Lawrence's dislike for swagger sticks and compulsory church parades, as well as their common desire to abolish the death penalty for cowardice.

The period at Mount Batten, which lasted with interruptions until 1933, would seem to have been peaceful and happy. Lawrence, for part of the time (up till October, 1931), had the company of his adorers, Wing-Commander and Mrs. Smith, whose friendship with him is narrated in a work by Mrs. Smith, entitled *The Golden Reign*. One daughter of the house was nicknamed " Squeak," and Mrs. Smith had a delicious sense of humour which could not help " giggling like a naughty child in church " whenever anyone played Bach, in which mirth " Tes " thoughtfully joined. He had also a new interest in speed boats, and seems also to have learned to fly. He had a brand-new and " apolaustic " motor-cycle given him by the Shaws, his friends to see again, new books and new records to enjoy. And yet at times there came on him—or he said there did—a deep sense of weariness and tædium vitæ,[93] " . . . how tired I am of bikes and books and music and food and drink and words and work."[94] This was the man who some months later claimed that he had never been bored.

He was but forty when he wrote those words of discouragement. Were they the expression of a passing mood or the more serious statement of his nihilism?[95] With such a histrion who can tell? Yet it is the fact that such expressions of weariness and boredom thread his later letters, ending in the rather too conscious pathos of his too brief days after discharge from the R.A.F. when he declaims:

> " Days seem to dawn, suns to shine, evenings to follow, and then I sleep. What I have done, what I am doing, what I am going to do, puzzle me and bewilder me. Have you ever been a leaf and fallen from your tree in autumn and been really puzzled about it? That's the feeling."[96]

Of course we may connect that with the " lost " feeling of complete—and vacant—liberty after so many years of military service.

But the feeling of life's emptiness and his own weariness had been just as keen six years before. Again one thinks once more of his sicknesses and accidents as at least a contributory if not a chief cause. He told Graves that he had had malaria " so often that it's hardly worth mentioning," and also " Malta fever, Dysentery, Typhoid, Blackwater, Smallpox, etc."[97] That was in 1927. What was meant by the " etc." is anyone's guess, and there is no other mention of blackwater fever or smallpox. How could he have come through smallpox unmarked? Then there were his airplane and motor-cycle accidents, and his wounds, which had a tendency to increase, like Falstaff's men in buckram, from nine to " over sixty."[98] All these would explain moods of depression and the not infrequent expressions of weariness and disgust with life, though it must be recognised that his whole attitude towards life was so falsely mental and mechanical that he automatically hated almost everything which really makes up a man's life and gives it savour. A man cannot with impunity allow himself to be so completely " super-cerebral " for so long, despising or recoiling in disgust from all the " animal " experience common to us all, despising work, avoiding responsibility, wanting to be kept and to do nothing. As Martin Luther so rightly said:

> ' *Who loves not women, wine and song,*
> *He lives a fool his whole life long.*'

Lawrence was one of Mr. Eliot's hollow men, and both make a virtue of the same unwholesome incapacity for living—that genius for accepting the world which was so greatly the gift of D. H. Lawrence and, in a quite different but equally authentic way, is the gift of Roy Campbell.

After allowing Lawrence to moulder for several years as a Q.M. storeman, mechanic, airman clerk and runner, the Air people at last made some use of his mechanical bent in these Mount Batten years, although his service at the Schneider Cup race brought him into the limelight again. Lawrence's story is that Italo Balbo asked him to see that the slipway for the Italian planes was as clean as that of the R.A.F. Liddell Hart says Balbo " knew T. E. of old."[99] Where and how? Mussolini and his party did not come into power until October, 1922, when Lawrence was already out of " the world " and an Uxbridge recruit. At the date of the race, September, 1929, there was a Labour government with Lord Thomson as Secretary of State for Air, and it is claimed that he was annoyed because various members of the late government talked to Lawrence. He was therefore again dismissed from the Air Force, and only reinstated because, immediately afterwards, he met in Whitehall " a public personage " (unnamed) who, learning that Lawrence was free, suggested that they " make a trip across the desert." Terrified at this the " Foreign Office " rang up the " Air Ministry " to persuade them to allow Lawrence to remain, " which," Graves reflects, " was what Lawrence had foreseen."[100] A condition of his reinstatement was that he should not visit or speak to any " great men—e.g., Winston, Austen, Birkenhead, Sassoon, Lady Astor," but was permitted Bernard Shaw, who was annoyed at not being included.[101] Such was this very true-to-type Lawrence story, based so far as I can discover on no evidence but his own. Lawrence liked to boast of such triumphs to his humbler friends, and wrote to Aircraftman Hayter: " In November I had a tiff with Lord T., our present boss. He tried to sling me out: I double-crossed him. So am airmanning on. Our C.O. is a treat."[102]

A priori, the Balbo tale is suspicious, and it seems unlikely that Lawrence would be discharged from the R.A.F. a second time, and then immediately be reinstated because he threatened to go to Irak. He could have gone to Jericho for all Thomson cared. What does seem possible is that Thomson was annoyed by Lawrence's persistent and officious efforts to " reform " the R.A.F. from the ranks, through the influence of his political friends, and told Lawrence to shut up or get out. The story would then be manufactured to hide the discomfiture of a reprimand.

More interesting is the story of Lawrence's Biscayne Baby fast motor-boat, given him by a Major Colin Cooper. This is introduced impressively as " one of six made by the Purdy Boat Company, the six best things that the United States have made."[103] From this the unwary reader might imagine that only six such perfect and speedy machines existed, whereas in fact the United States was then far ahead of England in such manufactures, and, in the late 1920's, one American firm alone was turning out 1,500 such boats with speeds between 25 and 35 m.p.h., and others as fast as 55 m.p.h. were manufactured. Those who visited the United States in those years will remember such boats rushing out to meet the liners from New

York harbour, and even in the waters round Bermuda. The British were slow in following up, and Lawrence claimed that it was through him and the performance of his boat that the R.A.F. were induced to design and to build a fast flat-bottomed speed-boat of similar type, in order to pick up airmen who had crashed or been forced to parachute into the sea. During the period when the boats were in the trial stage, Lawrence was employed as one of those engaged in running and reporting on them. We have the familiar type of tale that through his C.O., Lawrence succeeded in imposing these craft on a Ministry which otherwise would have remained blind to their merits. The claim is also made that these boats " saved hundreds of lives " during the last war, which let us hope is true. But whatever the extent of Lawrence's share in causing these speed-boats to be adopted by the R.A.F. for picking up fallen airmen (impossible to determine without official papers), he cannot exclusively be credited without some injustice to the original American builders, the Major who introduced them to an ignorant England (were they so unknown in 1929?) and the English adaptors or improvers, boat-builders and engineers.

Lawrence's own claims for the boats went a good deal further than that they might and could save the lives of airmen forced to come down on the sea. In 1933, Liddell Hart took Lawrence to see Mr. Lloyd George, then of course long since out of office, and surviving only as the ghost of the great Liberal Party sitting uncrowned on the ruins thereof. Lawrence importantly informed the ex-Prime Minister that with " his " new speed boats it would no longer be possible for a submarine to operate near the coast of Britain.[104] Would he had been right! And if indeed they did anything to curb the bitter danger, then all honour to him for whatever share he had in it. But Lawrence —like nearly everybody—was not happy in his predictions of future warfare. " As for physicists," he wrote, " rot 'em."[105] Why certainly, but let us admit that sub-atomic weapons which frighten dictators and bureaucrats as much as soldiers and human beings have their sinister good side. Moreover, Lawrence thought tanks clumsy and obsolete, a view which is said to have been shared by General Gamelin.

Certain irrelevant but interesting little events must be here recorded. In March, 1930, the University of St. Andrews (Scotland) offered Lawrence the honorary degree of Doctor of Laws, which he wittily pretended to believe was a students' hoax. In August, 1930, a flash of wit lights up the enormous mausoleum of Lawrence's Letters, which would not contribute much to a new La Rochefoucauld, Voltaire or Oscar Wilde. Lawrence had formed (very rightly) a high opinion of Noël Coward's plays, and by way of cheering his favourite dramatist, had sent him a copy of the somewhat lugubrious *Mint*. In replying, Mr. Coward began: "Dear 338171" (may I call you 338?) . . ." Of course, "T. E." laughed heartily at it, but on which side of his now cherubic countenance? And in 1932, Yeats for reasons known to himself, nominated Lawrence for the Irish Academy of Letters. By way of showing his respect to the poet and the Academy, Lawrence delayed his reply for eight months, but then turned on the blarney tap full cock:

> "I set eyes on you once, in Oxford, many years ago, and wanted then to call the street to attention (for lack of the power to make the sun blaze out appropriately, instead) but fortunately did nothing!"[106]

Lawrence appears to have agreed with Disraeli that everyone likes flattery, but that with some people you should lay it on with a trowel.

In September of 1932, Lawrence was "returned to duty" from his task of testing speed boats, but on consideration he felt indisposed to accept this without a fight, and accordingly brought the R.A.F. to their senses by a request to be released from service from 6th April, 1933. He did not wish to continue if it meant that he would be employed on routine station duties.*[107]   Of course, the Ministry capitulated. He was posted to Felixstowe, where he was attached to some contractors' yards and ordered to wear plain clothes to avoid publicity, or so he said. A confidential report stated that his ideas on high-speed craft were worth considering.[108] This is why he was sent to Messrs. White, at Cowes. The Under Secretary of State for Air at the time was his friend Sir Philip Sassoon. He was never weary of wire-pulling, and knew all the right people.

During the final years of Lawrence's service, his Clouds Hill cottage was gradually fitted up against the time when he would have to take his discharge. The money earned by his translation of the *Odyssey* went towards furnishing the cottage with a distant approximation to his boyhood's dreams of a William Morris "hall." Outside

---

* Lawrence's letter of resignation exists, but was it ever sent in ?

the door was carved a well-known but rather cryptic phrase from Herodotus, which might be called a learned way of naming his home Sans Souci. There were carved teak doors brought back from Jidda after the luckless embassy to Hussein. There were a water supply and a bath, and, if there were no " shut-beds," there were the sleeping-bags marked " Meum " and " Tuum." If the artistic decorations he introduced are a little disconcerting, we must remember that in taste there are always great differences. Outside he had rhododendrons set, and his mother put in quantities of daffodils and other flowers close up to the house.[109] He grew much attached to the place, and felt great resentment when he had to lend it to a married couple, for, as he said, he didn't like having women there.[110]

The cottage housed his collection of gramophone records and his books. It is rather a surprise that a poor man with only his airman's three shillings a day and a small income could have afforded so many expensive records, until we learn from Miss Patch that many were given to him by Charlotte Shaw. Lawrence was not a musician, but a music-lover apparently without any training, so that to try to criticise the collection from the point of view of a professional or trained musician would be unfair and irrelevant. Moreover, his choice was necessarily limited by the records then available, which are far from being almost unlimited like books. He had records of early music, but said he found the Dolmetsch concerts " pretty poisonous," though he approved the gift of a Dolmetsch clavicord to Bridges. His main collections, as is almost inevitable, were of Bach, Beethoven, Brahms, Handel, Haydn, Mozart and Schubert, but he had some Wagner and Schumann; and a good deal of Delius and Elgar. French, Spanish, Russian and Italian music are poorly represented. It is, in fact, an average sort of collection such as might be found in any musically-minded middle-class family. On the other hand, it is probably the best and largest collection of classical music records ever made by a ranker during service.

More interest attaches to the books, since Lawrence was or wanted to be both scholar and writer; and his library is usually an indication of such a one's interests and culture. In Lawrence's case we must remember that if he had read at Oxford half of what he claimed, and his memory was half as " phenomenal " as asserted, his mind must have been a miniature London Library, and his need for books less than that of other men.   Moreover, his wandering life was not conducive to book collecting, and he complained that some of his pre-1914 books had been lost or stolen.   The catalogued collection amounts to about 1,250 books, about half of which are by contemporaries, many are presentation copies and others were Hand Press books collected for their printing rather than their contents.   The largest collection of any author is of D. H. Lawrence (26) followed by Robert Graves, Bernard Shaw, W. H. Hudson (17), William Morris (16), Conrad and Maurice Baring (14), S. Sassoon and Thomas Hardy (13), Doughty, Norman Douglas and James Hanley (12).   The English poets are well but not exceptionally represented, for there are many gaps.   There are a certain number of French texts, but few medieval and not one Provençal.   Otherwise, foreign books, even French, are nearly all in translations.   It is in no sense a scholar's library nor a carefully selected choice of the world's books, but the haphazard collection of a dilettante who knew a considerable number of contemporary authors.

The passage of time and Lawrence's reiterated protestations that one of his reasons for enlisting in the ranks was to be " ordinary " among ordinary men did not prevent him from telling them extraordinary and unfounded stories designed to show how important he was.   Perhaps the most striking of these was his reiterated claims that he had been offered and had refused the great office of High Commissioner for Egypt, advanced so often and with such confidence that it seems quite likely that he came to believe it himself, as the august " Prinney " came to believe that he had led the cavalry charge at Salamanca.   (What a very English character Falstaff is!)   I ask the reader's indulgence for going rather more deeply into this little episode than it seems to deserve, since it was this which first aroused my suspicions of Lawrence's veracity and led me to find proof after proof that much he reports of himself—including and especially his Arabian experiences —was heightened, exaggerated, faked, boastful and sometimes entirely without foundation.   I have tried, but perhaps not always successfully, to give the evidence in the whole of this book fairly and in such a way that it can be instantly verified, though not without some indignation that such a man should have been given the fame and glory of the real heroes of 1914-1918.

The post of High Commissioner for Egypt was a great one, and the man to whom it was offered might (if he chose) boast that he had the full trust of the King's government. It was not in the gift of the Colonial Secretary, like the post of Chief British Resident at Amman, or of Governor of Cyprus or of the Bahamas, but was a Cabinet appointment. When it was camouflaged as Consul-General, it had been held by Kitchener; and before him by Lord Cromer and Sir Eldon Gorst. After them, as High Commissioners, came Sir Henry McMahon, Sir Reginald Wingate, Allenby, Lord Lloyd. Was it possible that such a post had been offered to Colonel Lawrence, let alone to Private Ross or A.C. Shaw? First, let us look at Lawrence's claim. On the 30th September, 1934, Lawrence wrote to the first Lord Lloyd some comments on his book, *Egypt Since Cromer*, and among them Lawrence said:

> " My statement, when they offered me the succession to Allenby, was that I'd shut up the Residency, except as offices, take a room at Shepheard's, and ride about Cairo and the Delta on my motor-bike; and yet ' run ' the Government of Egypt, from underneath! Out-Eldoning Gorst, if I may put it so. T. E. S. . . .Winston tried to get my consent to take Allenby's place, and so to accept his resignation at this moment."[111]

In December of 1926, Lawrence more briefly but confidently made the same claim to Charlotte Shaw, again saying that it was Winston Churchill who made the offer at the time of Allenby's threatened resignation early in 1922. Moreover, in that extraordinary collection or hotch-potch of recollections, *T. E. Lawrence by his Friends*, we find the following reminiscence from Mr. Alec Dixon, who was a corporal in the Tank Corps with Lawrence in 1923-5:

> " Once or twice during his service at Bovington, T. E. was offered official posts in the Near East and elsewhere, all of which he refused flatly. Only once did he show any interest in these offers. One day at Clouds Hill he said to me: ' They've offered me Egypt.' I suggested he was just the man for the job. ' No,' he said decisively; ' Egypt would make me vicious. I believe they're talking of Ronaldshay as an alternative. If so, they're barking up the wrong tree. George Lloyd's the man for Egypt, and I'm going to tell them so.' This I believe he did."[112]

The facts are that Allenby went to London early in 1922 prepared to resign as High Commissioner unless Egypt was granted independence; which was done, and he remained as High Commissioner until May, 1925, being succeeded by Lord Lloyd in October of that year. And yet Lawrence and his friends would have us believe first, that in 1922 the Lloyd George government was prepared, if Lawrence would only agree, to accept the resignation of a Field Marshal and entrust to a 34-year-old, temporary civil servant in the Colonial Office an incipient revolt in Egypt which the conqueror of Palestine and Syria felt unable to control ; secondly, that in 1925 another Cabinet, presided over by Stanley Baldwin, made a similar offer to Private Ross of the Tanks.

According to Mr. Winston Churchill's recollections in *T. E. Lawrence by his Friends*: " . . . governorships and great commands were then (1921) at my disposal. Nothing availed. *As a last resort* I sent him (Lawrence) out to Transjordania . . . "[113] It must be repeated that Mr. Churchill, though Secretary for the Colonies, had not the " disposal " of so high an office as " Egypt," and that Lawrence, whatever else was then offered, was sent by Mr. Churchill to Amman " as a last resort " in July, 1921, seven months before the crisis of Allenby's threatened resignation. To quote Mr. Churchill again: " One day I said to Lawrence: ' What would you like to do when all this is smoothed out? The greatest employments are open to you *if you care to pursue your new career in the Colonial service.*' " The italics are mine ; Egypt came under the Foreign, not the Colonial Office. Lord Curzon as Foreign Secretary would certainly have had to be consulted, and he had little reason to favour Lawrence who, as we have seen, had tried to bring him into ridicule and contempt.

Again, if the government were prepared to accept Allenby's resignation, it would only be because they were opposed to granting Egypt a greater measure of independence and were looking for a man prepared, if necessary, to crush the national uprising which Allenby foresaw. Is it likely that they would choose, to carry out such a repressive, Imperialist policy, one who was uncompromisingly committed to be the champion of Arab freedom?

In a letter of March, 1922, Lawrence says he left the Colonial Office on 28th February, but had been there daily since; in another of the 31st March, he announces that he may be leaving England not for Cairo but for Baghdad, which would hardly be the residence of the High Commissioner for Egypt. On the 10th April, he says his "tenth resignation" had been rejected, but that he was sitting in Barton Street working at his book.[114]

I felt that I should try to obtain some authoritative statements on this, without disclosing the fact that I thought the claim suspicious or giving away the passages in which Lawrence made it. Through my friend John Browning, and Mr. Colin Mann, then Public Relations Officer of the Conservative Party, I caused this and one or two others of Lawrence's claims to be submitted to Mr. L. S. Amery, who was a Cabinet Minister; to the second Lord Lloyd; and to Lawrence's friend Sir Ronald Storrs.

Mr. Amery replied:

> "I should think it extremely unlikely that Lawrence was asked to succeed Allenby as High Commissioner in Egypt. My recollection is that the Foreign Office were very keen to secure the post for a diplomat, while Sir Austen Chamberlain and others of us favoured George Lloyd, who was actually appointed."[115]

It will be noted that this applies only to 1925. Lord Lloyd replied:

> "I was on extremely good terms with my father and he talked to me frequently about Egypt, on which he was a great authority, and about Lawrence, whom he knew well. Considering how much he told me on both these subjects I think it unlikely that, had he known that such an offer had ever been made to Lawrence, he would not have told me about it. In fact, I never remember hearing him mention it."[116]

Sir Ronald Storrs, who was also asked about Lawrence's claim (we shall glance at it later) that he had been asked to reorganise Home Defence, wrote:

> "Here is a strange question. My answer to both (1) and (2) is an emphatic NO. Indeed I regard both suggestions as grotesquely improbable. I saw a good deal of T. E. and was, I believe, more in his confidence than most and he never mentioned anything of this nature."[117]

In the ranks

Of course he didn't. Sir Ronald knew the facts. But from 1918 until 1923, Lord Lloyd was away in Bombay, and Mrs. Shaw and Corporal Dixon were easy game. By way of making sure, I inspired another intermediary to put the Egypt question to One Whom I will only designate as a Much Greater Man, who was understood to growl that the assertion that Lawrence had ever officially been offered the post of High Commissioner for Egypt was " certainly unfounded."* Good enough! The assertion was never made by *me*. But it is surely interesting that the great authority on Lawrence and author of the *Dictionary of National Biography* notice on him—Sir Ronald Storrs— had overlooked these interesting passages in his hero's letters and in the book by his " Friends " to which Sir Ronald is himself a distinguished contributor.

This habit of attributing offers of imaginary grandeurs to himself rather grew on Lawrence as the time for his final discharge from the R.A.F. came nearer. It is true that he was offered by a banker, and refused, a position in the City of London,[118] where at one time he had also reserved for himself the position of night-watchman at the Bank of England. He also talked of starting a printing press at Clouds Hill. But these things were mixed up with such fantasies as his telling his neighbour, ex-Sergeant Knowles, that the printing press might have to be postponed for years " since he might again be asked to undertake the reorganisation of Home Defence, and if so would feel that he had no alternative but to take the job, as it was work of such national importance."[119] The distinguished persons who were asked about the Egypt myth also brushed aside the idea that Lawrence had ever been offered " Home Defence." Yet he told Liddell Hart that he had received " approaches " to become successor to Sir Maurice Hankey, afterwards Lord Hankey, who was Clerk to the Privy Council from 1919 to 1938, and Secretary to the Committee of Imperial Defence from 1912-1938. Lawrence added negligently that he had answered he " would only do so if the normal Cabinet side was removed from the Committee of Imperial Defence! "[120] On which Captain Hart reflects that it was " interesting to see him even contemplating the latter role." Yes, indeed, but what evidence is there that he was ever offered such a post, especially since in 1935

---

* Sir Winston Churchill has since affirmed that although he never offered the post of High Commissioner to Lawrence officially he *may* have talked over the possibility of his being offered it unofficially with Lawrence.

Lord Hankey still had three or four years of office ahead? Lawrence's friends, Hart especially, played up to the megalomania of the self-important egotist who made these claims, although one of his favourite poses was that he had joined the ranks in order " to degrade himself " and make it impossible for him to be employed in any responsible post.

Liddell Hart informed him that many people were approaching him (Hart) to get Lawrence to become " dictator." Lawrence said the Fascists had been after him, and he had replied that he would not help them to power, but if they gained it, he would agree to become " dictator " of the press for a fortnight. Lawrence went on to say that a new lead would be popular and that it would be Fascist only till power was gained. He thought Mosley would not " tolerate any really good chief of staff," but " his " (whose?) " chance might come if someone really big took him " (whom?) " under their wing." Hart then asked " T. E." if he would contemplate leading any movement? To which Lawrence replied " No," and said he still intended to settle down in his cottage, but that there were many jobs for him to do if he tired of life in the cottage. On which Liddell Hart noted that his attitude was changing, perhaps more than he knew.[121]

When in 1935 Lawrence took his discharge from the R.A.F. and retired to Clouds Hill, it is not surprising that among the reporters who tried to interview him was one whose questionnaire began: " Do you intend to make yourself Dictator of England? "[122] An idiotic question, of course, but if a man with a newspaper reputation tells his friends that he has been " offered Egypt " and " offered Hankey's jobs " and " offered Home Defence," and discusses with a London *Times* correspondent the possibility of leadership of the Fascist Party, what is to be expected? Once more the sensationalism is to be traced, not to the journalists, but to Lawrence who started it. And, when a man starts such rumours about himself, it is ridiculous to complain of being " persecuted by the press," and something worse than ridiculous to assault a newspaper photographer, as Lawrence did.

Strangely enough, Lawrence's sudden death was directly involved in this toying with the idea of Fascist dictatorship. A friend had written to him suggesting a meeting between Lawrence and Hitler. Apparently, the idea was that Lawrence, being " the natural leader of that age in England," should meet the late but by-few-regretted Adolf, and that together they would fix up the future of the world for the next thousand years. The snag about this was, that while Hitler certainly commanded Germany, Lawrence didn't command anything, while most people will agree that the English have a strong antipathy to all dictators except the Trades Union Council, Mrs. Grundy and the yellow press. Even if the interview had taken place, it would scarcely have ranked as even a pre-view of Munich. Lawrence dashed off on his motor-cycle and sent a telegram fixing an appointment (with the letter-writer, not with Hitler) for the next day, wet or fine. He then remounted and dashed off home.[123]

He had said that his motor-cycle speeding would end tragically one day. Already he had had several warnings. He told Liddell Hart that he had skidded when taking sausages to his comrades at Cranwell, and again on the slippery tram-lines on Highgate Hill.[124] More serious smashes are mentioned in the *Letters*. In April, 1923, he damaged his cycle badly, but himself escaped unhurt;[125] in December, 1925, he skidded on ice going at 55 m.p.h., damaged the cycle, and hurt his knee, ankle and elbow. A year later he wrecked his motor-cycle and lamed himself by an accident in Islington. And there were others. From which one might infer he was rather a fast than a good rider.

Coming back fast from the post-office after having sent the telegram, on the 13th May, 1935, Lawrence ignored the salutary rule that the crest of even a shallow hill is a blind corner if the road is hidden, and came full speed on two errand boys whose cycles took up too much of the road. Lawrence swerved to avoid them, lost control, and was hurled to the ground. His brain was dreadfully injured, and the surgeon who attended him believed that if he had lived he would have been paralysed, and would have lost the power of speech and all memory. He lingered a few days, and died of pneumonia on the 19th May, 1935.[126]

On the 21st May he was buried at Moreton Church in a plain, unmarked coffin, and, at Captain Hart's suggestion, the mourners did not wear formal clothes. There was no parade or particular ceremonial, but his pall-bearers were Sir Ronald Storrs, Colonel Newcombe and Eric Kennington; Pat Knowles, Aircraftman Bradbury and Russell of the Tank Corps.[127] Through the efforts of his friends, an inscription to Lawrence's memory was placed in St. Paul's Cathedral, London, and a bust in the crypt. In the church of St.

Martin, Wareham (Dorset), there is a large funeral monument by Mr. Eric Kennington, showing Lawrence in Arab dress, with his hand on his crooked dagger and a camel saddle under his head—a sort of Crusader *à rebours*. Lawrence was the appropriate hero for his class and epoch. *Requiescat*.

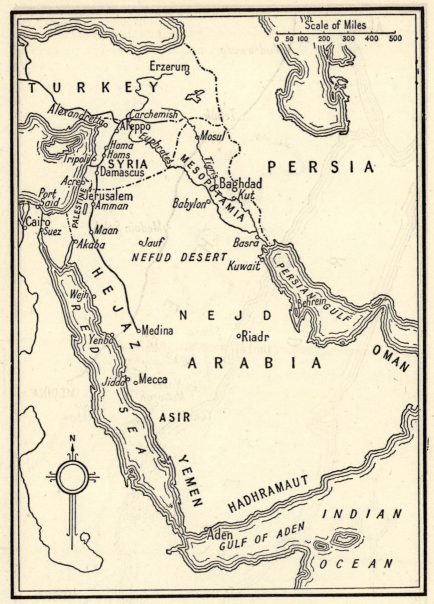

ARABIA AND THE MIDDLE EAST

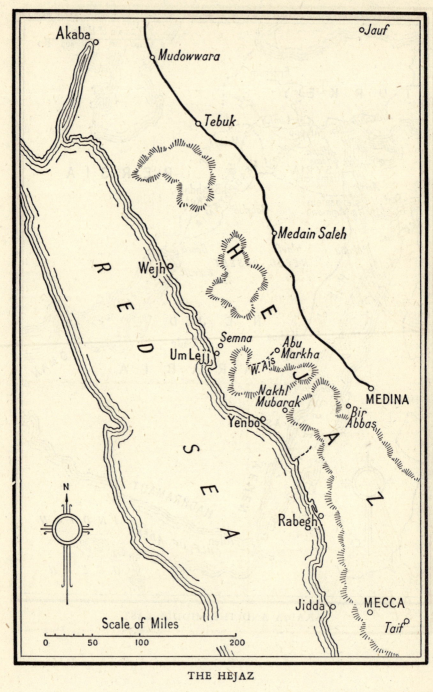

Akaba

Jauf

Mudowwara

Tebuk

Medain Saleh

H E

Wejh

J E

Semna

Abu
Markha

Um Lejj

W. Aïs

Nakhl
Mubarak

A

MEDINA

R E D

Yenbo

Bir
Abbas

Z

S E A

Rabegh

N

Scale of Miles

Jidda

MECCA

0   50   100   200

Taif

THE HEJAZ

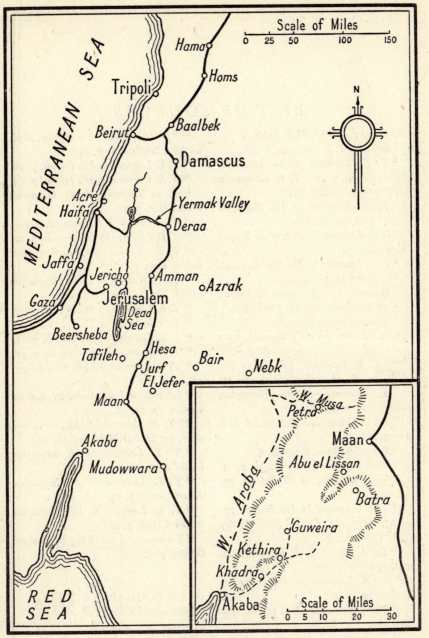

THE PALESTINE CAMPAIGN

LIST OF SOURCES

PART I: CHAPTER ONE

[1] *Letters of T. E. Lawrence*, p. 491.

[2] *T. E. Lawrence to his Biographer Robert Graves*, p. 59. *T. E. Lawrence to his Biographer Liddell Hart*.

[3] *T. E. Lawrence to his Biographer Liddell Hart*, pp. 27, 180.

[4] *With Lawrence in Arabia* by Lowell Thomas, p. 21.

[5] *T. E. Lawrence by His Friends*, p. 25.

[6] Somerset House Records.

[7] *Debrett's Peerage*, 1919. *Burke's Peerage and Baronetage*, 1917 and 1921.

[8] Somerset House Records.

[9] *Burke's Peerage and Baronetage*, 1917 and 1921.

[10] '*T. E. Lawrence.*' In *Arabia and After*, by B. H. Liddell Hart, p. 13. *T. E. Lawrence to his Biographer, Liddell Hart*, p. 78.

[11] British Museum. Additional MS. 45903, 4.

[12] Somerset House Records.

[13] *T. E. Lawrence by His Friends*, p. 25.

[14] *T. E. Lawrence by His Friends*, pp. 31, 32.

[15] *T. E. Lawrence by His Friends*, pp. 25-27. *Crusader Castles* (Vol. I) by T. E. Lawrence, p. 5.

[16] *The Letters of T. E. Lawrence*, pp. 147, 148.

[17] *T. E. Lawrence to his Biographer Liddell Hart*, p. 51.

[18] *The Letters of T. E. Lawrence*, pp. 381, 382.

[19] *The Letters of T. E. Lawrence*, p. 721.

[20] "*Be it Cosiness.*" *The Pageant*, 1896, by Max Beerbohm, p, 230.

[21] *T. E. Lawrence by His Friends*, p. 36.

[22] *T. E. Lawrence by His Friends*, p. 34.

[23] *T. E. Lawrence to his Biographer Liddell Hart*, p. 51.

[24] *The Letters of T. E. Lawrence*, p. 491.

[25] *T. E. Lawrence by His Friends*, p. 26.

[26] *T. E. Lawrence to his Biographer Liddell Hart*, p. 51.

[27] *T. E. Lawrence to his Biographer Liddell Hart*, p. 51.

[28] *T. E. Lawrence by His Friends*, p. 41.

[29] *T. E. Lawrence by His Friends*, p. 26.

[30] *T. E. Lawrence by His Friends*, p. 26.

[31] *T. E. Lawrence by His Friends*, p. 57.

[32] *T. E. Lawrence by His Friends*, pp. 52, 54.

[33] *Lawrence and the Arabs*, by Robert Graves, pp. 24, 25.

[34] '*T. E. Lawrence*'. In *Arabia and After*, by Liddell Hart, pp. 18, 19.

[35] *T. E. Lawrence to his Biographer Liddell Hart*, p. 210.

[36] *T. E. Lawrence to his Biographer Robert Graves*, p. 59.

[37] *T. E. Lawrence to His Biographer Robert Graves*, p. 64.

[38] *Lawrence and the Arabs*, by Robert Graves, p. 5.

PART I: CHAPTER TWO

[1] *Crusader Castles* (Vol. 2) by T. E. Lawrence, pp. 9-10.

[2] *T. E. Lawrence by His Friends*, pp.

26, 28; *Lawrence and the Arabs*, by Robert Graves, p. 14; *Oriental Assembly*, by T. E. Lawrence, p. 38.

[3] *Crusader Castles* (Vol. 2) by T. E. Lawrence, p. 47.

[4] *T. E. Lawrence by His Friends*, p. 48; *Seven Pillars of Wisdom*, by T. E. Lawrence, p. 566.

[5] *The Letters of T. E. Lawrence*, pp. 244, 246.

[6] *The Letters of T. E. Lawrence*, p. 191.

[7] *Seven Pillars of Wisdom*, by T. E. Lawrence, p. 171.

[8] *T. E. Lawrence to his Biographer Robert Graves*, p. 132.

[9] *T. E. Lawrence to his Biographer Robert Graves*, p. 89.

[10] *The Letters of T. E. Lawrence*, p. 429.

[11] *Lawrence and the Arabs*, by Robert Graves, p. 11.

[12] *With Lawrence in Arabia*, by Lowell Thomas, pp. 21, 22.

[13] *With Lawrence in Arabia*, by Lowell Thomas, pp. 24, 25.

[14] *Lawrence and the Arabs*, by Robert Graves, pp. 12, 13.

[15] ' *T. E. Lawrence* '. *In Arabia and After*, by B. H. Liddell Hart, pp. 13, 14.

[16] ' *T. E. Lawrence* '. *In Arabia and After*, by B. H. Liddell Hart, pp. 13, 14.

[17] British Museum. Additional MS. 45903,4.

[18] *T. E. Lawrence to his Biographer Robert Graves*, p. 7.

[19] *T. E. Lawrence to his Biographer Robert Graves*, p. 5.

[20] *T. E. Lawrence to his Biographer Liddell Hart*, p. 67.

[21] *T. E. Lawrence to his Biographer Robert Graves*, p. 70.

[22] *The Letters of T. E. Lawrence*, p. 398.

[23] *T. E. Lawrence to his Biographer Liddell Hart*, p. 27.

[24] *Portrait of T. E. Lawrence, The Lawrence of The Seven Pillars of Wisdom*, by Vyvyan Richards, p. 28.

[25] *The Letters of T. E. Lawrence*, p. 816.

[26] *T. E. Lawrence to his Biographer Liddell Hart*, p. 163.

[27] *T. E. Lawrence to his Biographer Liddell Hart*, p. 208.

[28] *T. E. Lawrence to his Biographer Robert Graves*, p. 15.

[29] *The Letters of T. E. Lawrence*, p. 449.

[30] ' *T. E. Lawrence* '. *In Arabia and After*, by B. H. Liddell Hart, p. 17.

[31] *T. E. Lawrence to his Biographer Liddell Hart*, pp. 24, 51.

[32] *T. E. Lawrence to his Biographer Liddell Hart*, p. 51.

[33] *T. E. Lawrence by His Friends*, p. 28. Private Communication.

[34] *T. E. Lawrence by His Friends*, p. 28; *T. E. Lawrence* by Vyvyan Richards, p. 16; *Lawrence and the Arabs* by Robert Graves, p. 14.

[35] *Portrait of T. E. Lawrence, The Lawrence of The Seven Pillars of Wisdom*, by Vyvyan Richards, p. 24.

[36] British Museum. Additional MS. 45903, 4.

PART I: CHAPTER THREE

[1] *T. E. Lawrence by His Friends*, p. 67.

[2] *With Lawrence in Arabia*, by Lowell Thomas, p. 22; *T. E. Lawrence by His Friends*, p. 43.

[3] *T. E. Lawrence to his Biographer Liddell Hart*, p. 51.

[4] *T. E. Lawrence by His Friends*, p. 41.

[5] ' *T. E. Lawrence* '. *In Arabia and After*, by B. H. Liddell Hart, p. 17.

[6] *T. E. Lawrence by His Friends*, p. 62.

[7] *Lawrence and the Arabs*, by Robert Graves, pp. 16, 17.

[8] *T. E. Lawrence by His Friends*, p. 383.

[9] *T. E. Lawrence by His Friends*, p. 494.

[10] *T. E. Lawrence by His Friends*, p. 62.

[11] ' *T. E. Lawrence* '. *In Arabia and After*, by B. H. Liddell Hart, p. 17.

[12] *Portrait of T. E. Lawrence, The Lawrence of The Seven Pillars of Wisdom*, by Vyvyan Richards, p. 26.

[13] *Portrait of T. E. Lawrence, The Lawrence of The Seven Pillars of Wisdom*, by Vyvyan Richards, p. 19.

[14] *T. E. Lawrence to his Biographer Robert Graves*, p. 48.

[15] *The Letters of T. E. Lawrence*, p. 109.

[16] *Lawrence and the Arabs*, by Robert Graves, p. 16.

[17] *T. E. Lawrence by His Friends*, pp. 62, 63.

[18] *Seven Pillars of Wisdom*, by T. E. Lawrence. Synopsis. p. 7.

[19] Private Communication.

[20] *The Letters of T. E. Lawrence*, p. 109.

[21] *The Letters of T. E. Lawrence*, p. 148.

[22] *T. E. Lawrence by His Friends*, pp. 97, 47, 42. *Portrait of T. E. Lawrence, The Lawrence of The Seven Pillars of Wisdom*, by Vyvyan Richards, p. 36. Private Communication.

[23] *Lawrence and the Arabs*, by Robert Graves, p. 16.

[24] *T. E. Lawrence to his Biographer Liddell Hart*, p. 52.

[25] *T. E. Lawrence by His Friends*, p. 57.

[26] *T. E. Lawrence by His Friends*, pp. 41, 35. *Portrait of T. E. Lawrence, The Lawrence of The Seven Pillars of Wisdom*, by Vyvyan Richards, pp. 40, 41.

[27] *Portrait of T. E. Lawrence, The Lawrence of The Seven Pillars of Wisdom*, byVyvyan Richards, p. 21.

[28] *Lawrence and the Arabs*, by Robert Graves, p. 437.

[29] *The Roots of the Mountains*, by William Morris.

[30] *T. E. Lawrence by His Friends*, p. 385.

[31] *Portrait of T. E. Lawrence, The Lawrence of the Seven Pillars of Wisdom*, by Vyvyan Richards, p. 43.

[32] *T. E. Lawrence by His Friends*, p. 68.

[33] *The Letters of T. E. Lawrence*, p. 146.

[34] *The Letters of T. E. Lawrence*, p. 161.

[35] *T. E. Lawrence by His Friends*, p. 284.

[36] *T. E. Lawrence by His Friends*, p. 327.

[37] *T. E. Lawrence by His Friends*, p. 431.

[38] Unpublished letter to Henry Williamson, 2nd April 1928.

[39] *T. E. Lawrence to his Biographer Robert Graves*, p. 78.

[40] *T. E. Lawrence by His Friends*, p. 27.

[41] *T. E. Lawrence by His Friends*, pp. 34, 35.

[42] *The Letters of T. E. Lawrence*, pp. 456, 665, 669.

[43] *The Letters of T. E. Lawrence*, p. 496.

[44] British Museum. Additional MS. 45903, 4.

PART I: CHAPTER FOUR

[1] *T. E. Lawrence by His Friends*, p. 67.

[2] *T. E. Lawrence by His Friends*, p. 54.

[3] *T. E. Lawrence by His Friends*, p. 54.

[4] *The Letters of T. E. Lawrence*, pp. 43, 47, 48.

[5] *The Letters of T. E. Lawrence*, p. 47. *Crusader Castles* (Vol. 2), by T. E. Lawrence, p. 17. *T. E. Lawrence by His Friends*, p. 29.

[6] *Crusader Castles* (Vol. 2), by T. E. Lawrence, p. 18.

[7] *The Letters of T. E. Lawrence*, p. 50.

[8] *The Letters of T. E. Lawrence*, p. 51.

[9] *The Letters of T. E. Lawrence*, p. 52.

[10] *The Letters of T. E. Lawrence*, p. 48.

11 *Crusader Castles* (Vol. 2), by T. E. Lawrence, p. 41.

12 ' *T. E. Lawrence* '. *In Arabia and After*, by B. H. Liddell Hart, p. 18.

13 *Crusader Castles* (Vol. 2), by T. E. Lawrence, p. 57.

14 *Crusader Castles* (Vol. 2), by T. E. Lawrence, p. 49.

15 *The Letters of T. E. Lawrence*, p. 60.

16 *The Letters of T. E. Lawrence*, p. 62.

17 Footnote to *Letters of T. E. Lawrence*, p. 44.

18 *Crusader Castles* (Vol. 2), by T. E. Lawrence, p. 35.

19 *T. E. Lawrence to his Biographer Robert Graves*, p. 56.

20 *T. E. Lawrence by His Friends*, p. 54.

21 *T. E. Lawrence*, by Vyvyan Richards, p. 15.

22 *T. E. Lawrence by His Friends*, p. 44.

23 *Crusader Castles* (Vol. 1), by T. E. Lawrence, p. 3.

24 Footnote to *Letters of T. E. Lawrence*, p. 44.

25 *T. E. Lawrence*, by Vyvyan Richards, p. 14.

26 *The Letters of T. E. Lawrence*, p. 57.

27 ' *T. E. Lawrence* '. *In Arabia and After*, by B. H. Liddell Hart, pp. 15, 16. *The Letters of T. E. Lawrence*, pp. 53-57, 81. Footnote to p. 56.

28 *Lawrence and the Arabs*, by Robert Graves, p. 14.

29 *Portrait of T. E. Lawrence, The Lawrence of The Seven Pillars of Wisdom*, by Vyvyan Richards, p. 47.

30 *The Letters of T. E. Lawrence*, p. 53.

31 *The Letters of T. E. Lawrence*, p. 59.

32 *Crusader Castles* (Vol. 2), by T. E. Lawrence, p. 56.

33 *With Lawrence in Arabia*, by Lowell Thomas, p. 24.

34 *The Letters of T. E. Lawrence*, p. 78.

35 *Lawrence and the Arabs*, by Robert Graves, p. 17.

36 ' *T. E. Lawrence* '. *In Arabia and After*, by B. H. Liddell Hart, p. 20.

37 *T. E. Lawrence to his Biographer Robert Graves*, pp. 48, 57.

38 *The Letters of T. E. Lawrence*, p. 79.

39 *Portrait of T. E. Lawrence, The Lawrence of The Seven Pillars of Wisdom*, by Vyvyan Richards, p. 53.

40 *T. E. Lawrence to his Biographer Robert Graves*, p. 61. Note to *The Letters of T. E. Lawrence*, p. 63.

41 *T. E. Lawrence by His Friends*, pp. 73, 74.

42 *The Letters of T. E. Lawrence*, p. 81.

43 ' *T. E. Lawrence* '. *In Arabia and After*, by B. H. Liddell Hart, p. 20.

44 *The Letters of T. E. Lawrence*, p. 94.

45 *The Letters of T. E. Lawrence*, pp. 73, 74.

46 *The Letters of T. E. Lawrence*, pp. 65-73. *T. E. Lawrence by His Friends*, p. 76.

47 *The Letters of T. E. Lawrence*, p. 81.

48 *Military Operations, Egypt and Palestine*, Vol. 2, p. 597.

49 *The Letters of T. E. Lawrence*, p. 79.

50 *Lawrence and the Arabs*, by Robert Graves, p. 18.

51 *T. E. Lawrence by His Friends*, pp. 76, 77.

52 *T. E. Lawrence by His Friends*, p. 92.

53 *Portrait of T. E. Lawrence, The Lawrence of The Seven Pillars of Wisdom*, by Vyvyan Richards, p. 54.

54 *T. E. Lawrence by His Friends*, p. 74.

55 *The Letters of T. E. Lawrence*, pp. 81, 82.

56 *Portrait of T. E. Lawrence, The Lawrence of The Seven Pillars of Wisdom*, by Vyvyan Richards, p. 54.

[57] *Lawrence and the Arabs,* by Robert Graves, p. 19.

[58] *Lawrence and the Arabs,* by Robert Graves, pp. 19, 20. ' *T. E. Lawrence* '. *In Arabia and After,* by B. H. Liddell Hart, p. 21.

[59] *T. E. Lawrence by His Friends,* p. 74.

[60] *The Letters of T. E. Lawrence,* p. 109.

[61] *Crusader Castles* (Vol. 1), by T. E. Lawrence, p. 13. *The Letters of T. E. Lawrence,* p. 110.

[62] *Memories of Victorian Oxford and of Some Early Years,* by Sir Charles Oman, p. 149.

[63] *T. E. Lawrence,* by Vyvyan Richards, p. 22. (Great Lives.)

[64] *Lawrence and the Arabs,* by Robert Graves, p. 20.

[65] *Crusader Castles* (Vol. 1), by T. E. Lawrence, p. 4.

[66] ' *T. E. Lawrence* '. *In Arabia and After,* by B. H. Liddell Hart, p. 21.

[67] *The Letters of T. E. Lawrence,* p. 93.

[68] *Crusader Castles. A Brief Study of the Military Architecture of the Crusades,* by Robin Fedden, p. 64, pp. 22-3.

[69] *Style Romane.* Louis Bréhier de l'Institut (Larousse, 1941), p. 37.

PART I: CHAPTER FIVE

[1] *The Letters of T. E. Lawrence,* p. 86.

[2] *T. E. Lawrence by His Friends,* p. 139.

[3] *Crusader Castles* (Vol. 2), by T. E. Lawrence, *frontispiece.*

[4] *The Letters of T. E. Lawrence,* pp. 84, 85. *Portrait of T. E. Lawrence, The Lawrence of The Seven Pillars of Wisdom,* by Vyvyan Richards, pp. 23-4.

[5] *T. E. Lawrence by His Friends,* p. 49.

[6] *The Letters of T. E. Lawrence,* p. 85.

[7] *The Letters of T. E. Lawrence,* p. 86.

[8] *The Letters of T. E. Lawrence,* p. 86.

[9] *The Letters of T. E. Lawrence,* p 84.

[10] *The Letters of T. E. Lawrence,* p. 87.

[11] *T. E. Lawrence to his Biographer* Liddell Hart, p. 24.

[12] *Memoirs,* by Lady Gregory.

[13] *The Letters of T. E. Lawrence,* p. 87.

[14] *The Letters of T. E. Lawrence,* p. 102.

[15] *The Letters of T. E. Lawrence,* p. 97.

[16] *The Letters of T. E. Lawrence,* p. 97.

[17] *T. E. Lawrence to his Biographer* Robert Graves, p. 49.

[18] *Lawrence and the Arabs,* by Robert Graves, p. 19. ' *T. E. Lawrence* '. *In Arabia and After,* by B. H. Liddell Hart, p. 19. *T. E. Lawrence by His Friends,* p. 29.

[19] *Reminiscences,* by A. H. Sayce, p. 161.

[20] *T. E. Lawrence to his Biographer* Robert Graves, p. 50.

[21] *T. E. Lawrence to his Biographer* Robert Graves, p. 66.

[22] *Portrait of T. E. Lawrence, The Lawrence of The Seven Pillars of Wisdom,* by Vyvyan Richards, p. 46.

[23] *The Letters of T. E. Lawrence,* p. 89.

[24] *The Letters of T. E. Lawrence,* p. 91.

[25] *The Letters of T. E. Lawrence,* p. 104.

[26] *Reminiscences,* by A. H. Sayce, p. 328.

[27] *The Letters of T. E. Lawrence,* p. 99.

[28] *T. E. Lawrence to his Biographer* Robert Graves, p. 49.

[29] *T. E. Lawrence to his Biographer* Liddell Hart, p. 83.

[30] *T. E. Lawrence to his Biographer* Liddell Hart, p. 67.

[31] *T. E. Lawrence by His Friends,* p. 87.

[32] *T. E. Lawrence by His Friends,* p. 87.

[33] *The Letters of T. E. Lawrence,* p. 101.

[34] *The Letters of T. E. Lawrence,* p. 147.

[35] *The Letters of T. E. Lawrence,* p. 102.

[36] *The Letters of T. E. Lawrence,* p. 114.

[37] Baedeker's *Syria and Palestine* (1912), p. 419.

[38] Note to *Letters of T. E. Lawrence*, p. 103.

[39] *T. E. Lawrence by His Friends*, pp. 80, 89.

[40] *The Letters of T. E. Lawrence*, pp. 114, 115.

[41] *T. E. Lawrence by His Friends*, p. 89.

[42] *T. E. Lawrence*, by Vyvyan Richards, p. 32 (Great Lives).

[43] *Dead Towns and Living Men*, by C. Leonard Woolley, p. 112.

[44] *T. E. Lawrence by His Friends*, p. 95.

[45] *T. E. Lawrence by His Friends*, p. 97.

[46] *Oriental Assembly*, by T. E. Lawrence, pp. 5-54.

[47] *T. E. Lawrence by His Friends*, pp. 95-9.

[48] *The Letters of T. E. Lawrence*, p. 120.

PART I: CHAPTER SIX

[1] *The Letters of T. E. Lawrence*, p. 125.

[2] *T. E. Lawrence by His Friends*, p. 137.

[3] ' *T. E. Lawrence* '. *In Arabia and After*, by B. H. Liddell Hart, p. 22.

[4] *Lawrence and the Arabs*, by Robert Graves, p. 23. ' *T. E. Lawrence* '. *In Arabia and After*, by B. H. Liddell Hart, p. 22.

[5] *The Letters of T. E. Lawrence*, pp. 132-5.

[6] *T. E. Lawrence by His Friends*, p. 82.

[7] *Lawrence and the Arabs*, by Robert Graves, p. 23.

[8] *The Letters of T. E. Lawrence*, p. 136.

[9] *The Letters of T. E. Lawrence*, p. 126.

[10] *Dead Towns and Living Men*, by C. Leonard Woolley, pp. 150-77.

[11] *Oriental Assembly*, by T. E. Lawrence, pp. 57, 58.

[12] *Lawrence and the Arabs*, by Robert Graves, p. 31. ' *T. E. Lawrence* '. *In Arabia and After*, by B. H. Liddell Hart, p. 29.

[13] *Dead Towns and Living Men*, by C. Leonard Woolley, p. 109.

[14] *The Letters of T. E. Lawrence*, p. 145.

[15] *Lawrence and the Arabs*, by Robert Graves, pp. 32-4. ' *T. E. Lawrence* '. *In Arabia and After*, by B. H. Liddell Hart, pp. 29, 30.

[16] *Dead Towns and Living Men*, by C. Leonard Woolley, pp. 111-20.

[17] *The Letters of T. E. Lawrence*, p. 160.

[18] *The Letters of T. E. Lawrence*, p. 161.

[19] *The Letters of T. E. Lawrence*, p. 161.

[20] *T. E. Lawrence to his Biographer Liddell Hart*, p. 67.

[21] *T. E. Lawrence by His Friends*, pp. 86, 87.

[22] *T. E. Lawrence by His Friends*, pp. 50, 62, 63.

[23] *T. E. Lawrence by His Friends*, pp. 50, 62, 63.

[24] *T. E. Lawrence to his Biographer Liddell Hart*, p. 90.

[25] *The Wilderness of Zin*, by Leonard Woolley and T. E. Lawrence, p. 20.

[26] *T. E. Lawrence to his Biographer Liddell Hart*, p. 27.

[27] *T. E. Lawrence to his Biographer Robert Graves*, pp. 23, 24.

[28] *T. E. Lawrence by His Friends*, pp. 586, 587.

[29] *T. E. Lawrence to his Biographer Liddell Hart*, p. 24.

[30] *T. E. Lawrence by His Friends*, p. 180.

[31] *T. E. Lawrence by His Friends*, p. 587.

[32] *The Letters of T. E. Lawrence*, p. 137.

[33] *T. E. Lawrence by His Friends*, p. 90.

[34] *The Letters of T. E. Lawrence*, p. 527.

[35] *T. E. Lawrence by His Friends*, p. 89.

[36] *T. E. Lawrence by His Friends*, pp. 89, 90.

[37] *T. E. Lawrence by His Friends*, p. 90.

[38] *T. E. Lawrence by His Friends*, pp. 90, 91.

[39] *T. E. Lawrence by His Friends*, p. 132.

[40] *T. E. Lawrence by His Friends*, p. 91.

[41] *T. E. Lawrence by His Friends*, p. 104.

[42] *T. E. Lawrence by His Friends*, p. 91.

[43] *Lawrence and the Arabs*, by Robert Graves, p. 36.

[44] ' *T. E. Lawrence* '. *In Arabia and After*, by B. H. Liddell Hart, p. 23.

[45] ' *T. E. Lawrence* '. *In Arabia and After*, by B. H. Liddell Hart, p. 27.

[46] *Seven Pillars of Wisdom*, by T. E. Lawrence, p. 564.

[47] *A Paladin of Arabia*, by Major N. N. E. Bray, pp. 133-255.

[48] *The Letters of T. E. Lawrence*, pp. 139, 140, 144.

[49] *The Letters of T. E. Lawrence*, p. 149.

[50] *The Letters of T. E. Lawrence*, p. 159.

[51] *Seven Pillars of Wisdom*, by T. E. Lawrence, p. 446.

[52] ' *T. E. Lawrence* '. *In Arabia and After*, by B. H. Liddell Hart, p. 27. *T. E. Lawrence to his Biographer Liddell Hart*, p. 141.

[53] *Oriental Assembly*, by T. E. Lawrence, p. 42.

[54] *The Independent Arab*, by Major Sir Hubert Young, p. 18.

[55] *The Independent Arab*, by Major Sir Hubert Young, pp. 19, 20.

[56] *Portrait of T. E. Lawrence, The Lawrence of The Seven Pillars of Wisdom*, by Vyvyan Richards, pp. 59, 60. *The Letters of T. E. Lawrence*, p. 167.

[57] *The Letters of T. E. Lawrence*, pp. 158, 159.

[58] *Dead Towns and Living Men*, by C. Leonard Woolley, pp. 188, 189. *The Letters of T. E. Lawrence*, p. 158.

[59] *The Letters of T. E. Lawrence*, pp. 150, 151.

[60] *T. E. Lawrence to his Biographer Robert Graves*, p. 81.

[61] *The Letters of T. E. Lawrence*, p. 246.

[62] *T. E. Lawrence by His Friends*, p. 104.

[63] ' *T. E. Lawrence* '. *In Arabia and After*, by B. H. Liddell Hart, p. 27.

[64] ' *T. E. Lawrence* '. *In Arabia and After*, by B. H. Liddell Hart, p. 23.

[65] ' *T. E. Lawrence* '. *In Arabia and After*, by B. H. Liddell Hart, p. 23.

[66] *Portrait of T. E. Lawrence, The Lawrence of The Seven Pillars of Wisdom*, by Vyvyan Richards, p. 58.

[67] ' *T. E. Lawrence* '. *In Arabia and After*, by B. H. Liddell Hart, p. 23.

[68] *Lawrence and the Arabs*, by Robert Graves, p. 36.

[69] ' *T. E. Lawrence* '. *In Arabia and After*, by B. H. Liddell Hart, p. 34.

[70] *T. E. Lawrence by His Friends*, pp. 77, 78.

[71] *T. E. Lawrence by His Friends*, p. 84.

[72] *T. E. Lawrence by His Friends*, p. 115.

[73] *The Independent Arab*, by Sir Hubert Young, pp. 14-22.

[74] *Lawrence and the Arabs*, by Robert Graves, p. 36.

[75] *Seven Pillars of Wisdom*, by T. E. Lawrence, pp. 46, 47, 55.

[76] ' *T. E. Lawrence* '. *In Arabia and After*, by B. H. Liddell Hart, p. 16. *Letters of T. E. Lawrence*, p. 152.

[77] *T. E. Lawrence by His Friends*, pp. 131, 132.

[78] *T. E. Lawrence by His Friends*, p. 132.

[79] *The Wilderness of Zin*, by C. Leonard Woolley and T. E. Lawrence, p. 11. *The Letters of T. E. Lawrence*, p. 176.

[80] *T. E. Lawrence by His Friends*, p. 132.

[81] Notes to *Letters of T. E. Lawrence,* p. 163.

[82] *The Wilderness of Zin,* by C. Leonard Woolley and T. E. Lawrence, p. 17.

[83] *The Letters of T. E. Lawrence,* p. 188.

[84] *The Wilderness of Zin,* by C. Leonard Woolley and T. E. Lawrence, pp. 23-9.

[85] *T. E. Lawrence by His Friends,* p. 106.

[86] *The Wilderness of Zin,* by C. Leonard Woolley and T. E. Lawrence, pp. 86, 88.

[87] *The Wilderness of Zin,* by C. Leonard Woolley and T. E. Lawrence, pp. 71-4.

[88] *T. E. Lawrence by His Friends,* p. 106.

[89] *T. E. Lawrence by His Friends,* pp. 106, 107.

[90] *The Wilderness of Zin,* by C. Leonard Woolley and T. E. Lawrence, pp. 145-147. *The Letters of T. E. Lawrence,* p. 165. *T. E. Lawrence by His Friends,* p. 107.

[91] *Palestine and Syria,* by Karl Baedeker (1912), p. 213. *T. E. Lawrence by His Friends,* p. 107. Notes to *The Letters of T. E. Lawrence,* p. 167.

[92] *The Letters of T. E. Lawrence,* pp. 165, 166.

[93] *Dead Towns and Living Men,* by C. Leonard Woolley, pp. 111-6. *The Letters of T. E. Lawrence,* pp. 171-5. *Men in Print,* by T. E. Lawrence.

[94] *Dead Towns and Living Men,* by C. Leonard Woolley, p. 278.

PART I: CHAPTER SEVEN

[1] *Lawrence and the Arabs,* by Robert Graves, p. 55.

[2] *The Golden Reign,* by Clare Sydney Smith, p. 79.

[3] *T. E. Lawrence,* by Vyvyan Richards, p. 14 (Great Lives).

[4] *With Lawrence in Arabia,* by Lowell Thomas, p. 14.

[5] Private letter from Lowell Thomas, December 1950.

[6] *Lawrence and the Arabs,* by Robert Graves, p. 5.

[7] *T. E. Lawrence to his Biographer Robert Graves,* p. 59.

[8] *T. E. Lawrence to his Biographer Robert Graves,* p. 128.

[9] *T. E. Lawrence to his Biographer Robert Graves,* p. 5.

[10] *T. E. Lawrence by His Friends,* p. 214.

[11] *T. E. Lawrence to his Biographer Robert Graves,* p. 45.

[12] *T. E. Lawrence to his Biographer Robert Graves,* pp. 181, 184.

[13] *Seven Pillars of Wisdom,* by T. E. Lawrence, p. 322.

[14] *Allenby, a Study in Greatness,* by Colonel A. P. Wavell, p. 193, footnote.

[15] *The Truth about the Peace Treaties,* by David Lloyd George (Vol. 2), p. 1028.

[16] *With Lawrence in Arabia,* by Lowell Thomas, p. 33.

[17] *With Lawrence in Arabia,* by Lowell Thomas, p. 33.

[18] *Lawrence and the Arabs,* by Robert Graves, pp. 36-8.

[19] *T. E. Lawrence to his Biographer Liddell Hart,* p. 55.

PART II: CHAPTER ONE

[1] *The Letters of T. E. Lawrence,* p. 161.

[2] *The Letters of T. E. Lawrence,* p. 176.

[3] *The Wilderness of Zin,* by C. Leonard Woolley and T. E. Lawrence, p. 17.

[4] Notes to *The Letters of T. E. Lawrence*, p. 181.

[5] *The Palestine Campaigns*, by Colonel A. P. Wavell, p. 9.

[6] *The Letters of T. E. Lawrence*, p. 188.

[7] *The Letters of T. E. Lawrence*, p. 188.

[8] *The Letters of T. E. Lawrence*, p. 190.

[9] *Seven Pillars of Wisdom*, by T. E. Lawrence, p. 562.

[10] *The Letters of T. E. Lawrence*, p. 185.

[11] *The Letters of T. E. Lawrence*, p. 187.

[12] *T. E. Lawrence by His Friends*, p. 225.

[13] *With Lawrence in Arabia*, by Lowell Thomas, p. 23.

[14] *Lawrence and the Arabs*, by Robert Graves, p. 151.

[15] *Seven Pillars of Wisdom*, by T. E. Lawrence, p. 114.

[16] *T. E. Lawrence to his Biographer Liddell Hart*, pp. 50–1.

[17] '*T. E. Lawrence*'. *In Arabia and After*, by Liddell Hart, pp. 164–6.

[18] '*T. E. Lawrence*'. *In Arabia and After*, by B. H. Liddell Hart, p. 165.

[19] *T. E. Lawrence to his Biographer Liddell Hart*, p. 96.

[20] *Memories of Victorian Oxford and Some Early Years*, by Sir Charles Oman, pp. 108–9.

[21] Notes to The *Letters of T. E. Lawrence*, p. 184.

[22] *The Letters of T. E. Lawrence*, p. 185.

[23] *With Lawrence in Arabia*, by Lowell Thomas, p. 37.

[24] *Lawrence and the Arabs*, by Robert Graves, p. 81.

[25] *The Dictionary of National Biography*, 1949–50.

[26] *T. E. Lawrence by His Friends*, pp. 107–8.

[27] *T. E. Lawrence*, by Vyvyan Richards, p. 37 (Great Lives).

[28] *T. E. Lawrence to his Biographer Liddell Hart*, p. 94.

[29] *T. E. Lawrence to his Biographer Liddell Hart*, p. 55.

[30] Notes to *The Letters of T. E. Lawrence*, p. 181.

[31] Letter from Sir Coote Hedley, 17th May, 1933. *T. E. Lawrence to his Biographer Liddell Hart*, p. 192.

[32] '*T. E. Lawrence*'. *In Arabia and After*, by B. H. Liddell Hart, p. 95.

[33] *The Letters of T. E. Lawrence*, p. 187.

[34] *The Letters of T. E. Lawrence*, p. 188.

[35] *The Letters of T. E. Lawrence*, p. 187.

[36] *Lawrence and the Arabs*, by Robert Graves, p. 81. '*T. E. Lawrence*'. *In Arabia and After*, by B. H. Liddell Hart, p. 96.

[37] Notes to *The Letters of T. E. Lawrence*, p. 181.

[38] '*T. E. Lawrence*'. *In Arabia and After*, by B. H. Liddell Hart, p. 95. *T. E. Lawrence to his Biographer Liddell Hart*, pp. 55, 125, 192.

[39] *T. E. Lawrence to his Biographer Liddell Hart*, p. 192.

[40] *The Letters of T. E. Lawrence*, p. 391.

[41] '*T. E. Lawrence*'. *In Arabia and After*, by B. H. Liddell Hart, p. 96.

[42] *T. E. Lawrence to his Biographer Liddell Hart*, p. 24.

[43] *T. E. Lawrence to his Biographer Robert Graves*, p. 49.

[44] *Seven Pillars of Wisdom*, by T E. Lawrence, p. 106.

[45] *The Letters of T. E. Lawrence*, p. 192.

[46] *T. E. Lawrence by His Friends*, p. 132.

[47] *T. E. Lawrence by His Friends*, p. 136.

[48] *T. E. Lawrence by His Friends*, p. 137.

[49] Letters in London *Times*, June 22, July 20, 1951. *The Letters of T. E. Lawrence*, p. 684.

[50] *Seven Pillars of Wisdom*, by T. E. Lawrence, p. 25.

[51] *T. E. Lawrence by His Friends*, pp. 136-7.

[52] *T. E. Lawrence by His Friends*, p. 138.

[53] *T. E. Lawrence by His Friends*, p. 158.

[54] *T. E. Lawrence by His Friends*, pp. 133-41.

[55] *The Letters of T. E. Lawrence*, p. 191.

[56] *The Letters of T. E. Lawrence*, p. 192.

[57] *Lawrence and the Arabs*, by Robert Graves, p. 82. ' *T. E. Lawrence* '. *In Arabia and After*, by B. H. Liddell Hart, pp. 97, 98.

[58] *The Letters of T. E. Lawrence*, p. 199.

[59] *The Letters of T. E. Lawrence*, p. 196.

[60] *Military Operations, Egypt and Palestine* (Vol. 1), pp. 37-51.

[61] *T. E. Lawrence by His Friends*, p. 140.

[62] *The Letters of T. E. Lawrence*, p. 203, footnote.

[63] *Seven Pillars of Wisdom*, by T. E. Lawrence, p. 56.

[64] *With Lawrence in Arabia*, by Lowell Thomas, p. 38.

[65] *Lawrence and the Arabs*, by Robert Graves, p. 82.

[66] ' *T. E. Lawrence* '. *In Arabia and After*, by B. H. Liddell Hart, p. 98.

[67] ' *T. E. Lawrence* '. *In Arabia and After*, by B. H. Liddell Hart, p. 98.

[68] *Lawrence and the Arabs*, by Robert Graves, p. 83.

[69] Notes to *The Letters of T. E. Lawrence*, p. 183.

[70] Notes to *The Letters of T. E. Lawrence*, p. 203.

[71] *Seven Pillars of Wisdom*, by T. E. Lawrence, p. 59.

[72] *Lawrence and the Arabs*, by Robert Graves, p. 85.

[73] ' *T. E. Lawrence* '. *In Arabia and After*, by B. H. Liddell Hart, p. 98.

[74] *War and Revolution in Asiatic Russia*, by M. Philips Price.

[75] *Encyclopaedia Britannica*, 14th Ed., Vol. 5, p. 59.

[76] *T. E. Lawrence by His Friends*, pp. 93, 94.

[77] *The Letters of T. E. Lawrence*, p. 192.

[78] *The Letters of T. E. Lawrence*, p. 193.

[79] *The Letters of T. E. Lawrence*, pp. 193-4.

[80] *T. E. Lawrence to his Biographer Liddell Hart*, p. 17. *The Letters of T. E. Lawrence*, p. 195.

[81] *Military Operations, Egypt and Palestine*, Vol. 1, p. 20.

[82] *Sir J. Maxwell*, by Sir G. Arthur, p. 153.

[83] *Military Operations, Egypt and Palestine*, Vol. 1, pp. 76-85.

[84] ' *T. E. Lawrence* '. *In Arabia and After*, by B. H. Liddell Hart, pp. 46-7.

[85] *The Arab Awakening*, by George Antonius, pp. 184, 191-2.

[86] Notes to *The Letters of T. E. Lawrence*, p. 195.

[87] *The Letters of T. E. Lawrence*, p. 197.

[88] *The Letters of T. E. Lawrence*, pp. 195-6.

[89] *The Letters of T. E. Lawrence*, p. 196.

[90] *Military Operations, Egypt and Palestine*, Vol. 1, p. 210.

[91] *The Letters of T. E. Lawrence*, p. 197.

[92] *Le Hedjaz dans la Guerre Mondiale*, by Général Ed. Brémond.

PART II: CHAPTER TWO

[1] *Orientations*, by Sir Ronald Storrs, p. 196-9. *Seven Pillars of Wisdom*, by T. E. Lawrence, p. 250.

[2] *Orientations*, by Sir Ronald Storrs, p. 196.

[3] *Le Hedjaz dans la Guerre Mondiale*, by Général Ed. Brémond, p. 160.

[4] *The Letters of Gertrude Bell*, 30th November, 1915.

[5] *The Letters of T. E. Lawrence*, p. 199.

[6] *The Letters of T. E. Lawrence*, p. 551.

[7] *The Letters of T. E. Lawrence*, p. 191.

[8] *The Desert and the Sown*, by Gertrude Lowthian Bell, p. 160.

[9] *Orientations*, by Sir Ronald Storrs, p. 16.

[10] *Orientations*, by Sir Ronald Storrs, pp. 129-30. *Military Operations, Egypt and Palestine*, Vol. 1, p. 213.

[11] *Orientations*, by Sir Ronald Storrs, p. 156.

[12] *Military Operations, Egypt and Palestine*, Vol. 1, pp. 212-4. *Orientations*, by Sir Ronald Storrs, pp. 157-8.

[13] *Orientations*, by Sir Ronald Storrs, p. 183.

[14] *The Letters of T. E. Lawrence*, p. 201.

[15] *Orientations*, by Sir Ronald Storrs, p. 197.

[16] *Orientations*, by Sir Ronald Storrs, p. 180.

[17] *Military Operations, Egypt and Palestine*, Vol. 1, p. 215.

[18] *Orientations*, by Sir Ronald Storrs, p. 159.

[19] *The Arab Awakening*, by George Antonius, p. 158.

[20] *Military Operations, Egypt and Palestine*, Vol. 1, p. 215. *The Truth about the Peace Treaties*, by David Lloyd George, Vol. 2, p. 1018.

[21] *The Truth about the Peace Treaties*, by David Lloyd George, Vol. 2, p. 1019.

[22] *Military Operations, Egypt and Palestine*, Vol. 1, p. 217.

[23] *The Independent Arab*, by Sir Hubert Young, p. 271.

[24] *Orientations*, by Sir Ronald Storrs, p. 163.

[25] *Secret Despatches from Arabia*, p. 5.

[26] *Loyalties. Mesopotamia 1914-1917*, by Sir A. T. Wilson, p. 97.

[27] *Loyalties. Mesopotamia 1914-1917*, by Sir A. T. Wilson, p. 97.

[28] *The Letters of T. E. Lawrence*, p. 203.

[29] '*T. E. Lawrence*'. *In Arabia and After*, by B. H. Liddell Hart, pp. 98-9. *Lawrence and the Arabs*, by Robert Graves, pp. 86-7.

[30] *Lawrence and the Arabs*, by Robert Graves, p. 97.

[31] *Seven Pillars of Wisdom*, by T. E. Lawrence, p. 60.

[32] *The Letters of Gertrude Bell*, 9th April, 1916.

[33] *The Letters of Gertrude Bell*, 4th May, 1916.

[34] *The Letters of T. E. Lawrence*, pp. 205, 208-10.

[35] *Lawrence and the Arabs*, by Robert Graves, p. 87.

[36] *The Independent Arab*, by Sir Hubert Young, pp. 72-3. *T. E. Lawrence by His Friends*, p. 123.

[37] '*T. E. Lawrence*'. *In Arabia and After*, by B. H. Liddell Hart, p. 99.

[38] *Lawrence and the Arabs*, by Robert Graves, p. 87,

[39] *The Arab Awakening*, by George Antonius, p. 416.

[40] *Seven Pillars of Wisdom*, by T. E. Lawrence, p. 591.

[41] '*T. E. Lawrence*'. *In Arabia and After*, by B. H. Liddell Hart, p. 101.

[42] *The Letters of T. E. Lawrence*, p. 202.

[43] *Three Persons*, by Sir Andrew Macphail, p. 207.

[44] '*T. E. Lawrence*'. *In Arabia and After*, by B. H. Liddell Hart, p. 104.

[45] *The Letters of T. E. Lawrence,* p. 208.

[46] *Seven Pillars of Wisdom,* by T. E. Lawrence, p. 106.

[47] *Seven Pillars of Wisdom,* by T. E. Lawrence, p. 114.

[48] *The Arab Awakening,* by George Antonius, p. 191.

[49] *Le Hedjaz dans la Guerre Mondiale,* by Général Ed. Brémond, p. 28.

[50] *The Arab Awakening,* by George Antonius, p. 191.

[51] *Military Operations, Egypt and Palestine,* Vol. 1, p. 230.

[52] *Orientations,* by Sir Ronald Storrs, pp. 160-1.

[53] *Memoirs of King Abdulla of Transjordan,* pp. 132-8. *Orientations,* by Sir Ronald Storrs, pp. 163-70.

[54] *Orientations,* by Sir Ronald Storrs, pp. 167, 195.

[55] *Memoirs of King Abdulla of Transjordan,* pp. 142-53. *Military Operations, Egypt and Palestine,* Vol. 1, pp. 225-8. *Le Hedjaz dans la Guerre Mondiale,* by Général Ed. Brémond, p. 57. *The Arab Awakening,* by George Antonius, pp. 194-200.

[56] *Le Hedjaz dans la Guerre Mondiale,* by Général Ed. Brémond, p. 31.

[57] *Le Hedjaz dans la Guerre Mondiale,* by Général Ed. Brémond, p. 32.

[58] *Le Hedjaz dans la Guerre Mondiale,* by Général Ed. Brémond, p. 68.

[59] *Le Hedjaz dans la Guerre Mondiale,* by Général Ed. Brémond, pp. 67-73.

[60] *The Arab Awakening,* by George Antonius, p. 214.

[61] *Le Hedjaz dans la Guerre Mondiale,* by Général Ed. Brémond, p. 68.

[62] *Orientations,* by Sir Ronald Storrs, p. 192.

[63] *Le Hedjaz dans la Guerre Mondiale,* by Général Ed. Brémond, p. 74. *Orientations,* by Sir Ronald Storrs, pp. 193-4.

[64] *Orientations,* by Sir Ronald Storrs, p. 198.

[65] *Orientations,* by Sir Ronald Storrs, p. 180.

[66] *Orientations,* by Sir Ronald Storrs, pp. 182-3.

[67] *Seven Pillars of Wisdom,* by T. E. Lawrence, pp. 66-75. *Orientations,* by Sir Ronald Storrs, pp. 181-7. *Memoirs of King Abdulla of Transjordan,* pp. 157-8.

[68] *Orientations,* by Sir Ronald Storrs, pp. 198-9.

[69] *Secret Despatches from Arabia,* pp. 12-45; *Seven Pillars of Wisdom,* by T. E. Lawrence, p. 106.

PART II: CHAPTER THREE

[1] *Lawrence and the Arabs,* by Robert Graves, p. 89.

[2] *Military Operations, Egypt and Palestine,* Vol. 1, p. 248.

[3] *Seven Pillars of Wisdom,* by T. E. Lawrence, pp. 99-101.

[4] *Seven Pillars of Wisdom,* by T. E. Lawrence, p. 91.

[5] *Orientations,* by Sir Ronald Storrs, p. 198.

[6] *Seven Pillars of Wisdom,* by T. E. Lawrence, p. 63.

[7] *Seven Pillars of Wisdom,* by T. E. Lawrence, pp. 70-1.

[8] *Seven Pillars of Wisdom,* by T. E. Lawrence, p. 63.

[9] *Seven Pillars of Wisdom,* by T. E. Lawrence, p. 61.

[10] *Seven Pillars of Wisdom,* by T. E. Lawrence, p. 97.

[11] *Seven Pillars of Wisdom,* by T. E. Lawrence, pp. 51-2. *The Arab Awakening,* by George Antonius, p. 132.

[12] *T. E. Lawrence to his Biographer Liddell Hart*, pp. 188-9.

[13] *T. E. Lawrence by His Friends*, p. 125.

[14] *T. E. Lawrence by His Friends*, p. 94.

[15] *The Letters of T. E. Lawrence*, p. 196.

[16] *The Letters of T. E. Lawrence*, p. 196.

[17] *Seven Pillars of Wisdom*, by T. E. Lawrence, p. 111.

[18] *Seven Pillars of Wisdom*, by T. E. Lawrence, p. 132.

[19] *Seven Pillars of Wisdom*, by T. E. Lawrence, p. 132.

[20] *Seven Pillars of Wisdom*, by T. E. Lawrence, p. 168.

[21] *Seven Pillars of Wisdom*, by T. E. Lawrence, pp. 168-9; *Le Hedjaz dans la Guerre Mondiale*, by Général Ed. Brémond, p. 84.

[22] *Le Hedjaz dans la Guerre Mondiale*, by Général Ed. Brémond, p. 42.

[23] *Orientations*, by Sir Ronald Storrs, pp. 174, 185.

[24] *With Lawrence in Arabia*, by Lowell Thomas, *passim*.

[25] *T. E. Lawrence by His Friends*, p. 149.

[26] *Le Hedjaz dans la Guerre Mondiale*, by Général Ed. Brémond, p. 76.

[27] *Military Operations, Egypt and Palestine*, Vol. 1, p. 231.

[28] *Le Hedjaz dans la Guerre Mondiale*, by Général Ed. Brémond, p. 96.

[29] *Secret Despatches from Arabia*, p. 24.

[30] *Secret Despatches from Arabia*, p. 22.

[31] *Lawrence and the Arabs*, by Robert Graves, p. 109.

[32] *Secret Despatches from Arabia*, pp. 41-51.

[33] *Secret Despatches from Arabia*, p. 51.

[34] *The Letters of T. E. Lawrence*, p. 212.

[35] *Seven Pillars of Wisdom*, by T. E. Lawrence, p. 126.

[36] *Secret Despatches from Arabia*, p. 51.

[37] *T. E. Lawrence by His Friends*, p. 208.

[38] *Orientations*, by Sir Ronald Storrs, p. 195; *Secret Despatches from Arabia*, p. 53; *Seven Pillars of Wisdom*, by T. E. Lawrence, pp. 128-30.

[39] *Orientations*, by Sir Ronald Storrs, pp. 195-6.

[40] *Secret Despatches from Arabia*, pp. 53-4; *Seven Pillars of Wisdom*, by T. E. Lawrence, pp. 131-9.

[41] *Seven Pillars of Wisdom*, by T. E. Lawrence, p. 132.

[42] *Le Hedjaz dans la Guerre Mondiale*, by Général Ed. Brémond, pp. 95-7.

[43] *Seven Pillars of Wisdom*, by T. E. Lawrence, p. 166.

[44] *Le Hedjaz dans la Guerre Mondiale*, by Général Ed. Brémond, p. 98.

[45] *Le Hedjaz dans la Guerre Mondiale*, by Général Ed. Brémond, pp. 195-7.

[46] *Secret Despatches from Arabia*, p. 64; *Seven Pillars of Wisdom*, by T. E. Lawrence, p. 140.

[47] *Military Operations, Egypt and Palestine*, Vol. 1, p. 237.

[48] *Seven Pillars of Wisdom*, by T. E. Lawrence, p. 111.

[49] *Seven Pillars of Wisdom*, by T. E. Lawrence, p. 153.

[50] *Seven Pillars of Wisdom*, by T. E. Lawrence, p. 160.

[51] *Seven Pillars of Wisdom*, by T. E. Lawrence, p. 161.

[52] *Shifting Sands*, by Major N. N. E. Bray, pp. 122-3.

[53] *Shifting Sands*, by Major N. N. E. Bray, p. 123.

[54] *Shifting Sands*, by Major N. N. E. Bray, pp. 120-32.

[55] *Lawrence and the Arabs*, by Robert Graves, p. 141.

⁵⁶ *Shifting Sands*, by Major N. N. E. Bray, p. 127.

⁵⁷ *Travels in Arabia Deserta*, by Chas. M. Doughty, Vol. 1, p. 576; Vol. 2, p. 36.

⁵⁸ *Lawrence and the Arabs*, by Robert Graves, p. 117.

⁵⁹ ' *T. E. Lawrence* '. In *Arabia and After*, by B. H. Liddell Hart, pp. 120-1.

⁶⁰ *Seven Pillars of Wisdom*, by T. E. Lawrence, p. 167.

⁶¹ *The Arab Awakening*, by George Antonius, pp. 214-5.

⁶² *Military Operations, Egypt and Palestine*, Vol. 1, p. 227.

⁶³ *Le Hedjaz dans la Guerre Mondiale*, by Général Ed. Brémond, p. 117.

⁶⁴ *Les Armées Françaises dans la Grande Guerre*, Tome 9; p. 190.

⁶⁵ *Military Operations, Egypt and Palestine*, Vol. 1, p. 225.

⁶⁶ *Le Hedjaz dans la Guerre Mondiale*, by Général Ed. Brémond, pp. 88-9.

⁶⁷ *Les Armées Françaises dans la Grande Guerre*, Tome 9, p. 190.

⁶⁸ *Les Armées Françaises dans la Grande Guerre*, Tome 9, Annexe 335.

⁶⁹ *Military Operations, Egypt and Palestine*, Vol. 1, p. 260.

PART II: CHAPTER FOUR

¹ *Seven Pillars of Wisdom*, by T. E. Lawrence, p. 201.

² *Military Operations, Egypt and Palestine*, Vol. 1, pp. 26-7. *The Palestine Campaigns*, by Col. A. P. Wavell, pp. 11-2.

³ *Le Hedjaz dans la Guerre Mondiale*, by Général Ed. Brémond, pp. 18-9.

⁴ *Military Operations, Egypt and Palestine*, Vol. 1, p. 407.

⁵ *Le Hedjaz dans la Guerre Mondiale*, by Général Ed. Brémond, p. 265.

⁶ *Gegenspieler des Obsten Lawrence*, 1936, by Hans Luhrs, p. 65.

⁷ *Military Operations, Egypt and Palestine*, Vol. 2, pp. 407-8.

⁸ *Le Hedjaz dans la Guerre Mondiale*, by Général Ed. Brémond, pp. 18-9.

⁹ *Le Hedjaz dans la Guerre Mondiale*, by Général Ed. Brémond, p. 19.

¹⁰ *Seven Pillars of Wisdom*, by T. E. Lawrence, p. 229.

¹¹ *Seven Pillars of Wisdom*, by T. E. Lawrence, p. 103.

¹² *With Lawrence in Arabia*, by Lowell Thomas, p. 124.

¹³ *Seven Pillars of Wisdom*, by T. E. Lawrence, p. 192.

¹⁴ *Seven Pillars of Wisdom*, by T. E. Lawrence, p. 194.

¹⁵ *Lawrence and the Arabs*, by Robert Graves, p. 152.

¹⁶ *Lawrence and the Arabs*, by Robert Graves, p. 116.

¹⁷ *Military Operations, Egypt and Palestine*, Vol. 2, p. 399.

¹⁸ *Military Operations, Egypt and Palestine*, Vol. 2, p. 238. *Le Hedjaz dans la Guerre Mondiale*, by Général Ed. Brémond, p. 118.

¹⁹ *Le Hedjaz dans la Guerre Mondiale*, by Général Ed. Brémond, p. 122.

²⁰ *Seven Pillars of Wisdom*, by T. E. Lawrence, pp. 192-203.

²¹ *Le Hedjaz dans la Guerre Mondiale*, by Général Ed. Brémond, p. 155.

²² *Le Hedjaz dans la Guerre Mondiale*, by Général Ed. Brémond, p. 152.

²³ *Les Armées Françaises dans la Grande Guerre*, Tome 9, p. 192.

²⁴ *Seven Pillars of Wisdom*, by T. E. Lawrence, p. 229.

²⁵ *T. E. Lawrence by His Friends*, p. 124.

26 *T. E. Lawrence by His Friends*, p. 124.

27 *With Lawrence in Arabia*, by Lowell Thomas, p. 83.

28 *Lawrence and the Arabs*, by Robert Graves, p. 161.

29 *Seven Pillars of Wisdom*, by T. E. Lawrence, p. 227.

30 *Seven Pillars of Wisdom*, by T. E. Lawrence, p. 300-4. *Military Operations, Egypt and Palestine*, Vol. 1, p. 240.

31 *The Independent Arab*, by Sir Hubert Young, pp. 147-8.

32 *Travels in Arabia Deserta*, by Chas. M. Doughty, Vol. 1, p. 423.

33 *Travels in Arabia Deserta*, by Chas. M. Doughty, Vol. 1, p. 437.

34 *Orientations*, by Sir Ronald Storrs, pp. 251-61.

35 *Military Operations, Egypt and Palestine*, Vol. 1, p. 240. *Secret Despatches from Arabia*, pp. 122-3.

36 *Le Hedjaz dans la Guerre Mondiale*, by Général Ed. Brémond, p. 163; *Secret Despatches from Arabia*, pp. 123-7; *Seven Pillars of Wisdom*, by T. E. Lawrence, pp. 315-9.

37 *Seven Pillars of Wisdom*, by T. E. Lawrence, p. 377; *Le Hedjaz dans la Guerre Mondiale*, by Général Ed. Brémond.

38 *Le Hedjaz dans la Guerre Mondiale*, by Général Ed. Brémond, p. 95.

39 *Le Hedjaz dans la Guerre Mondiale*, by Général Ed. Brémond, p. 119.

40 *Le Hedjaz dans la Guerre Mondiale*, by Général Ed. Brémond, p. 121.

41 *Seven Pillars of Wisdom*, by T. E. Lawrence, pp. 167-8, 664.

42 *Le Hedjaz dans la Guerre Mondiale*, by Général Ed. Brémond, p. 133.

43 *Seven Pillars of Wisdom*, by T. E. Lawrence, p. 664.

44 *Le Hedjaz dans la Guerre Mondiale*, by Général Ed. Brémond, pp. 123-33.

45 *With Lawrence in Arabia*, by Lowell Thomas, pp. 83-4.

46 *Lawrence and the Arabs*, by Robert Graves, pp. 161-2.

47 *Seven Pillars of Wisdom*, by T. E. Lawrence, p. 228.

48 *Seven Pillars of Wisdom*, by T. E. Lawrence, p. 234.

49 *Seven Pillars of Wisdom*, by T. E. Lawrence, p. 235.

50 *Seven Pillars of Wisdom*, by T. E. Lawrence, p. 258.

51 ' *T. E. Lawrence* '. *In Arabia and After*, by B. H. Liddell Hart, p. 183.

52 *With Lawrence in Arabia*, by Lowell Thomas, p. 84.

53 *Seven Pillars of Wisdom*, by T. E. Lawrence, p. 228.

54 *Seven Pillars of Wisdom*, by T. E. Lawrence, p. 228.

55 *Seven Pillars of Wisdom*, by T. E. Lawrence, p. 277.

56 *Lawrence and the Arabs*, by Robert Graves, p. 190.

57 *T. E. Lawrence to his Biographer Robert Graves*, p. 90.

58 *The Arab Awakening*, by George Antonius, pp. 220-1.

59 *The Arab Awakening*, by George Antonius, p. 221.

60 *The Arab Awakening*, by George Antonius, p. 221.

61 *The Letters of T. E. Lawrence*, pp. 225-30.

62 ' *T. E. Lawrence* '. *In Arabia and After*, by B. H. Liddell Hart, p. 194.

63 *Seven Pillars of Wisdom*, by T. E. Lawrence, p. 321.

64 *Le Hedjaz dans la Guerre Mondiale*, by Général Ed. Brémond, pp. 209-10.

65 *The Arab Awakening*, by George Antonius, p. 322.

PART II: CHAPTER FIVE

[1] *The Fire of Life*, by General Sir George Barrow, p. 44.

[2] *Seven Pillars of Wisdom*, by T. E. Lawrence, p. 322.

[3] *Seven Pillars of Wisdom*, by T. E. Lawrence, p. 321.

[4] *Seven Pillars of Wisdom*, by T. E. Lawrence, p. 380.

[5] *Seven Pillars of Wisdom*, by T. E. Lawrence, p. 383.

[6] *Seven Pillars of Wisdom*, by T. E. Lawrence, p. 527.

[7] *Seven Pillars of Wisdom*, by T. E. Lawrence, p. 322.

[8] *Seven Pillars of Wisdom*, by T. E. Lawrence, p. 584.

[9] *Seven Pillars of Wisdom*, by T. E. Lawrence, p. 643.

[10] *T. E. Lawrence by His Friends*, p. 145.

[11] *T. E. Lawrence by His Friends*, p. 145.

[12] *The Times*, 29th May, 1935.

[13] *The Times*, 29th May, 1935.

[14] *Allenby—A Study in Greatness*, by A. P. Wavell, p. 193.

[15] *The Fire of Life*, by General Sir George Barrow, p. 215.

[16] *Seven Pillars of Wisdom*, by T. E. Lawrence, p. 323.

[17] *Seven Pillars of Wisdom*, by T. E. Lawrence, p. 323.

[18] *Seven Pillars of Wisdom*, by T. E. Lawrence, p. 328.

[19] *Le Hedjaz dans la Guerre Mondiale*, by Général Ed. Brémond, p. 229.

[20] *Military Operations, Egypt and Palestine*, Vol. 1, p. 224.

[21] *Military Operations, Egypt and Palestine*, Vol. 1, p. 210.

[22] *The Palestine Campaigns*, by A. P. Wavell, p. 19.

[23] *Seven Pillars of Wisdom*, by T. E. Lawrence, p. 380.

[24] *Military Operations, Egypt and Palestine*, Vol. 1, p. 401.

[25] *Le Hedjaz dans la Guerre Mondiale*, by Général Ed. Brémond, p. 218.

[26] *Seven Pillars of Wisdom*, by T. E. Lawrence, p. 368.

[27] *Seven Pillars of Wisdom*, by T. E. Lawrence, pp. 369–70.

[28] *Secret Despatches from Arabia*, p. 136.

[29] *T. E. Lawrence by His Friends*, p. 41.

[30] *Oriental Assembly*, by T. E. Lawrence, p. 144.

[31] *Seven Pillars of Wisdom*, by T. E. Lawrence, p. 384.

[32] *The Letters of T. E. Lawrence*, pp. 237–8; *Lawrence and the Arabs*, by Robert Graves, p. 246.

[33] *Seven Pillars of Wisdom*, by T. E. Lawrence, p. 379.

[34] *Secret Despatches from Arabia*, p. 140.

[35] *Seven Pillars of Wisdom*, by T. E. Lawrence, p. 380.

[36] *Secret Despatches from Arabia*, p. 140.

[37] *Les Armées Françaises dans la Grande Guerre*, Tome 9, Annexe 454.

[38] *Les Armées Françaises dans la Grande Guerre*, Tome 9, Annexe 454.

[39] *Seven Pillars of Wisdom*, by T. E. Lawrence, p. 387.

[40] *Secret Despatches from Arabia*, p. 142.

[41] *The Letters of T. E. Lawrence*, p. 239.

[42] *Seven Pillars of Wisdom*, by T. E. Lawrence, pp. 422–3.

[43] *Desert Mounted Corps*, by Lt.-Col. R. M. Presto, quoted by General Sir George Barrow, pp. 187–8.

[44] *Seven Pillars of Wisdom*, by T. E. Lawrence, pp. 441–6.

[45] British Museum. Additional MS. 45903, 4.

[46] *Sunday Times*, W. E. Johns, 8th April, 1951.

[47] *T. E. Lawrence to his Biographer Liddell Hart*, p. 71.

[48] *Arabian Days*, by St. John Philby, p. 210.

[49] *Seven Pillars of Wisdom*, by T. E. Lawrence, p. 445.

[50] *Seven Pillars of Wisdom*, by T. E. Lawrence, p. 447.

PART II: CHAPTER SIX

[1] *Military Operations, Egypt and Palestine*, Vol. 2, p. 262.

[2] *Secret Despatches from Arabia*, pp. 121-2.

[3] *The Truth about the Peace Treaties*, by David Lloyd George, p. 1040.

[4] *The Truth about the Peace Treaties*, by David Lloyd George, p. 1067.

[5] *The Truth about the Peace Treaties*, by David Lloyd George, p. 1067.

[6] *Seven Pillars of Wisdom*, by T. E. Lawrence, p. 453.

[7] *Seven Pillars of Wisdom*, by T. E. Lawrence, p. 453.

[8] *Seven Pillars of Wisdom*, by T. E. Lawrence, p. 453.

[9] *Military Operations, Egypt and Palestine*, Vol. 2, p. 260.

[10] *T. E. Lawrence by His Friends*, p. 147.

[11] *Seven Pillars of Wisdom*, by T. E. Lawrence, p. 455.

[12] *Orientations*, by Sir Ronald Storrs, p. 307.

[13] *Le Hedjaz dans la Guerre Mondiale*, by Général Ed. Brémond, p. 140.

[14] *Orientations*, by Sir Ronald Storrs, p. 287.

[15] *Orientations*, by Sir Ronald Storrs, p. 289.

[16] *The Truth about the Peace Treaties*, by David Lloyd George, p. 1025.

[17] *Seven Pillars of Wisdom*, by T. E. Lawrence, p. 455.

[18] *The Truth about the Peace Treaties*, by David Lloyd George, p. 1023.

[19] *Seven Pillars of Wisdom*, by T. E. Lawrence, p. 537.

[20] *Le Hedjaz dans la Guerre Mondiale*, by Général Ed. Brémond, pp. 209-10; *Military Operations, Egypt and Palestine*, Vol. 2, p. 294.

[21] *Seven Pillars of Wisdom*, by T. E. Lawrence, p. 456.

[22] *Secret Despatches from Arabia*, p. 152.

[23] *Secret Despatches from Arabia*, pp. 150-3; *Military Operations, Egypt and Palestine*, Vol. 2, pp. 402-4; *Seven Pillars of Wisdom*, by T. E. Lawrence, pp. 474-82.

[24] *Secret Despatches from Arabia*, p. 152; *Seven Pillars of Wisdom*, by T. E. Lawrence, p. 481; *Encyclopaedia Britannica*, 14th Ed., Vol. 16, p. 860; ditto, Vol. 20, article: *Small Arms*.

[25] *Secret Despatches from Arabia*, p. 149.

[26] *Military Operations, Egypt and Palestine*, Vol. 2, p. 404, footnote.

[27] *Secret Despatches from Arabia*, p. 149.

[28] *Le Hedjaz dans la Guerre Mondiale*, by Général Ed. Brémond, p. 234.

[29] *Military Operations, Egypt and Palestine*, Vol. 2, p. 404.

[30] *The Arab Awakening*, by George Antonius, p. 225.

[31] *Military Operations, Egypt and Palestine*, Vol. 2, p. 404.

[32] *The Palestine Campaigns*, by A. P. Wavell, p. 179, footnote.

[33] *Lawrence and the Arabs*, by Robert Graves, p. 307.

[34] ' *T. E. Lawrence* '. In *Arabia and After*, by B. H. Liddell Hart, p. 277.

[35] *Seven Pillars of Wisdom*, by T. E. Lawrence, p. 483.

[36] *Secret Despatches from Arabia*, p. 152.

[37] *Seven Pillars of Wisdom*, by T. E. Lawrence, pp. 485-7.

[38] *Seven Pillars of Wisdom*, by T. E. Lawrence, pp. 490-501; *Military Operations, Egypt and Palestine*, Vol. 2, pp. 302-9.

[39] *Seven Pillars of Wisdom*, by T. E. Lawrence, pp. 501-2.

[40] *Seven Pillars of Wisdom*, by T. E. Lawrence, p. 479.

[41] *Military Operations, Egypt and Palestine*, Vol. 2, p. 405.

[42] *Le Hedjaz dans la Guerre Mondiale*, by Général Ed. Brémond, pp. 237-8.

PART II: CHAPTER SEVEN

[1] *Army List*, June-August 1918; *Seven Pillars of Wisdom*, by T. E. Lawrence, p. 505.

[2] *The Golden Carpet*, by Somerset de Chair, p. 175.

[3] *The Independent Arab*, by Sir Hubert Young, p. 178.

[4] *The Independent Arab*, by Sir Hubert Young, pp. 170-1.

[5] *The Independent Arab*, by Sir Hubert Young, p. 155.

[6] *Orientations*, by Sir Ronald Storrs, p. 160, footnote.

[7] *The Independent Arab*, by Sir Hubert Young, p. 155.

[8] *The Letters of T. E. Lawrence*, p. 320.

[9] *The Letters of T. E. Lawrence*, p. 519.

[10] *The Letters of T. E. Lawrence*, p. 423.

[11] *The Independent Arab*, by Sir Hubert Young, p. 194.

[12] *Military Operations, Egypt and Palestine*, Vol. 2, p. 405; *The Independent Arab*, by Sir Hubert Young, pp. 145-6.

[13] *The Independent Arab*, by Sir Hubert Young, pp. 151-2.

[14] *The Independent Arab*, by Sir Hubert Young, p. 142.

[15] *Seven Pillars of Wisdom*, by T. E. Lawrence, p. 490.

[16] *Le Hedjaz dans la Guerre Mondiale*, by Général Ed. Brémond, p. 236.

[17] *Seven Pillars of Wisdom*, by T. E. Lawrence, p. 460.

[18] *Military Operations, Egypt and Palestine*, Vol. 2, p. 396.

[19] *Military Operations, Egypt and Palestine*, Vol. 2, pp. 407-8.

[20] *T. E. Lawrence to his Biographer Liddell Hart*, p. 25.

[21] *Seven Pillars of Wisdom*, by T. E. Lawrence, p. 527.

[22] *The Independent Arab*, by Sir Hubert Young, pp. 195-200.

[23] *The Independent Arab*, by Sir Hubert Young, p. 198.

[24] *Fünf Jahre Turkei*, by General Liman von Sanders, p. 330.

[25] *Fünf Jahre Turkei*, by General Liman von Sanders, p. 330.

[26] *Fünf Jahre Turkei*, by General Liman von Sanders, p. 330.

[27] *Seven Pillars of Wisdom*, by T. E. Lawrence, p. 556.

[28] *T. E. Lawrence by His Friends*, p. 125.

[29] *Seven Pillars of Wisdom*, by T. E. Lawrence, p. 111.

[30] *Orientations*, by Sir Ronald Storrs, pp. 159-61.

[31] *The Arab Awakening*, by George Antonius, p. 433.

[32] *The Arab Awakening*, by George Antonius, pp. 433-4.

[33] *The Independent Arab*, by Sir Hubert Young, p. 277.

[34] *T. E. Lawrence to his Biographer Liddell Hart*, p. 149.

[35] *T. E. Lawrence to his Biographer Robert Graves*, p. 103.

[36] *Secret Despatches from Arabia*, pp. 155-61

[37] *Secret Despatches from Arabia*, p. 159.

[38] *Le Hedjaz dans la Guerre Mondiale*, by Général Ed. Brémond, pp. 282-3.

[39] *Seven Pillars of Wisdom*, by T. E. Lawrence, pp. 533-4; *Le Hedjaz dans la Guerre Mondiale*, by Général Ed. Brémond, pp 278-9.

[40] *Le Hedjaz dans la Guerre Mondiale*, by Général Ed. Brémond, p. 287; *The Independent Arab*, by Sir Hubert Young, p. 209.

[41] *The Independent Arab*, by Sir Hubert Young, p. 201.

[42] *Seven Pillars of Wisdom*, by T. E. Lawrence, p. 579.

[43] *Military Operations, Egypt and Palestine*, Vol. 2, pp. 563-5.

[44] *Military Operations, Egypt and Palestine*, Vol. 2, pp. 565-6; *Secret Despatches from Arabia*, p. 166.

[45] *Military Operations, Egypt and Palestine*, Vol. 2, pp. 466-7.

[46] *Military Operations, Egypt and Palestine*, Vol. 2, p. 566.

[47] *Military Operations, Egypt and Palestine*, Vol. 2, pp. 566-7.

[48] *Secret Despatches from Arabia*, p. 168.

[49] *Seven Pillars of Wisdom*, by T. E. Lawrence, p. 631.

[50] *Secret Despatches from Arabia*, p. 168.

[51] *History of Jerusalem*, by Besant and Palmer, p. 116.

[52] *Le Hedjaz dans la Guerre Mondiale*, by Général Ed. Brémond, p. 301.

[53] *T. E. Lawrence to his Biographer Liddell Hart*, p. 152.

[54] *Military Operations, Egypt and Palestine*, Vol. 2, pp. 582-3; *The Fire of Life*, by General Sir George Barrow, pp. 210-11.

[55] *Seven Pillars of Wisdom*, by T. E. Lawrence, pp. 635-6.

[56] *The Fire of Life*, by General Sir George Barrow, p. 211.

[57] *Military Operations, Egypt and Palestine*, Vol. 2, pp. 555-8.

[58] *The Fire of Life*, by General Sir George Barrow, p. 211.

[59] *The Fire of Life*, by General Sir George Barrow, p. 209.

[60] *Seven Pillars of Wisdom*, by T. E. Lawrence, p. 434.

[61] *Seven Pillars of Wisdom*, by T. E. Lawrence, p. 640.

[62] *Seven Pillars of Wisdom*, by T. E. Lawrence, p. 640.

[63] *Military Operations, Egypt and Palestine*, Vol. 2, p. 586.

[64] *Military Operations, Egypt and Palestine*, Vol. 2, p. 586.

[65] *The Palestine Campaigns*, by A. P. Wavell, p. 229.

[66] *Military Operations, Egypt and Palestine*, Vol. 2, p. 588.

[67] *Military Operations, Egypt and Palestine*, Vol. 2, pp. 588-9.

[68] *Military Operations, Egypt and Palestine*, Vol. 2, pp. 590-1.

[69] *Allenby—A Study in Greatness*, by A. P. Wavell, p. 285, footnote.

[70] *Seven Pillars of Wisdom*, by T. E. Lawrence, p. 628.

[71] *Secret Despatches from Arabia*, p. 170; *T. E. Lawrence by His Friends*, pp. 154-8.

[72] *Secret Despatches from Arabia*, p. 171.

[73] *Secret Despatches from Arabia*, p. 171; *The Fire of Life*, by General Sir George Barrow, pp. 212-14.

[74] *Seven Pillars of Wisdom*, by T. E. Lawrence, p. 653.

[75] *Seven Pillars of Wisdom*, by T. E. Lawrence, p. 653.

[76] *The Independent Arab*, by Sir Hubert Young, p. 257.

[77] ' *T. E. Lawrence* '. *In Arabia and After*, by B. H. Liddell Hart, p. 372.

[78] *Memoirs and Reflections*, H. H. Asquith.

[79] *The Arab Awakening*, by George Antonius, p. 275.

[80] *Le Hedjaz dans la Guerre Mondiale*, by Général Ed. Brémond, p. 307.

[81] *The Arab Awakening*, by George Antonius, p. 275.

[82] *The Letters of T. E. Lawrence*, p. 670.

[83] *The Letters of T. E. Lawrence*, p. 671.

[84] *The Letters of T. E. Lawrence*, p. 269.

[85] *Le Hedjaz dans la Guerre Mondiale*, by Général Ed. Brémond, p. 307.

[86] *Le Hedjaz dans la Guerre Mondiale*, by Général Ed. Brémond, p. 319; French F.O. telegram, No. 682 (Picot).

[87] *Le Hedjaz dans la Guerre Mondiale*, by Général Ed. Brémond, p. 323; French F.O. telegram, No. 3 (Pontalis).

PART III: CHAPTER ONE

[1] *Seven Pillars of Wisdom*, by T. E. Lawrence, p. 661.

[2] *Oriental Assembly*, by T. E. Lawrence, p. 132.

[3] *T. E. Lawrence to his Biographer Liddell Hart*, p. 49.

[4] *Bibliophiles' Almanack*, by Herbert Read, 1928.

[5] *Military Operations, Egypt and Palestine*, Vol. 2, pp. 618-47.

[6] *Seven Pillars of Wisdom*, by T. E. Lawrence, p. 586.

[7] *T. E. Lawrence to his Biographer Liddell Hart*, p. 165.

[8] *Seven Pillars of Wisdom*, by T. E. Lawrence, p. 660.

[9] *The Independent Arab*, by Sir Hubert Young, p. 253.

[10] *Seven Pillars of Wisdom*, by T. E. Lawrence, p. 651.

[11] *Seven Pillars of Wisdom*, by T. E. Lawrence, p. 653.

[12] *Le Hedjaz dans la Guerre Mondiale*, by General Ed. Brémond, p. 318.

[13] *The Letters of T. E. Lawrence*, p. 258.

[14] *The Independent Arab*, by Sir Hubert Young, p. 265.

[15] ' *T. E. Lawrence* '. *In Arabia and After*, by B. H. Liddell Hart, p. 385; *Lawrence and the Arabs*, by Robert Graves, p. 291.

[16] *Army List*, August, 1918.

[17] *T. E. Lawrence to his Biographer Liddell Hart*, p. 165.

[18] *With Lawrence in Arabia*, by Lowell Thomas, p. 256.

[19] *Lawrence and the Arabs*, by Robert Graves, p. 292.

[20] *T. E. Lawrence to his Biographer Liddell Hart*, p. 166.

[21] *Lawrence and the Arabs*, by Robert Graves, p. 293.

[22] *T. E. Lawrence to his Biographer Liddell Hart*, p. 166.

[23] *The Letters of T. E. Lawrence*, p. 270.

[24] *Secret Despatches from Arabia*, p. 161.

[25] *The Letters of T. E. Lawrence*, p. 268.

[26] *The Independent Arab*, by Sir Hubert Young, p. 257.

[27] *The Letters of T. E. Lawrence*, p. 268.

[28] *The Letters of T. E. Lawrence*, p. 268.

[29] *Le Hedjaz dans la Guerre Mondiale*, by Général Ed. Brémond, pp. 308-9.

[30] *With Lawrence in Arabia*, by Lowell Thomas, p. 257.

[31] *Le Hedjaz dans la Guerre Mondiale,* by Général Ed. Brémond, p. 311.

[32] '*T. E. Lawrence*'. *In Arabia and After,* by B. H. Liddell Hart, p. 386.

[33] *T. E. Lawrence by His Friends,* p. 301.

[34] *T. E. Lawrence to his Biographer Liddell Hart,* p. 157.

[35] *The Letters of T. E. Lawrence,* p. 273.

[36] *Le Hedjaz dans la Guerre Mondiale,* by Général Ed. Brémond, p. 317.

[37] *T. E. Lawrence by His Friends,* p. 195.

[38] *Lawrence and the Arabs,* by Robert Graves, p. 390.

[39] *T. E. Lawrence by His Friends,* p. 195.

[40] *Fünf Jahre Turkei,* by General Liman von Sanders.

[41] *Military Operations, Egypt and Palestine,* Vol. 2, p. 294.

[42] *The Letters of T. E. Lawrence,* p. 269.

[43] *The Truth about the Peace Treaties,* by David Lloyd George, p. 1038.

[44] *The Truth about the Peace Treaties,* by David Lloyd George.

[45] *The Truth about the Peace Treaties,* by David Lloyd George, p. 1041.

[46] *The Truth about the Peace Treaties,* by David Lloyd George, p. 1043.

[47] *T. E. Lawrence by His Friends,* p. 195.

[48] *T. E. Lawrence to his Biographer Liddell Hart,* p. 101.

[49] *The Truth about the Peace Treaties,* by David Lloyd George, pp. 1038-9.

[50] '*T. E. Lawrence*'. *In Arabia and After,* by B. H. Liddell Hart, p. 392.

[51] *The Truth about the Peace Treaties,* by David Lloyd George, pp. 1053-4.

[52] *The Truth about the Peace Treaties,* by David Lloyd George, pp. 1052-3.

[53] *The Truth about the Peace Treaties,* by David Lloyd George, p. 1058.

[54] *The Truth about the Peace Treaties,* by David Lloyd George, p. 1079.

[55] Burton's *Nights,* Vol. X, pp. 203-4, footnote.

[56] Papers relating to the Foreign Relations of the United States, Vol. XII, p. 750.

PART III: CHAPTER TWO

[1] *The Truth about the Peace Treaties,* by David Lloyd George, p. 1098.

[2] *The Truth about the Peace Treaties,* by David Lloyd George, p. 1098.

[3] *The Truth about the Peace Treaties,* by David Lloyd George, pp. 1100-13.

[4] *Syria. An Historical Appreciation,* by Robin Fedden, p. 271.

[5] *The Letters of T. E. Lawrence,* p. 291.

[6] *The Letters of T. E. Lawrence,* p. 289.

[7] *The Letters of T. E. Lawrence,* p. 290.

[8] *The Letters of T. E. Lawrence,* p. 293.

[9] *T. E. Lawrence by His Friends,* pp. 193-4.

[10] *T. E. Lawrence to his Biographer Liddell Hart,* p. 131.

[11] *T. E. Lawrence to his Biographer Robert Graves,* p. 54.

[12] *Lawrence and the Arabs,* by Robert Graves, pp. 392-3.

[13] *T. E. Lawrence by His Friends,* p. 300.

[14] *T. E. Lawrence to his Biographer Liddell Hart,* p. 131; *T. E. Lawrence by His Friends,* pp. 194, 301.

[15] *T. E. Lawrence by His Friends,* p. 301.

[16] *The Letters of T. E. Lawrence,* p. 332.

[17] *Memories of Victorian Oxford and Some Early Years,* by Sir Charles Oman, pp. 116-30.

[18] *Seven Pillars of Wisdom,* by T. E. Lawrence, p. 388.

[19] *T. E. Lawrence by His Friends,* p. 325.

[20] Somerset House Records.

[21] *T. E. Lawrence by His Friends,*

p. 161; *The Letters of T. E. Lawrence*, p. 276.

[22] *The Letters of T. E. Lawrence*, p. 277.
[23] *T. E. Lawrence by His Friends*, p. 147.
[24] *The Truth about the Peace Treaties*, by David Lloyd George, p. 1047
[25] *Le Hedjaz dans la Guerre Mondiale*, by Général Ed. Brémond, p. 325.
[26] Papers relative to the Foreign Relations of the United States, Vol. XI, p. 123.
[27] *Arabian Days, an Autobiography*, by H. St. J. Philby, p. 176.
[28] *Arabian Days, an Autobiography*, by H. St. J. Philby, p. 178.
[29] *Arabia*, by H. St. J. Philby, p. 270.
[30] *Le Hedjaz dans la Guerre Mondiale*, by Général Ed. Brémond, p. 328.
[31] *Arabian Days, an Autobiography*, by H. St. J. Philby, p. 182.

PART III: CHAPTER THREE

[1] *The Independent Arab*, by Sir Hubert Young, p. 279.
[2] Private letter from Lowell Thomas, December 8th, 1950.
[3] *T. E. Lawrence by His Friends*, p. 193.
[4] '*T. E. Lawrence*'. *In Arabia and After*, by B. H. Liddell Hart.
[5] *Shifting Sands*, by Major N.N.E. Bray, pp. 65-9.
[6] *The Independent Arab*, by Sir Hubert Young, pp. 142-3.
[7] *Lawrence and the Arabs*, by Robert Graves, p. 337.
[8] *Military Operations, Egypt and Palestine*, Vol. 2, p. 408.
[9] *Lawrence and the Arabs*, by Robert Graves, p. 336.

[10] *The Golden Carpet*, by Somerset de Chair, M.P., p. 33.
[11] *T. E. Lawrence by His Friends*, p. 206.
[12] *T. E. Lawrence by His Friends*, pp. 205-7.
[13] *With Lawrence in Arabia*, by Lowell Thomas, pp. 16-7.
[14] *With Lawrence in Arabia*, by Lowell Thomas, p. 19.
[15] *With Lawrence in Arabia*, by Lowell Thomas, p. 19.
[16] Lowell Thomas, private letter of December, 1950.
[17] *T. E. Lawrence by His Friends*, p. 208.
[18] *With Lawrence in Arabia*, by Lowell Thomas, pp. 97-8.
[19] *With Lawrence in Arabia*, by Lowell Thomas, pp. 97-104.
[20] *The Letters of T. E. Lawrence*, p. 545.
[21] *Orientations*, by Sir Ronald Storrs, p. 315.
[22] *The Independent Arab*, by Sir Hubert Young, p. 23.
[23] *With Lawrence in Arabia*, by Lowell Thomas, p. 167.
[24] *With Lawrence in Arabia*, by Lowell Thomas, p. 167.
[25] Letter from Lowell Thomas of 16th October, 1950.
[26] Letter from Lowell Thomas of 16th October, 1950.
[27] *T. E. Lawrence by His Friends*, p. 212.
[28] Letter from Lowell Thomas, 27th December, 1950.
[29] *T. E. Lawrence by His Friends*, pp. 211-3; Letter of Lowell Thomas of December 27th, 1950.
[30] Letter of Lowell Thomas of 27th December, 1950.
[31] *T. E. Lawrence by His Friends*, p. 262.
[32] *With Lawrence in Arabia*, by Lowell Thomas, p. 174.

[33] *With Lawrence in Arabia*, by Lowell Thomas, p. 92.

[34] *With Lawrence in Arabia*, by Lowell Thomas, p. 118.

[35] *With Lawrence in Arabia*, by Lowell Thomas, p. 121.

[36] *With Lawrence in Arabia*, by Lowell Thomas, p. 121.

[37] *With Lawrence in Arabia*, by Lowell Thomas, p. 118.

[38] *With Lawrence in Arabia*, by Lowell Thomas, p. 199.

[39] *With Lawrence in Arabia*, by Lowell Thomas, p. 187.

[40] *With Lawrence in Arabia*, by Lowell Thomas, p. 232.

[41] *With Lawrence in Arabia*, by Lowell Thomas, p. 317.

[42] *With Lawrence in Arabia*, by Lowell Thomas, p. 304.

[43] *Portrait of T. E. Lawrence, The Lawrence of The Seven Pillars of Wisdom*, by Vyvyan Richards, p. 228.

[44] '*T. E. Lawrence*'. *In Arabia and After*, by B. H. Liddell Hart, pp. 120-1.

[45] *The Golden Reign*, by Clare S. Smith, p. 36.

[46] *Steel Chariots in the Desert*, by S. C. Rolls, p. 56.

[47] *Seven Pillars of Wisdom*, by T. E. Lawrence, p. 563.

[48] Lowell Thomas, letter of December 27th, 1950.

[49] *With Lawrence in Arabia*, by Lowell Thomas, p. 14.

[50] *T. E. Lawrence to his Biographer Robert Graves*, p. 59.

[51] *T. E. Lawrence by His Friends*, pp. 213-4.

[52] *With Lawrence in Arabia*, by Lowell Thomas, p. 160.

[53] *The Letters of T. E. Lawrence*, p. 520.

[54] *Secret Despatches from Arabia*, pp. 130-1; *With Lawrence in Arabia*, by Lowell Thomas, pp. 198-9.

[55] *T. E. Lawrence by His Friends*, p. 208.

[56] *T. E. Lawrence by His Friends*, pp. 207-8.

[57] *T. E. Lawrence by His Friends*, p. 208.

[58] Letter of Lowell Thomas of 27th December, 1950.

[59] *T. E. Lawrence by His Friends*, p. 209.

[60] *T. E. Lawrence by His Friends*, p. 209.

[61] Lowell Thomas, letter of December 27th, 1950.

[62] *T. E. Lawrence by His Friends*, p. 226.

[63] Letter from Messrs. A. & C. Black, 31st January, 1951.

[64] *Who's Who*, 1921.

[65] *The Letters of T. E. Lawrence*, p. 363.

[66] *Who's Who* of years quoted.

[67] *T. E. Lawrence by His Friends*, pp. 214-15.

[68] *The Letters of T. E. Lawrence*, p. 301.

[69] *The Letters of T. E. Lawrence*, pp. 298-9.

[70] *The Letters of T. E. Lawrence*, p. 429.

[71] *Lawrence and the Arabs*, by Robert Graves, p. 403.

[72] *T. E. Lawrence by His Friends*, p. 397.

[73] *T. E. Lawrence by His Friends*, p. 245.

PART III: CHAPTER FOUR

[1] *The Letters of T. E. Lawrence*, p. 280.

[2] '*T. E. Lawrence*'. *In Arabia and After*, by B. H. Liddell Hart, p. 400.

[3] *T. E. Lawrence to his Biographer Robert Graves*, p. 50.

[4] *The Golden Reign*, by Clare S. Smith, p. 36.

[5] *The Letters of T. E. Lawrence*, p. 301.

[6] *The Letters of T. E. Lawrence*, p. 280.
[7] *The Letters of T. E. Lawrence*, p. 300.
[8] *The Letters of T. E. Lawrence*, p. 301.
[9] *The Letters of T. E. Lawrence*, p. 653.
[10] British Museum, Additional MS. 45903,4.
[11] *The Letters of T. E. Lawrence*, p. 333.
[12] *The Letters of T. E. Lawrence*, p. 333.
[13] *Portrait of T. E. Lawrence, The Lawrence of The Seven Pillars of Wisdom*, by Vyvyan Richards, p. 179.
[14] *T. E. Lawrence to his Biographer Robert Graves*, p. 12.
[15] *T. E. Lawrence by His Friends*, p. 117.
[16] *The Letters of T. E. Lawrence*, pp. 267-8.
[17] *Arabian Days, an Autobiography*, by H. St. J. Philby, p. 178.
[18] *The Independent Arab*, by Sir Hubert Young, p. 287.
[19] *T. E. Lawrence by His Friends*, p. 63.
[20] *Lawrence and the Arabs*, by Robert Graves, pp. 402-3.
[21] *The Letters of T. E. Lawrence*, p. 555.
[22] *T. E. Lawrence to his Biographer Robert Graves*, p. 108.
[23] *T. E. Lawrence to his Biographer Robert Graves*, pp. 140-1.
[24] *T. E. Lawrence to his Biographer Robert Graves*, p. 161.
[25] *Memoirs of King Abdulla of Transjordan*, pp. 258-60.
[26] *Memories of Victorian Oxford and of Some Early Years*, by Sir Charles Oman.
[27] *The Letters of T. E. Lawrence*, p. 301.
[28] *With Lawrence in Arabia*, by Lowell Thomas, p. 308.
[29] *T. E. Lawrence to his Biographer Robert Graves*, p. 15.
[30] *Arabian Days, An Autobiography*, by H. St. J. Philby, p. 184.
[31] *T. E. Lawrence by His Friends*, pp. 187-9.
[32] *The Letters of T. E. Lawrence*, p. 329.
[33] *T. E. Lawrence by His Friends*, pp. 197-8.
[34] *T. E. Lawrence by His Friends*, p. 230.
[35] *T. E. Lawrence to his Biographer Liddell Hart*, p. 143.
[36] *The Times Literary Supplement*, 22nd June, 1951.
[37] *Arabian Days, An Autobiography*, by H. St. J. Philby, p. 187.
[38] *Arabian Days, An Autobiography*, by H. St. J. Philby, p. 186.
[39] *T. E. Lawrence to his Biographer Liddell Hart*, p. 144.
[40] *Arabian Days, An Autobiography*, by H. St. J. Philby, p. 198.
[41] *Arabian Days, An Autobiography*, by H. St. J. Philby, p. 205.
[42] ' *T. E. Lawrence* '. *In Arabia and After*, by B. H. Liddell Hart, p. 410.
[43] *Arabia*, by H. St. J. Philby, p. 284.
[44] *T. E. Lawrence to his Biographer Liddell Hart*, p. 142 ; ' *T. E. Lawrence* '. *In Arabia and After*, by B. H. Liddell Hart, p. 412.
[45] *T. E. Lawrence by His Friends*, p. 236.
[46] *Arabian Days, An Autobiography*, by H. St. J. Philby, p. 207.
[47] ' *T. E. Lawrence* '. *In Arabia and After*, by B. H. Liddell Hart, p. 412.
[48] *Memoirs of King Abdulla of Transjordan*, pp. 200-4.
[49] *Arabia*, by H. St. J. Philby, p. 284.
[50] *Arabian Days, An Autobiography*, by H. St. J. Philby, p. 228.
[51] *The Arab Awakening*, by George Antonius, p. 331.
[52] *T. E. Lawrence by His Friends*, p. 199.
[53] *The Letters of T. E. Lawrence*, p. 336.
[54] *Memoirs of King Abdulla of Transjordan*, p. 226.
[55] *Arabian Days, An Autobiography*, by H. St. J. Philby, p. 208.

[56] British Museum. Additional MS. 45903,4.

[57] *Arabian Days, An Autobiography*, by H. St. J. Philby, pp. 208–9.

[58] *Seven Pillars of Wisdom*, by T. E. Lawrence, p. 171.

[59] *The Arab Awakening*, by George Antonius, pp. 220–3.

[60] *The Letters of T. E. Lawrence*, p. 191.

PART III: CHAPTER FIVE

[1] *The Letters of T. E. Lawrence*, p. 469.

[2] *Lawrence and the Arabs*, by Robert Graves, p. 406.

[3] 'T. E. Lawrence'. In *Arabia and After*, by B. H. Liddell Hart, p. 399; *T. E. Lawrence to his Biographer Liddell Hart*, p. 145.

[4] *Lawrence and the Arabs*, by Robert Graves, p. 406.

[5] *The Letters of T. E. Lawrence*, p. 319.

[6] *The Letters of T. E. Lawrence*, p. 296.

[7] *Lawrence and the Arabs*, by Robert Graves, p. 406.

[8] 'T. E. Lawrence'. In *Arabia and After*, by B. H. Liddell Hart, p. 400; *T. E. Lawrence to his Biographer Liddell Hart*, p. 145.

[9] 'T. E. Lawrence'. In *Arabia and After*, by B. H. Liddell Hart, p. 400.

[10] *T. E. Lawrence by His Friends*, p. 249.

[11] *Portrait of T. E. Lawrence, The Lawrence of The Seven Pillars of Wisdom*, by Vyvyan Richards, pp. 184–5.

[12] *Lawrence and the Arabs*, by Robert Graves, p. 406.

[13] *The Letters of T. E. Lawrence*, p. 300.

[14] *The Letters of T. E. Lawrence*, p. 318.

[15] *Three Persons*, by Sir Andrew Macphail, p. 198.

[16] *Lawrence and the Arabs*, by Robert Graves, p. 406.

[17] *The Letters of T. E. Lawrence*, p. 356.

[18] *The Letters of T. E. Lawrence*, p. 360.

[19] *T. E. Lawrence to his Biographer Robert Graves*, p. 5.

[20] *Thirty Years with G.B.S.*, by Blanche Patch, p. 78.

[21] *The Letters of T. E. Lawrence*, pp. 386–7.

[22] *The Letters of T. E. Lawrence*, pp. 387–8.

[23] *Thirty Years with G.B.S.*, by Blanche Patch, p. 78.

[24] *Thirty Years with G.B.S.*, by Blanche Patch, p. 78; *The Letters of T. E. Lawrence*, p. 469.

[25] *T. E. Lawrence by His Friends*, p. 388.

[26] Unpublished letter to Henry Williamson, 2nd April, 1928.

[27] *Portrait of T. E. Lawrence, The Lawrence of The Seven Pillars of Wisdom*, by Vyvyan Richards, pp. 188–9.

[28] *T. E. Lawrence by His Friends*, pp. 389–90.

[29] *T. E. Lawrence by His Friends*, p. 391.

[30] *The Letters of T. E. Lawrence*, p. 295.

[31] *The Letters of T. E. Lawrence*, p. 469.

[32] *The Letters of T. E. Lawrence*, p. 465.

[33] *The Letters of T. E. Lawrence*, pp. 468–9, 498; *Seven Pillars of Wisdom*, by T. E. Lawrence, p. 318.

[34] *T. E. Lawrence to his Biographer Liddell Hart*, p. 129.

[35] *The Letters of T. E. Lawrence*, p. 428.

[36] *The Letters of T. E. Lawrence*, p. 361.

[37] *The Letters of T. E. Lawrence*, p. 369.

[38] *The Letters of T. E. Lawrence*, p. 373.

[39] *The Letters of T. E. Lawrence*, p. 388.

[40] *The Letters of T. E. Lawrence*, p. 397.

[41] *The Letters of T. E. Lawrence*, p. 397.

[42] *The Letters of T. E. Lawrence*, pp. 399–400.

43 *The Letters of T. E. Lawrence*, p. 514.

44 *The Letters of T. E. Lawrence*, p. 519.

45 *The Letters of T. E. Lawrence*, pp. 524-5.

46 *The Letters of T. E. Lawrence*, pp. 527, 535, 528.

47 *Lawrence and the Arabs*, by Robert Graves, p. 409.

48 *Le Hedjaz dans la Guerre Mondiale*, by Général Ed. Brémond, p. 9.

49 *The Golden Reign*, by Clare S. Smith, p. 77.

50 *Lawrence and the Arabs*, by Robert Graves, p. 408.

51 *T. E. Lawrence to his Biographer Robert Graves*, p. 180.

52 *Lawrence and the Arabs*, by Robert Graves, p. 409.

53 *T. E. Lawrence by His Friends*, p. 396.

54 *T. E. Lawrence to his Biographer Robert Graves*, p. 180.

55 *The Letters of T. E. Lawrence*, p. 472.

56 *The Letters of T. E. Lawrence*, p. 529.

57 *T. E. Lawrence to his Biographer Liddell Hart*, p. 25.

58 *Seven Pillars of Wisdom*, by T. E. Lawrence, p. 64.

PART III: CHAPTER SIX

1 *T. E. Lawrence to his Biographer Robert Graves*, pp. 15-6.

2 *Lawrence and the Arabs*, by Robert Graves, p. 47.

3 *T. E. Lawrence to his Biographer Robert Graves*, p. 8.

4 *The Letters of T. E. Lawrence*, p. 788.

5 *T. E. Lawrence by His Friends*, p. 285.

6 *T. E. Lawrence by His Friends*, p. 89.

7 *T. E. Lawrence by His Friends*, p. 214.

8 *The Letters of T. E. Lawrence*, p. 93.

9 *The Letters of T. E. Lawrence*, p. 57.

10 *Seven Pillars of Wisdom*, by T. E. Lawrence, p. 5.

11 *T. E. Lawrence to his Biographer Robert Graves*, p. 15.

12 *T. E. Lawrence to his Biographer Robert Graves*, p. 16.

13 *T. E. Lawrence to his Biographer Robert Graves*, pp. 16-7.

14 *T. E. Lawrence*, by Vyvyan Richards, p. 32 (Great Lives).

15 *T. E. Lawrence to his Biographer Liddell Hart*, p. 156.

16 *T. E. Lawrence to his Biographer Liddell Hart*, p. 169.

17 *T. E. Lawrence to his Biographer Liddell Hart*, p. 64.

18 *T. E. Lawrence by His Friends*, p. 592.

19 *Seven Pillars of Wisdom*, by T. E. Lawrence, p. 19.

20 *Seven Pillars of Wisdom*, by T. E. Lawrence, p. 30.

21 *Seven Pillars of Wisdom*, by T. E. Lawrence, p. 214.

22 *Seven Pillars of Wisdom*, by T. E. Lawrence, p. 40.

23 *Seven Pillars of Wisdom*, by T. E. Lawrence, p. 348.

24 *Seven Pillars of Wisdom*, by T. E. Lawrence, pp. 147-8, 161.

25 *Travels in Arabia Deserta*, by Charles Doughty, Vol. 2, p. 376.

26 *The Penetration of Arabia*, by D. G. Hogarth, p. 93; *Terminal Essay*, by Richard Burton, Vol. 10, p. 201.

27 *Seven Pillars of Wisdom*, by T. E. Lawrence, p. 171.

28 *Seven Pillars of Wisdom*, by T. E. Lawrence, pp. 236-7.

29 *Seven Pillars of Wisdom*, by T. E. Lawrence, pp. 243, 553, 269.

30 *Seven Pillars of Wisdom*, by T. E. Lawrence, p. 311.

31 *The Letters of T. E. Lawrence*, p. 450.
32 *The Letters of T. E. Lawrence*, p. 527.
33 *The Letters of T. E. Lawrence*, p. 458.
34 *The Letters of T. E. Lawrence*, p. 524.
35 *The Letters of T. E. Lawrence*, p. 649.
36 *The Letters of T. E. Lawrence*, p. 652.
37 *The Letters of T. E. Lawrence*, p. 667.
38 British Museum. Additional MS. 45903,4.
39 *The Letters of T. E. Lawrence*, p. 652.

PART III: CHAPTER SEVEN

1 *T. E. Lawrence by His Friends*, p. 162.
2 *Lawrence and the Arabs*, by Robert Graves, p. 45.
3 *T. E. Lawrence to his Biographer Robert Graves*, pp. 50-1.
4 *The Letters of T. E. Lawrence*, p. 364.
5 *The Letters of T. E. Lawrence*, p. 362.
6 *The Letters of T. E. Lawrence*, p. 398.
7 *The Letters of T. E. Lawrence*, p. 425.
8 *The Letters of T. E. Lawrence*, p. 411.
9 *The Letters of T. E. Lawrence*, p. 416.
10 *The Letters of T. E. Lawrence*, p. 416.
11 *T. E. Lawrence to his Biographer Robert Graves*, p. 22.
12 *T. E. Lawrence to his Biographer Robert Graves*, p. 52.
13 *The Letters of T. E. Lawrence*, p. 416.
14 *The Letters of T. E. Lawrence*, p. 414.
15 *T. E. Lawrence to his Biographer Liddell Hart*, p. 51.
16 *T. E. Lawrence to his Biographer Liddell Hart*, p. 24.
17 *T. E. Lawrence by His Friends*, p. 247.
18 *T. E. Lawrence to his Biographer Robert Graves*, p. 20.

PART III: CHAPTER EIGHT

1 *The Letters of T. E. Lawrence*, p. 363.
2 *The Letters of T. E. Lawrence*, p. 363.
3 *The Letters of T. E. Lawrence*, p. 363.
4 *The Letters of T. E. Lawrence*, p. 364.
5 W. E. Johns, *Sunday Times*, April 8th, 1951.
6 *The Letters of T. E. Lawrence*, p. 365.
7 *The Letters of T. E. Lawrence*, pp. 365-6.
8 *The Letters of T. E. Lawrence*, p. 368.
9 *The Letters of T. E. Lawrence*, pp. 390-1.
10 *The Letters of T. E. Lawrence*, p. 392.
11 *T. E. Lawrence to his Biographer Robert Graves*, p. 25; *Lawrence and the Arabs*, by Robert Graves, p. 419; *The Letters of T. E. Lawrence*, p. 398.
12 *The Letters of T. E. Lawrence*, p. 393-4.
13 *The Letters of T. E. Lawrence*, p. 363.
14 *The Letters of T. E. Lawrence*, p. 363.
15 *T. E. Lawrence to his Biographer Liddell Hart*, p. 160.
16 *T. E. Lawrence to his Biographer Liddell Hart*, p. 160.
17 *The Golden Reign*, by Clare S. Smith, pp. 8-185.
18 *The Letters of T. E. Lawrence*, p. 364.
19 *The Letters of T. E. Lawrence*, p. 405.
20 *The Letters of T. E. Lawrence*, p. 405.
21 *The Letters of T. E. Lawrence*, p. 409.
22 *The Letters of T. E. Lawrence*, pp. 411-2.
23 *The Letters of T. E. Lawrence*, p. 431.
24 *The Letters of T. E. Lawrence*, p. 439.
25 *The Letters of T. E. Lawrence*, p. 464.
26 *The Letters of T. E. Lawrence*, p. 554.
27 *The Letters of T. E. Lawrence*, p. 728.
28 *T. E. Lawrence by His Friends*, p. 377.
29 *T. E. Lawrence by His Friends*, p. 339.
30 *T. E. Lawrence by His Friends*, p. 340.

[31] *T. E. Lawrence by His Friends*, p. 361.

[32] *T. E. Lawrence by His Friends*, p. 373.

[33] *T. E. Lawrence by His Friends*, p. 390.

[34] *T. E. Lawrence by His Friends*, p. 366.

[35] *T. E. Lawrence by His Friends*, p. 521.

[36] *T. E. Lawrence by His Friends*, p. 375.

[37] *Thirty Years with G.B.S.*, by Blanche Patch, p. 85.

[38] *Lawrence and the Arabs*, by Robert Graves, pp. 43-4.

[39] *Genius of Friendship, 'T. E. Lawrence,'* by Henry Williamson, p. 10.

[40] *Genius of Friendship, 'T. E. Lawrence,'* by Henry Williamson, p. 10.

[41] *T. E. Lawrence to his Biographer Robert Graves*, p. 73.

[42] *T. E. Lawrence to his Biographer Robert Graves*, p. 54.

[43] *The Letters of T. E. Lawrence*, p. 613.

[44] *The Letters of T. E. Lawrence*, p. 447.

[45] *Lawrence and the Arabs*, by Robert Graves, p. 423.

[46] *The Letters of T. E. Lawrence*, p. 772.

[47] *T. E. Lawrence by His Friends*, p. 486.

[48] *The Letters of T. E. Lawrence*, pp. 475, 479.

[49] *The Letters of T. E. Lawrence*, p. 420.

[50] *The Letters of T. E. Lawrence*, p. 425.

[51] *The Letters of T. E. Lawrence*, p. 458.

[52] *The Letters of T. E. Lawrence*, p. 471.

[53] *The Letters of T. E. Lawrence*, p. 474.

[54] *The Letters of T. E. Lawrence*, p. 476.

[55] *The Letters of T. E. Lawrence*, p 477.

[56] *The Letters of T. E. Lawrence*, p. 485.

[57] *The Letters of T. E. Lawrence*, p. 477.

[58] *The Letters of T. E. Lawrence*, pp. 480-1.

[59] *The Letters of T. E. Lawrence*, p. 482.

[60] *The Letters of T. E. Lawrence*, pp. 502-3.

[61] *The Letters of T. E. Lawrence*, p. 505.

[62] *The Letters of T. E. Lawrence*, p. 516.

[63] *Thirty Years with G.B.S.*, by Blanche Patch, p. 86.

[64] *T. E. Lawrence by His Friends*, p. 246.

[65] Lawrence's translation of *Odyssey*, Translator's Note.

[66] *The Letters of T. E. Lawrence*, p. 607.

[67] *The Letters of T. E. Lawrence*, p. 632.

[68] *T. E. Lawrence by His Friends*, pp. 401-18; Private communication.

[69] Private communication.

[70] *The Letters of T. E. Lawrence*, p. 570.

[71] *T. E. Lawrence by His Friends*, p. 406.

[72] *The Letters of T. E. Lawrence*, p. 615.

[73] *The Letters of T. E. Lawrence*, p. 728.

[74] *The Letters of T. E. Lawrence*, p. 728.

[75] *The Letters of T. E. Lawrence*, p. 522.

[76] *The Letters of T. E. Lawrence*, p. 522.

[77] *T. E. Lawrence by His Friends*, pp. 407-8.

[78] *T. E. Lawrence to his Biographer Liddell Hart*, p. 191.

[79] *T. E. Lawrence by His Friends*, p. 285.

[80] *The Letters of T. E. Lawrence*, p. 632.

[81] *The Letters of T. E. Lawrence*, p. 515.

[82] *The Letters of T. E. Lawrence*, p. 514.

[83] *The Letters of T. E. Lawrence*, pp. 632-3.

[84] *The Letters of T. E. Lawrence*, p. 634.

[85] *The Golden Reign*, by Clare S. Smith, p. 25.

[86] *T. E. Lawrence by His Friends*, p. 351.

[87] *T. E. Lawrence by His Friends*, p. 353.

[88] *T. E. Lawrence by His Friends*, p. 355.

[89] *Women in Love*, by D. H. Lawrence, pp. 60, 131.

[90] *The Letters of T. E. Lawrence*, p. 642.

[91] *The Letters of T. E. Lawrence*, p. 653.

[92] *T. E. Lawrence to his Biographer Liddell Hart*, p. 187.

[93] *The Letters of T. E. Lawrence*, p. 659.

[94] *The Letters of T. E. Lawrence*, p. 660.

[95] *T. E. Lawrence to his Biographer Robert Graves*, p. 78.

[96] *The Letters of T. E. Lawrence*, p. 871.

[97] *T. E. Lawrence to his Biographer Robert Graves*, p. 61.

[98] *The Letters of T. E. Lawrence*, p. 346.

[99] '*T. E. Lawrence*'. *In Arabia and After*, by B. H. Liddell Hart, p. 429.

[100] *The Letters of T. E. Lawrence*, p. 673; *T. E. Lawrence to his Biographer Robert Graves*, p. 164.

[101] *The Letters of T. E. Lawrence*, p. 673.

[102] *The Letters of T. E. Lawrence*, p. 677.

[103] *The Letters of T. E. Lawrence*, p. 637.

[104] *T. E. Lawrence to his Biographer Liddell Hart*.

[105] *The Letters of T. E. Lawrence*, p. 610.

[106] *The Letters of T. E. Lawrence*, p. 744.

[107] *The Letters of T. E. Lawrence*, p. 763.

[108] *The Letters of T. E. Lawrence*, p. 765.

[109] *The Letters of T. E. Lawrence*, p. 768.

[110] *The Letters of T. E. Lawrence*, p. 841.

[111] *The Letters of T. E. Lawrence*, p. 820.

[112] *T. E. Lawrence by His Friends*, p. 376.

[113] *T. E. Lawrence by His Friends*, p. 199.

[114] *The Letters of T. E. Lawrence*, pp. 337, 339, 340.

[115] Letter from Mr. Colin Mann, of 2nd January, 1951.

[116] Letter from Mr. Colin Mann, of 2nd January, 1951.

[117] Letter from Mr. Colin Mann, of 2nd January, 1951.

[118] *The Letters of T. E. Lawrence*, p. 830.

[119] *The Letters of T. E. Lawrence*, pp. 844-5.

[120] *T. E. Lawrence to his Biographer Liddell Hart*, p. 230.

[121] *T. E. Lawrence to his Biographer Liddell Hart*, pp. 222-3.

[122] *T. E. Lawrence by His Friends*, p. 455

[123] *T. E. Lawrence by His Friends*, p. 455.

[124] *T. E. Lawrence to his Biographer Liddell Hart*, p. 35.

[125] *The Letters of T. E. Lawrence*, p. 407.

[126] *T. E. Lawrence to his Biographer Liddell Hart*, p. 231; *The Letters of T. E. Lawrence*, pp. 872-3.

[127] *T. E. Lawrence to his Biographer Liddell Hart*, pp. 232-3.

BIBLIOGRAPHY

1. *Crusader Castles*, by T. E. Lawrence. The Golden Cockerel Press, 1936. Two vols. Edition limited to 1000 numbered copies.

2. *The Letters of T. E. Lawrence*. Edited by David Garnett. London. Jonathan Cape. 1938.

3. *T. E. Lawrence's Letters to H. S. Ede*, 1927-1935. Foreword and Running Commentary by H. S. Ede. The Golden Cockerel Press. Printed by Christopher Sandford and Owen Rutter at the Golden Cockerel Press, Rolls Passage, London, E.C.4, in 14 pt. Perpetua type on Arnold's mould-made paper, and finished on the 4th day of September, 1942. The edition is limited to 500 numbered copies, of which numbers 1-30 are bound in full morocco and accompanied by facsimile reproductions of five of the letters. Numbers 31-500 are bound in quarter-morocco.

4. *The Wilderness of Zin*, by Leonard Woolley and T. E. Lawrence. With a chapter on the Greek Inscriptions by M. N. Tod. Introduction by Sir Frederick Kenyon. Jonathan Cape, 1936.

5. *Seven Pillars of Wisdom: a Triumph*, by T. E. Lawrence. London, Jonathan Cape, 1935.

6. *Revolt in the Desert*, by ' T. E. Lawrence.' George H. Doran Company. New York, 1927.

7. *Secret Despatches from Arabia published by permission of the Foreign Office.* Foreword by A. W. Lawrence. Printed by Christopher Sandford and Owen Rutter at the Golden Cockerel Press in Perpetua type on Arnold's mould-made paper. The Edition is limited to 1000 numbered copies, of which numbers 1-30 are bound in white pig-skin and accompanied by a collotype reproduction of part of T. E. Lawrence's manuscript of *Seven Pillars of Wisdom*. Numbers 31-1000 are bound in quarter-Niger.

8. *Oriental Assembly*, by T. E. Lawrence. Edited by A. W. Lawrence. With Photographs by the Author. London. Williams and Norgate, Ltd., 1939.

9. *The Mint*. Notes made in the R.A.F. Depot between August and December, 1922, and at Cadet College in 1925 by 352087 A/C Ross. Regrouped and copied in 1927 and 1928 at Aircraft Depot, Karachi. Garden City, New York, Doubleday, Doran & Company, 1936. Limited to 50 copies, of which 10 are for sale.

10. *An Essay on Flecker*, by T. E. Lawrence. Thirty copies of this book have been printed on J. B. Green unsized parchment paper at the Corvinus Press.

11. *Men in Print. Essays in Literary Criticism*, by T. E. Lawrence. Introduction by A. W. Lawrence. Printed in the midst of war by Christopher Sandford and Owen Rutter at the Golden Cockerel Press, in Perpetua type on Arnold's hand-made paper, and finished on the 16th day of July, 1940. The edition is limited to 500 numbered copies, of which numbers 1-30 are bound in full Niger and accompanied by a facsimile reproduction of T. E. Lawrence's manuscript of one of his essays. Numbers 31-500 are bound in quarter-Niger.

12. *T. E. Lawrence to his Biographer, Robert Graves* and *T. E. Lawrence to his Biographer, Liddell Hart*. Limited to 500 copies at 5 guineas each. Faber and Faber. 1938.

13. *The Odyssey of Homer; newly translated into English Prose*. Introduction by John Finlay. Translator's Note by T. E. Shaw. New York. Oxford University Press. 1932.

14. *Fifty-Five Years at Oxford. An Unconventional Autobiography*, by G. B. Grundy. Methuen. 1945.

15. *Memories of Victorian Oxford and of Some Early Years* by Sir Charles Oman. Methuen. 1941.

16. *Palestine and Syria. Handbook for Travellers.* By Karl Baedeker. Leipzig: Karl Baedeker. 1912.

17. *Dead Towns and Living Men, being Pages from an Antiquary's Notebook.* By C. Leonard Woolley. Jonathan Cape. 1932.

18. *With Lawrence in Arabia.* By Lowell Thomas. With Frontispiece and 64 other Illustrations. London: Hutchinson and Co. No date. (1924.)

19. *Lawrence and the Arabs.* By Robert Graves. Illustrations edited by Eric Kennington. Maps by Herry Perry. Jonathan Cape. 1927.

20. *Portrait of T. E. Lawrence, the Lawrence of the Seven Pillars of Wisdom.* By Vyvyan Richards. Jonathan Cape. 1936.

21. *T. E. Lawrence.* By Vyvyan Richards. Great Lives. Duckworth. 1939.

22. '*T. E. Lawrence.*' *In Arabia and After.* By Liddell Hart. Jonathan Cape. 1934.

23. *T. E. Lawrence by His Friends.* Edited by A. W. Lawrence. Jonathan Cape. 1937.

24. *The Golden Reign. The Story of my Friendship with* '*Lawrence of Arabia*'. Clare Sydney Smith. Cassell, 1940.

25. *Genius of Friendship.* '*T. E. Lawrence.*' Henry Williamson. Faber and Faber. 1941.

26. *Military Operations, Egypt and Palestine. From the Outbreak of War with Germany to June,* 1917. Compiled by Lieut.-General Sir George MacNunn and Captain Cyril Falls. Vol. 1. 1928; *Military Operations, Egypt and Palestine. From June,* 1917, *to the End of the War.* Vol. 2, in two parts, compiled by Captain Cyril Falls. Maps by Major A. F. Becke. 1930. Published by His Majesty's Stationery Office.

27. *The Palestine Campaigns.* By Colonel A. P. Wavell. Constable. 1928.

28. *The Fire of Life,* by General Sir George de S. Barrow. Hutchinson and Co. No date. (1942.)

29. *Le Hedjaz dans la Guerre Mondiale.* By Général Ed. Brémond. Préface du Maréchal Franchet d'Espérey. Payot. 1931.

30. *Allenby—a Study in Greatness.* By A. P. Wavell. Harrap. 1940.

31. *Memories of a Turkish Statesman—*1913-1919. By Djemal Pasha. Formerly Governor of Constantinople. Imperial Ottoman Naval Minister, and Commander of the Fourth Army in Sinai, Palestine and Syria. Hutchinson. No date.

32. *Fünf Jahre Turkei.* By General Liman von Sanders.

33. *Gegenspieler des Obsten Lawrence.* By Hans Lührs. 1936.

34. *Zwishen Kaukasus und Sinai. Jahrbuch des Bundes der Asienkämpfer.* 1921.

35. *Memoirs of King Abdulla of Transjordan.* Edited by Philip P. Graves. With an Introduction by R. J. C. Broadhurst. Cape. 1950.

36. *Three Persons.* By Sir Andrew Macphail. London; Murray. 1929.

37. *The Letters of Gertrude Bell.* Selected and Edited by Lady Bell. Ernest Benn. 1927.

38. *Loyalties. Mesopotamia, 1914-1917. A Personal and Historical Record,* by Lt.-Col. Sir Arnold T. Wilson. Oxford University Press. 1930.

39. *Shifting Sands.* By Major N. N. E. Bray. Foreword by Sir Austen Chamberlain. Unicorn Press. 1934.

40. *A Paladin of Arabia.* By Major N. N. E. Bray. The Biography of Brevet Lieutenant-Colonel G. E. Leachman. Foreword by Sir Samuel Hoare. Unicorn Press. 1936.

41. *Steel Chariots in the Desert. The Story of an Armoured-Car Driver with the Duke of Westminster in Libya and in Arabia with T. E. Lawrence.* By S. C. Rolls. Cape. 1937.

42. *Lawrence of Arabia.* By R. H. Kiernan. Harrap. 1935.

43. *Lawrence the Rebel.* By Edward Robinson. Lincolns-Prager (Publishers) Ltd. 1946.

44. *Lawrence: The Story of his Life.* By Edward Robinson. Oxford University Press. 1935.

45. *In the Steps of Lawrence of Arabia.* By Douglas Glen. Rich and Cowan, Ltd. No date.

46. *Orientations.* By Sir Ronald Storrs. Ivor Nicholson and Watson. 1939.

47. *The Independent Arab.* By Major Sir Hubert Young. Murray. 1933.

48. *The Arab Awakening. The Story of the Arab National Movement.* By George Antonius. Hamish Hamilton. 1938.

49. *Arabian Days.* An Autobiography of H. St. J. B. Philby. Robert Hale, Ltd. 1948.

50. *The Truth about the Peace Treaties.* By David Lloyd George. Gollancz. 1938.

51. *Too True to be Good,* etc. By Bernard Shaw. Constable.

52. *Thirty Years with G.B.S.* By Blanche Patch. Gollancz. 1951.

53. *Travels in Arabia Deserta.* By Charles M. Doughty. With an Introduction by T. E. Lawrence. Cape. Two vols. 1936. (First published 1888.)

54. *A Wandering Scholar in the Levant.* By David G. Hogarth. Murray. 1896.

Bibliography

55. *The Penetration of Arabia. A Record of the Development of Western Knowledge Concerning the Arabian Peninsula.* By David George Hogarth. Alston Rivers. 1905.

56. *Arabia.* By D. G. Hogarth. Oxford. At the Clarendon Press. 1922.

57. *Arabia.* By H. St. J. B. Philby. Ernest Benn, Ltd. 1930.

58. *A Pilgrim in Arabia.* By H. St. J. B. Philby. Robert Hale, Ltd. 1946.

59. *Syria. The Desert and the Sown.* By Gertrude Lowthian Bell. Heinemann. 1908.

60. *Arabia Phoenix.* By Gerald de Gaury. Harrap. 1946.

61. *In Unknown Arabia.* By Major R. E. Cheesman. Macmillan. 1926.

62. *Letters from Syria.* By Freya Stark. Penguin Books.

63. *Crusader Castles. A Brief Study of the Military Architecture of the Crusades.* By Robin Fedden. Art and Technics. 1950.

64. *Syria. An Historical Appreciation* by Robin Fedden. Robert Hale, Ltd. 1946.

65. *The Shaw–Shaw Letters.* British Museum Additional MS. 45922 and 45903, 4.

(Other books referred to or briefly quoted from are included in the Lists of Sources attached to each chapter or in footnotes.)

ACKNOWLEDGMENTS

THE AUTHOR and publishers wish to express their indebtedness to the following for permission to include in this book passages from the books listed below :

MILITARY OPERATIONS, EGYPT AND PALESTINE vols. I and II : The Controller, H. M. Stationery Office.

SECRET DESPATCHES FROM ARABIA (The Golden Cockerel Press): The Foreign Office.

THE ARAB AWAKENING by George Antonius : Hamish Hamilton Ltd.

THE INDEPENDENT ARAB by Sir Hubert Young : John Murray (Publishers) Ltd.

GENIUS OF FRIENDSHIP: 'T. E. LAWRENCE,' by Henry Williamson (Faber): Henry Williamson.

THE LETTERS OF GERTRUDE BELL selected and edited by Lady Bell: Ernest Benn Ltd.

SHIFTING SANDS by Major N. N. E. Bray: Unicorn Press (London) Ltd.

THE FIRE OF LIFE by General Sir George de S. Barrow: Hutchinson & Co. (Publishers) Ltd.

ARABIAN DAYS. An Autobiography by H. St. John Philby : Robert Hale Ltd. and H. St. John Philby.

ARABIA by H. St. John Philby: Ernest Benn Ltd. (*Sa'udi Arabia* by the same author has yet to appear).

THE TRUTH ABOUT THE PEACE TREATIES by David Lloyd George : Victor Gollancz, Ltd.

SYRIA : An Historical Apprecation by Robin Fedden : Robert Hale Ltd. & Robin Fedden.

LE HEDJAZ DANS LA GUERRE MONDIALE by Général Ed. Brémond: Editions Payot-Paris.

INDEX

Index

Index

Index

436